VICARIOUS LIABILITY: CRITIQUE AND REFORM

The scope of vicarious liability has significantly expanded since its original conception. Today employers are being found liable for actions of employees that they did not authorise, and never would have authorised if asked. They are being held liable for an employee's criminal activity. In the related strict liability field of non-delegable duties, they are being held liable for wrongdoing of independent contractors. Notions of strict liability have grown increasingly isolated in the law of tort, given the exponential growth in the tort of negligence. They require intellectual justification. Such a justification has proven to be elusive and largely unsatisfactory in relation to vicarious liability and to concepts of non-delegable duty. The law of three jurisdictions studied has now apparently embraced the 'enterprise risk' theory to rationalise the imposition of vicarious liability. This book subjects this theory to strong critique by arguing that it has many weaknesses, which the courts should acknowledge. It suggests that a rationalisation of the liability of an employer for the actions of an employee lies in more traditional legal doctrine which would serve to narrow the circumstances in which an employer is legally liable for a wrong committed by an employee.

Volume 28 in the series Hart Studies in Private Law

Vicarious Liability

Critique and Reform

Anthony Gray

•HART•
OXFORD • LONDON • NEW YORK • NEW DELHI • SYDNEY

HART PUBLISHING
Bloomsbury Publishing Plc
Kemp House, Chawley Park, Cumnor Hill, Oxford, OX2 9PH, UK

HART PUBLISHING, the Hart/Stag logo, BLOOMSBURY and the Diana logo are trademarks of Bloomsbury Publishing Plc

First published in Great Britain 2018

A catalogue record for this book is available from the British Library.

Library of Congress Cataloging-in-Publication data

Names: Gray, Anthony (Law teacher)

Title: Vicarious liability : critique and reform / Anthony Gray.

Description: Oxford, UK ; Portland, Oregon : Hart Publishing, 2018. | Series: Hart studies in private law; volume 28 | Includes bibliographical references and index.

Identifiers: LCCN 2018018274 (print) | LCCN 2018019805 (ebook) | ISBN 9781509920242 (Epub) | ISBN 9781509920235 (hardback : alk. paper)

Subjects: LCSH: Respondeat superior—English-speaking countries.

Classification: LCC K962 (ebook) | LCC K962 .G73 2018 (print) | DDC 346/.152103—dc23

LC record available at https://lccn.loc.gov/2018018274

ISBN: HB: 978-1-50992-023-5
ePDF: 978-1-50992-025-9
ePub: 978-1-50992-024-2

Typeset by Compuscript Ltd, Shannon

To find out more about our authors and books visit www.hartpublishing.co.uk. Here you will find extracts, author information, details of forthcoming events and the option to sign up for our newsletters.

TABLE OF CONTENTS

INTRODUCTION

One of the most venerable doctrines of the common law is vicarious liability, by which an employer is said to be legally liable for the actions of their employees. While there is a long case history reflecting such a doctrine, a satisfactory unifying rationale for the imposition of such liability remains elusive. Discussion of vicarious liability takes place as part of the bigger picture of tort law in terms of fault-based liability as opposed to principles of strict liability, and the broader objectives of tort law, such as distributive or corrective justice.

While the law of fault-based doctrines such as negligence have grown substantially in the common law, and tort law has moved away from notions of strict liability, two important pockets of strict liability remain: vicarious liability and non-delegable duties. As they have become further isolated and removed from the mainstream of tort law, the question of their justification and explanation, and indeed their proper place in the future of tort law, looms larger. This need to provide such an explanation has moved three jurisdictions studied in this book, the United States, United Kingdom and Canada, to adopt an 'enterprise risk' theory, which is said to explain and justify the imposition of strict liability upon an employer for the misdeeds of their employees, regardless of the employer's personal fault. This theory will be critiqued.

It is thought that legal critique is best informed by a thorough understanding of the case law as it is, and how it has developed. Thus, Part I of the book is devoted to a thorough explanation of the development of vicarious liability in the jurisdictions chosen for further study: the United States, United Kingdom, Canada and Australia. These jurisdictions have been chosen because they clearly share an important common law basis. More importantly, developments in one jurisdiction have inevitably influenced developments elsewhere. It is always good, including for legal scholars, to stick close to what the judges are actually doing. Judges in the jurisdictions chosen routinely refer to what their colleagues in the other chosen jurisdictions have decided. It is not considered ideal for legal theorists or academics to get too far ahead of themselves in their analysis of the legal landscape. My legal education has taught me to pay close attention to the reality of decision making.

Further, there has been a lot of development in vicarious liability principle over the years. It is believed that we can gain a deeper understanding of how and why the principles are as they are if we consider a broad timeline of developments, rather than just the most recent few cases. There is much wisdom in the historical case law. It was thought to be imperative to succinctly capture as much of this as possible in order to do a current discussion of the topic justice.

In Part II of the book I tackle the question of rationalisation and explanation for the doctrine of vicarious liability. At present, three of the jurisdictions chosen for study have adopted the 'enterprise risk' model, a law and economics construct which justifies the imposition of costs upon an enterprise on the basis it is efficient to properly cost an activity, to ensure it is provided at the optimal level. This is a theory which largely emanated from the United States, with very limited historical support in the United Kingdom, before being accepted in Canada and eventually the United Kingdom. Although the Australian court has flirted with such a doctrine, it ended up discarding it.

I do not believe that the courts have subjected the enterprise risk theory to the kind of in-depth analysis that is warranted, if it is sought to justify vicarious liability upon such a basis. Accordingly, chapter five of this book will explain the idea of enterprise risk theory, before subjecting it to what I consider to be serious, sustained criticism in chapter six. The doctrine is weak. It is ahistorical, it is piecemeal, it relies on vague concepts and doubtful assumptions, and it fails the test of any model, in that it does not accurately describe its subject. These faults are considered fatal. Other attempted justifications are also considered.

In chapter eight I develop my preferred model of conceptualising the liability of an employer for actions of their employees, which is an agency model. I use the word 'agency' here in a broad sense to mean that ability of an individual (employee) to affect the legal position of another (employer). An employer should be liable for actions of their employee agent which were for the purposes of the employer and for their benefit. The notion of vicarious liability as agency based, and the idea that an employer's liability for actions of an employee are limited to circumstances in which an employee was acting for the employer's purposes and benefit, find substantial historical support in the vicarious liability case law. They are considered to provide appropriate limits on the extent to which an employer is liable for actions of an employee.

It will be seen that such limits are sorely needed. There are difficulties with the existing case law. It will be seen that I am highly critical of case outcomes where an employer is held legally liable for actions of an employee that they did not authorise and never would have authorised, including deliberate, criminal wrongdoing. They have been liable for things which they specifically prohibited an employee from doing. They have been held liable for wrongful activity of independent contractors over whom they had very little control. In these senses, I believe that the law of vicarious liability and its sister doctrine of non-delegable duties has gone too far. I do not generally believe that the law should punish the innocent. The fact someone is wealthy, or may have insurance, is no basis upon which to visit liability upon them.

Though I view vicarious liability and non-delegable duties as sister doctrines, in an important way the current conception of them is strangely contradictory. Some of those jurisdictions that have apparently accepted vicarious liability upon the basis that the cost of risks of a business must be internalised to it have also apparently accepted that the cost of risks of a business must be allocated to an external body, namely the firm engaging an independent contractor. This will be further explored in chapter ten. The law risks incoherence.

As I develop in Part III of the book, I believe that the law should only visit consequences upon a person or organisation that is morally blameworthy. The law should not punish the innocent. For this reason, I believe that vicarious liability is best reconceptualised as a doctrine making an employer liable for actions they expressly or impliedly authorised, actions that were within the scope of the employee's employment and carried out for the purposes and benefit of the employer. Where the employee does this and commits a legal wrong, and a victim is injured, that victim may legitimately claim against the employer. The employer should be held liable as if they had committed the wrongdoing themselves, because they authorised the action. In other circumstances, for instance the employee was engaged in a 'frolic' and/or was acting for their own purposes, the law should not visit liability upon the employer. They have not done anything wrong. They do not deserve society's opprobrium. The law risks losing its moral force if it punishes the innocent. For similar reasons, I have grave reservations with the current law under which an employer can be held liable for paying punitive damages for the wrongdoing of an employee, including for activities not done for the purposes or benefit of the employer.

It has been an ambitious task to review what has been decided and what has been written about vicarious liability over the centuries, to try to determine trends in the law, to consider criticisms and alternative theories and, in the end, to try to improve it. Of course, it is always easy to criticise; it is more difficult to make constructive suggestions for improvement. As a result, while I have made very serious criticisms of the existing use of the enterprise risk theory, I have also proposed a model which, while no doubt imperfect, will produce what I consider to be better outcomes than the current state of affairs, where more and more costs are being imposed upon employers, on highly questionable and generalised assumptions about the financial and social implications. My aim in writing the book has been twofold: to assist readers in understanding the current law of vicarious liability, what it is and why it is, and where it came from, and then to invite them to consider the current doctrine, and its supposed rationalisations, with a critical eye, and to consider alternatives. We must always strive to improve the law. We should seek to find a theoretical basis to explain current doctrine where we can. Faulty models do not assist and may obscure and mislead. We must be wary of models which purport to explain current law, but which are really an ideological view of where their adherents wish to shift the common law. And proponents of the law must have the historical awareness to understand why it has developed in the way it has, and that in some cases, the reasons for the law being the way it is no longer holds and must be reconsidered. Only historical awareness and breadth of learning can hope to give us this perspective.

I trust readers will find that this book makes a modest contribution to this debate.

Part I

Outline of Development of Vicarious Liability in Chosen Jurisdictions

Introduction to Part I

It is considered to be essential, prior to providing any critique on the law as it is or how it could be improved, to first understand the law as it is. This includes a consideration of how it got to where it is today. The axis of time gives us a much broader understanding of the legal principles as they stand today, what they used to be, why and when they changed, and whether the changes are, in hindsight, defensible and supported. Thus, Part I of this book will to a large extent be descriptive, setting out the detail of the history of development of vicarious liability through the ages, in the select jurisdictions of the United Kingdom, United States, Canada and Australia. Once the law in each jurisdiction is understood, some critique and reflection will be provided. Obviously, to some extent pathologies in one jurisdiction are similar to pathologies in others; it will not come as a surprise that some of the issues that have bedevilled us in one jurisdiction have also troubled courts elsewhere. The beauty of a comparative approach is that it allows us to see this, and to consider several possible approaches to deal with such situations, given clear divergence among the jurisdictions being studied here. Importantly, they share a common law basis, and their law, at least initially, started at a broadly similar position. However, their development differed, as this part will see.

1

Developments in English Legal History

Historical Development of Vicarious Liability Until the Early Twentieth Century

That area of law which we now refer to as vicarious liability has an extensive history. It has adapted very substantially from its original roots, more so than many other legal doctrines. As this is intended to be a book that is critical of the current law of vicarious liability, it makes logical sense to first trace the development of the doctrine from its early days to the present. Thus, Part I of the book considers development of the law of vicarious liability in England, Australia, Canada and the United Kingdom. The law must be properly understood before it can be properly critiqued.

It may be that, in hindsight, we might find that some of the turns that the law in this area took have proven to be counterproductive. It may be that we should return to the state of the law of vicarious liability which existed at some time in its past. Or it may be that we support and defend the way in which the principles have morphed, broadly reflective of changes in society through the years, and in particular changes in how business and enterprise is conducted, changes in how the law views productive enterprise and its risks, and changes in attitudes towards individual versus collective responsibility. Tort law is unlikely to be immune from changes of the latter variety. As Atiyah noted in his classic work on vicarious liability, the doctrine seems anomalous given that it conflicts with two fundamental principles of tort law, that a person should only be liable for loss or damage they caused by their own acts or omissions, and that liability is fault based.[1]

In tracing the historical roots of the vicarious liability doctrine, we are assisted by the work of two esteemed legal scholars, John Wigmore and Oliver Wendell Holmes, who both wrote multi-part articles discussing vicarious liability in its historical context in the *Harvard Law Review* in the latter years of the nineteenth century. I am grateful for their references to some of the historical material to which I refer below.

Wigmore argues that the law of vicarious liability can be traced to Germanic law. He quotes Brunner to the effect that in Germanic law, a housemaster was

[1] PS Atiyah, *Vicarious Liability in the Law of Torts* (London, Butterworths, 1967) 12.

liable to third parties for the actions of those connected to his house.[2] This could include slaves, half-free and free persons. It included liability for the actions of the housemaster's wife.[3] Such a law exonerated the housemaster if they could prove that they played no part in the deeds of which complaint had been made.

Holmes says that the principle of vicarious liability can be traced to both Germanic and Roman law. He said that it was originally sourced in terms of liability for slaves, that a slave owner (a housemaster, as in the German context) might be liable for actions committed by their slave(s). This was extended to family members of the household through the concept of the *paterfamilias*.[4] United Kingdom[5] and Australian cases have reflected this history in a different context.[6] He says that Roman law did not develop a sophisticated concept of agency, but recognised exceptions, in cases involving innkeepers and shipowners. It did not originally accept that an individual could incur obligations or acquire rights through the acts of third parties.[7] Holmes says that around the time of the Norman Conquest the *frithborth*, or frankpledge, was recognised in English law. This made the master the pledge of his servants. If they committed wrongdoing, their master either had to turn them over or to make amercement for the wrong.[8] Pollock and Maitland view this as a softening of the initial approach to the liability of an individual for their slaves.[9]

[2] 'The ambit of vicarious liability may best be understood as ultimately influenced by, even derived from, medieval notions of headship of a household': *Sweeney v Boylan Nominees Pty Ltd* (2006) 226 CLR 161, 169–70 (Gleeson CJ; Gummow, Hayne, Heydon and Callinan JJ).

[3] *Scott v Davis* (2000) 204 CLR 333, 409 (Gummow J).

[4] 'When slaves or children in power had committed a delict, it was, in classical Roman law, their paterfamilias whom the victim had to sue ... the paterfamilias was ... vicariously liable for the wrongful act of persons in his power, but his liability was of a noxal character' (limited to the value of the slave or child): R Zimmermann, *The Law of Obligations: Roman Foundations of the Civilian Tradition* (Oxford, Clarendon Press, 1996) 1118; P Giliker, *Vicarious Liability in Tort: A Comparative Perspective* (Cambridge, Cambridge University Press, 2010) 7.

[5] *Admiralty Commissioners v SS Amerika* [1917] AC 38, 45 (Lord Parker) and 54 and 60 (Lord Sumner) (in the context of an action by an employer for loss of services); *Fisher v Oldham Corporation* [1930] 2 KB 364, 375 where McCardie J noted the action for loss of services 'rested on the old rule that a master had some sort of property in the service of one who is a servant'. The point here is simply the connection between employees, household members and notions of slavery. The action for loss of services is said to be of much earlier origin than vicarious liability: *Commonwealth v Quince* (1944) 68 CLR 227, 235 (Latham CJ).

[6] *Attorney-General for NSW v Perpetual Trustee Co* (Ltd) (1952) 85 CLR 237, 272: 'when the legal right or interest of the master ... was of a proprietary nature and the master therefore had complete control of those services' (Webb J); 276: 'the head of a household was regarded as having a quasi-proprietary interest in the members of his family, his apprentices, his hired servants, and their services' (Fullagar J); 298: 'the particular situation of master and servant ... was formerly a matter of status' (Kitto J); *Commonwealth v Quince* (n 6) 236–37 who states the action for loss of services rested 'on the idea that the master had a quasi-proprietary interest in his servant's services; and that idea is connected with ideas as to the status of a servant, which originated in the rules of law applicable to villein status' (quoting W Holdsworth, *The History of English Law Volume VIII* 2nd edn (London, Sweet & Maxwell, 1937); see also McTiernan J (250).

[7] OW Holmes, 'Agency' (1891) 4 *Harvard Law Review* 345, 350.

[8] Holmes, 'Agency' (n 7) 355.

[9] F Pollock and FW Maitland, *The History of English Law Volume 2: Before the Time of Edward I* (Cambridge, Cambridge University Press, 1895) 470. The learned authors also include within this

Wigmore argues that these principles were recognised in Norman England. He cites numerous cases from the Selden Society's *Court Baron* (1250–1300 AD). Case 36 involves William of Street's Case. In it an accusation is made against a father whose son trespassed onto another's property to take their fruit. The report says the father 'deni(es) that the son ever did so at his bidding', but the trial proceedings seem to reflect the father's admission he is liable for what his son did. Case 55, William Lorimer's Case, involved the defendant being alleged to be responsible for actions of workers who cut stubble in the field of another. The defendant denies responsibility on two fronts, claiming that the workers did not cut the stubble 'by my commandment', and also claiming that the workers were only day labourers, for which he should not be held liable. Apparently 'either defence was good'.

Pollock and Maitland also take this position regarding the law at the time:

> We may take for granted that the man who commands a trespass, which is committed in obedience to his command, is himself a trespasser. About this our law of the thirteenth century and of much earlier times had no doubt whatsoever ... what is done by a man's command may be imputed to him as though it were his own act.[10]

Note the slight inconsistency in wording in the passage by the learned authors. The first sentence seems to convey the idea that the wrongdoing is deemed to be the act of the principal. The second says that the wrong is imputed to them 'as though' it were their act. This difference is important and will be discussed in greater detail later in the book.

In a case in AD 1231 against defendant fishermen for allegedly taking the plaintiff's fishing nets, the defendants were asked whether they did the taking 'by the authority of Abbot of St Edmund's, whose men they are'. Bracton states that 'it must be inquired of the master whether he has avowed the deed of his servants or not ... if he has avowed it ... he makes the wrong his own, if there was a wrong'.

Wigmore says that in this period a crude distinction was being made between penal consequences and mere consequences to pay amercement or compensation. A master could avoid penal consequences by denying that he had commanded or consented to the actions of the wrongdoer. He says that in this period the master would still sometimes be liable to pay amercement for what the worker had done, but that eventually the 'defence' based on lack of command or consent would extend from the 'criminal' context to the 'civil' context.[11] Bracton takes a similar

category the liability that an individual had for the wrongdoing of their beasts, and for their inanimate objects.

[10] Pollock and Maitland (n 9) 526–27; see also D Ibbetson, *A Historical Introduction to the Law of Obligations* (Oxford, Oxford University Press, 1999) 69: 'the specific acts of servants must have been commanded or at least assented to by the master (in order to make the master liable for those actions)'.

[11] J Wigmore, 'Responsibility for Tortious Acts: Its History' (1894) 7 *Harvard Law Review* 315, 335: 'by the end of the 1200s the general civil rule was as indicated by Bracton's statement ... in other words, so far as any penal results were concerned, the master could pretty generally exonerate himself by pleading that he had not commanded or consented to the act, while nevertheless this was only a growing exception to a responsibility which the moral sense of the community was still inclined to predicate

position.[12] It fits with Pollock and Maitland's observation that in the context of master and servant liability, and more generally, 'the king's courts were approaching the field of tort through the field of crime'.[13]

Wigmore refers to numerous cases in the fourteenth and fifteenth centuries reflecting the increasing acceptance in what we would understand to be 'civil law' of an argument from the master that they were not liable for actions of a servant because they did not command or consent to them. He cites a 1353 case as pivotal in acceptance by the civil law of such a doctrine.[14] A 1354 statute seems to reflect the command and consent theory.[15] This approach was continued early in the fifteenth century.[16]

This approach continued in the seventeenth century. In *Waltham v Mulgar* the question arose of the liability of a shipowner for the actions of a contractor who worked for them. Popham CJ stated that:

> Where a master put his servant to do an illegal act, the master shall answer for the servant if he mistakes in the doing of the act; but where he put his servant to do a legal

generally and accordingly the liability to make good any harm done ie the civil liability—still continued without regard to command or consent. As we shall see later the test of command or consent was soon after extended generally to civil liability also; and even in the 1200s we seem to see it coming. Yet as that century was not thoroughly conscious of the distinctions 'civil' and 'criminal' it can only be said that, at the point to which we have now traced the topic … the test of command or consent was applied in some cases and not applied in others, the general notion being that absence of command or consent excused from correctional or penal consequences'.

[12] Holmes, 'Agency' (n 7) 355: 'Even in Bracton, who writes under the full influence of the Roman law, I have failed to find any passage which distinctly asserts the civil liability of masters for their servants' torts, apart from command or ratification'.

[13] Pollock and Maitland (n 9) 529.

[14] 'No merchant nor other … shall lose or forfeit his goods or merchandizes for the trespass and forfeiture of his servant, unless he do it by the command or procurement of his master, or that he hath offended in the office in which his master hath set him': St 27 Edw III, 2, c 19 (referred to in J Wigmore 'Responsibility for Tortious Acts: Its History—II' (1894) 7 *Harvard Law Review* 383, 385). See also 9 H VI, 53, pl 37 (1431): 'if your servant by your covin and commandment sells bad wine, (the buyer) shall have action against you; for it is your own selling; and if the case is that you did not command your servant to sell to that person, then you may allege that you did not sell to the plaintiff' (from counsel, but which has been accepted as the precedent from the case); 11 Edw IV, 6, pl 10 (1472): 'if he undertakes to shoe my horse, and orders his servant to do it … the action lies against the master' (Choke J, with whom Brian J agreed); 13 H VII, 15, pl 10 (1498): 'it was held in Common Bench, if my servant, against my desire, chases my beasts into the land of a stranger, I may not be punished for this, but my servant'; 21 H VII, 22, pl 21 (1506): 'where I command my servant to take the distress legally, and he rides on the distress, I this case he shall be punished, and I excused, for that when I command him to do a thing legally, and he does contrary to the commandment, he does a wrong to which I did not assent; it is reason to punish him and to excuse me' (Rede CJ); *Doctor and Student*, II, c 42 (Muchall's Ed, 233)1518): 'for trespass or battery, or wrongful entry into lands or tenements … the master shall not be charged for his servant, unless he did it by his commandment … but that an host or keeper of a tavern shall answer for their guests, unless it be done by their assent and commandment, I do not remember that I have read it in the laws of England'.

[15] 'That no merchant nor other, of what condition that he be, shall lose or forfeit his goods nor merchandises for the trespass and forfeiture of his servant, unless he do it by the commandment or procurement of his master': Stat 27 Edw III stat 2 cap 19.

[16] In *Beaulieu v Finglam* (1401) B & M 557 the Court found that a homeowner could be liable for the actions of another who 'by my leave or my knowledge' did something resulting in fire damage to a neighbouring property, but not if the culprit did it 'against my will'.

act, as here to take the goods of the king's enemies, and he has taken the goods of friends, the master shall not answer.[17]

Similarly, in *Southern v How* it was found that a jeweller whose servant provided counterfeit jewels to the plaintiff was not liable for the wrongdoing because the servant had exceeded his authority.[18] In *Kingston v Booth* three members of the court stated that:

> If I command my servant to do what is lawful, and he misbehave himself, or do more, I shall not answer for my servant, but my servant for himself, for that it was his own act; otherwise it was in the power of every servant to subject his master to what actions or penalties he pleased. Thirdly, if I command my servant to do a lawful act, as in this case to pull down a little wooden house (wherein the plaintiff was …) and bid them take care they hurt not the plaintiff, if in this doing my servants wound the plaintiff, in trespass of assault and wounding brought against me, I may plead not guilty, and give this in evidence, for that I was not guilty of the wounding, and the pulling down of the house was a lawful act.[19]

Wigmore writes that these principles were challenged by developments in commerce,[20] a point also noted by the United Kingdom Supreme Court in 2016.[21] As the size of business enterprise grew, it became less likely that a master would specifically authorise particular actions of a servant. The master and the servant were more remote from each other than was the position at the time the doctrine was first conceived. The law needed to respond to these developments in business. However, it was not entirely clear how, if at all, the test could evolve to meet the changing environment of business, but also provide the kind of certainty needed.

The seeds of a new approach appear at the very end of the seventeenth century.[22] In *Turberville v Stampe* the court considered the liability of a master for the actions of his servant which led to fire damage to a neighbouring property.[23] Holt CJ stated that if a stranger set fire to the defendant's house, and it led to the burning of the plaintiff's house, the defendant would not be liable. However,

> [i]n this case if the defendant's servant kindled the fire in the way of husbandry, and proper for his employment, though he had no express command of his master, yet the master shall be liable … for it shall be intended that the servant had authority from his master, it being for his master's benefit.

[17] *Waltham v Mulgar* (1606) Moo KB 1076; 72 ER 1606.

[18] *Southern v How* (1618) 15 Cro Jac 468; 79 ER 400, 401.

[19] *Kingston v Booth* (1685) Skinner, 228; 90 ER 105, 105 (Withins, Holloway and Walcot JJ).

[20] Wigmore 'Responsibility for Tortious Acts: Its History—II' (n 14) 392–93.

[21] *Mohamud v Wm Morrison Supermarkets Plc* [2016] AC 677, 684: 'the 17th century was a century of expansion of commerce and industry, and vicarious liability began to be broadened' (Lord Toulson, with whom Lord Neuberger, Baroness Hale, Lord Dyson and Lord Reed agreed).

[22] Pollock and Maitland state that prior to the revolution of 1688 'there are exceedingly few hints … given to us of any responsibility of a master for acts that he has not commanded': Pollock and Maitland (n 9) 527. The learned authors say that first hint of change was couched in terms of 'implied command'.

[23] *Turberville v Stampe* (1698) 1 Ld Raym 264; 91 ER 1072.

This passage is important for at least two reasons. First, it specifically moves away from the specific command or consent requirement, holding that a master could be liable although he did not expressly command the actions of the servant. Instead, it was enough if the servant had 'authority', though this concept was not explained. Secondly, Holt CJ linked the concept of authority with whatever could be characterised as 'being for the master's benefit'. This is the first case that I can find where this concept was used as a basis for finding a master liable.

The move from a specific command basis to an implicit command basis had important implications at a time when the forms of action ruled. The plaintiff's choice to proceed in trespass or case was critical; an incorrect choice would be fatal to their claim. When the employer was liable for actions they had specifically authorised, commanded or ratified, it was possible to say their liability for their servant's actions was in trespass, being a direct act.[24] However, when it was sought to make the master liable for actions that were not specifically authorised, commanded or ratified, it became more difficult to justify an action in trespass against the employer, and the court began to accept that the proper action against the employer was in case, they being indirectly liable for what the servant did.

Holt CJ also decided *Middleton v Fowler*,[25] involving the question of liability of a stagecoach owner for the actions of the driver in losing a passenger's luggage. Holt CJ again expressed the principles in terms of what authority the servant had been given by the master. He said where a servant acted within such authority the 'act of the servant is the act of the master'.[26] This concept is also evident in the judgment in *Boucher v Lawson*,[27] where Hardwicke CJ stated that the owner of a vessel would not be liable where a servant was given control of the ship for a particular purpose. The servant used the ship for another purpose. The court was satisfied the shipowner could not be held liable for those actions. Other examples where courts found that the act of the servant was the act of the master include *Lane v Cotton*,[28] *Ackworth v Kempe*,[29] *Laugher v Pointer*[30] and *Williams v Jones*.[31] It is encompassed by the Latin phrase *qui facit per alium facit per se*.[32] It is evident

[24] *Scott v Davis* (n 3) 390 (Gummow J).

[25] *Middleton v Fowler* (1699) 1 Salk 282; 91 ER 247.

[26] This reasoning is also evident in *Jones v Hart* (1699) 2 Salk 441; 90 ER 1295.

[27] *Boucher v Lawson* (1815) Cas t Hard 194; 95 ER 125.

[28] 'What is done by the deputy is done by the principal, and it is the act of the principal' (*Lane v Cotton* (1701) 1 Salk 17, 18; 91 ER 17 (Holt CJ)).

[29] *Ackworth v Kempe* (1778) 1 Doug 41, 43; 99 ER 30: 'for all civil purposes the act of the sheriff's bailiff is the act of the sheriff' (Lord Mansfield). See also YB 49 Ed III, 25, 26, pl 3 where it was held that an abbot would be liable for actions of their underlings 'for that is adjudged the deed of the abbot'.

[30] *Laugher v Pointer* (1826) 5 B & C 547; 108 ER 204: 'such servants represent the master himself, and their acts stand upon the same footing as his own' (Littledale J, 554 and 207); 'whatever is done for the working of my mine or the repair of my house, by persons mediately or immediately employed by me, may be considered as done by me' (Abbott CJ, 576 and 215).

[31] *Williams v Jones* (1865) 3 H & C 602, 609; 159 ER 668, 671: 'where the relation of master and servant exists between one directing a thing to be done and those employed to do it, the master is considered in law to do it himself' (Blackburn J).

[32] In other words, 'the direct act of one is treated as if it were the direct act of another': OW Holmes, 'Agency II' (1891) 5 *Harvard Law Review* 1, 21.

in the summary of Bacon.[33] Holmes said that this idea was originally conceived in relation to public service employees, but came to be applied to cases of master and servant generally.[34] The principle was also recognised by Blackstone.[35]

On the other hand, some cases seem to deny that the servant's acts are in effect deemed to be the acts of the master: 'the maxim "qui facit per alium facit per se" renders the master liable for all the negligent acts of the servant in the course of his employment; but that liability does not make the direct act of the servant the direct act of the master'.[36] At one time, this had an important bearing on whether the action against the master should be brought in trespass or case. At that time, plaintiffs were required to elect to proceed either in trespass or case, and an incorrect choice would be fatal to their case. According to Baron Parke's comments in *Sharrod*, a plaintiff proceeding against a master for the claimed wrongful actions of a servant within the course of employment should proceed in case, rather than trespass. This difference is material and will be explored later in the book.

Where courts attempted to justify why a master was liable for the actions of their servant within authority, there sometimes appears statements that as between two innocent individuals (the person suffering injury and the master), it is somehow 'better' or 'more reasonable' that the master should suffer the loss, given that they engaged the servant.[37] In other words, somewhat anomalously crude notions of blame were utilised to justify the imposition of (strict) liability on the master.

Sir William Blackstone made the following summary of the English law in the late eighteenth century:

> As for those things which a servant may do on behalf of his master, they seem all to proceed upon this principle, that the master is answerable for the act of his servant, if done by his command, either expressly given or implied: *nam qui facit per alium facit*

[33] 'The reason why the acts of the servant are, in many instances, esteemed the acts of the master arises from the relation between a master and servant; for as in strictness everybody ought to transact his own affairs, and it is by the favour and indulgence of the law that he can delegate the power of acting for him to another, it is highly reasonable that he should answer for such substitute, at least civiliter; and that his acts, being pursuant to the authority given him, should be deemed acts of the master': M Bacon, *A New Abridgment of the Law*, 5th edn (London, A Strahan, 1798) 583.

[34] He cites *Woodgate v Knatchbull* (1787) 2 TR 148, 154 where Ashurst J says that the principle Lord Mansfield applied in *Ackworth* applies to master and servant cases generally: Holmes, 'Agency' (n 7) 362. Pollock and Maitland warn of the dangers of extrapolating from the rules applied to royal officers to general legal principle: (n 9) 531.

[35] Sir William Blackstone, *Commentaries on the Laws of England 1765–1769*: 'the wrong done by the servant is looked upon in law as the wrong of the master himself' (431–32).

[36] *Sharrod v London and North Western Railway Co* (1849) 4 Ex 579, 586; 154 ER 1345, 1347–48 (Parke B, for the Court).

[37] *Hern v Nichols* (1700) 1 Salk 289, 289: 'seeing somebody must be a loser by this deceit, it is more reason, that he that employs and puts a trust and confidence in the deceiver should be a loser, than a stranger' (Holt CJ); *Sir Robert Wayland's Case* (1706) 3 Salk 234: 'the master at his peril ought to take care what servant he employs; and it is more reasonable that he should suffer for the cheats of his servant than strangers or tradesmen'; *Udell v Atherton* (1861) 7 H & N 170, 191; 158 ER 437, 445: 'the rule ought to apply, that, as between two innocent persons, he who has trusted must take the consequence' (Lord Bramwell); cited with evident approval by Lord Scarman in *Rose v Plenty* [1976] 1 WLR 141, 148; *George Whitechurch Ltd v Cavanagh* [1902] AC 117, 137.

> *per se*. Therefore, if the servant commit a trespass by the command or encouragement of his master, the master shall be guilty of it … so likewise if the drawer at a tavern sells a man bad wine, whereby his health is injured, he may bring an action against the master; for although the master did not expressly order the servant to sell it to that person in particular, yet his permitting him to draw and sell it at all is impliedly a general command … in the same manner, whatever a servant is permitted to do in the usual course of his business, is equivalent to a general command … the principal must answer for (the conduct of his servants) for the law implies that they act under a general command … (provided the damage is done) while he is actually employed in the master's service … the wrong done by the servant is looked upon in law as the wrong of the master himself.[38]

We see further reference to the concept of whether the servant was acting for the benefit of the master. Some courts seem to prefer this approach, as opposed to one making the master liable for anything that occurred within the scope of employment. In *Bush v Steinman* Eyre CJ said that the 'general proposition that a person shall be answerable for any injury which arises in carrying into execution that which he has employed another to do seems to me to be too large and loose'.[39] He referred to another case (*Littledale v Lord Lonsdale*), and he said that case referred to the question whether the work was being 'carried on for his (the master's) benefit'.[40] Rooke J took a similar view: 'he who has work going on for his benefit and on his premises must be civilly answerable for the acts of those whom he employs'.[41]

There are many other case examples which consider as being relevant to a master's liability whether the servant's actions were for the benefit of the master. They include *Williams v Jones*,[42] *Stone v Cartwright*,[43] *Laugher v Pointer*[44] and *Duncan v Findlater*.[45] Several judges refer to it in *Limpus v London General Omnibus Company*.[46] Other examples of its use include *British Mutual Banking*

[38] Blackstone (n 35) 429. The master would also be liable for actions of the servant which were not initially authorised, but which were subsequently ratified by them: *Lewis v Read* (1845) 13 M & W 834; 153 ER 350, or perhaps where the master 'acquiesced' in the acts: *Ward v Evans* 2 Salk 442; 91 ER 383.

[39] *Bush v Steinman* (1799) 1 B & P 404; 126 ER 978, 979.

[40] ibid.

[41] ibid 981.

[42] (1865) 3 H & C 602, 612; 159 ER 668, 672: 'nor was the act of lighting the pipe in any way whatever for the benefit of his master' (Blackburn J).

[43] *Stone v Cartwright* (1795) 6 TR 411, 413; 101 ER 622, 623: 'the present defendant has no interest in the colliery, nor was it worked for his benefit' (Lord Kenyon CJ).

[44] (1826) 5 B & C 547, 554; 108 ER 204, 207 (Littledale J)

[45] *Duncan v Findlater* (1839) 6 Cl & F 894, 910; 7 ER 934, 940: 'what he does, being done for my benefit and under my direction, I am responsible for the consequences of doing it' (Lord Brougham). That case is also noteworthy for use of the rationale for the imposition of liability on the master that he is liable because he 'set the whole thing in motion' (940).

[46] *Limpus v London General Omnibus Company* (1862) 1 H & C 526; 158 ER 993: 'the master is responsible for any misconduct of the servant in driving and managing it which must be considered as having resulted from the performance of the duty entrusted to him, and especially if he was acting for his master's benefit' (537, 997–98 (Williams J)); 'he left it to the jury to say whether the injury resulted from an act done by the driver in the course of the service and for his masters' purposes' (538, 998 (Crompton J)); 'the proper question is whether the servant was acting at the time in the course of his master's service and for his master's benefit' (540, 999 (Willes J)); 'if a servant acts in the prosecution of

Company Limited v Charnwood Forest Railway Company.[47] Here it is clearly used as an additional requirement to concepts of scope. Lord Esher MR stated that 'although what the secretary stated related to matters about which he was authorised to give answers, he did not make the statements for the defendants but for himself'.[48] It is also referred to in *Dyer v Munday*.[49]

Relatedly, there is evidence in some cases of reference to the purpose or purposes for which the relevant servant was acting. The courts have tried to distinguish cases where the servant was purporting to act to further the employer's interests, and cases where the servant was not purporting to do so, but rather to advance a personal, private interest of their own.[50] There are obvious analogies between this distinction and the previous discussion of whether a servant was acting for their master's benefit. A person acting for their master's benefit will be acting for the purposes of the employer; a person not acting for the master's benefit will not be acting for the employer's purposes.

Some examples of the court's interest in the purpose or purposes for which the relevant servant acted include *Williams v Jones*, where there is reference to questions regarding whether the servant's actions were 'in furtherance of the object of the employment', 'in furtherance of the master's business', or 'for the purposes of the master'.[51] Further case examples include *British Mutual Banking Company Limited v Charnwood Forest Railway Company*,[52] *Dyer v Munday*,[53] *Cheshire v Bailey*[54] and *Ruben v Great Fingall Consolidated*.[55] Academic writing at the

his master's business for the benefit of his master … the master is liable' (541, 999 (Byles J)); 'if the jury should (conclude) that he did the act, not to further his master's interest … but from private spite … the defendants were not responsible' (543, 1000 (Blackburn J)).

[47] *British Mutual Banking Company Limited v Charnwood Forest Railway Company* (1887) 18 QBD 714 (CA).

[48] ibid 716. Bowen LJ also held the master (company) derived no benefit from the servant's acts (719); see also *Bolingbroke v Swindon Local Board* (1874) 9 LR (Common Pleas) 575, 578 (Keating J) and 579 (Grove J).

[49] *Dyer v Munday* [1895] 1 QB 742, 747 (Lopes LJ).

[50] *Croft v Alison* (1821) 4 B & Ald 589; 106 ER 1052, where the Court distinguished factual situations on this basis: 'if a servant driving a carriage, in order to effect some purpose of his own, wantonly strikes the horses of another person, and produces the accident, the master will not be liable. But if, in order to perform his master's orders, he strikes (the horse) but injudiciously … that will be negligent and careless conduct for which the master will be liable, being an act done in pursuance of the servant's employment'; see similarly *Wheatley v Patrick* (1837) 2 M & W 649; 150 ER 917.

[51] (1865) 3 H & C 602, 612; 159 ER 668, 672 (Keating J, for Erle CJ and Smith J); in *Patten v Rea* (1857) 2 CBNS 605, 615 there is a reference to the servant 'going about his master's business' (Willes J).

[52] (1887) 18 QBD 714, 716–17 where Lord Esher MR found the servant 'did not make the statements for the defendant but for himself … as he made them in his own interest or to assist his friend, he was not acting for the defendants'.

[53] [1895] 1 QB 742, 746 where Lord Esher MR said the question was whether the servant 'did the acts complained of for the purpose of furthering that employment, and not for private purposes of his own'; Lopes LJ asked whether the servant's actions were 'in furtherance of (their) employment' (747).

[54] *Cheshire v Bailey* [1905] 1 KB 237, 245: 'any departure by the servant for his own purposes from the discharge of his ordinary duties would relieve his master from responsibility' (Mathew LJ).

[55] *Ruben v Great Fingall Consolidated* [1906] AC 439, 446: 'where … the (servant) is acting fraudulently for his own illegal purposes, no representation by him relating to the matter will bind his employers. And … it would be a matter of reproach if the law were otherwise' (Lord Davey).

time reflected its importance.[56] Subsequent cases have referred to such matters differently, for instance by considering whether the employee was engaged on a 'frolic' at the time of the events in question, in which case the employer would not be vicariously liable for the servant's actions.[57]

Without wishing to interrupt the historical flow of this chapter, I must make reference at this point to a much more recent case, that of *Rose v Plenty*.[58] There, ironically with respect, is a reference to the purpose(s) for which the servant acted in the judgment of Lord Denning:

> [I]n considering whether a prohibited act was within the course of the employment, it depends very much on the purpose for which it is done. If it is done for his employer's business, it is usually done in the course of his employment, even though it is a prohibited act.[59]

This passage is puzzling, because it occurs after Lord Denning points out that in the decision of *Lloyd v Grace, Smith and Co* in 1912, to be discussed below, the House of Lords jettisoned the requirement that in order for vicarious liability to be applied, the servant had to be acting for the benefit of the employer. Evidently, Lord Denning approved of this move in *Lloyd*. In that vein, it is strange that in the same judgment he should refer to the issue of whether the servant was acting for the purposes of the employer. Clearly, the issue of whether the employee was acting for the *purposes* of the employer, and whether they were acting for the master's *benefit*, are closely correlated. It seems incongruous, with respect, to accept the relevance of one, but not the relevance of the other.

Again, in the nineteenth century we see references in the case law to consideration of whether the servant was acting at the command of the master. This occurs in cases such as *Morley v Gaisford*,[60] *Savignac v Roome*,[61] *Stone v Cartwright*,[62] *McManus v Crickett*,[63] *Goodman v Kennell*[64] and *Sharrod v London and North Western Railway Co*.[65] It was emphasised by Cockburn CJ in *Patten v Rea*.[66] The direction and command principle also appears in *Duncan v Findlater*.[67]

[56] F Pollock, *Essays in Jurisprudence and Ethics* (London, FB Rothman, 1882) 126: 'a man is liable for harm done by the use of his property without due care, but for his purposes and in a generally authorized manner, but not for harm done by the use of it in an unauthorized manner and for the wrongdoer's purposes alone'.

[57] *Morris v CW Martin and Sons Ltd* [1966] 1 QB 716, 733–34 (Lord Diplock).

[58] 1976] 1 WLR 141.

[59] ibid 144 (Lord Denning MR).

[60] *Morley v Gaisford* (1795) 2 HB 443.

[61] *Savignac v Roome* (1795) 6 TR 125.

[62] (1795) 6 TR 411.

[63] *McManus v Crickett* (1800) 1 East 106: 'if a servant quits sight of the object for which he is employed, and without having in view his master's orders, pursues that which his own malice suggests, he no longer acts in pursuance of the authority given him' (Kenyon CJ).

[64] *Goodman v Kennell* (1828) 1 Moore & P 241.

[65] (1849) 4 Ex 581.

[66] *Patten v Rea* (1857) 2 CBNS 606; 140 ER 554, 556: 'the servant must be driving with his master's authority and upon his business'.

[67] 'I am liable for what is done for me and under my orders by the man I employ … and the reason that I am liable is this, that by employing him I set the whole thing in motion, and what he does,

Yet we also find in cases in this area further reference to concepts of scope of employment. Cases on point include *McManus v Crickett*,[68] *Laugher v Pointer*,[69] *Coleman v Riches*[70] and *Patten v Rea*.[71] In *Patten*, Williams J explicitly acknowledged the shift from concepts of command to the concept of scope of employment: 'now it clearly is not necessary in cases of this sort that there should be any express request; the jury may imply a request or assent from the general nature of the servant's duty and employment'. Williams J also conceived of the obligation in terms of agency principle.[72] This is clearly a reference to an agency concept that is broader than an ability of the person seen as agent to contract on behalf of the purported principal, since the context was the liability of the owner of a horse and buggy where his servant drove the horse and buggy in a manner which injured the plaintiff's horse. Acceptance of the scope of employment doctrine seemed to contradict the view of Eyre CJ in *Bush v Steinman* that the 'general proposition that a person shall be answerable for any injury which arises in carrying into execution that which he has employed another to do, seems to be too large and loose'.[73]

Apart from the repeated use of the 'benefit of the master' concept in *Limpus*,[74] the case is also important for at least two other reasons. Firstly, because it dealt with conduct that had been specifically prohibited by the employer, and secondly, that the employer might reasonably have been expected to have sufficient resources to meet any judgment. Of the judges in this case, only Willes J and Byles J in the majority, and Wightman J dissenting, referred to the relevance of these factors. Willes J made two contentious findings here; first, that 'there ought to be a remedy against some person capable of paying damages to those injured by improper driving'.[75] I have not found this kind of reasoning expressed in previous cases, though it may have been implicitly part of the reasoning. Secondly, he found it 'immaterial that the defendants directed their servant not to do the act'.[76]

On the other hand, there are suggestions in the case law that the liability of a master for the acts of their servants does not apply in cases of deliberate

being done for my benefit and under my direction, I am responsible for the consequences of doing it' (*Duncan v Findlater* (n 45) 910, Lord Brougham).

68 (1800) 1 East 106.

69 (1826) 5 B & C 547; 108 ER 204: 'I admit the principle, that a man is answerable for the conduct of his servants in matters done by them in the exercise of the authority that he has given them' (Lord Kenyon).

70 *Coleman v Riches* (1855) SC 3 CLR 795; 139 ER 702.

71 (1857) 2 CBNS 606.

72 ibid: 'the real question is whether the servant while doing the negligent act complained of was acting as the agent of the defendant'.

73 (1799) 1 B & P 404, 407; 126 ER 978, 979.

74 (1862) 1 H & C 526; 158 ER 993.

75 ibid 535, 539; ER 998.

76 ibid; to like effect Byles J (541, 999): 'it is said that what was done was contrary to the master's instructions; but that might be said in ninety-nine out of a hundred cases in which actions are brought for reckless driving. It is also said that the act was illegal. So, in almost every action for negligent driving an illegal act is imputed to the servant'; *cf* Wightman J (dissenting) who found this precluded the employee being seen as acting within the scope of their employment: 'I cannot consider the express prohibition to the coachman to do what he did as immaterial in considering what was the course of his service in that respect' (1 H & C 535, 536; 150 ER 993, 997).

wrongdoing. For example, Holt CJ in *Jones v Hart* suggested that a postmaster would be liable for the negligence of one of their servants resulting in mail being lost. However, he suggested the result would be different if the servant had stolen the mail, because in such cases 'he was a wrongdoer'. He said the same rule would apply if a jailer deliberately permitted an escape. The master would not be liable, because the action was deliberate. He contrasted this with the position if the escape was due to mere negligence.[77] Similarly, for Wightman J (dissenting) in *Limpus* one of the reasons the employer was not liable for what the employee did was the 'wilful' nature of the employee's actions.[78] The idea that wilful acts are not within the 'scope of employment' principle also appears in judgments in *Bolingbroke v Swindon Local Board*.[79]

Another interesting case in this period is *Poulton v London and South Western Railway Company*.[80] It is interesting because the reasoning tends to suggest that the scope of any employee's employment is constrained by what their employer was/would have been lawfully entitled to do. The plaintiff was a passenger on the defendant's railway. He was on his way back from an agricultural show and was entitled to have his horse ride on the train as well without further payment. When he reached the end of his journey, an employee of the defendant demanded that the plaintiff pay a further fare for the horse. The plaintiff refused, and the employee detained him. The law permitted the railway company to detain those who had not paid due fares. The plaintiff sued the defendant for false imprisonment. False imprisonment was established; in fact, the defendant was not legally permitted to detain the plaintiff as they did. One issue was whether the defendant railway company was liable for the false imprisonment.

All members of the court found the defendant not liable for the false imprisonment. This was because the defendant did not have the legal power to detain the plaintiff. This affected the servant's scope of employment, according to the court. Blackburn J found that 'having no power themselves, they cannot give the station master any power to do the act'.[81] Mellor J took the same position, finding an employer could not be liable where the employee 'acts in a manner in which the company themselves would not be authorized to act'.[82] Shee J agreed that 'an authority cannot be implied to have been given to a servant to do an act, which, if his master were on the spot, the master would not be justified in doing'.[83] Blackburn J said the railway company was no more liable than they would have been had the employee committed an assault on the plaintiff.[84]

[77] (1699) 2 Salk 441; 91 ER 382, 383.
[78] (1862) 1 H & C. 526, 534.
[79] (1874) 9 LR (Common Pleas) 575, 578 (Keating J) and 579 (Grove J).
[80] *Poulton v London and South Western Railway Company* (1867) 2 QB 534.
[81] ibid 540.
[82] ibid 541.
[83] ibid.
[84] ibid 539. This is interesting given that subsequently the Court would hold an employer liable for assaults committed by their servants: *Dyer v Munday* (n 49).

An important statement of the law at this time was made by leading common lawyer Willes J in *Barwick v English Joint Stock Bank*.[85] The simple facts involved the question of whether a bank was liable for the actions of their bank manager in apparently guaranteeing a particular debt. Willes J stated that:

> With respect to the question, whether a principal is answerable for the act of his agent in the course of his master's business, and for his master's benefit, no sensible distinction can be drawn between the case of fraud and the case of any other wrong. The general rule is that the master is answerable for every such wrong of the servant or agent as is committed in the course of the service and for the master's benefit, though no express command or privity of the master be proved.[86]

This statement of the law in the latter part of the nineteenth century is considered important for several reasons. First, it was made by a judge whom some regard as one of the finest common law judges in English history,[87] and certainly one of the leading proponents. Secondly, it continues the trend away from the express command theory that had previously been thought to justify the imposition of liability upon a master. And thirdly, it appears to condition a master's liability for the actions of their servants on a dual requirement. Firstly, that the act took place in the course of the master's business, and secondly that it occurred for the benefit of the employer. That this is Willes J's position is evident by his use of the conjunction 'and' in two places within this passage to link the requirements of the servant acting in the course of their master's business, and the fact that their actions are for the benefit of the master. A natural reading of the passage suggests they are separate, individual requirements. A master would not be liable for the actions of their employee unless both were satisfied. It was possible that, upon the facts, one could be satisfied and not the other. In such a case, it seems that the master would not be liable for what their servant did. As indicated earlier, many cases prior to *Barwick* had cited and applied the principle of whether the relevant actions were done for the benefit of the master.

While this summary of the law at that time was authored by one justice, a unanimous Privy Council in *Mackay v Commercial Bank of New Brunswick*[88] cited it as the 'best definition' of the circumstances in which a master would be liable for actions of their servant that they had not specifically authorised. It was also cited with approval by the House of Lords in *Houldsworth v City of Glasgow Bank and Liquidators*.[89] There Lord Selborne, with whom Lord Hatherley agreed (three Law Lords decided the case) stated that the principle discussed by Willes J in *Barwick*

[85] *Barwick v English Joint Stock Bank* (1867) LR 2 Ex 259.

[86] ibid 265.

[87] *Scott v Davis* (n 3) 348 (McHugh J).

[88] *Mackay v Commercial Bank of New Brunswick* (1874) 5 LR (PC) 394, 411 (Sir Montague E Smith, for the Council).

[89] *Houldsworth v City of Glasgow Bank and Liquidators* (1880) 5 AC 317, 326 (Lord Selborne, who after citing the judgment of Willes J in *Barwick*, added that 'to the principle so stated no exception can, in my opinion, be taken'; Lord Hatherley agreed with Lord Selborne's judgment (331)).

was 'a principle, not of the law of torts, or of fraud and deceit, but of the law of agency'.[90]

The view that Willes J in *Barwick* was expressing a dual requirement was taken in *British Mutual Banking Company Limited v Charnwood Forest Railway Company*[91] and in *Ruben v Great Fingall Consolidated*.[92] In *George Whitechurch Ltd v Cavanagh* cited with apparent approval a comment by Bowen LJ in *British Mutual Banking Company* to the effect that no precedent which remained good law had held a principal liable in an action for deceit for unauthorised and/or fraudulent acts of a servant or agent committed not for the principal's benefit but that of the employee's private ends.[93]

However, the late nineteenth century also saw suggestions that both of the elements described by Willes J in *Barwick* may not in fact be needed in order to hold a master liable for what a servant did. This suggestion effectively appears in the judgment of Blackburn J in *McGowan v Dyer*.[94] There Blackburn J cites *Story on Agency* to the effect that a principal is liable for fraud, deceit, misrepresentation, tort and other omission of duty by an agent in the course of employment, although the master did not authorise, justify, participate in or know of the conduct, or even if the master had forbidden it.[95] He did not mention any requirement that the action or omission of the servant be for the benefit of the employer.

Matters came to a head in *Lloyd v Grace, Smith and Co*.[96] The facts of this case forced the House of Lords to squarely address the question of whether a master was liable for the actions of an employee that were clearly for the employee's own benefit, and not for the benefit of the employer. The relatively simple facts involved the plaintiff attending at the offices of the defendant with a view to obtaining advice on her property investments. She spoke with the firm's conveyancing manager, Sandles, and gave him instructions to sell her property and to call in a mortgage. Sandles gave her documents to sign. She did not read or understand them. Unknown to her, they effected a transfer of the title to her properties and the benefit of the mortgage to Sandles. The question was the liability of the employer for the actions of Sandles. The employer derived no benefit from Sandles' behaviour. As a result, the correct interpretation to be given to the statement of the law by Willes J in *Barwick* became critical. If the success of the plaintiff's case were to turn on whether the actions in question were committed for the defendant's benefit, her claim would be unsuccessful. However, if it were not necessary, her claim was much stronger.

[90] ibid 326.
[91] (1887) 18 QBD 714, 718 (Lord Bowen).
[92] [1906] AC 439, 465 (Lord Davey).
[93] [1902] AC 117, 141.
[94] *McGowan v Dyer* (1873) LR 8 QB 141.
[95] ibid 145.
[96] *Lloyd v Grace, Smith and Co* [1912] AC 716.

All members of the Court found in favour of the plaintiff. Lord Macnaghten delivered the leading judgment. He interpreted the judgment of Willes J in *Barwick* as not to require that the acts in question were for the master's benefit. He claimed that Willes J was merely dealing with the factual scenario in *Barwick*, where the principal had in fact benefited by the actions of the servant. However, Lord Macnaghten said it was a very different proposition to suggest that in all cases where it was sought to make an employer liable for the actions of their employees, it was necessary to show that the employer benefited.[97] He read the judgment of Willes J in *Barwick* as not requiring that to be shown in all cases. He found that suggestions to the contrary by Lord Bowen and Lord Davey were incorrect and should be overruled.

With respect, the court in *Lloyd* seriously understated the support for a requirement that the relevant actions be for the benefit of the employer and for their purposes. There was substantial authority over more than two centuries where the concept had been used, commencing in the late seventeenth century decision in *Turberville v Stampe*. It was somewhat disingenuous, with respect, to focus on the decision in *Barwick*, and claim that Willes J never meant there to be a dual requirement of acting for the master's benefit and within the scope of employment, and to effectively abandon the first requirement. That first requirement actually pre-existed the scope of employment doctrine and had been recognised and applied in case law over 200 years. Rejection of it really required a much fuller articulation and justification than what is evident in *Lloyd*. The court should have squarely faced the seriousness of the action they proposed to take, rather than seek to downplay and minimise it in the way it did.

Lord Macnaghten also apparently based his decision on other grounds, and it is of course not known the extent, if any, to which these other grounds affected his interpretation of what Willes J had said in *Barwick*. For instance, Lord Macnaghten seemed to adopt reasoning based on a lesser of two evils type approach, asking 'who is to suffer for this man's fraud? The person who relied on the (defendant's) accredited representative, or the defendant, who put his rogue in his own place and clothed him with his own authority?'[98] The Earl of Halsbury took a similar position, pointing out that 'seeing somebody must be a loser in the case', it was 'more reason' that the one who employed the dishonest individual should bear the loss than the innocent third party.[99] In other words, fault-based reasoning was used to support a decision about strict liability. Lord Macnaghten also referred to the fact that it was open for an employer to obtain insurance to protect themselves against the risk of employee wrongdoing.[100] Earl Loreburn

[97] ibid 732; to like effect Lord Halsbury (726) and Lord Shaw (741); Earl Loreburn (725) agreed with what Lord Macnaghten said about *Barwick*, and Lord Atkinson agreed generally with Lord Macnaghten's judgment (739).

[98] ibid 738.

[99] ibid 727, citing *Hern v Nichols* (1700) 1 Salk 289 (Holt CJ).

[100] ibid 738.

viewed the matter as a case of breach of contract and tort, both committed by the defendant's agent.[101]

In the early years of the twentieth century, as the concept of 'scope of employment' became the dominant principle in describing the circumstances in which an employer would be liable for the actions of their employee, Salmond's scholarly articulation of the principle became critical. He stated that an employer would be liable for authorised acts, and for unauthorised acts provided they were considered to be modes—albeit improper modes, of doing that which was authorised.[102] In contrast, the employer would not be liable for the servant's independent acts. This summary may have been intended to reflect the case law described above which sought to distinguish 'wilful' acts, and acts not done for the purposes of the master, from the scope of the employer's liability.

Cases subsequent to *Lloyd* have continued to apply the idea that it is not necessary to show that the relevant act of the servant was for the master's benefit. Cases in this period will be discussed at greater length in chapter two and just a brief summary will be provided here for current purposes. Employers have been liable for the consequences of actions of the servant which were specifically prohibited by the employer,[103] and for criminal behaviour of the servant.[104] Arguably, the principles of vicarious liability are most difficult in their application to intentional wrongs. Past concerns in the case law about making an employer liable for 'wilful' actions of a servant appear to have been either ignored or rejected. Vicarious liability has been applied to make employers liable for behaviour that is on any view grossly negligent, such as lighting a cigarette while unloading fuel from a tanker and dropping the struck match onto the ground.[105] The closeness of the connection between the employee's actions and their employment is extremely important in determining the employer's liability for their employee's actions.[106] More recently, the English courts have apparently based the imposition of vicarious liability on cases in which it is 'fair, just and reasonable' to do so,[107] though

[101] ibid 724.

[102] JW Salmond, *The Law of Torts: A Treatise on the English Law of Liability for Civil Injuries*, 1st edn (London, Stevens & Haynes, 1907) 95. In the 1936 version he explains that: 'the master is responsible for acts actually authorised by him (and) … is liable even for acts which he has not authorised, provided they are so connected with acts that he has authorised that they may be regarded as modes—although improper modes—of doing them. In other words, a master is responsible not merely for what he authorises his servant to do, but also for the way in which he does it … on the other hand, if the unauthorised and wrongful act of the servant is not so connected with the authorised act as to be a mode of doing it, but is an independent act, the master is not responsible: for in such a case the servant is not acting in the course of his employment, but has gone outside of it'.

[103] *Rose v Plenty* (n 37) (employer liable for injuries 13-year-old plaintiff suffered after falling from a milk truck; employees had been specifically directed not to permit young people to assist with the milk run in this way).

[104] *Morris v CW Martin and Sons Ltd* (n 57); *Mohamud* (n 21); *Various Claimants v WM Morrisons Supermarket PLC* [2017] EWHC 3113.

[105] *Century Insurance Company Limited v Northern Ireland Road Transport Board* [1942] AC 509.

[106] *Lister and Others v Hesley Hall Ltd* [2002] 1 AC 215.

[107] *Various Claimants v Catholic Child Welfare Society* [2013] 2 AC 1.

that concept appears to have been borrowed from the law of negligence,[108] a fault-based tort with very different contours from the strict liability notion of vicarious liability.

It is fair to say that it has proven to be extremely difficult to articulate a unifying rationale for the law regarding vicarious liability.[109] This has long been noted by scholars, and more recently by judges. Understandably, the early cases discussed in this chapter contain either no or very bare reasoning to support their assertions of principle; more recent cases have attempted to articulate a unifying rationale, although many are sceptical that this is possible. The *Mohamud* possible rationales for vicarious liability will be discussed in a later chapter. At this point it is sufficient to note that a search for a unifying rationale to explain and rationalise the historical case law developments enumerated above has been and continues to be futile. In a generally coherent system of legal rules when most legal principle can be rationally articulated and defended, this sticks out.

Vicarious Liability in the Context of Other Developments in Tort Law

It is considered essential to read and digest all of the above developments in the law of vicarious liability in the broader context of tort law. Developments in one area of tort law are not, and should not be, immune from developments elsewhere in tort law.[110]

Various doctrines of nineteenth-century English tort law made it very difficult for an employee injured at work to claim compensation from their employer. Most notorious was the doctrine of common employment, precluding an injured employee from obtaining compensation against an employer where their injuries were caused by the actions of another employee.[111] Further, robust application of the doctrine of *volenti non fit injuria* inhibited the ability of injured employees to claim compensation, as did the doctrine of contributory negligence, which were

[108] *Caparo Industries Plc v Dickman* [1990] 2 AC 605; P Giliker, 'Comparative Perspectives on Vicarious Liability: Defining the Scope of Employment' in J Neyers, E Chamberlain and S Pitel (eds), *Emerging Issues in Tort Law* (Oxford, Hart Publishing, 2007) 426 notes this standard is reminiscent of the *Caparo* approach.

[109] *Prince Alfred College Inc v ADC* (2016) 258 CLR 134, 148 (French CJ; Kiefel Bell Keane and Nettle JJ); *Lister v Hesley Hall Ltd* (n 106) 232 (Lord Clyde).

[110] R Merkin and J Steele, *Insurance and the Law of Obligations* (Oxford, Oxford University Press, 2013) 316: 'while the abolition (I suggest the learned authors may have meant "introduction" rather than "abolition", reading their text here in context) of workers' compensation was accompanied by the repeal of the doctrine of common employment, so that *Priestley v Fowler* is no more, we have seen that the core principles of vicarious liability are the work of the same group of judges, during the same era, and dealing with issues which they will have correctly perceived to be related'.

[111] *Priestley v Fowler* (1837) 3 M & W 1; 150 ER 1030.

complete defences open to a defendant employer. Further, a workers' compensation scheme was not available until 1897.[112] In addition, the law of negligence was in a truncated state, where any plaintiff had to show that their relationship was within a category of recognised case in which a duty of care had been recognised, as opposed to the generalised duty of care which was introduced in 1932, and which has since buttressed a large expansion in negligence claims.

It is somewhat difficult to make too much of this position in the nineteenth century, and the extent to which it led to an expansion of employer vicarious liability, in particular through the jettisoning of the requirement that the relevant actions be for the employer's benefit or for a purpose of the employer, and the expansion of vicarious liability to wilful and/or criminal actions of the employee. This is because the courts typically did not use this (expressly) as a justification for their liberalisation of the liability rules in the area of vicarious liability. They used, to a limited extent, other rationalisations and justifications, which will themselves be subject to critique later in the book. However, it is fair to say that typically the existence and state of other principles of the law of tort did not feature in these attempted express rationalisations and justifications.

So my argument is acknowledged to some extent to be speculative. However, Ibbetson notes that frustration with some of the then rules of tort led judges to development of relatively novel principles, including the non-delegable duty, and *Ryland v Fletcher* strict liability. My argument in a sense mirrors Ibbetson's observations of other developments in tort law at the time. The point of the argument, that vicarious liability grew substantially in the late nineteenth century and early twentieth century in order to avoid strictures elsewhere in the law of tort, is that perhaps this cause and effect relationship has been forgotten over time. Specifically, the law has now abolished the doctrine of common employment. It no longer views the voluntary assumption of risk and/or contributory negligence as complete defences, and workers' compensation is much more readily available. It is much easier now than it was in the nineteenth century for a plaintiff to show that the defendant owed them a duty of care. It may be that a full appreciation of all of these developments may cause us to question the utility of the expansion of vicarious liability throughout the late nineteenth and twentieth and twenty-first centuries. Specifically, that it may now be unnecessarily broad, given developments elsewhere in the law of tort. This will be a theme explored throughout the book.

A final point should be made about the relation of vicarious liability to developments elsewhere in tort law. The House of Lords determined that United Kingdom law should apply a three-stage test in determining whether or not a defendant owes a duty of care. At the third stage, the court will consider whether it is 'fair, just and reasonable' to impose the asserted duty.[113] Interestingly, as will be explored

[112] Workmen's Compensation Act 1897 (UK).
[113] *Caparo Industries Plc v Dickman* (n 108) 617–18.

in a later chapter, it also considers whether it is fair and reasonable to impose vicarious liability upon an employer. At one level there is congruence across the United Kingdom law of tort in considering whether the imposition of liability upon a defendant is fair, just and reasonable. At another level, one may question the practical efficacy of law based on such a standard, given its inherent subjectivity. And clearly, vicarious liability involves strict liability, which is the antithesis of fault-based negligence liability, there is no necessary correlation in the principles which the two areas apply in determining liability. Canada applies a two-stage test which also considers the fairness and reasonableness of recognising that a duty of care exists in a particular situation.[114]

In contrast, the Australian High Court has rejected the use of either the three-stage or two-stage test in formulating whether a duty of care is owed. It has pointedly declined to consider whether imposition of a duty of care would be 'fair, just and reasonable'.[115] And interestingly, it has also declined to use such principles in justifying the imposition of vicarious liability, as will be seen in chapter three. So this congruence is interesting, though as indicated, to my mind there is no inevitability about applying the fair, just and reasonable requirement in either both contexts of fault and no-fault liability, or in neither.

Summary and Reflections on Historical Development of Vicarious Liability

The historical development of the principles of vicarious liability discussed above can be succinctly stated as follows:

— The relevant principles appear to be sourced in German law and were accepted in England post-conquest.
— They were originally based in the liability of the head of a household for the actions of their servants, before being expanded; they may also have a source in the liability of an individual for slaves, and liability with respect to public servants.
— The principles were originally rationalised on an express command or consent theory, but as the size of businesses grew beyond the level of a household, this narrow view of the scope of liability became untenable.
— The law thus turned to an implied command theory but struggled to articulate the precise parameters of liability.

[114] *Cooper v Hobart* [2001] 3 SCR 537; adopting a revised version of the two-stage test articulated in *Anns v Merton London Borough Council* [1978] AC 728.

[115] *Sullivan v Moody* (2001) 207 CLR 562, 579 (Gleeson CJ; Gaudron, McHugh, Hayne and Callinan JJ).

- Initially the law embraced a concept that the relevant actions of the servant had to be for the master's benefit; this was complemented by consideration of the purpose(s) for which the servant acted, and consideration of whether they were on a 'frolic'.
- This was later complemented by a focus on the scope of the servant's authority; apparently both were required in order for the master to be liable for the servant's actions.
- Suggestions appeared that it should not be necessary in all cases that the servant be acting for the master's benefit, a position which the law would eventually adopt in the early twentieth century.
- The law accepted that an employer would be liable for the actions of a servant that were authorised, and those which were unauthorised where they were merely an unauthorised mode of performing something which was authorised.
- The law initially did not accept that an employer could be liable for actions of the servant that were 'wrongful' and/or 'wilful', but eventually accepted an employer could be liable for such actions.
- The law initially did not accept that an employer could be liable for actions of a servant that the employer had specifically prohibited, but eventually accepted that an employer could be liable for such actions.
- There has been ambivalence regarding whether, if vicarious liability exists, the actions of the servant are deemed to be the actions of the master, or whether the master's liability is determined 'as if' the servant's actions are theirs; that is a difference which will be discussed later in the book.
- At some points blame appears to intrude unexpectedly, with suggestions that it is 'better' that the employer wear the loss because they chose the servant.
- At some points, questions of whether the employer is likely to have the means to make good the plaintiff's loss, and/or the availability of insurance, appear to buttress conclusions.
- Sometimes agency concepts are used to explain the liability of the master.
- The cases typically do not dwell in detail on the rationale for the imposition of vicarious liability; many rationales have been suggested, all are contested, and none may satisfactorily explain all principle in this area.
- The law of vicarious liability began to expand at a time where elsewhere in the law of tort various principles made it extremely difficult for an injured plaintiff, and in particular an injured employee, to obtain compensation from an employer; a cause and effect relationship can be suggested although the evidence is limited.
- A suggestion that it was not within the scope of employment for an employee to do something that their employer was not legally permitted to do has not been carried forward in the case law.

It is understandable and was perhaps inevitable that as the size and nature of businesses expanded beyond the home or farm-based business level, a theory of liability of the head of household, the 'master', would need to expand beyond the express command or consent theory. The search for a test that was more realistic and could be practically applied to the realities of the business environment is fully justified.

However, the challenge for the law was what this new test should be. As indicated above, at first a theory seemed to be applied based on whether the relevant actions of the servant were for the benefit of the principal or, in other words, whether the servant was acting for the purposes of the principal. Now, the cases as I read them do not generally deign to ever articulate why this is the principle to be applied. Obviously, cases of the relevant era—the late seventeenth century through to the early nineteenth century—were typically very lightly reported and lightly reasoned. In the absence of explicit reasoning and justification by the judges, at least a couple of possibilities may be canvassed.

First, it may be thought that an employer should only be liable for the actions of a servant done for their benefit, or to further their purposes, because it was thought that only in such cases could it be rationally said that the actions of the servant were the actions of the master, or that the law should view them as such. If the servant were really acting for themselves, arguably it becomes incoherent to say that they were the actions of the employer. This can explain the focus on the purpose of the servant in doing what they did, and whether they were acting for the benefit of the employer. If I am generally only liable for my own actions, liability for the actions of another needs to be carefully justified. If that person is really acting for me, it becomes easier to justify my being liable for what they did. Here agency theory fits. Agency theory holds that I am liable for what someone else did on my behalf. It is consistent and analogous with the historical roots of the vicarious liability doctrine in terms of command, but adapted to the changed realities of business.

Secondly, it could reflect a crude enterprise risk theory that has become fashionable in more recent years in the law of vicarious liability. In other words, that someone who runs an enterprise should fairly bear the costs of that enterprise, and that loss associated with what an employee did for the purposes of the business were among those costs. This draws some support from the cases which talk about someone 'setting something in motion'[116] and being liable for the fall-out, in the sense of the commencement of a business being setting something in motion.

Perhaps the other realisation, apparent scattered through a couple of the cases, was that, of itself, the 'for the benefit of the employer' principle may not be a sufficient way to place appropriate boundaries around an employer's liability. For instance, what if an employee kills a competitor to the employer's business? The employee might think this will benefit the employer; however most would say that the employer should not be liable for such an action. It was extreme. It was

[116] *Duncan v Findlater* (n 45) 910 (Lord Brougham).

unauthorised. It was beyond the scope of that for which the servant was engaged. Obviously, the answer to this question would turn upon whether an objective or subjective view were taken of the issue of whether the employee was acting for the benefit of the employer. Would it be sufficient that the employee believed they were acting for their employer's benefit, or would it need to appear to a reasonable observer that the employee was so acting?

Hence, the law eventually realised that, by itself, the concept of whether the employee was acting for the benefit or purposes of the employer was insufficient in determining vicarious liability boundaries. It had to be accompanied by something else, and that something else proved to be the 'scope of employment' doctrine.

However, while this apparently solved a problem like the one identified in the above paragraph, that 'benefit and purpose' did not always lead to palatable results; it created other problems. How should the scope of an employee's employment be determined? It was an inherently ambiguous concept, and different minds could reasonably come to different conclusions as to what the scope of an employee's employment was, as is evidenced by some of the case outcomes. For a time, the law seemed to require both that the relevant actions be for the employer's benefit/purpose, and that the actions be within the scope of employment, evidenced for instance by the judgment of Willes J for the court in *Barwick*, and Blackstone's summation of the position.

However, while it might have solved some problems, the scope of employment concept created others. Specifically, the concept of 'scope of employment' was particularly difficult in relation to actions of the employee that were wilful. Should an employer be held liable in cases of deliberate wrongdoing by the employee, where they might reasonably argue they never would have authorised the servant's actions? If the answer were yes, this would take the doctrine well beyond its original moorings of command. Yet some judges in the late nineteenth century, in cases like *Limpus*, apparently countenanced a suggestion that an employer could be liable in such circumstances. This became antagonistic to and impossible to reconcile with an ongoing requirement that the servant act for the benefit of the master and/or for the master's purposes. Something had to give. In 1912 in *Lloyd* the requirement that the relevant action be for the employer's benefit and for the employer's purposes was jettisoned.

As indicated above, this occurred without a full disclosure of the significance of the step being taken. The 'employer benefit' had been a requirement of the law since the 1698 *Turberville* decision; it seems disingenuous to focus merely on the *Barwick* articulation of it, and then claim that Willes J did not intend the master's benefit concept to be required in all cases, before adopting the scope of employment doctrine. The master's benefit requirement clearly predated the scope of employment concept. It sought to keep the vicarious liability doctrine within reasonable bounds, to avoid the 'looseness' of which Eyre CJ presciently warned in *Bush v Steinman*. Frankly, its interment deserved a much fuller discussion of the risks and benefits of such a significant change to the law. The judgment should have acknowledged that an important change to the law, with serious consequences, was being taken. The fact that an important change to be law was being made by the judges should not have been misrepresented as in fact not presenting a change at all. The judges should not have misread what was decided in *Barwick*. Their explanation of what it decided was, to be brutally frank, disingenuous.[117]

Nevertheless, the reality is that this step was taken. As a result, past concerns expressed in previous cases, that an employer should not be liable for 'wilful' actions of an employee,[118] and that a principle that made an employer liable for everything the employee did in the workplace was 'too loose',[119] were effectively either ignored or rejected. The finding that it could not be within the scope of an employee's liability to do something that their employer would not have been lawfully entitled to do was also effectively overruled.[120]

However, this took vicarious liability further away from its original moorings in the context of command, and that the servant's actions were considered to be really those of the master, which justified the master being answerable for them. When that rationale disappeared, and that connection to original history was severed, judges immediately searched for other justifications for the imposition of liability in such cases, including in the *Lloyd* decision itself. These included the lesser of two evils theory, which had appeared in the odd earlier case, that as between two innocent people, it was 'better' that the employer be liable, which inevitably invited in notions of blame and fault to a doctrine that was supposedly strict in nature, rather than fault based. It invited consideration of which party had deeper pockets and/or access to insurance, which is considered to be questionable legal reasoning. And it resorted to notions of what was 'fair, just and reasonable', a concept again borrowed from the fault area of tort law, yet apparently applied here to justify the imposition of no-fault, strict liability on an employer. We will see how the law of vicarious liability developed in the United Kingdom in the twentieth century in the following chapter.

[117] Atiyah opines that the *Lloyd* decision 'came as a surprise' to the profession: Atiyah (n 1) 196.
[118] *Bolingbroke v Swindon Local Board* (n 48).
[119] *Bush v Steinman* (n 39).
[120] (1867) 2 QB 534.

2

Developments in United Kingdom Vicarious Liability Law: Twentieth and Twenty-First Centuries

Development

The traditional law of vicarious liability essentially applied a two-stage test. At the first stage, the court considered whether the relationship between the defendant and the wrongdoer was of a type where vicarious liability could potentially apply (the threshold question). At the second stage, the court would consider whether the defendant was in fact liable for the wrongdoer's actions. Issues such as scope of employment, authorised and unauthorised modes, and more recently closeness of connection were relevant to this second stage. As most of the difficulty has involved the second question, I will first discuss how the United Kingdom law has developed on that question. I will briefly summarise how the law has developed on the first question in this chapter, and subject it to more detailed consideration in chapter nine.

I have dealt with the development of the vicarious liability doctrine in the United Kingdom up until the *Lloyd* decision in detail in chapter one. I have indicated that the doctrine was sourced in a conception of a business as a family-based enterprise, where the head of the household was liable for the actions of members of that household. It was initially conceived of in terms of an express command theory, but as the size of business grew, this became untenable. The law thus developed an implied command theory, and the scope of employment doctrine developed as part of this theory. For a significant time, the law considered whether the relevant actions of the servant were for the benefit of the employer or were otherwise directed towards the employer's purpose. This is best exemplified in the decision of Willes J for the Court in *Barwick v English Joint Stock Bank*,[1] who expressly included a requirement, in order that vicarious liability be held to apply, that the employee be acting for the benefit of the employer. This position had also been taken by many previous cases. Many past cases had sought

[1] *Barwick v English Joint Stock Bank* (1867) LR 2 Ex 259.

to distinguish from vicarious liability cases where the employee was on a 'frolic' of their own, as opposed to acting for the purposes of the employer.[2]

As I indicated in chapter one, I believe the House of Lords was disingenuous in *Lloyd v Grace, Smith and Co*[3] in how they dealt with the *Barwick* precedent. The claim of several of the Law Lords that *Barwick* did not mean to lay down a requirement that in all cases of vicarious liability it was necessary to show that the employee was acting for the benefit of the employer[4] is belied by the fact that many other decisions had also spoken of the need for the employee's actions to be seen to be for the benefit of the employer.[5] Other cases had endorsed the careful wording of Willes J in *Barwick*, emphasising that in order to make an employer liable for what an employee had done, it was necessary to find the employee was acting for the purposes of the employer.[6] In retrospect the court in *Lloyd* should have squarely addressed what it was doing, which was effecting a major extension and enlargement of the vicarious liability principle, which subsequent cases have reflected upon.[7] Salmond apparently agreed that the court in *Lloyd* significantly changed the law.[8]

Apart from its treatment of *Barwick*, and the United Kingdom law as it was understood prior to the decision, other aspects of the reasoning in the case are problematic. Earl Loreburn appeared to base his reasoning on a suggested breach of contract by the agent to apply diligence and honesty in carrying out the business.[9] I have not read another case where the imposition of vicarious liability on an employer is justified on the basis of such a contract, and none that

[2] *Bayley v Manchester, Sheffield and Lincolnshire Railway Company* (1872) LR 7 CP 415, 420 where Willes J distinguished cases where what was done was based on the 'caprice' of the employee, as opposed to being in the course of employment.

[3] *Lloyd v Grace, Smith and Co* [1912] AC 716.

[4] ibid 732 (Lord Macnaghten), with whom Earl Loreburn (725) and Lord Atkinson (739) agreed; to like effect Lord Shaw (741).

[5] Examples include *Glasgow Corporation v Lorimer* [1911] AC 209, 214.

[6] *Ruben v Great Fingall Consolidated* [1906] AC 439, 446: 'where therefore (as in the present case) the secretary is acting fraudulently for his own illegal purposes, no representation by him relating to the matter will bind his employers. And in my opinion it would be a matter of reproach if the law were otherwise' (Lord Davey); *British Mutual Banking Company Limited v Charnwood Forest Railway Company* (1887) 18 QBD 714 (CA) where Bowen LJ said he was 'aware of no precedent (apart from an overruled one) for holding that a principal is liable in an action of deceit for the unauthorized and fraudulent act of a servant or agent committed, not for the general or special benefit of the principal, but for the servant's own private end', cited with approval in *George Whitechurch Ltd v Cavanagh* [1902] AC 117, 141 (Lord Brampton).

[7] eg, Lord Denning stated that the *Lloyd* decision had 'revolutionised' the law in this area: *Morris v CW Martin and Sons Ltd* [1966] 1 QB 716, 723; in the same case, Lord Diplock referred to it as a 'landmark' (735).

[8] 'It was long supposed that where the fraud or other wilful wrongdoing of the servant was committed for his own benefit and not for his master's benefit, his master was not responsible. It has now been decided by the House of Lords, however, in *Lloyd v Grace Smith and Co*, that this is not the case': JW Salmond, *The Law of Torts: A Treatise on the English Law of Liability for Civil Injuries*, 4th edn (London, Stevens & Haynes, 1916) 99 (*Salmond on Torts*).

[9] *Lloyd* (n 3) 724.

I have read since this case have done so. Two of the other justices appeared to adopt the reasoning of Holt CJ in *Hern v Nichols* that given a choice between two innocent parties bearing the loss associated with the wrongdoing, the employer should be the one doing so.[10] The Earl of Halsbury simply said 'it is more reason' that the employer should bear the loss because they chose the employee.[11] Lord Macnaghten, with whom Lord Atkinson agreed, took a similar view, asking: 'who is to suffer for this man's fraud? The person who relied on (the) accredited representative, or (the employer), who put this rogue in his own place and clothed him with his own authority?'.[12] Others have also said the case is probably better seen as a case not involving vicarious liability.[13]

Also influential in the early twentieth century was the summary of the law of vicarious liability provided by Salmond in his *Salmond on Torts*. Given its pivotal importance in this area, unusual for a textbook summary, it is considered essential to directly quote it at length:

> It is clear that the master is responsible for acts actually authorised by him: for liability would exist in this case, even if the relation between the parties was merely one of agency, and not one of service at all. But a master, as opposed to the employer of an independent contractor, is liable even for acts which he has not authorized, provided they are so connected with acts which he has authorized that they may rightly be regarded as modes—although improper modes—of doing them. In other words, a master is responsible not merely for what he authorizes his servant to do, but also for the way in which he does it … On the other hand, if the unauthorized and wrongful act of the servant is not so connected with the authorized act as to be a mode of doing it, but is an independent act, the master is not responsible: for in such a case the servant is not acting in the course of his employment, but has gone outside of it.[14]

In *Goh Choon Seng v Lee Kim Soo* the Privy Council distinguished three different types of case in the area of vicarious liability:

— Where the servant was using their master's time or place or equipment for their own purposes, in which case the master was not responsible.

— Where the servant was employed only to do a particular work or kind of work, and does something outside of that scope of employment, in which case again the master is not responsible.

[10] *Hern v Nichols* (1709) 1 Salk 289.

[11] *Lloyd* (n 3) 727.

[12] ibid 738.

[13] JW Neyers, 'A Theory of Vicarious Liability' (2005) 43 *Alberta Law Review* 287, 315: 'it is submitted that a better view of Lloyd is that it is an instance of personal liability'; J Murphy, 'Juridical Foundations of Common Law Non-Delegable Duties' in J Neyers, E Chamberlain and S Pitel (eds), *Emerging Issues in Tort Law* (Oxford, Hart Publishing, 2007) 376–77.

[14] JW Salmond, *The Law of Torts: A Treatise on the English Law of Liability for Civil Injuries*, 9th edn (London, Sweet & Maxwell, 1935) 95. It is often said that Salmond's first limb in fact describes a case of direct, rather than vicarious, liability: C McIvor, 'The Use and Abuse of the Doctrine of Vicarious Liability' (2006) 35 *Common Law World Review* 268, 280.

— Where the servant is doing some work they were engaged to do, but does it in a way that the master did not authorise and would never have authorised, in which case the master is responsible.[15]

Subsequent cases seemed to take a very broad view of the employer's liability under the rules established in *Lloyd*. An employer was held liable for the gross negligence of an employee in lighting a match while unloading fuel from a fuel tanker to underground tanks at a service station.[16] This was specifically tied back to the *Lloyd* extension. Lord Wright concluded that:

> The act of a workman in lighting his pipe or cigarette is an act done for his own comfort and convenience and, at least generally speaking, not for his employer's benefit, but that last condition is no longer essential to fix liability on the employer.[17]

In some cases, employer limits on the scope of an employee's employment seem to have been taken into account by the court in assessing whether vicarious liability principles made the employer liable. So in *Conway v George Wimpey and Co Ltd*,[18] the case involved a defendant company that was conducting work at an airport. It specifically instructed its employees driving to the workplace not to pick up workers employed by other employers. Contrary to these instructions, one of its employees picked up one such worker, the plaintiff. The plaintiff was injured as a result of the employee's negligence and wanted to make the defendant company vicariously liable for his injuries. All members of the Court of Appeal were satisfied that what the employee did was outside the scope of their employment; it was not merely a wrongful mode of performing an act they were employed to perform.[19] And in the slightly different context of the terms of a contract for services between the employer and a customer, limits on the liability of the employer for acts of their workers were enforced, such that the employer was not deemed vicariously liable for the wilful actions of one of their workers.[20]

Similarly, these limitations were given effect to by the Privy Council in *Kooragang Investments Pty Ltd v Richardson and Wrench Ltd*.[21] The defendant's servant was a valuer who conducted valuations for the defendant. The client who requested these valuations did not pay for the service, and the defendants directed the valuer not to perform any further valuations for that client. Defying

[15] *Goh Choon Seng v Lee Kim Soo* [1925] AC 550, 554 (Lord Phillimore, for the Council). See also *Plumb v Cobden Flour Mills Ltd* [1914] AC 62, 67 (where Lord Dunedin distinguished between prohibitions which limit the sphere of employment, and those which only deal with conduct within the sphere), applied in *Canadian Pacific Railway Co v Lockhart* [1942] AC 591 (express limitation on employees using uninsured private vehicle for delivery held to be of the latter kind, did not preclude an employer being vicariously liable where an employee did use his private uninsured vehicle, and caused injury to the plaintiff; the plaintiff could make the employer vicariously liable).

[16] *Century Insurance Company Limited v Northern Ireland Road Transport Board* [1942] AC 509.

[17] ibid 519.

[18] *Conway v George Wimpey and Co Ltd* [1951] 2 KB 266.

[19] ibid 276 (Asquith LJ), with whom Birkett LJ and Cohen LJ agreed.

[20] *Photo Production Ltd v Securicor Transport Ltd* [1980] AC 827.

[21] *Kooragang Investments Pty Ltd v Richardson and Wrench Ltd* [1982] AC 462.

his employer's specific instructions, the employee kept providing valuations for the customer. He used the defendants' letterhead and corporate name when he signed the valuations. The defendant did not receive a fee for these valuations. The plaintiff relied on these valuations to advance money to the client. Subsequently it was established that the valuations had been negligently prepared, and the plaintiff suffered loss as a result. The question was whether the defendant was liable for the valuations that the employee had conducted after being specifically directed not to do so.

The Privy Council, on appeal from the New South Wales Supreme Court, rejected the plaintiff's case. It was not sufficient to make the defendant liable in this case that the actions (valuations) were within a class of activity which the employer had (at least at one time) authorised the employee to conduct. Lord Wilberforce for the Council stated that: 'If committed for the benefit of the employer and while doing his business, principle and logic demand that the employer should be held liable (for an employee's fraud)'.[22] He acknowledged that in cases such as *Lloyd*, it had been found that it was not necessary that the employee be acting for the employer's benefit in order to make the employer vicariously liable for what the employee did. However, he rejected the suggestion that the law imposed vicarious liability on an employer merely because the employee was doing acts of the same kind as those which it was within their authority to do. He called a suggestion to the contrary 'extreme'.[23] He noted the employee was performing the valuations in issue 'not on behalf of the defendants but in his own interest'.[24] It was unconnected with the defendant's business. He said that to make an employer liable in such cases 'Would strain the doctrine of vicarious responsibility beyond the breaking point and in effect introduce into the law of agency a new principle equivalent to one of strict liability'.[25] Lord Wilberforce said that the employee's actions represented the clearest case of departure from the course of employment as could be imagined.[26] And although the Court of Appeal in *Ilkiw v Samuels* made an employer liable for the employee's negligence, Lord Diplock suggested that the result might have been different if the servant had used the relevant vehicle 'for some other purpose than his master's business, and the accident occurred while the vehicle was being used for that other purpose'.[27]

However, other courts had different ideas as to the significance of an express prohibition by the employer of the specific acts actually committed by the employee.[28] So for instance in *Rose v Plenty*[29] a milk delivery company specifically

22 ibid 472.
23 ibid 473.
24 ibid 475.
25 ibid.
26 ibid.
27 *Ilkiw v Samuels* [1963] 1 WLR 991, 1005.
28 The Court of Appeal found the employer vicariously liable for the employee's negligence in *Ilkiw v Samuels*, ibid, although what the employee did had been specifically prohibited by the employer.
29 *Rose v Plenty* [1976] 1 WLR 141.

directed its employees not to engage young people to assist in the delivery of milk bottles. The plaintiff, 13, was injured when he fell off the back of a milk truck. He had been assisting the employee with his delivery round, contrary to the employer's express direction to the employee that this must not occur. By a majority of 2:1, the Court of Appeal found for the plaintiff against the defendant company. Lord Denning in the majority relied on the earlier *Limpus* case, discussed in chapter one, to the effect that it was not necessarily a bar to employer vicarious liability that the act(s) complained of had been specifically forbidden by the employer. Denning MR stated that the employee was still acting within the course of their employment and for the master's purposes in doing what they did.[30] Scarman LJ referred to a distinction made in other cases between prohibitions which limited the sphere of employment, and those which dealt with conduct within that sphere. Scarman LJ said the limitation here was of the latter variety and did not preclude the employer being held vicariously liable.[31] Lawton LJ (dissenting) said that the decision in *Conway* remained good law and meant the plaintiff's case should be rejected. The employee was not authorised to subcontract work delegated to him.[32]

In *Broom v Morgan*[33] the Court of Appeal made some interesting reflections on the philosophy behind the vicarious liability concept. Somewhat surprisingly, Lord Denning there denied that the basis of vicarious liability was the 'mere economic reason' of the presumed deep pockets of the employer.[34] Rather, he said:

> It is the sound moral reason that the servant is doing the master's business, and it is the duty of the master to see that his business is properly and carefully done. Take the case of a master who sends a lorry out on to the road with his servant in charge. He is morally responsible for seeing that the lorry does not run down people on the pavement … it is his lorry, and it is his business that it is on. He takes the benefit of the work when it is carefully done, and he must take the liability of it when it is negligently done.[35]

The United Kingdom courts reached different positions in cases where, for some reason, the employee who committed the wrong was not ultimately liable to pay compensation to the plaintiff, for example because of some defence or immunity they enjoyed. Did this affect the (vicarious) liability of the employer? Specifically, if the employee had an immunity or defence, would the master similarly have such an immunity or defence? In *Broom v Morgan* the Court of Appeal found that the mere fact that the employee who committed the wrong had a legal

[30] ibid 144.
[31] ibid 149–50.
[32] ibid 145–46.
[33] *Broom v Morgan* [1953] 1 QB 597.
[34] ibid 607–08.
[35] ibid 608. Lord Denning's judgment also contains traces of the master's tort theory of vicarious liability: 'if the driver (employee) is negligent there is a breach of duty not only by the driver himself, but also by the master', as opposed to the preferred view of vicarious liability as being derivative in nature from the position of the employee.

defence, and would not be liable, did not preclude a successful action against the master.[36] In contrast, shortly after in *Staveley Iron and Chemical Co Ltd v Jones*, Lord Morton found that in true cases of vicarious liability, any immunity enjoyed by the employee who committed the wrong would also apply to the employer.[37] And in *Imperial Chemical Industries Ltd v Shatwell*, it was found that a defence of *volenti* to which an employee would be entitled, in the case where two employees committed a wrong in conjunction, could also be claimed by the employer. The court reasoned that if one of them had sued the other, a defence of *volenti* would have been available, and that this defence operated to preclude their employer being vicariously liable for the incident in question.[38]

This difference of opinion may be explained by the fact that Lord Denning appeared to adopt a master's tort approach to vicarious liability in *Broom*, as opposed to the derivative liability concept which was and remains the orthodox position, and is evidenced in *Staveley Iron*.[39] It makes logical sense for someone applying the derivative liability concept that if the employee committing the wrong has a defence or immunity, that defence or immunity should also be applicable and available to the employer.[40]

On occasions, a relatively strict view of the issue of whether the employee is acting within the scope of their employment is evident. For instance, this is evident in the Privy Council decision in *General Engineering Services v Kingston Corp*.[41] The simple facts involved the question whether a local authority was vicariously liable for the actions of their fire employees. The employees had deliberately driven slowly to a fire, pursuant to an industrial dispute. As a result, what should have been a journey of three-and-a-half minutes became a journey of 17 minutes. As a result of the delay the plaintiff's premises were destroyed. All members of the Council found the employees were acting beyond the scope of their employment:

> The members of the fire brigade were not acting in the course of their employment … their mode and manner of driving, the slow progression of stopping and starting, was not so connected with the authorised act, that is driving to the scene of the fire as expeditiously as reasonably possible, as to be a mode of performing that act … here the unauthorised and wrongful act by the firemen was a wrongful repudiation of an essential obligation of their contract of employment, namely the decision and its implementation not to arrive at the scene of the fire in time to save the building and its contents. This decision was not in furtherance of their employer's business … such conduct was the

36 *Broom v Morgan* (n 33).

37 *Staveley Iron and Chemical Co Ltd v Jones* [1956] AC 627, with whom Lord Porter agreed (640).

38 *Imperial Chemical Industries Ltd v Shatwell* [1965] AC 656.

39 See also *Majrowski v Guy's and St Thomas's NHS Trust* [2007] 1 AC 224, 230 (Lord Nicholls, confirming that the master's tort theory is not part of the law of the United Kingdom).

40 G Williams, 'Vicarious Liability: Tort of the Master or of the Servant?' (1956) 72 *Law Quarterly Review* 522.

41 *General Engineering Services v Kingston Corp* [1988] 3 All ER 867.

very negation of carrying out some act authorised by the employer, albeit in a wrongful and unauthorised mode.[42]

Several vicarious liability cases involved the very different question of the possible liability of educational institutions for child abuse committed on children within their care. A leading case here is *Lister and Others v Hesley Hall Ltd*,[43] where survivors of child sexual abuse committed by a warden employed by the defendant sued the defendant for negligence and for vicarious liability. On appeal, the House of Lords found the defendant vicariously liable for the actions of the warden.

Lord Steyn delivered a judgment with which Lord Hutton agreed. Lord Steyn dismissed the pre-*Lloyd* position requiring that the relevant actions of the servant be for the benefit of the master as an 'overly restrictive view and hardly in tune with the needs of society'.[44] He viewed the *Lloyd* decision as providing a 'breakthrough' in this regard.[45] He cited the familiar Salmond statement of vicarious liability, stating that the law no longer struggles with the concept of vicarious liability in the context of intentional wrongdoing, but did not 'cope ideally' with such cases.[46] He said that the question was not whether the sexual abuse which occurred was an unauthorised mode of doing an act authorised by the master, as the Salmond approach suggested. Rather, it was whether there was a close connection between the wrongdoing and the employment. He found that there was, because the abuse was committed 'in the time and on the premises of the employers while the warden was also busy caring for the children'.[47] Speaking of the result in *Morris*, where the court had found an employer vicariously liable for the actions of an employee stealing a customer's property, he said that the 'law ought not to incur the reproach of showing greater zeal in protecting jewellery than in protecting children'.[48]

Lord Steyn indicated he had been greatly assisted by the decisions of the Canadian Supreme Court in *Bazley* and *Jacobi* but did not necessarily accept the full policy considerations discussed at length in those cases. He concluded that the sexual abuse was 'inextricably interwoven' with the carrying out of the wrongdoer's warden duties, such that the school authority was vicariously liable for what the warden did.[49]

Lord Clyde said that a consideration of the history of vicarious liability was not useful in seeking guidance for its modern application. Remarkably, he concluded that there was not 'any reason of principle or policy' which could guide resolution of its application in particular cases.[50] He agreed that deliberately wrongful acts

[42] ibid 869–70 (Lord Ackner, for the Council).
[43] *Lister and Others v Hesley Hall Ltd* [2002] 1 AC 215.
[44] ibid 224.
[45] ibid.
[46] ibid 226.
[47] ibid 227.
[48] ibid 228.
[49] *Bazley v Curry* [1999] 2 SCR 534; *Jacobi v Griffiths* [1999] 2 SCR 570; *Lister*, ibid, 230.
[50] ibid 232; similarly, Lord Pearce in *Imperial Chemical Industries Ltd v Shatwell* (n 38) 685: 'the doctrine of vicarious liability has not grown from any very clear, logical or legal principle but from

could not easily be seen as wrongful modes of doing authorised acts, within the words of the classic Salmond formulation. He acknowledged that Salmond had sought to distinguish between, on the one hand, authorised acts, and wrongful and unauthorised modes of doing an act authorised by the master and, on the other, independent acts of the employee, for which the employer would not be vicariously liable.

He agreed with Lord Steyn that what mattered was the closeness of the connection between the wrongful act and the employment. He said it was relevant to consider whether the wrongful acts were 'ways of carrying out the work which the employer had authorised'.[51] He indicated a broad view should be taken to the concept of 'scope of employment',[52] though the mere fact that the employment provided the opportunity for the wrongdoing to take place was not sufficient.[53] As a result, issues of time and place did not determine whether an employer was vicariously liable for the wrongdoing.

On the facts, Lord Clyde found the school authority was vicariously liable for the acts of the warden. While the fact that the employment provided the warden with the opportunity to commit the abuse was not sufficient, in addition the nature of the warden's employment involving close contact with the students, in the view of Lord Clyde, created sufficient connection between the abuse and the work he had been engaged to do. As Lord Clyde summarised it:

> The respondents gave the warden a quite general authority in the supervision and running of the (school) as well as some particular responsibilities. His general duty was to look after and to care for, among others, the appellants. That function was one which the respondents had delegated to him. That he performed that function in a way which was an abuse of his position and an abnegation of his duty does not sever the connection with his employment. The particular acts which he carried out upon the boys have to be viewed not in isolation but in the context and the circumstances in which they occurred.[54]

Lord Hobhouse agreed that sexual abuse, being a vile criminal act, could easily be seen as a paradigm example of something an employee could not conceivably be employed to do. However, he said that the employer had 'assumed a relationship' to the plaintiff. This is clearly language associated not with the context of vicarious liability, but of direct, personal liability, for instance in relation to negligent misstatement.[55]

Liability arose because the employer had chosen to delegate those responsibilities to an employee. For Lord Hobhouse, this meant that the employee's motive,

social convenience and rough justice. The master having (presumably for his own benefit) employed the servant, and being (presumably) better able to make good any damage, which may (result) … is answerable to the world at large for all torts committed by his servant in the course of it' (with whom Viscount Radcliffe agreed (678)).

[51] ibid 232.
[52] ibid 234.
[53] ibid 235; Lord Hobhouse made the same point (241).
[54] ibid 237.
[55] Murphy (n 13) 378.

and the fact he or she was doing something expressly forbidden and for their own ends, did not negative the possibility of vicarious liability.[56] Later he suggested that the correct approach to identifying the scope of the employment was to ask 'what was the duty of the servant towards the plaintiff which was broken by the servant and what was the contractual duty of the servant towards his employer'.[57] He said the second limb of the classic Salmond test was a convenient rule of thumb, but did not represent the fundamental principle to be applied, which was rather to 'compar(e) the duties respectively owed by the servant to the plaintiff and to his employer'.[58] Lord Hobhouse agreed with Lord Steyn that the policy discussion by the Canadian Supreme Court in *Bazley* did not necessarily apply as an explanation of United Kingdom legal principle in this area.[59]

Lord Millett said vicarious liability was best explained as a loss distribution device. He seemed to accept an enterprise risk theory of vicarious liability, concluding that an employer would be liable for risks that were 'inherent in the nature of the business'.[60] Lord Millett said it was stretching language to breaking point to try to fit cases like this, involving intentional criminal wrongdoing, into the second limb of Salmond's test of unauthorised modes of performance for which the employer would be liable.[61]

Lord Millett also favoured use of the 'close connection' test.[62] He said that the 'heresy' that an employer could not be liable for an employee's deliberate wrongdoing was not exposed until the early twentieth century *Lloyd* decision.[63] He agreed there was no valid reason why the doctrine of vicarious liability should cease to operate at the border between tort and crime.[64] He discussed the Australian precedent in *Deatons Proprietary Limited v Flew*, and opined the result might have been different if the barmaid had been in charge of the bar and authorised to maintain order. He speculated it would not have been enough, to exclude the employer from being held liable, that the employee might have been settling a private score of her own.[65] Lord Millett appeared to abandon the scope of employment criterion:

> There is no a priori reason why an employer should not be vicariously liable for a sexual assault committed by his employee, although naturally such conduct will not normally be within the scope of employment.[66]

In schools, particularly boarding schools, as well as in prisons, nursing homes and other residential care for vulnerable individuals, there was an inherent risk that

[56] *Lister and Others v Hesley Hall Ltd* (n 43) 239.
[57] ibid 242.
[58] ibid.
[59] ibid; this course of action was criticised in McIvor (n 14) 276.
[60] *Lister and Others v Hesley Hall Ltd* (n 43) 244.
[61] ibid.
[62] ibid 245.
[63] ibid 246.
[64] ibid.
[65] ibid 249.
[66] ibid.

those charged with providing care might commit abuse on vulnerable residents, particularly where they were in close proximity to them and in positions of trust. Lord Millett claimed it was not merely that the employment provided the opportunity for the abuse to occur:

> The school was responsible for the care and welfare of the boys. It entrusted that responsibility to the warden ... he did not merely take advantage of the opportunity which employment at a residential school gave him. He abused the special position in which the school had placed him to enable it to discharge its own responsibilities.[67]

As others have noted, Lord Miller's speech can be taken to be more consistent with other principles of liability, for instance non-delegable duties (to be discussed in chapter ten) as opposed to vicarious liability.[68]

Further endorsement of the enterprise risk approach, together with the lesser of two evils type rationale, was evident in *Dubai Aluminium Co Ltd v Salaam*.[69] There Lord Nicholls, with whom Lord Slynn and Lord Hutton agreed, stated that:

> The underlying legal policy is based on the recognition that carrying on a business enterprise necessarily involves risks to others. It involves the risk that others will be harmed by wrongful acts committed by the agents through whom the business is carried on. When those risks ripen into loss, it is just that the business should be responsible for compensating the person who has been wronged ... this policy reason dictates that liability for agents should not be strictly confined to acts done with the employer's authority ... negligence can be expected to occur from time to time ... sometimes agents may exceed the bounds of their authority or even defy express instructions. It is fair to allocate risk of losses thus arising to the businesses rather than leave those wronged with the sole remedy of doubtful value, against the individual employee.[70]

The decision also reflects an agency basis for the recognition of vicarious liability, in at least some types of case.[71]

The joint reasons noted the traditional distinction between cases where an employee is engaged, albeit misguidedly, in furthering their employer's interests, and cases where the employee is engaged in pursuing their own interests or, classically, on a frolic of their own. The joint reasons explained that in the former cases, it may be appropriate to attribute responsibility to the employer, whilst in the latter, it would not be. The reasons referenced with evident approval the statements of Lord Wilberforce in *Kooragang Investments*, discussed above, rejecting

[67] ibid 250.

[68] Murphy (n 13) 378; P Giliker, 'Comparative Perspectives on Vicarious Liability: Defining the Scope of Employment' in J Neyers, E Chamberlain and S Pitel (eds), *Emerging Issues in Tort Law* (Oxford, Hart Publishing, 2007) 426.

[69] *Dubai Aluminium Co Ltd v Salaam* [2003] 2 AC 366.

[70] ibid 377.

[71] Lord Nicholls, with whom Lord Slynn and Lord Hutton agreed, referred to the *Lloyd* decision as an example of vicarious liability where the plaintiff acted in reliance on the 'ostensible authority' of the employee (378).

the suggestion that as long as the employee was doing acts of the same kind as those for which they were employed, the employer would be liable.[72]

Lord Millett repeated his comments in *Lister* that vicarious liability was best seen as a loss distribution device based on social and economic policy.[73] He also reiterated that vicarious liability was justified on the basis of risks that could be considered 'reasonably incidental' to a particular kind of business.[74] Lord Millett said that in applying vicarious liability principles, matters such as whether the employee was acting in an improper manner, for an improper purpose or by an improper means were irrelevant.[75] The fact an employee was acting dishonestly and/or for their own benefit was not sufficient to exclude vicarious liability.[76]

In another case involving the possible liability of an educational institution for sexual abuse committed by its teachers,[77] members of the Supreme Court elaborated further on their views regarding vicarious liability. Lord Phillips, joined by all members of the Court, stated that 'The policy objective underlying vicarious liability is to ensure, in so far as it is fair, just and reasonable, that liability for tortious wrongs is borne by a defendant with the means to compensate the victim'.[78] The Court continued:

> There is no difficulty in identifying a number of policy reasons that usually make it fair, just and reasonable to impose vicarious liability on the employer when these criteria are satisfied:
>
> (i) the employer is more likely to have the means to compensate the victim than the employee and can be expected to have insured against that liability;
> (ii) the tort will have been committed as a result of activity being taken by the employee on behalf of the employer;
> (iii) the employee's activity is likely to be part of the business activity of the employer;
> (iv) the employer, by employing the employee to carry on the activity will have created the risk of the tort committed by the employee;
> (v) the employee will, to a greater or lesser degree, have been under the control of the employer.[79]

The Court noted that while traditionally a key characteristic of the employment relationship was control, in more recent times notions of control had been modified so as to include cases where an employer could direct what the

[72] *Dubai Aluminium* (n 69) 380–81.
[73] ibid 395.
[74] ibid 396.
[75] ibid 400.
[76] ibid 401.
[77] *Various Claimants v Catholic Child Welfare Society* [2013] 2 AC 1.
[78] ibid 15; this view of the rationale for vicarious liability also appears in *Majrowski v Guy's and St Thomas's NHS Trust* (n 39) 229 (Lord Nicholls). The deep pockets rationale was also adopted by Willes J in *Limpus v London General Omnibus Co* (1862) 1 H & C 526, 539. McIvor is critical of the use of concepts such as 'fairness' and 'justice' here, on the basis of their inherent subjectivity and uncertainty: (n 14) 279.
[79] *Various Claimants v Catholic Child Welfare Society* (n 77) 15.

employee did; it was not necessary that an employer could control how the employee did it.[80]

The Court noted that some of the precedents in this area were difficult. It stated that the *Lister* precedent did not provide precise criteria for determining whether an employer could be vicariously liable for sexual abuse by its employee. The test of 'close connection' was not particularly specific.[81] Only Lord Millett there had specifically endorsed the enterprise risk, though that theory gained more acceptance in *Dubai Aluminium*. The Court noted that the Australian High Court decision of *New South Wales v Lepore* showed a 'bewildering variety of analysis'.[82] The Court stated that in cases where an educational institution had been found liable for abuse committed by one of its employees, it had been because the employment relationship had 'facilitated the commission of the abuse by placing the abusers in a position where they enjoyed both physical proximity to their victims and the influence of authority over them both as teachers and as men of God'. Vicarious liability applied where the defendant had used the abuser to carry on their business, such that they 'created or significantly enhanced the risk' that the victims would suffer the relevant abuse.[83]

It is clear that vicarious liability can be imposed with respect to a breach of statutory duty by the employee, at least unless the relevant legislation makes it clear that there is no intention to make the employer liable for employees' failures.[84]

Most Recent Developments

The most recent United Kingdom decisions represent a continued application of the close connection approach. The more controversial of the decisions was *Mohamud v Wm Morrison Supermarkets Plc*,[85] where the court considered the liability of the owner of a petrol station for an assault committed by one of its customer service employees. The employee was in the sales kiosk at the station. A customer entered the kiosk and asked the attendant whether he could print off some documents from a USB stick. The employee refused the request in an offensive manner. He used racist, abusive and violent language in telling the customer to leave the kiosk. The customer left the kiosk and returned to his car. The attendant followed him out to the car and opened the front passenger door. He told the customer never to come back to the premises. The attendant punched the customer in the head. The customer got out of his car to close the front passenger door

[80] ibid 16.
[81] ibid 24.
[82] ibid 25.
[83] ibid 26.
[84] *Majrowski v Guy's and St Thomas's NHS Trust* (n 39); *Various Claimants v WM Morrisons Supermarket PLC* [2017] EWHC 3113 [153].
[85] *Mohamud v Wm Morrison Supermarkets Plc* [2016] AC 677.

the attendant had left open. The attendant punched him in the head again and punched and kicked him as he lay on the ground. The attendant ignored orders from a supervisor to stop the violent attack. The legal question was whether the owner of the service station was vicariously liable for the injuries caused to the customer by the attendant.

The joint reasons traced some of the historical development of vicarious liability, noting its roots in the command and consent theory, before being expanded. They noted without apparent disapproval sentiments of Holt CJ in 1708 in *Hern v Nichols* concerning the lesser of two evils rationale for the imposition of vicarious liability.[86] The reasons noted a New Zealand decision *Pettersson v Royal Oak Hotel Ltd*,[87] where a hotel owner was held liable for the actions of a barman. The barman had refused to serve an intoxicated customer. The customer threw a glass at the barman. The barman picked up a piece of the broken glass and threw it back towards the customer. Instead, it hit the plaintiff, another customer, in the eye, causing injury. The Court had found the hotel owner liable for the plaintiff's injuries. The United Kingdom Supreme Court explained the decision as being based on the notion that

> a barman needs to be capable of acting with restraint under provocation, for the safety of other customers, and if the proprietor engaged someone who was incapable of doing so and who injured an innocent customer, it would be wrong for the customer to be left with his only remedy against the barman.[88]

This is clearly reminiscent of Holt CJ's reasoning in *Hern v Nichols* and *Sir Robert Wayland's Case*.[89] The United Kingdom Supreme Court lauded the 'obvious justice' of the New Zealand decision.[90] The Court also later explained the *Lister* precedent as a case where 'the employee misused his position in a way which injured the claimant, and that is the reason why it was just that the employer who selected him and put him in that position should be held responsible'.[91]

Obviously, the facts in *Pettersson* were very similar to those considered by the Australian High Court in *Deatons v Flew*, where the High Court had found that a hotel owner was not legally liable for the actions of its employee throwing a glass into the face of a customer who had apparently insulted the employee. The Court found the barmaid was acting outside the scope of her employment, out of personal spite rather than in the interests of her employer.

The United Kingdom Supreme Court agreed that it was hard to describe the barmaid's actions as an improper mode of performing an authorised act, however 'that does not make the result just'. The Court claimed that 'members of the public would surely expect the company who employed her to serve customers to have

86 ibid 685.
87 *Pettersson v Royal Oak Hotel Ltd* [1948] NZLR 136.
88 *Mohamud* (n 85) 687.
89 (1709) 1 Salk 289; *Sir Robert Wayland's Case* (1707) 3 Salk 234; *Mohamud* (n 85) 687.
90 ibid.
91 ibid 693.

some responsibility for her conduct towards them'.[92] They added that 'it cannot be right that the measure of the company's responsibility should depend on whether she was the head barmaid or an assistant. The customer would have no knowledge what were the exact limits of her responsibilities'.[93] The Court noted that the Salmond formula created particular difficulties in application to cases where an employee had deliberately done wrong.[94]

Applying the 'close connection' test the joint reasons concluded the wrongdoer's job was to attend to customers. His response to the plaintiff was within the field of activity assigned to him. What occurred later around the bowser area was part of an unbroken chain of events. The joint reasons claimed the attendant's conduct in opening the passenger door of the plaintiff's car did not involve personal animosity between the two; rather it was an order to stay away from the employer's premises. It was thus in connection with the business in which he was employed.[95] Lord Dyson also applied the close connection test and also found the employer vicariously liable for the employee's actions.[96]

To some extent, there is conflicting precedent on the question of the liability of an employer for unauthorised violence by an employee. The employer was held liable for such violence in *Mohamud*, and the employer of a nightclub bouncer was held liable when the bouncer stabbed a patron (after having returned home specifically to fetch his knife after an earlier altercation with the victim).[97] Further, the Crown was held vicariously liable for one of their officers shooting a victim who would not turn over a public phone to the officer.[98] On the other hand, recently an employer was not held vicariously liable for a fight between employees that broke out in the early hours of the morning, after a work Christmas party, and where the protagonists were arguing over work issues.[99]

The other vicarious liability case at this time involved an action against the government.[100] A catering manager working at a government prison was injured when a prisoner carrying a large bag of rice dropped it on her back. Just prior to the incident, another prisoner had dropped a bag of rice. The manager told prisoners to stop work until that rice was cleaned up. Another prisoner ignored the direction, and it was while in the course of trying to navigate around the mess that the prisoner dropped the rice onto the catering manager. The question was of the government's vicarious liability for the actions of the prisoner in dropping the rice onto the catering manager. Obviously, the case was unusual in not

[92] ibid 688.
[93] ibid.
[94] ibid 687.
[95] ibid 694.
[96] ibid 696.
[97] *Mattis v Pollock* [2003] 1 WLR 2158 (CA).
[98] *Bernard v Attorney General of Jamaica* [2004] UKPC 47 (PC).
[99] *Bellman v Northampton Recruitment Limited* [2016] EWHC 3104 (QB) (Cotter J).
[100] *Cox v Ministry of Justice* [2016] AC 660.

reflecting a traditional employer–employee case, but one concerning the liability of the government for the actions of a resident involuntarily detained in one of its facilities.

The unanimous court here took the opportunity to consider Lord Phillips' five factors in *Dubai Aluminium*. They took particular issue with the first factor, stating it was not likely to be significant in most cases. They said that the ability of a defendant to meet a judgment against them was not a principled justification for imposing vicarious liability.[101] Regarding insurance, the court said that issues of liability should not depend on whether or not the person sued had insurance, though conceding it might be relevant in some cases.[102] As to the fifth element, they noted that the existence of the ability of an employer to exert control over the employee did not have the significance that it had in previous cases involving vicarious liability questions.[103]

The Court essentially maintained the enterprise risk approach to vicarious liability questions, holding that an employer should be liable for torts that could fairly be regarded as risks associated with its business activities, whether done for the purpose of furthering those activities or not.[104] The court lauded such an approach as reflecting the realities of the modern working environment, where flexible work practices meant that increasing numbers of workers may not have a contract of employment with the organisation engaging them. It said it represented an extension of the traditional rule making an employer liable for the actions of their employees acting in the course of their employment.

Again, the contentious 'benefit' concept arose: 'The individual for whose conduct it may be vicariously liable must carry on activities assigned to him by the defendant as an integral part of its operation and for its benefit'.[105] The Court continued to refer to the 'benefit' concept, concluding that on the facts of the case, the prisoners' work was integrated into prison operations. It concluded that 'the activities assigned to them are not merely of benefit to themselves'.[106]

However, given it decided *Mohamud* at the same time, where the employer was liable for an employee's violent assaults, perhaps too much should not be made of this re-appearance of the benefit concept. In saying that, it should be conceded that the court claimed in *Mohamud* that the employee was acting in furtherance of the employer's interests, rather than out of some kind of personal vendetta. It is not entirely clear, but doubted that the Court intended to go back to the pre-*Lloyd* days, where the benefit concept assumed real importance within the law of vicarious liability. Perhaps the Court regards it as one factor to be considered in the factual milieu. Its use retains scholarly support.[107] The Court noted that the factors

[101] ibid 669.
[102] ibid.
[103] ibid.
[104] ibid 670.
[105] ibid 672.
[106] ibid 674.
[107] P Morgan, 'Recasting Vicarious Liability' (2012) 71 *Cambridge Law Journal* 615, 639.

mentioned by Lord Phillips should be applied to individual cases. They should not generally be subject to an overriding question as to whether a particular conclusion in a given case was 'fair, just and reasonable', but in novel cases, that concept could be useful in determining whether or not vicarious liability should apply in a given situation.[108]

A further example of the United Kingdom's acceptance of the enterprise risk approach to vicarious liability appears in *Armes v Nottinghamshire County Council*.[109] There Lord Reed, with whom Lady Hale, Lord Kerr and Lord Clarke agreed, noted that:

> The most influential idea in modern times has been that it is just that an enterprise which takes the benefit of activities carried on by a person integrated into its organisation should also bear the cost of harm wrongfully caused by that person in the course of those activities.[110]

The Court applied Lord Phillips five factor test in finding the authority vicariously liable for abuse committed by a foster carer to whom they had entrusted the care of minors.

Regarding the so-called threshold question of whether a relationship was such that vicarious liability could potentially exist, the United Kingdom courts have traditionally had less trouble distinguishing an employee (for whose acts the employer will generally be vicariously liable) from an independent contractor (for whose acts the employer will generally not be vicariously liable).[111] Issues of control have loomed large in this discussion. The ability of the one who engaged the worker to control not only what is to be done, but the manner in which it will be done, is critical.[112] The focus will typically be on the right to control, not whether actual control is exercised.[113] However, this test is applied flexibly, recognising that employees will often have high levels of skill in the area in which they work, such that a narrow application of a control test might exclude such workers who ought to be regarded as employees.[114] Issues around the circumstances in which

[108] *Cox v Ministry of Justice* (n 100) 675.

[109] *Armes v Nottinghamshire County Council* [2017] UKSC 60.

[110] ibid [67].

[111] The United Kingdom courts have exceptionally recognised liability of an engaging firm for some actions of an independent contractor, but this tends to be rationalised on the grounds that the contractor is engaged in an extra-hazardous activity, in which case a non-delegable duty, not vicarious liability, will or may ground liability upon the engaging firm: *McDermid v Nash Dredging and Reclamation Co Ltd* [1987] AC 906; see E McKendrick 'Vicarious Liability and Independent Contractors—A Re-Examination' (1990) 53 *Modern Law Review* 770.

[112] *Yewens v Noakes* (1880) 6 QBD 530, 532 (Bramwell LJ); *Mersey Docks and Harbour Board v Coggins and Griffith (Liverpool) Ltd* [1947] AC 1, 12 (Viscount Simon); 17 (Lord Porter); 18 (Lord Simons); 21 (Lord Uthwatt); the extent to which the worker is accountable to the employer for the manner in which the work was done is analogous: *E v English Province of Our Lady of Charity and Another* [2013] QB 722, 770 (Ward LJ).

[113] *Yewens v Noakes*, ibid, 530 (Bramwell LJ).

[114] *Viasystems (Tyneside) Ltd v Thermal Transfer (Northern) Ltd and Others* [2006] QB 510, 530 (Rix LJ); *E v English Province of Our Lady of Charity* (n 112) 766 (Ward LJ).

a power of dismissal will be important,[115] as will the payment arrangements.[116] Whether or not the worker uses their own equipment, and has their own staff, will be relevant.[117] The courts have also been prepared to extend vicarious liability to relationships that are sufficiently akin to employment.[118]

Courts have also taken a so-called entrepreneur test to questions of whether a worker is an employee or independent contractor, considering issues such as whether the worker has the chance to profit from the work, and risks loss.[119] In turn, this relates to a subsequent 'organisation test', which effectively considers whether the worker should be considered to be part of the employer's organisational business structure, or whether the worker effectively has their own business.[120] These matters will be considered further in chapter nine.

More recently in *Armes v Nottinghamshire County Council*[121] the Supreme Court found that a government authority could be held vicariously liable for the actions of foster carers in whose care the victim had been placed by the government authority. It noted, as had previous decisions, that vicarious liability could be found to apply to relationships that were not strictly employment relationships, but which were sufficiently akin to employment relationships. It found that the relationship between government authority and foster carer was sufficiently akin to an employment relationship to justify the imposition of vicarious liability upon the government. In so finding, the Court applied the five indicia that Lord Phillips had provided in *Catholic Child Welfare Society and Others* to help determine whether or not it was 'fair, just and reasonable' to impose vicarious liability, to the slightly different, but related, question of whether the relationship between the engager and the person who had been engaged to perform functions was such as could attract the operation of vicarious liability.

In applying Lord Phillips' five factors, the Supreme Court gave most prominence to the last four. It found that the foster parents were not carrying on an independent 'business' of their own. In contrast, they were an integral part of the local authority's organisation and the childcare services it provided.[122]

Regarding the fourth of Lord Phillips' factors, the Court found that the employer had created the risk of the tort being committed. On the one hand, it found that the local authority's placement of children in the care of foster parents created

[115] *Performing Right Society Ltd v Mitchell and Booker Ltd* [1924] 1 KB 762, 767 (McCardle J).

[116] ibid 767 (McCardle J).

[117] *Lee Ting Sang v Chung Chi-Keung* [1990] 2 AC 374, 382 (PC).

[118] *Armes v Nottinghamshire County Council* (n 109); *Cox v Ministry of Justice* (n 100).

[119] *Montreal v Montreal Locomotive Works Ltd* [1947] 1 DLR 161, 169 (Lord Wright) (PC).

[120] *Stevenson Jordan & Harrison Ltd v Macdonald and Evans* [1952] 1 TLR 101, 111 (Lord Denning); *Market Investigations Ltd v Minister of Social Security* [1969] 2 QB 173 (Cooke J); R Flannigan, 'Enterprise Control: The Servant–Independent Contractor Distinction' (1987) 37 *University of Toronto Law Journal* 25; R Kidner, 'Vicarious Liability: For Whom Should the Employer be Liable?' (1995) 15 *Legal Studies* 47, 59–60.

[121] [2017] UKSC 60.

[122] ibid [59] (Lord Reed, with whom Lady Hale, Lord Kerr and Lord Clarke agreed).

a relationship of authority and trust between the foster parents and children 'in circumstances where close control cannot be exercised by the local authority'.[123] This made the children vulnerable to abuse. Risk was inherent in the choice of the local authority. The Court considered it fair that the authority compensate children where that risk materialised, given children were under the control of the authority.[124]

Regarding the fifth of Lord Phillips' factors, the Court found that the local authority 'exercised a significant degree of control over both what the foster parents did and how they did it'.[125] This contrasts with their finding two paragraphs earlier that the local authority could not exercise close control over the foster carers.[126] The Court added that the extent to which control was necessary to impose vicarious liability should not be overemphasised.[127]

It noted that its finding in this case differed from the decision of the Supreme Court of Canada in *KLB v British Columbia*, where that Court had found the state not to be vicariously liable for actions of foster carers. It sought to explain this difference by pointing out that while deterrence had been a prime consideration justifying the Canadian court's decisions in cases such as *Bazley*, *Jacobi* and *KLB*, that the United Kingdom courts had never particularly embraced the deterrence rationale of vicarious liability. It made fleeting reference to the fact that suggestions that the structuring of vicarious liability in a particular way might lead to desired changes in practice, including vetting and supervision, were 'empirically untested'.[128] Rather, the Court noted the United Kingdom's (eventual) acceptance of the enterprise risk approach:

> The most influential idea in modern times has been that it is just that an enterprise which takes the benefit of activities carried on by a person integrated into its organisation should also bear the cost of harm wrongfully caused by that person in the course of those activities.[129]

Again, the Court referred to the concept of benefit. In concluding that the local authority was vicariously liable for the foster carer's actions, the Court concluded that the abuse took place in the course of an activity carried on for the benefit of the local authority.[130]

[123] ibid [61].
[124] ibid.
[125] ibid [62].
[126] 'close control cannot be exercised by the local authority': ibid [61].
[127] ibid [65].
[128] ibid [69].
[129] ibid [67].
[130] ibid [60]; Chief Justice of the High Court of Australia, Susan Kiefel, noted that in relation to vicarious liability 'the fact that generally speaking an enterprise benefits from the acts of an employee is accorded importance by some common law courts today': 'Vicarious Liability in Tort—A Search for Policy, Principle or Justification' (New South Wales Supreme Court Judges Conference, August 2017) 11.

Recently, some judges have considered whether it is 'fair, just and reasonable' to consider a particular worker to be an employee.[131] It is possible that more than one employer might be vicariously liable for the same incident.[132] Relationships which are not employer–employee, but sufficiently analogous to such a relationship, might attract the vicarious liability principle.[133] I will consider relationships that should give rise to vicarious liability in more detail in chapter nine.

Some Critique and Reflection on United Kingdom Case Law

The first observation concerns the evident inability of the United Kingdom courts to agree upon a consistent rationale for the imposition of vicarious liability. This was most candidly admitted by Lord Clyde in *Lister*, who observed no principle or policy could satisfactorily explain the existing state of precedent on vicarious liability. This is considered to be an unacceptable state of affairs. In most areas of law, it is possible to articulate the principles upon which the current law stands. It is to be lamented that the courts have been unable to agree upon a single rationale or set of principles here. Currently, at least, the United Kingdom Supreme Court has appeared to agree on an 'enterprise risk' approach to assessing vicarious liability, liberally referring to the Canadian Supreme Court decisions in *Jacobi* and *Bazley* in doing so. However, interestingly members of the United Kingdom Supreme Court, while adopting the enterprise risk approach evident in *Bazley* and *Jacobi*, at the same time decline to accept the policy analysis that is at the heart of these decisions. It is somewhat puzzling that a country can wholeheartedly adopt the approach taken in the leading courts of a comparable nation, while at the same time refusing to sign up to the policy analysis that fundamentally underpinned those decisions.[134]

The second observation is the Court's inconsistent attitude to issues such as whether the employee guilty of wrongdoing was acting for the benefit of the employer (in which case vicarious liability could apply), or whether they were acting for their own purposes (in which case vicarious liability would not apply). This distinction is also evident in the writings of Salmond on the subject, writings

[131] *E v English Province of Our Lady of Charity* (n 112) 769 (Ward LJ) and 784 (Davis LJ). Davis LJ also considered whether the 'worker' considered there was appointed to further the aims and purposes of the 'employer' (785).

[132] *Viasystems (Tyneside) Ltd v Thermal Transfer (Northern) Ltd and Others* (n 114) 510 (May LJ and Rix LJ).

[133] *E v English Province of Our Lady of Charity* (n 112); *Armes v Nottinghamshire County Council* (n 109).

[134] McIvor (n 14) 276; P Giliker, 'Rough Justice in an Unjust World' (2002) 65 *Modern Law Review* 269, 274.

which have had a very significant effect on the development of vicarious liability in a variety of nations.

Specifically, as indicated in chapter one, for many years it was relevant for the court to consider whether the employee was acting for the benefit and/or purposes of the employer, in determining whether or not the employer should be legally liable for their actions. This requirement in order for vicarious liability to apply was removed in the 1912 decision in *Lloyd*. I have made critical comments about that decision earlier in the chapter and will not repeat them here.

What has been interesting has been that, despite the decision in *Lloyd*, subsequent case law has continued to refer to whether the employee's actions benefited the employer and/or were for the purposes of the employer, in determining whether vicarious liability should apply to given facts.[135] This has occurred basically ever since the *Lloyd* decision. So in 1925, just a few years after *Lloyd*, the Privy Council considered it relevant to ask in *Goh Choon Seng* whether the employee was acting for their own purposes. Lord Wilberforce for the Council in *Kooragang Investments* in 1982 determined that the employee was acting for their own private interests in declining to find their employer vicariously liable for what they did. In 1988 the Council did the same, finding that firemen were not acting 'in furtherance of their employer's business', in rejecting a vicarious liability claim.[136]

In 2003 the joint reasons of a few judges in *Dubai Aluminium* in the Council appeared to endorse Lord Wilberforce's judgment in *Kooragang Investments*, and the distinction between circumstances where an employee was acting to further the employer's interests, and when they were acting on a frolic of their own. In 1953 in *Broom v Morgan* Lord Denning expressly rationalised vicarious liability on the basis that the employee was acting for the master's business and for their benefit. And recently again in 2016, a unanimous Supreme Court in *Cox v Ministry of Justice* referred to the issue of whether the 'employee' was acting for the benefit of the employer, in determining that the employer was vicariously liable for their negligent acts.[137] It was referred to in the same context in *Armes v Nottinghamshire County Council*[138] and in *Various Claimants v Barclays Bank Plc*.[139]

So, with great respect, the relevance (if any) of the question whether an employee was acting at the relevant time for the purposes of the employer, or was on a 'frolic' of their own, remains ambiguous. Despite the House of Lords' clear pronouncements to the contrary in *Lloyd* and *Century Insurance*, many examples

[135] The exception has been *Century Insurance*, where the House of Lords specifically noted that since the *Lloyd* decision, it was not necessary to show that the employee was acting for the benefit of the employer, in order that vicarious liability apply. And in *Dubai Aluminium* (n 69), Lord Millett concluded the purpose(s) for which the employee acted were irrelevant in considering the question of vicarious liability.

[136] *General Engineering Services v Kingston Corp* (n 41) 870 (Lord Ackner, for the Council).

[137] [2016] AC 660, 672, 674.

[138] [2017] UKSC 60, [60] (Lord Reed, with whom Lady Hale, Lord Kerr and Lord Clarke agreed).

[139] *Various Claimants v Barclays Bank Plc* [2017] EWHC 1929, [45] (Davies J).

since show the Court attempting to make the distinction. For the record, I support the making of the distinction, as I will elaborate upon in chapter eight.

The points for now are first the evident inconsistency in the precedents regarding the engagement of such a principle, which I have shown. The second is the difficulty in reconciling use of this principle with the actual decisions arrived at in some cases, and in particular those cases involving intentional wrongdoing. If the distinction between occasions when an employee is acting for the purposes of the employer, and when they are acting independently on a frolic of their own is supported, and I do support it for reasons that will be amplified in a later chapter, then it becomes very difficult to find an employer liable for sexual abuse committed by one of its employees. I think it is clearly evident that sexual abuse by a teacher is not committed for the purposes of the employer and/or for their benefit. It is clearly for the personal gratification of the teacher wrongdoer. So in terms of the line between acts done for the employer's purposes (to which vicarious liability can apply) and independent acts, I would have thought that sexual abuse by a teacher would very clearly be in the 'independent act' category.[140] Yet, this theory is confounded by the decisions of the court in *Lister* and *Various Claimants*, where the employer was found vicariously liable for such acts.

Further, members of the United Kingdom Supreme Court tried in *Mohamud* to tie the employee's violent actions to a purpose of the employment, claiming he was purporting to act for the employer's purposes in discouraging (with his fists) the victim from returning to the premises. Now, the Court did not find the need to do this in the sexual abuse cases, and it would have been extremely difficult to have done so. And the factual finding that a violent, aggressive employee by punching a customer was acting in furtherance of the employer's interests is, with respect, highly questionable.

In other words, the Court's sometimes use of the 'purposes of the employer' concept is criticised here. It is criticised because it is seemingly inconsistent with the 1912 decision in *Lloyd* that it was not necessary in order to attract vicarious liability to show that the employee was acting for the benefit of the employer. It is criticised because sometimes the purpose concept is lauded by the Court; at other times ignored. It is criticised because clearly there are examples where the Court is arriving at a decision that an employer is vicariously liable for what an employee did when it does not seem reasonably open, with respect, to find that the employee was acting for the employer's purposes (*Lister*, *Various Claimants*). And it is criticised because the Court seems very ready to find an employee was

[140] I must express my agreement here with Robert Stevens: R Stevens, *Torts and Rights* (Oxford, Oxford University Press, 2007) 270: 'a child is abused by a teacher whilst at school. The teacher's conduct is clearly intentional wrongdoing, which is prohibited by his employer. Can there be vicarious liability for this tort? Although the Salmond test is open-textured, it is not arguable that child abuse comes within it. Teachers are employed to care for children, not to abuse them. It is the very opposite of what they have been authorised to do'.

acting for the employer's purposes, when others might just see a violent, aggressive employee who is apparently looking for a victim upon whom to unload his anger, rather than any serious attempt to serve their employer's purposes (*Mohamud*). Now, as I say, I actually support the use of the purpose of the employer concept in the context of vicarious liability law, but to do so requires the court to squarely address the *Lloyd* principle, be consistent with its use, apply it properly rather than ignore it when it might not lead to the result that the court favours, or strain the concept to claim that an employee was acting for their employer's purposes when most reasonable observers would conclude that they were clearly not.

Another point to note about the precedent is that, sometimes, issues of blame tend to seep into the analysis. This is technically incorrect. Given that vicarious liability is a principle of strict liability, it would not be correct legal analysis to seek to buttress conclusions about an issue of strict liability by resort to matters that pertained to blame or fault.[141] We see evidence of this seepage in *Lloyd*, where three justices appeared to ascribe blame to the employer because they chose to engage the employee who in that case turned out to be dishonest.[142] It again appears most recently in *Mohamud*, where the joint reasons discuss various cases, including *Lister*, and conclude that they were cases where it was just to make the employer liable because the employer had 'selected (the employee) and put him in th(e) position'.[143] With respect, and no pun intended, this is faulty reasoning.[144]

This issue of bad employee selection would be relevant in a case against the employer for negligence in the selection of employees; it is hard to justify its relevance to the strict liability concept of vicarious liability. These reasoning problems in the judgments of three justices in *Lloyd* are troubling for this reason. Problematically, *Lloyd* is one of the leading cases in this area, regularly cited for the fact that an employer can be vicariously liable for deliberate criminal actions of an employee, and that there is no need to show that the employee was acting for the purpose(s) of the employer. And the continued resort to such reasoning today

[141] Rix LJ was correct, with respect, in *Viasystems (Tyneside) Ltd v Thermal Transfer (Northern) Ltd* (n 114) 529: 'the concept of vicarious liability does not depend on the employer's fault but on his role. Liability is imposed by a policy of the law upon an employer, even though he is not personally at fault', as was Ward LJ in *E v English Province of Our Lady of Charity* (n 112) 745: '(vicarious liability) is … a form of strict liability'.

[142] Earl of Halsbury (727); Lord Macnaghten (788); and Lord Atkinson (789); see also *Mersey Docks and Harbour Board v Coggins and Griffith* (n 112) 18: 'the doctrine of the vicarious responsibility of the "superior", whatever its origin, is today justified by social necessity, but, if the question is where that responsibility should lie, the answer should surely point to that master in whose act some degree of fault, though remote, may be found' (Lord Simonds).

[143] [2016] AC 677, 693 (Lord Toulson, for Lord Neuberger, Baroness Hale, Lord Dyson and Lord Reed).

[144] McIvor also criticises the English courts for confusing issues relating to vicarious liability with fault-based concepts: (n 14) 288; as does Giliker, 'Rough Justice in an Unjust World' (n 134) 275–76; and N McBride, *Vicarious Liability Cases McBride's Guides*, available at: mcbridesguides.com/category/tort-law/, 2: 'now—it seems that the House of Lords was completely incapable of grasping this point; that … liability in … situations (involving intentional misconduct by employees are) examples of personal liability rather than vicarious liability'.

in *Mohamud* by five members of the United Kingdom Supreme Court is even more troubling.

Similar concerns can be raised with the lesser of two evils type argument, which appealed to the court in *Hern v Nichols*, a decision evidently approved of by members of the House of Lords in *Lloyd* itself, and in the joint reasons in *Mohamud.*[145] This reasoning is that it is 'better' that as between two innocent persons, the employer and the third party, it is somehow 'better' that the loss be borne by the employer. Sometimes it is not entirely clear why such an outcome is in fact better, and it is tempting to think that such reasoning might be masking a search for deep pockets, it being better because the employer is better able to absorb such a loss. However, a reading of the early cases suggests, albeit based on the scant reasoning in *Hern v Nichols* itself and progeny, that the 'lesser of two evils' argument comes down to a crude form of blame.[146] That somehow, it is better to place the loss with the employer because they chose the employee who did the wrongful act. However, it remains problematic to justify the imposition of no-fault strict liability on a fault principle. It is understandable perhaps in the early eighteenth century that a judge might mix notions of strict liability with notions of fault and negligence, given the relatively primitive state of tort law at that time. It is much less forgivable today.

I should add that this book will not consider in depth the question of an employer's direct liability in negligence to the third party, if they were in fact in breach of a duty of care owed to the third party by choosing an unsuitable employee. As I indicated in chapter one, this action is much more readily available currently than it was in past centuries, and indeed prior to 1932. However, it is appropriate to acknowledge that, today, any argument about fault in the employer for choosing an inappropriate employee is appropriately placed within a negligence claim. It has no place buttressing a vicarious liability argument. Thus, it is suggested that the courts should not be looking to *Hern v Nichols* and progeny to try to justify the imposition of vicarious liability, as occurred most recently in the joint judgment in *Mohamud*. That line of reasoning should no longer be regarded as legitimate.

Another issue is that the law of the United Kingdom seems to have an ambivalent attitude towards the question of the relevance, if any, of any express limitations placed by the employer on an employee. In some cases, those limitations have been relevant in assessing whether an employer is vicariously liable for something the employee did that might be implicated in such limits. Examples here include *Conway v George Wimpey*, *Kooragang Investments* and *Photocorp Production.* The court used specific prohibitions, and in the latter case an exclusion clause, to determine the scope of an employee's employment. In *Shatwell* Lord Hodson

145 *Mohamud* (n 85) 684–85.

146 'Seeing somebody must be a loser by this deceit, it is more reason that he that employs and puts a trust and confidence in the deceiver should be a loser, than a stranger': (1709) 1 Salk 289; *Sir Robert Wayland's Case* (n 89)7; *Udell v Atherton* (1861) 7 H & N 170, 191.

referred to the 'manifest unjustness' if an employee who acted in defiance of an employer's orders was able to claim against their employer vicariously because another employee was involved in the conduct.[147] Lord Hobhouse in *Lister* said that it was relevant in determining the application of vicarious liability to consider what contractual duty the employee owed to the employer. With respect, I agree. It surely makes intuitive sense that in determining what is the scope of an employee's employment, one would have regard to the written terms under which they were engaged.

However, in other cases, the court has simply found that the fact that an employer has specifically forbidden the acts concerned did not preclude the employer being vicariously liable when the employee does the forbidden act(s), and a third party is injured as a result. Prime examples here include *Rose v Plenty*, where the employer prohibited the specific act complained of, yet was still held liable for the consequences to a third party of the employee ignoring that prohibition. And in *Mohamud*, somewhat surprisingly, members of the Supreme Court stated, in discussing *Deatons v Flew*, that the liability of the hotel owner for what the barmaid did should not depend on whether she was head barmaid or merely an assistant. With respect, why not? Surely, what the employee was actually engaged to do is highly relevant to a consideration of the scope of their duties.

The Supreme Court sought to justify its position by stating that the injured party in such a case would not know what were the precise responsibilities of the particular employee. So much may be conceded. But it is strange reasoning to make the plaintiff's knowledge of the liability position or employment or contractual relationships of others the determinant of liability. The plaintiff in *Hedley Byrne and Partners v Heller*[148] was not successful, because of a limitation clause in the advice given by the defendants. They may well not have known of that limitation at the time. However, their lack of knowledge did not mean they were entitled to claim, or that the exclusion clause was irrelevant to their case. If I have a car accident with someone, I do not know whether they are insured. I do not know what the terms of their insurance policy are. I do not know whether they are driving as part of an employment obligation, or privately. However, my (lack of) knowledge of all of these things does not affect how the law treats the accident. Similarly, a plaintiff's lack of knowledge of whether an employee has significant or minor responsibilities should not affect the liability of the employer for that employee's actions.

Another potential example of inconsistency relates to the courts' repeated insistence that the mere fact that the employment created the opportunity for the wrongdoing to occur is not sufficient in order to justify the imposition of vicarious liability on the defendant employer. This is considered to be correct. However, in this light, development of some of the vicarious liability doctrine, particularly

[147] *Imperial Chemical Industries Ltd v Shatwell* (n 38) 682–83.
[148] *Hedley Byrne and Partners v Heller* [1964] AC 465.

in the context of sexual abuse misconduct by employees, is considered to be somewhat problematic. Specifically, the view of Lord Steyn (with whom Lord Hutton agreed) in *Lister*, that in determining whether or not an employer was vicariously liable for the employee's actions, it was relevant to consider that the relevant acts took place in the employer's time and on their premises. With respect, this is considered to be the equivalent of 'opportunity'. It is not possible to claim that it is not enough to find vicarious liability to say that the employment created the opportunity for the abuse to occur, but then say it is relevant that the abuse took place during the employee's working hours and on the premises where they were engaged. Surely, they are two sides of the one coin. In this respect, I agree with Lord Clyde in that case who made comments to that effect. Time and place issues are not sufficient to justify the imposition of vicarious liability.

Still, the 'opportunity' doctrine remains fraught. How can Lord Clyde say, on the one hand, that the fact the employment provided the opportunity for the abuse to occur is not enough in order to attract vicarious liability, but then focus on the fact that the employee's employment provided them with the chance of close contact with students, and eventually for abuse to occur? How is that not a case of the employment providing the 'opportunity' for the abuse to occur? A concept which some judges, including Lord Clyde himself, admits is not sufficient in order to justify vicarious liability? Surely, it was in fact the person's engagement as a warden at the school, with pastoral care responsibilities for students, which gave him the opportunity to commit the abuse? It does seem difficult, with respect, to deny that providing the opportunity for abuse to occur is not sufficient, but then focus on the fact that the wrongdoer's specific employment tasks allowed them close contact with vulnerable students in a trusting environment.

I will reserve my critical consideration of various rationales the United Kingdom courts have provided for the imposition of vicarious liability, including the enterprise risk theory, deep pockets, insurance aspects, and the concept of fairness and justice, for Part II of the book, which is devoted to a consideration of rationales.

3

Developments in Australian Case Law

Historical Development

One point should be made before discussing the Australian case law on vicarious liability. It is that until 1963 the High Court considered itself bound by decisions of the House of Lords.[1] In that year the Court finally decided it should no longer be so bound. In addition, for many years the High Court considered itself bound by decisions of the Privy Council, regardless of the source country from which the appeal was heard.[2] Readers should read the Australian decisions recounted below in that light.[3] There will thus be no surprise in the fact that much of the principle applied in the cases is take from the English cases discussed in chapter one and chapter two, and there are many references to English case law. It is fair to say that in the years after 1963, the law of Australia has begun to diverge from the law of England in relation to vicarious liability, as of course it has in other areas of tort law, and law generally. United Kingdom decisions still remain influential and persuasive to an Australian court, but they do not enjoy the kind of unquestioning adherence to which they were once accorded.

The High Court first considered the question of vicarious liability in 1919 in *Bugge v Brown*.[4] The case involved a defendant grazier who employed a servant to work on his land. Under the terms of engagement, the grazier agreed to provide the servant with cooked meat. On a day when the servant was due to work some distance away from the farmhouse, the defendant supplied the servant with raw meat and cooking implements. They were instructed to cook the meat at other premises on the grazier's property. Instead, the servant lit a fire elsewhere on the premises in order to cook the meat. The fire got out of control and damaged the neighbouring premises of the plaintiff. The question was the defendant's liability for the admittedly negligent conduct of the servant in starting the fire where he

[1] *Parker v The Queen* (1963) 111 CLR 610, 632–33 (Dixon CJ, for all members of the Court).

[2] *Viro v The Queen* (1978) 141 CLR 88, 93 (Barwick CJ); 118–19 (Gibbs J); 129 (Stephen J); 135 (Mason J); 167 (Murphy J); and 174 (Aickin J).

[3] *Parker v The Queen* (n 1) 632–33 (Dixon CJ, for all members of the Court). Appeals from the High Court to the Privy Council were abolished in 1975 (Privy Council (Appeals from the High Court) Act 1975 (Cth)) and appeals from State Supreme Courts to the Privy Council were abolished in 1986: s 11 Australia Act 1986 (UK).

[4] *Bugge v Brown* (1919) 26 CLR 110.

did. By a majority of 2:1, the High Court found the defendant grazier vicariously liable for the servant's actions.

The influence of the English law on the majority judgments is clearly evident. They cite English cases extensively, including *Lloyd* and *Limpus*. The majority observed that these cases permitted a master to be found vicariously liable for the actions of the servant, although they were acts forbidden by the employer, or even criminal acts. The question was whether the servant was acting within the scope of their employment in doing what they did. Isaacs J in the majority based his reasoning on the judgment of *Hern v Nichols* and the lesser of two evils rationale:

> The principle on which the responsibility rests is that it is more just to make the person who has entrusted his servant with the power of acting in his business responsible for injury occasioned to another in the course of so acting, than that the other and entirely innocent party should be left to bear the loss.[5]

Not every action of a servant would be legally binding on their employer. An employer would not be liable where the employee did not 'assume to act' within the scope of employment, or if the act was sufficiently remote from what he was employed to do,[6] and not related to the purpose of the employment.[7]

The other judge in the majority stated that 'the employer is liable for damage resulting from the negligent use of a fire on his land if he has sanctioned the lighting of the fire anywhere on his property for the occasion'.[8]

In *Colonial Mutual Life Assurance Society Limited v Producers and Citizens Co-Operative Assurance Company of Australia Limited*[9] (*CML*) the issue arose of the liability of the appellant, an insurance company, for the statements of their canvasser and agent. The agent was engaged pursuant to a written agreement. One of the terms of the engagement was that the agent would not make a statement, oral or written, likely to reflect on the character, integrity or conduct of another person or institution, or which might tend to bring them into disrepute. It was alleged that the agent in fact disparaged a rival of the firm that engaged him, suggesting they were insolvent. The question was the liability of the appellant company for the agent's statements.

A majority of the High Court of Australia (4:2) found that the appellant was responsible under the principles of vicarious liability for the agent's statements. Gavan Duffy CJ and Starke J found that the appellants had placed the agent in a position to do the kind of acts of which complaint was made. It was within the scope of his authority to canvas for new customers, and that included making the kinds of comments he had, in order to attract their business.[10] Gavan Duffy CJ and

[5] ibid 117.
[6] ibid 118.
[7] ibid 122.
[8] ibid 132 (Higgins J).
[9] *Colonial Mutual Life Assurance Society Limited v Producers and Citizens Co-Operative Assurance Company of Australia Limited* (1931) 46 CLR 41.
[10] ibid 46–47.

Starke J found that if an unlawful act were within the scope of an agent's authority, the fact that the employer had specifically prohibited what the agent actually did was irrelevant. They cited to *Limpus* for this point.[11]

Dixon J, with whom Rich J agreed, first stated the relevant law of vicarious liability as he understood it. The fact that Australian law mirrored English case will again be evident. Dixon J stated that usually where

> [a] tort is committed in the course of the performance of work for the benefit of another person, (the employer) cannot be vicariously responsible if the actual tortfeasor is not his servant and he has not directly authorized the doing of the act which amounts to a tort. The work, although done at his request and for his benefit, is considered as the independent function of the person who undertakes it, and not as something which the person obtaining the benefit does by his representative standing in his place.[12]

This passage is noteworthy for its acceptance and use of both of the principles of (a) whether the employee was acting within the scope of what they were authorised to do; and (b) whether the relevant act was for the 'benefit' of the employer. As indicated in chapter one, this was at one time the position in English law, as reflected by the late nineteenth century *Barwick* decision, but that position changed in 1912 with the *Lloyd* decision. Yet here, in 1931, a leading Australian justice is still referring to the concept of benefit.

Three other points from the judgment of Dixon J are noteworthy. First, his conception of how vicarious liability applied in the case was to the effect that the appellant company should be considered 'as itself conducting the negotiation in his person'.[13] Secondly, he dismissed the relevance of the exclusion clause in the agent's terms of engagement, concluding it was not a limitation on authority, but a promise as to how it would be exercised.[14] Finally, Dixon J noted that 'the rule which imposes liability upon a master for the wrongs of his servant committed in the course of his employment is commonly regarded as part of the law of agency'.[15]

Evatt and McTiernan JJ dissented, finding that the appellant should not be held liable for the agent's statements. Evatt J focused on the motive of the agent. He distinguished acts done in the course of employment from acts done due to 'caprice' of the servant. He said nothing in *Lloyd* indicated that the motive of the employee was irrelevant in determining whether what they did was within the scope of employment. He found that if the wrongdoing were motivated by the ill-will of the servant, that would be relevant in determining whether they were acting within scope.[16] Here the agent was acting from 'spite and malice'.

[11] ibid 47.
[12] ibid 48.
[13] ibid 49.
[14] ibid 50.
[15] ibid 49.
[16] ibid 62–64.

Evatt J rejected the suggestion that an employer could not effectively limit the scope of an employee's authority by appropriate inclusions in the written terms of engagement:

> It is difficult to suppose that a master who puts another in his place to do a class of act in his absence can never define or delimit such 'class of act'. Indeed the very first question that arises in applying the classical passage of Willes J is 'what is the authorised class of acts'? It is fallacious to assert that, as a matter of law and despite everything contained in his contract of service, every person who is sent out to prospective customers to procure orders for his master's goods is empowered to utter criticisms upon the goods and business methods of (competitors).[17]

The High Court next considered the matter in *Deatons Proprietary Limited v Flew*.[18] The case involved an action against a hotel owner. His barmaid had thrown a glass at the plaintiff, a patron of the hotel, after he made an unpleasant comment to her. As a result, the plaintiff lost sight in one eye. He sought to make the hotel vicariously responsible for the actions of the barmaid.

All members of the Court dismissed the claim. They all agreed that the appropriate test focused on the scope of the employee's employment and found that what the barmaid did here was outside that scope. It was not an act incidental to employment.[19] It was not performed on behalf of the employer.[20] It was not done in furtherance of the employer's interests.[21] Her actions were likely motivated by private spite.[22]

Dixon J seemed to engage the principle of 'occasion'. This is particularly important, since the High Court in its most recent case in this area, to be discussed below, also utilised this concept. Dixon J said that this was not a case involving 'a wrongful act done for the servant's own benefit for which the master is liable when they are acts to which the ostensible performance of his master's work gives occasion',[23] citing *Lloyd*. He then added that the barmaid's act was a 'spontaneous act of retributive justice. The occasion for administering it and the form it took may have arisen from the fact that she was a barmaid', however retribution was not part of the course of her employment.[24]

Some difference of opinion regarding the theoretical basis of vicarious liability became evident in *Darling Island Stevedoring and Lighterage Co Ltd v Long*.[25] The case involved the possible liability of a defendant for their employee's actions in breaching a statute. The statute provided for a penalty for breach to be paid by the 'person in charge'. The Court found it was not intended that the

[17] ibid 67–68.
[18] *Deatons Proprietary Limited v Flew* (1949) 79 CLR 370.
[19] ibid 378 (Latham CJ).
[20] ibid 379 (Latham CJ).
[21] ibid 379 (Latham CJ) and 381 (Dixon J).
[22] ibid 380 (Dixon J) and 387 (Williams J).
[23] ibid 381.
[24] ibid 382.
[25] *Darling Island Stevedoring and Lighterage Co Ltd v Long* (1957) 97 CLR 36.

statutory provision create a liability on the employer for the employee's breach. Some divergence of views was evident regarding the theoretical justification of an employer's liability for their servant's actions. Fullagar J described the 'true vicarious liability' involved, that the master was liable not because they breached a duty, but because another breached a duty, and the master was liable for the acts of the other.[26] He said vicarious liability was based on policy and was justified by agency principle.[27] In contrast, Kitto J seemed to conceive of vicarious liability as being based on a breach of duty that the *employer* owed.[28] He opined that the Court asked whether the servant's actions were within the scope of employment in order to determine whether the employer owed the injured party a duty of care.[29] He placed this in the context of the previously important question as to whether the action against the master should proceed in trespass or case. The Court determined that the action against the master should generally proceed in case, unless the master had specifically commanded the action of which complaint was made. For Kitto J, this reflected the 'distinct and independent' liability of the employer for the breach of a duty they themselves owed, as opposed to a liability derivative of that of the servant.[30] Subsequent cases would not adopt Kitto J's master's tort theory of vicarious liability; rather the view of vicarious liability as being derivative of the position of the servant has been applied.[31]

Soblusky v Egan was Australia's motor vehicle vicarious liability case.[32] It involved the question of the liability of the appellant, a person entitled to possession of a vehicle. He had given permission for another to drive the vehicle. He remained in the vehicle but had fallen asleep. The vehicle was involved in an accident. The court found the appellant was liable for the driving, because he was entitled to direct and control the motion of the vehicle. The court noted the possible rationales of the vicarious liability principle, including the deep pockets rationale, and the need to find a defendant with the ability to satisfy a judgment.[33] Of these, the court noted that they 'explain but they do not justify a development of the law if it really involves a departure from principle'.[34] The court decided the case on agency principles, that the driver was driving as the agent of the appellant.

[26] ibid 57.

[27] ibid.

[28] *Darling Island* (n 25): 'In the common case of damage caused to a stranger by a careless driving on a highway by a servant in the course of his employment, the principle requires that the driving of the servant be treated as the driving of the master; but the result is to hold the master liable, not for the servant's breach of a duty of care which he, the servant, owed to the stranger, but for a breach of a duty of care which the master himself owed to the stranger' (61), with whom Taylor J agreed.

[29] ibid 63 (with whom Taylor J agreed).

[30] ibid 64–65.

[31] L Klar, 'Vicarious Liability' in C Sappideen and P Vines (eds), *Fleming's The Law of Torts*, 10th edn (Pyrmont, NSW, Thomson Reuters/Lawbook Co, 2011); *New South Wales v Lepore* (2003) 212 CLR 511.

[32] *Soblusky v Egan* (1960) 103 CLR 215.

[33] ibid 229 (Dixon CJ; Kitto and Windeyer JJ).

[34] ibid 229 (Dixon CJ; Kitto and Windeyer JJ).

The appellant had full legal authority to direct what was to be done with the vehicle, and he had delegated this to the driver, with full ability to reassert the power of control.[35] It was irrelevant that the appellant was in fact asleep during the journey.

The limits of the so-called motor vehicle doctrine were explored subsequently in *Scott v Davis.*[36] The plaintiff, a child, attended a birthday party on the defendant's premises. The defendant owned a number of vintage aeroplanes. The plaintiff asked whether he could have a ride in one of them. The defendant asked a pilot who had attended the party to take the plaintiff up in one of the aircraft. The pilot agreed. The plane crashed due to the pilot's negligence, and the plaintiff was injured. He sued the defendant, arguing that he should be liable for the pilot's negligence. A majority of the court rejected the plaintiff's claim.

Gleeson CJ denied that the pilot was acting as the agent of the defendant. The defendant could not assert a power of control or direction over the manner in which the pilot was flying the aircraft.[37] The pilot was not an employee. He rejected a suggestion that the defendant should be liable because the pilot was acting at the request of the defendant, and for his purposes.[38] It was relevant that the context was a social, rather than commercial, occasion.[39]

Gummow J seemed to embrace an 'enterprise risk' theory of vicarious liability:

> The doctrine of vicarious liability in modern times derives support from the notion that a party who engages others to advance that party's economic interests should be placed under a liability for losses incurred by third parties in the course of the enterprise.[40]

He also sought to justify vicarious liability on an insurance footing, stating that the employer 'was seen as a suitable means for the passing on of those losses through such means as liability insurance and higher prices for the goods and services supplied by the enterprise'.[41]

In dissent, McHugh J took an agency approach. He found the pilot was acting as the agent of the defendant owner and was subject to his general direction and control. The precedent of *Soblusky*, where the driver was held to be acting on behalf of the defendant although the defendant was sleeping, was somewhat analogous. The pilot was acting within the scope of the authority conferred upon him by the defendant.

McHugh J cited various policy rationales for making a principal vicariously liable for the actions of their agent. It would provide principals with an incentive to be careful in selecting, training and defining the scope of engagement of the agent.

[35] ibid 231 (Dixon CJ; Kitto and Windeyer JJ).
[36] *Scott v Davis* (2000) 204 CLR 333.
[37] ibid 341; Gummow J made the same observation (420); as did Hayne J (440) and Callinan J (459).
[38] ibid 342; see also Hayne J (440).
[39] ibid 343; see also Hayne J (438–39) and Callinan J (458).
[40] ibid 418–19.
[41] ibid 419; Hayne J agreed that the question of insurance and the availability of deep pockets had influenced the direction of vicarious liability (436, 439), as did Callinan J (450).

The principal would have a right to be indemnified by the agent. Liability would not be indeterminate. Finally, he opined it was 'fairer' that the person who engaged the wrongdoer as their representative or delegate should bear the loss, as opposed to the innocent third party.[42]

The High Court considered the liability of the operators of a courier business for the negligent actions of one of their couriers in *Hollis v Vabu Pty Limited*.[43] One of the disputed questions was whether the courier involved was an employee or independent contractor. This was a question that the Court had considered on many occasions. Typically, matters such as the extent to which the organisation engaging the worker retained control over matters such as what was to be done and how it was to be done were important.[44] The potential for control, rather than actual control, was important.[45] The extent to which the worker used their own resources was relevant, as was whether the person was paid for a particular result.[46]

The Court noted the law had long made this distinction; it was important because typically a defendant was liable for actions of their employees committed within the scope of employment but was not liable for actions of independent contractors.[47] The joint reasons noted it was difficult to articulate a rationale for vicarious liability, but broad policy considerations were at play.[48]

The joint reasons seemed to embrace an enterprise risk theory of vicarious liability:

> Under contemporary Australian conditions, the conduct by the defendant of an enterprise in which persons are identified as representing that enterprise should carry an obligation to third persons to bear the cost of injury or damage to them which may fairly be said to be characteristic of the conduct of that enterprise.[49]

The joint reasons accepted that the imposition of vicarious liability on enterprises could play a useful role in deterring undesirable activity.[50]

McHugh J continued to apply his agency basis of vicarious liability. He agreed with the joint reasons that the doctrine had its basis in policy considerations.[51] He also applied the enterprise risk theory of vicarious liability.[52] McHugh J eschewed the traditional distinction between employees and independent

[42] ibid 367.

[43] *Hollis v Vabu Pty Limited* (2001) 207 CLR 21.

[44] *Humberstone v Northern Timber Mills* (1949) 79 CLR 389, 404.

[45] *Zuijs v Wirth Brothers Pty Ltd* (1955) 93 CLR 561, 571.

[46] *Marshall v Whittaker's Building Supply Co* (1963) 109 CLR 210; *Stevens v Brodribb* (1986) 160 CLR 16.

[47] *Hollis* (n 43) 36 (Gleeson CJ; Gaudron, Gummow, Kirby and Hayne JJ). The distinction was subsequently affirmed in *Sweeney v Boylan Nominees Pty Ltd* (2006) 226 CLR 161, 172 (Gleeson CJ; Gummow, Hayne, Heydon and Crennan JJ).

[48] *Hollis* (n 43) 37.

[49] ibid 40.

[50] ibid 43.

[51] ibid 54.

[52] ibid 55–56.

contractors, on the basis it no longer reflected the realities of the modern workplace.[53] For McHugh J, it was enough that the negligent courier was acting as the agent of the courier company.

Callinan J sharply rejected the enterprise risk approach. He said it was based on assumptions which may have been made by those with incomplete information and by those who may not be qualified to assess the relevant evidence. There was little concrete evidence to support an assumption of a link between increases in insurance premiums and the taking of steps to mitigate risk.[54] Here, couriers themselves also had an incentive to be careful. The Court should be wary of imposing an employer-employee regime in cases where neither party might wish it.[55]

A very significant case for the development of vicarious liability in Australia was the conjoined appeals case of *State of New South Wales v Lepore; Samin v State of Queensland; Rich v State of Queensland*.[56] The cases involved the question of the liability of educational providers for abuse committed by teachers on students. The discussion here will focus on that part of the case that dealt with the educational provider's possible vicarious liability for the actions of the teachers; the question of non-delegable duty will be considered in chapter ten.

Gleeson CJ discussed the 'scope of employment' aspect of vicarious liability, contrasting that with circumstances in which an employee was considered to be on a 'frolic' of their own.[57] An employer was not liable for 'independent acts' of employees.[58] He stated that the fact that the employment situation created the opportunity for the wrongdoing to occur was insufficient.[59] He referred to the well-known Salmond test, that an employer was liable for authorised acts, and unauthorised acts if they were so connected with authorised acts as to amount to modes—albeit improper modes—of doing them. Gleeson CJ noted the difficulty with the application of the test was that the answer to the question of whether impugned acts were merely improper modes of carrying out authorised acts would depend on the level of generality at which 'authorised acts' were defined.[60]

Gleeson CJ said that many variables attended the relationship between school authority and student. He said this meant no absolute answer could be given as

[53] ibid 57.
[54] ibid 68.
[55] ibid 69.
[56] *State of New South Wales v Lepore; Samin v State of Queensland; Rich v State of Queensland* (2003) 212 CLR 511. For discussion see J Wangmann, 'Liability for Institutional Child Sexual Assault: Where Does Lepore Leave Australia?' (2004) 28 *Melbourne University Law Review* 169; P Vines, '*New South Wales v Lepore; Samin v Queensland; Rich v Queensland*—Schools' Responsibility for Teachers' Sexual Assault: Non-Delegable Duty and Vicarious Liability' (2003) 27 *Melbourne University Law Review* 612; C Beuermann, 'Conferred Authority, Strict Liability and Institutional Child Sexual Abuse' (2015) 37 *Sydney Law Review* 113.
[57] *State of New South Wales v Lepore; Samin v State of Queensland; Rich v State of Queensland*, ibid, 535.
[58] ibid 537.
[59] ibid.
[60] ibid 539.

to the possible vicarious liability of a school for abuse by a teacher; much would depend on the context. He said that in the past, sexual abuse by a teacher of a student would be regarded as purely an independent act, for which the school authority would not be vicariously liable. However, today the answer was not so easy. He said there could be a legal difference between an 'opportunistic act of serious and random violence which might be different in terms of its connection with employment, from improper touching by a person whose duties include intimate contact with another'.[61]

Gleeson CJ claimed that the 'enterprise risk' theory of vicarious liability had not been taken up in Australia, despite what the High Court had reasoned in *Hollis*. However, he stated that in practice there might not be a lot of difference in results if the enterprise risk theory were adopted, since in most cases 'considerations that would justify a conclusion as to whether an enterprise materially increases the risk of an employee's offending would also bear upon an examination of the nature of the employee's responsibilities, which are regarded as central in Australia'.[62] He said that usually the risk of sexual abuse would not be regarded as an incident of the conduct of most schools, or that ordinary responsibilities of teachers were such that sexual assaults on students would not usually be regarded as conduct, albeit serious misconduct, that would be considered to be within the scope of employment. However, there were exceptions involving staff who had 'personal protection' (for the sake of simplicity, I will subsequently refer to these as 'pastoral') responsibilities, and a relationship of power and intimacy. In such cases, sexual abuse committed by them on children within their care could be regarded as sufficiently connected with that employment as to give rise to vicarious liability upon their employer for their actions.[63] He emphasised the 'power and intimacy' that would characterise such situations. The age of the students, any particular vulnerability they had, the tasks allocated to teachers, and the number of staff allocated to the responsibility of student supervision would all be relevant, as would the nature and circumstances of the sexual misconduct.[64]

Gaudron J noted the unsatisfactory doctrinal underpinnings of the law of vicarious liability, and that some decisions may have been influenced by unidentified policy considerations.[65] Like McHugh J in previous cases, she preferred to place vicarious liability on the footing of principal and agent, together with notions of estoppel.[66]

Gaudron J criticised some of the language in decisions making an employer vicariously liable for criminal actions of their employees, including *Lloyd* and *Morris*. Speaking of the decision in *Morris*, where an employer was held liable

61 ibid 540–41.
62 ibid 544.
63 ibid.
64 ibid 546.
65 ibid 553.
66 ibid 554.

for an employee's theft, she noted that 'precisely how it could be said that the employee was acting in the scope or course of his employment in stealing the coat was not explained. Nor is it easy to postulate on what basis it might be so said'.[67] She concluded it was a 'misuse of language' to say that deliberate criminal acts were committed within the course of employment.[68]

She preferred to cast the liability of an educational institution for abuse committed by staff in terms of a non-delegable duty, and was strongly critical of the use of vicarious liability in such cases:

> If vicarious liability is to be imposed so that a person is to be held liable in damages for injury suffered without fault on his or her part, it ought to be imposed only in circumstances where it can be justified by reference to legal principle. To do otherwise is to invite disrespect for the law. As already indicated, to hold an employer liable for the authorised acts of an employee for acts done in the course of his or her employment is simply to apply the ordinary law of agency … where the issues concern the doing of an authorised act in an unauthorised way, it will ordinarily be the case that vicarious liability results from the ostensible authority of the person whose acts caused injury to the plaintiff. The difficulties that have arisen in relation to vicarious liability concern the absence of any real test for determining whether an act occurred in the course of or within the scope of employment. That difficulty is exacerbated in the case of deliberate criminal acts which, save perhaps, for some temporal connection, cannot ordinarily be described as acts done in the course of or within the scope of employment.[69]

Gaudron J said the only principled basis on which vicarious liability could be imposed for deliberate criminal activity of another was to argue the defendant was estopped from asserting the person was not acting within their employment. This doctrine was equally applicable to employee and independent contractor.[70] This would occur when the plaintiff would reasonably assume that the wrongdoer was acting as the servant, agent or representative of the defendant.[71]

Gummow and Hayne JJ agreed that a fully satisfactory rationale for the vicarious liability doctrine had been slow to appear, and that policy considerations explained much of it.[72] At least one of the posited rationales was to deter an employer from poor choices regarding employees.[73] They adopted a negative stance towards the enterprise risk theory underpinning developments in Canadian law, suggesting that it might distract a court from considering whether the employee's actions were within the scope of employment, instead focusing on the extent to which the defendant increased a risk that abuse would occur, for example by opening a school. Gummow and Hayne JJ emphasised that conducting a school might 'provide the occasion or the opportunity' for a teacher

[67] ibid 556.
[68] ibid 557.
[69] ibid 560–61.
[70] ibid 561.
[71] ibid.
[72] ibid 580.
[73] ibid 581–82.

to assault a pupil.[74] However, the school authority should not be held liable for this simple fact.

Likewise, Gummow and Hayne JJ did not appear to support Gleeson CJ's distinction between different teaching staff, some with greater pastoral care roles than others, in terms of vicarious liability. Gummow and Hayne JJ said sexual assaults by teachers were not confined to those with pastoral roles.[75] They said that in every school, teachers exercised authority and power. The environment created the risk of abuse, regardless of whether the teacher had a pastoral role or not. The Canadian authorities had also appeared to draw this distinction, suggesting that a school authority was more likely to be held vicariously liable for sexual abuse committed by a teacher who had pastoral care responsibilities with respect to a child, than a teacher who did not have such responsibilities.

Gummow and Hayne JJ effectively rejected such a distinction. They said that it 'gives no significance to three facts'. These were that the conduct concerned was intentional conduct by the employee, it contravened the employee's contract of employment, and was contrary to the core of the task for which the teacher was employed. Further, evidently the teacher had not been deterred from such activity by the possibility of criminal sanction.[76] As a result, the imposition of vicarious liability on an employer for the wrongdoing could not be justified on the basis of deterrence.[77] Gummow and Hayne JJ said it was speculative at best to suggest the imposition of vicarious liability on an educational institution would make them more careful in choosing staff, and in any event, vicarious liability was not (should not) be about the negligence of the defendant.[78]

Gummow and Hayne JJ said that Pollock had supported a version of the 'enterprise risk' approach to vicarious liability. However, a critical aspect of Pollock's argument was that the employer would be liable for risks created that were associated with an employee's pursuing the employer's business interests. In that vein, it was said to be fair that the employer bore those costs. They argued that the Canadian decisions had taken this theory too far, by seeking to use it to justify the imposition of liability on an employer where the employee was not acting in furtherance of the employer's business, but in a way that was the antithesis of those interests.[79] They were worried that by simply focusing on 'enterprise risk' vicarious liability would morph into something like a 'but for' test, in the sense of asking whether the wrong would have occurred but for the defendant's enterprise. Gummow and Hayne JJ said this could distract from questions about the scope of the employee's employment.[80] Gummow and Hayne JJ seemed to share

[74] ibid 586.
[75] ibid 587.
[76] ibid.
[77] ibid.
[78] ibid.
[79] ibid 588.
[80] ibid 589.

Gaudron J's ambivalence about criminal acts being held to be within the scope of employment, as well as acts that had been specifically prohibited by the employer. However, they did not reject those suggestions; they merely conceded it was contrary to what the phrase 'course of employment' might be thought to mean.[81]

Gummow and Hayne JJ attempted to distil the case law which had attempted to clarify the 'scope of employment' principle in the context of wrongful acts, including the decision of Dixon J in *Deatons*. Their interpretation was that vicarious liability could be imposed where:

a. The wrongful act was done in intended pursuit of the employer's interests or in intended performance of the contract of employment; or
b. The wrongful act was done in ostensible pursuit of the employer's business or in the apparent execution of authority which the employer held out the employee as having.[82]

They added that sometimes the question of who benefited from the employee's conduct would be relevant.[83] Applying these tests, Gummow and Hayne JJ found that the school authority was not vicariously liable for what the teachers did. Their actions were not done in intended pursuit of the interests of the state in conducting educational classes. They were not done in intended pursuit of the contract of employment. They were not done ostensibly in the interests of the state or the educational system. They were not done in apparent execution of the teachers' authority.[84] Gummow and Hayne JJ found sexual assault of a pupil was not an 'unintended by-product' of performance of the teacher's role.[85] It was irrelevant whether the teacher's role comprised a pastoral care requirement or not. They held that to find here that the teachers' actions were within the scope of their employment would 'strip any content' from that requirement, and amount simply to a rule that the employer was liable for all of the actions of their employees. The fact that the school authority had deep pockets was not a reason to hold them liable.[86]

Kirby J also noted that a unifying rationale for the imposition of vicarious liability had been slow to emerge.[87] However, he agreed with the enterprise risk approach, evident in the Canadian cases in particular. He also agreed with the deterrence rationale. He claimed that the 'only truly effective way' of encouraging employers in the educational setting to reduce the risk of sexual abuse of students was to impose economic damages on such employers.[88] He said that from the point of view of the wronged victim, they were typically innocent of any wrongdoing.

[81] ibid.
[82] ibid 591–92.
[83] ibid 592.
[84] ibid 594–95.
[85] ibid 594.
[86] ibid.
[87] ibid 611.
[88] ibid 613.

The perpetrator may not have sufficient assets to meet any judgment. The victims had suffered serious harm. He concluded that the common law 'does not usually disappoint legitimate and reasonable expectations in such matters'.[89]

Kirby J noted that vicarious liability had in the past, and should continue, to be applied in cases of intentional wrongdoing by the employee, including actions contrary to express employer instructions. He interpreted the 'scope of employment' test to mean that an employer would be liable for their employee's wrongdoing where (a) the employment materially and significantly enhanced or exacerbated the risk of the tort, (b) where there was significant connection between the creation or enhancement of the risk and the wrong it causes within the employer's enterprise, (c) where the conduct might fairly and properly be regarded as being done within the scope of employment.[90] Kirby J stated that ultimately, the question was whether it was 'just and reasonable' to impose on the relevant enterprise legal liability for the wrong committed by the employee.[91] Kirby J said that the employment must represent 'more than the occasion for the performance by the teacher of (their) … wrongs'.[92]

Callinan J stated that deliberate criminal misconduct would usually lie well outside the scope of an employee's duty.[93] Here nothing could be further from a teacher's duty than their sexual assault of a student. It was not reasonable to make an employer vicariously liable for such assaults.[94] It was an orthodox view that the mere fact the employment provided the 'opportunity' for the wrongdoing was insufficient to make the employer liable; however, if the connection test were applied broadly, it would in effect render an employer liable based on an opportunity-type analysis.[95] He rejected notions of 'fair and reasonable' on the basis they were impossibly subjective and uncertain in application.[96]

Most Recent Developments

Most recently the High Court reconsidered vicarious liability in *Prince Alfred College*.[97] The case involved abuse committed by a boarding master at the relevant school several decades before legal action was commenced. The plaintiff brought a case alleging both direct negligence and vicarious liability against the school.

[89] ibid 614.
[90] ibid 618.
[91] ibid 619.
[92] ibid 621.
[93] ibid 625.
[94] ibid.
[95] ibid 626.
[96] ibid. The other member of the Court, McHugh J, decided the case purely on the basis of the non-delegable duty, and did not discuss the possible application of vicarious liability here.
[97] *Prince Alfred College* (2016) 258 CLR 134.

He alleged the appellant was negligent for engaging the wrongdoer as boarding master. It had been discovered that the wrongdoer had a past conviction for sexual abuse against a child. He was engaged as a boarding master though he was a young and inexperienced teacher. The case alleged that the school had not arranged adequate supervision of the boarding master; specifically, often only one teacher was present during times where students were especially vulnerable to abuse. The plaintiff argued the school was vicariously liable for the abuse, because the offender committed the abuse while employed as a boarding master there. It was said that the abuse occurred within the course of his employment. Since the claimant brought the legal claim many years after the abuse occurred, he was according to ordinary limitation of actions rules prevented from continuing. He sought an exercise of the Court's discretion to grant an extension of time to permit his claim to proceed.

The High Court upheld an appeal against the decision of the state court which had found for the plaintiff. The lower court had granted an extension of time and had found the appellant vicariously liable for the actions of the boarding master. One (state) judge found the appellant was liable for direct negligence.[98]

The High Court decided too much time had elapsed between the time where the parties had apparently reached an accommodation on the dispute and these proceedings. The Court found the delay was not justified or excusable. It precluded the possibility of a fair trial.[99] It expressly declined to decide the substantive legal issues surrounding vicarious liability and/or possible direct negligence of the school.[100] However, given the uncertainty in this area of law, the Court decided to provide some indication of its views on the contours of the vicarious liability doctrine. Obviously, such comments were strictly obiter dicta in nature. These comments are likely to be influential. On the other hand, given the past differences of opinion among members of the Court and other courts on the scope of vicarious liability, it would hardly be surprising if the comments the High Court made in *Prince Alfred College* about vicarious liability do not represent the 'last word' on the doctrine's development in Australia.

The Court stated that the concept of 'scope of employment' had been used to frame the parameters of vicarious liability. The concept was supported, on the basis that it provided an objective, rational basis for liability.[101] The Court conceded that the question of 'connection' with employment had not assisted much in clarifying an employer's vicarious liability.[102] The Court developed a new principle in an effort to further clarify the Australian law. This was the notion of 'occasion'. The Court agreed with earlier case law to the effect that the mere fact employment

[98] A, *DC v Prince Alfred College Incorporated* [2015] SASC 12.

[99] *Prince Alfred College* (n 97) 142 (French CJ; Kiefel, Bell, Keane and Nettle JJ); 170–71 (Gageler and Gordon JJ).

[100] ibid 142–43 (French CJ; Kiefel, Bell, Keane and Nettle JJ); 171 (Gageler and Gordon JJ).

[101] ibid 148 (French CJ; Kiefel, Bell, Keane and Nettle JJ).

[102] ibid 156.

provided an opportunity for the wrongful act to be committed did not suffice in itself to justify vicarious liability. However, the Court stated that if the employment situation not only provided the *opportunity*, but was also the *occasion* for the commission of the wrongful act, vicarious liability could arise. The following is the critical passage:

> It may be sufficient to hold an employer vicariously liable for a criminal act committed by an employee where, in the commission of that act, the employee used or took advantage of the position in which the employment placed the employee vis-à-vis the victim … the relevant approach is to consider any special role that the employer has assigned to the employee and the position in which the employee is thereby placed vis-à-vis the victim. In determining whether the apparent performance of such a role may be said to give the occasion for the wrongful act, particular features (are relevant). They include authority, power, trust, control and the ability to achieve intimacy with the victim. The latter feature may be especially important. Where, in such circumstances, the employee takes advantage of (their) position with respect to the victim, that may (suggest) the wrongful act should be regarded as committed in the course or scope of employment … (rendering) the employer vicariously liable.[103]

The Court then proceeded to apply this new 'occasion' principle to the facts of the case. It considered whether the abuser's role as boarding master placed him in a position of power over and intimacy with the victim, such that it could be said that the abuser's role as boarding master 'gave the occasion' for the wrongful acts.[104]

Australian law has generally followed the law of the United Kingdom in this area in terms of making a strong distinction between an employer's liability for actions of their employees, on the one hand, and actions of an independent contractor. An employer is vicariously liable for actions of an employee; they are not generally vicariously liable for acts of an independent contractor.[105] This distinction has usually been less contentious than the scope of the liability for someone who is admitted to be an employee. Of course, this begs the question of how to distinguish between a true employee and a true independent contractor. Like the United Kingdom decisions, the Australian courts have applied the control test, considering the extent to which the employer controls the actions of the worker. There is some difference of view as to whether actual control,[106] or the potential for control,[107] is sufficient. It is sometimes said that where the employer can control not only what is to be done but how it shall be done, the worker

[103] ibid 159–60; with whom Gageler and Gordon JJ agreed (172).

[104] ibid 160–61; with whom Gageler and Gordon JJ agreed (172).

[105] *Sweeney v Boylan Nominees Pty Ltd* (2006) 226 CLR 161, 167 (Gleeson CJ; Gummow, Hayne, Heydon and Crennan JJ); *Hollis* (n 43) 36 (Gleeson CJ; Gaudron, Gummow, Kirby and Hayne JJ); *cf* McHugh J (dissenting) found that an employer could be liable for the actions of workers who were neither employees nor independent contractors (57).

[106] *Humberstone v Northern Timber Mills* (n 44) 396 (Latham CJ).

[107] ibid 404 (Dixon J); *Zuijs v Wirth Brothers Pty Ltd* (n 45) 571 (Dixon CJ; Williams, Webb and Taylor JJ); *Stevens v Brodribb* (n 46) 24 (Mason CJ).

is an employee.[108] A person who is paid for a particular result is likely to be an independent contractor.[109] The level of skill required to perform the task is not relevant.[110] A worker who supplies their own equipment and/or labour to do the work is more likely to be an independent contractor.[111] The High Court has been somewhat lukewarm on the 'organisation test' approach to establishing whether or not an employer–employee relationship exists, finding that it might be one factor in determining whether or not the requisite control exists, but that it was not an alternative test.[112] I will consider relationships that should give rise to vicarious liability in more detail in chapter nine.

Some Critique and Reflection on Australian Case Law

Given the relatively few Australian High Court cases on vicarious liability, some limited comments may be made with respect to it. Again, it needs to be understood in the context that while some of the cases were decided, the Australian High Court considered itself to be bound by decisions of the House of Lords, as well as the Privy Council.

The High Court has repeatedly observed that discerning a satisfactory rationale for the imposition of vicarious liability has been difficult. So much may be readily accepted. That said, the High Court has on some occasions attempted to articulate such a rationale. However, it is fair to say this has not always been successful. There has been evident confusion in the High Court as to whether to adopt the 'enterprise risk' theory that characterises the Canadian case law in this area. Specifically, the enterprise risk theory of vicarious liability was clearly adopted by five members of the High Court in *Hollis v Vabu Pty Limited*.[113] Yet in a case just two years later, three members of the Court in *Lepore* specifically rejected it. This included Gleeson CJ, who though a member of the joint judgment in *Hollis* which clearly accepted and applied enterprise risk, claimed in *Lepore* that the doctrine had never been accepted in Australia.[114] It included Gummow and Hayne JJ, also

[108] *Humberstone v Northern Timber Mills* (n 44) 404 (Dixon J); *Stevens v Brodribb*, ibid, 35 (Wilson and Dawson JJ).

[109] *Humberstone v Northern Timber Mills*, ibid, 396 (Latham CJ); *Marshall v Whittaker's Building Supply Co* (n 46) 214–15 (Kitto, Taylor, Menzies and Owen JJ).

[110] *Zuijs v Wirth Brothers Pty Ltd* (n 45) 570–71 (Dixon CJ; Williams, Webb and Taylor JJ).

[111] *Marshall v Whittaker's Building Supply Co* (n 46) 215 (Kitto, Taylor, Menzies and Owen JJ; 215 (Windeyer J); *Stevens v Brodribb* (n 46) 24 (Mason CJ) (with whom Brennan J agreed generally (47), and with whom Deane J agreed on that point (49).

[112] *Stevens v Brodribb*, ibid, 27–28 (Mason J) (with whom Brennan J agreed generally (47)) and with whom Deane J agreed on that point (49); 35–36 (Wilson and Dawson JJ).

[113] (2001) 207 CLR 21, 40 (Gleeson CJ; Gaudron, Gummow, Kirby and Hayne JJ); see also *Scott* (n 36) 418–19 (Gummow J).

[114] *Lepore* (n 31) 543. Gleeson CJ suggested that the doctrine had not been applied in Australia 'as a test for determining whether conduct is in the course of employment, as distinct from an explanation of the willingness of the law to impose vicarious liability'.

members of the joint reasons in *Hollis*, who now viewed the doctrine as potentially distracting from the key issue of course of employment.[115] Apart from Kirby J, other members of the Court in *Lepore* favoured a different rationale for the imposition of vicarious liability rather than enterprise risk.[116]

In its most recent pronouncements in 2016, the High Court did not seek to utilise the enterprise risk theory to explain or justify vicarious liability. What it did utilise was the concept of 'occasion', whether the employment provided the occasion, as opposed to the mere 'opportunity', for the wrongdoing to occur.

It is considered somewhat difficult to distinguish, as the Court attempted to do in *Prince Alfred College*, between cases where the employment provided the *opportunity* for the wrongful act(s) to occur, and cases where the employment provided the *occasion* for same. The distinction is important, because it has long been accepted that the fact the employment provided the *opportunity* for the wrongful act to occur is insufficient to attract vicarious liability, as the Court itself acknowledged in the case. In *Prince Alfred College* the Court claimed the 'occasion' principle explained and justified imposition of vicarious liability in particular cases. With respect, it is not entirely clear at this point precisely how the concept of 'occasion' adds to 'scope of employment' notions. If 'occasion' is informed by issues like power, control, trust and opportunity for intimacy with victims, as the High Court said, surely the existence of these elements would already be relevant in considering the scope of the employee's employment. As such, it is not clear what, if anything, the concept of 'occasion' adds. This observation is supported in the decision itself, where the joint reasons conclude, in discussing the recent United Kingdom decision in *Mohamud*, that 'the role assigned to the employee … did not provide the occasion for the wrongful acts which the employee committed outside the kiosk … what occurred after the victim left the kiosk was relevantly unconnected with the employee's employment'.[117] In other words, practically speaking 'occasion' and 'connection with employment' tend to run together. Somewhat paradoxically though, in the judgment of Dixon J in *Deatons*,[118] the judgment from which the High Court derived this 'occasion' principle, Dixon J himself *disaggregated* the concept of 'occasion' from scope questions: 'the occasion for administering (the throwing of the glass) and the form it took may have arisen from the fact that she was a barmaid, but retribution was not within the course of her employment as a barmaid'.[119] The fact that, of the court in *Deatons*, only Dixon J referred to the concept of 'occasion', and that he found no vicarious liability on the facts although admitting the 'occasion' for the barmaid's acts arose from her employment position, suggests the need for respectful scepticism as to the utility of the 'occasion' concept in clarifying the law here. The possible

[115] ibid 586.
[116] The High Court did not discuss the enterprise risk theory in *Prince Alfred*.
[117] *Prince Alfred College* (n 97) 160.
[118] (1949) 79 CLR 370.
[119] ibid 382.

use of the 'occasion' doctrine in order to clarify the contours of vicarious liability principle had also been rejected in other High Court decisions subsequent to *Deatons*.[120]

If this concept will be applied in future, much will turn on its further exposition. It may be, for example, that the High Court was attempting to contrast a situation where a school cleaner abuses a student, from a case where a boarding master does so. It is conceivable that the Court will utilise the 'occasion' principle to justify imposition of vicarious liability on the school authority with respect to the abuse of the latter, not the former. However, that would result in very fine and arguably arbitrary, incoherent distinctions. What if the abuse occurs while the school cleaner is cleaning the showers in the school dormitories? Can it justifiably be argued the employment was not the 'occasion' for the abuse, because pastoral care was not part of the cleaner's responsibilities, but if the same abuse were committed by the boarding master in the same place, the school authority would be liable? I am not sure that victims of abuse would have any time for such legal niceties. And again, what, if anything, does 'occasion' add here that considerations of the scope of employment have not already included? The difficulty of framing appropriate legal principle in this area is fully acknowledged. Having said that, the author is doubtful that the High Court's new 'occasion' principle is the answer and will provide any further clarity and workability in this difficult area of the law than existed prior to the case.

It is noteworthy that in the Australian case law there has been reasonable support for the proposition that vicarious liability principles might be seen best through concepts of agency. This appeared in *CML*,[121] *Darling Island*,[122] *Soblusky*,[123] and was maintained by McHugh J in cases such as *Scott*[124] and *Hollis*.[125] Most recently, it attracted the support of Gaudron in *Lepore*.[126] It was not considered in *Prince Alfred*. I will consider the possible agency basis of vicarious liability in more detail in chapter eight.

Only on limited occasions have members of the Court resorted to notions of fairness. An early example appeared in the judgment of Isaacs J in *Bugge*.[127] In *Scott*, McHugh J considered it relevant to ask whether it was fairer for the loss to be borne by the plaintiff or the employer.[128] To like effect, Kirby J in *Lepore* considered whether it was 'fair, just and reasonable' to impose vicarious liability

[120] *Lepore* (n 31) 621: 'the employment must represent more than the occasion for the performance by the teacher of his or her individual criminal and civil wrongs' (Kirby J); Gummow and Hayne JJ also referred to occasion and their discussion (586–87) makes clear they do not view the concept as helpful in determining the proper bounds of vicarious liability.

[121] (1931) 46 CLR 41, 49 (Dixon J).

[122] (1957) 97 CLR 36, 57 (Fullagar J).

[123] (1960) 103 CLR 215.

[124] (2001) 204 CLR 333, 345.

[125] (2001) 207 CLR 21, 57.

[126] (2003) 212 CLR 511, 554. McHugh J decided the case on other grounds.

[127] (1919) 26 CLR 110, 117.

[128] (2001) 204 CLR 333, 367.

upon the employer.[129] The parallels with the law of negligence here are interesting. As noted in chapter one, as part of establishing whether a duty of care is owed, the United Kingdom law considers whether it would be 'fair, just and reasonable' to do so, as part of the three-stage *Caparo* test. Kirby J applied this approach in several Australian negligence cases, but he abandoned it in 2002 when his colleagues continued to reject that approach.[130] However, in 2003 he utilised the same concept in the very different context of possible strict liability.

Only on limited occasions has the Court resorted to notions of fault in applying principles of vicarious liability, obviously a principle of strict liability. The judgment of Isaacs J in *Bugge*, in turn influenced by comments in *Hern v Nichols* discussed above, is a rare example.

Regarding liability of actions of the servant which were specifically prohibited by the employer, the High Court has on the occasions where it has considered factual scenarios involving that situation found that an employer could still be liable for such actions.[131] There is little exposition of the reasons for such a position, but the relevant cases were decided at a time when House of Lords decisions were binding on the High Court, and as has been seen, United Kingdom law does not consider that to be a bar to the imposition of vicarious liability. Evatt J was somewhat brave in *CML* to question this, given the extent of authority supporting it. There is considered to be much logic in his position that, in determining the scope of an employee's employment, that express limitations in the terms upon which the employee was engaged should be considered highly relevant, contrary to prevailing orthodoxy. Usually the law would pay close attention to the written terms of an agreement in terms of determining the parties' rights and obligations under it.

Rules of contract law, including the parol evidence rule, reflect the primacy that the law places on the written terms of engagement between parties, in determining their relative rights and responsibilities. When this is the typical pattern in relation to written contracts, it is somewhat questionable, with respect, for the law of vicarious liability to insist that in terms of the liability of one party to the contract, the master, the written terms do not necessarily impact on the extent to which they are legally responsible for the acts of another. The law regularly permits parties to exclude or limit liability, in terms of exclusion clauses and indemnity clauses. These are valid and are given effect to by the courts. The law generally respects and upholds parties' bargains, on the premise that the parties are in the best position to judge what is in their best interests. A court is (rightly) loath to interfere with parties' bargains and agreements, and generally strives in contract law to discern, and then give effect to, the parties' bargain. In this light in one area of civil obligations, namely contract law, it does seem anomalous to say the least that in another area of civil obligations, namely vicarious liability, the courts flagrantly ignore

[129] (2003) 212 CLR 511, 619.
[130] *Graham Barclay Oysters Pty Ltd v Ryan* (2002) 211 CLR 540, 626.
[131] *Bugge* (n 4); *CML* (n 9) 47 (Gavan Duffy CJ and Starke J); and 50 (Dixon J).

what might be specific clauses in an employment agreement that might otherwise have been thought to be highly relevant in determining the scope of an employer's responsibilities. This argument will be developed further in chapter eight.

While at one time the High Court would have considered itself bound by House of Lords decisions such as *Lloyd* to the effect that an employer could be liable for deliberate criminal actions of an employee, this limitation of course no longer applies. And in *Lepore* there is clear dissatisfaction with the principle that deliberate, criminal wrongdoing could be considered to be within the course of an employee's employment. It is perhaps most sharply rejected by Callinan J.[132] However, Gaudron J labelled it a 'misuse of language' to say that deliberate criminal acts were within the course of employment.[133] And Gummow and Hayne JJ said the situation that a criminal act could be within the course of employment was contrary to what the phrase might be thought to mean.[134] It is considered that a majority of the court in *Lepore* were clearly uncomfortable with a suggestion that a criminal act could be deemed to be within the course of employment. This is in sharp contrast with the United Kingdom law, reflected in the recent *Mohamud* decision, that reflects that the fact the employee's actions are clearly criminal is no bar at all to the employer being held vicariously liable for them. The court in *Prince Alfred* did not consider the issue. The argument that an employer should not be held liable for intentional, criminal actions of an employee will be developed further in chapter eight.

The High Court's jurisprudence generally reflects the traditional distinction between an employee and an independent contractor, although there have been exceptions. McHugh J rejected the utility of the distinction in *Hollis*, and Gaudron J clearly did not favour it in *Lepore*. That distinction will be considered in more detail in chapter nine.

There has also been some consideration of the purpose(s) for which the employee relevantly acted, in an effort to distinguish cases where an employer ought to be liable for what the employee did, and where the employee was acting on a 'frolic' of their own. Consideration of whether the employee purported to act for the employer's purposes is evident in *Bugge*,[135] in the dissenting judgment of Evatt J in *CML*,[136] and by members of the court in *Deatons*.[137] The court there considered it relevant that the employee was acting out of personal spite, and was not pursuing the employer's interests in doing what she did. Gleeson CJ in *Scott* suggested that the fact that the person whose acts were in question were done for the defendant's purposes was not sufficient to make the defendant vicariously liable for their actions.[138]

[132] *Lepore* (n 31) 625.
[133] ibid 557.
[134] ibid 589.
[135] (1919) 26 CLR 110, 122 (Isaacs J).
[136] (1931) 46 CLR 41, 62–64.
[137] (1949) 79 CLR 389, 379 (Latham CJ); 381 (Dixon J); and 387 (Williams J).
[138] (2001) 204 CLR 333, 342.

In *Lepore*, Gummow and Hayne JJ in particular seemed attracted to a vicarious liability principle that related to the purpose(s) for which the employee acted. In fact, one of the bases upon which they criticised the Canadian developments is that they had taken Pollock's work on enterprise risk too far, by applying it to a situation where the employee was clearly not acting for the purposes of the employer, whereas Pollock formulated the enterprise risk theory in that context.[139] In the two-pronged approach they developed to apply to vicarious liability cases, the law in this area would consider whether the employee was acting in the intended pursuit of the employer's interests and/or business.[140] This is considered to have great potential to appropriately limit the scope of vicarious liability. It enjoys significant historical support, as noted in chapter one. It will be further considered when the rationales for vicarious liability are considered in more detail in Part II.

There is also evidently some difference of opinion among the judges as to the correct principles to be applied in the specific context of the possible liability of an educational institution for sexual abuse committed by one of its staff members. On one view, it may be relevant in determining a school's responsibility for such an act as to the particular nature of the teacher offender's responsibilities. The suggestion has been that if the teacher has a specific pastoral care-type responsibility within the school, it is more likely that the school authority will be liable for abuse committed by that teacher, as opposed to a teacher with primarily teaching responsibilities. This distinction clearly appealed to Gleeson CJ in *Lepore*. In so accepting such a distinction, Gleeson CJ was clearly mirroring Canadian case law, to be discussed in chapter four, which made that distinction. However, it is noteworthy that Gleeson CJ did not share the same enthusiasm for the enterprise risk theory which clearly underpinned the Canadian authorities to which he referred. The distinction made by Gleeson CJ also apparently gained the support of the High Court most recently in *Prince Alfred*, where the Court considered the extent to which the teacher's specific responsibilities gave them the kind of power and intimacy over the victim of the abuse that arguably permitted the abuse to occur.

Yet, on the other hand, it can be hard to square this line of reasoning with the High Court's insistence that the fact the employment provided the opportunity for the abuse to occur was not sufficient, of itself, to justify making the employer liable for the abuse committed. Gummow and Hayne JJ clearly did not favour this supposed distinction between teachers with pastoral care roles, and so-called ordinary teachers, in terms of vicarious liability issues. They pointed out that any teaching responsibilities gave the recipient power and control over students, and it might be drawing a very fine line to treat as substantially legally different abuse committed by a teacher with pastoral care responsibilities, and a teacher who did

139 (2003) 212 CLR 511, 588.
140 ibid 591–92.

not have such responsibilities. As they pointed out, abuse can and has been committed by both types. Certainly, it would be a difficult conversation to explain to a survivor of abuse committed by a teacher without pastoral care responsibilities that he or she does not have a claim against the school based on vicarious liability, but if the abuse had been committed by the pastoral care leader at the school, they would have had such a case. Arguably, such fine distinctions do not reflect well on the law. It can be very difficult to rationalise such different treatment on defensible grounds.

Finally, the case law above has also referred to a number of possible rationales for the imposition of vicarious liability in particular cases. These have included the fact that the defendant has insurance against possible liability in such cases, or that the defendant has 'deep pockets'. There has been discussion of the possible deterrence effect of the imposition of vicarious liability in particular cases, and the positive impact that a legal principle making them vicariously liable for a broad range of employee activities might have in terms of more careful selection of staff. These various possible rationales for the imposition of vicarious liability will be discussed at length in Part II.

4

Developments in North American Case Law

Canadian Development

The Supreme Court of Canada has considered the possibility that an employee might be personally liable for wrongful actions at work which lead to a third-party plaintiff suffering loss. This occurred in *London Drugs Limited v Brassart and Vanwinkel and Others.*[1] There the question arose concerning possible personal liability of employees. The plaintiff had entrusted the employer with safe storage of some of their equipment. Due to the negligent forklift driving of some of the employer's employees, the equipment was damaged. There was an exclusion clause in the contract between the plaintiff and the employer limiting the employer's liability.

The case is important in the current context as confirming the possibility that an employee might owe, and obviously then might breach, a duty of care owed to third parties, such as the plaintiff in that case.[2] As a result, the case confirmed the possible personal liability of an employee for negligent actions which result in loss or damage to a third party. This possibility could be ameliorated, however, by liability limiting provisions in the contract between the employer and the plaintiff. In so deciding, the Supreme Court adopted a flexible approach to notions of privity of contract, to allow employees to take advantage of such provisions in contractual arrangements, though they were not expressly party to those arrangements.[3] Further, the doctrine of voluntary assumption of risk might effectively preclude the plaintiff from claiming against negligent employees in such cases.[4]

[1] *London Drugs Limited v Brassart and Vanwinkel and Others* [1992] 3 SCR 299.

[2] ibid, L'Heureux-Dube, Sopinka, Cory, Iacobucci and McLachlin JJ; La Forest J dissenting.

[3] ibid 439 (L'Heureux-Dube, Sopinka, Cory and Iacobucci JJ). This was provided (a) the limitation clause expressly or impliedly extended benefit to those employees seeking to rely on it, and (b) the employees seeking to have the benefit of the limitation clause were acting within the course of their employment and performing services provided for in the contract between employer and plaintiff when the loss occurred (448).

[4] ibid 460 (McLachlin J).

The so-called Salmond approach to vicarious liability was taken by the Privy Council in a Canadian case,[5] and by the Canadian Supreme Court in *WW Sales v City of Edmonton*.[6] At one time, Canadian justices expressed some ambivalence about the extension of vicarious liability principles to cases of deliberate wrongdoing. This has arisen in the context of the possible liability of an institution for child sexual abuse. So, for example, in *CA, CH, LK and MD v Critchley and Province of British Columbia*[7] the British Columbia Court of Appeal considered the vicarious liability of the state for abuse committed in a residential facility for troubled youth, run by Critchley under a contractual relationship with the state. McEachern CJ clearly was ambivalent about the application of vicarious liability in such cases:

> It seems to me that predatory sexual molestation is so totally different in kind and quality from what is reasonably to be expected from an experienced care giver that there may be room for distinguishing these various kinds of cases in a vicarious liability context … I raise these questions only because vicarious liability is such a harsh principle that its application to historic cases (of child sexual abuse) might possibly be reviewed … I question whether a principal without fault should be liable for the intentional crimes of an agent unless there was negligence in the actual employment of the agent or subsequently as may have been reasonably foreseen.[8]

In a similar era, that Court was required to consider the liability of a defendant firm hired to provide security for the plaintiff's business.[9] The firm employed a person as a security guard on night shift. While at work alone, that guard deliberately set fire to the plaintiff's premises, causing substantial damage and loss. By a majority of 2:1, the Court found the defendant vicariously liable for what the employee had deliberately done.[10]

For the majority, it was relevant that the employer had given the employee total control over security of the premises. As a result, it found it had 'put any employee who might be criminally inclined in a position to pursue that inclination, and is therefore vicariously liable'.[11] What happened was an inherent risk of the employment of security staff.[12] The majority noted the tort was committed on work premises and during work hours.[13]

Braidwood J authored a strong dissent. He concluded it could not be said the employee's actions were within the scope of employment; they were the antithesis

[5] *Lockhart v Stinson and CPR* [1942] 3 DLR 529, 536 (PC).

[6] *WW Sales v City of Edmonton* [1942] SCR 467.

[7] *CA, CH, LK and MD v Critchley and Province of British Columbia* [1998] CanLII 9129 (BC CA).

[8] ibid [108]–[109].

[9] *British Columbia Ferry Corporation v Invicta Security Service Corporation* [1998] CanLII 15029 (BC CA).

[10] ibid, Rowles and Donald JJ, Braidwood J dissenting.

[11] ibid [32].

[12] ibid: 'there would seem to be two types of risks that are in the ordinary course of running a security business … the second is that the people whom one entrusts to guard against external threats will misuse that trust to threaten the property themselves': [51].

[13] ibid [54].

of what he was employed to do—protect the premises. The employee's actions were not in furtherance of the employer's business.[14] Finding vicarious liability in cases such as this effectively rendered employers absolutely liable for criminal and tortious actions of their employees, whatever the circumstances.[15] The employment merely provided the opportunity for the abuse to occur, and it was common ground this was not sufficient to attract vicarious liability.[16]

The decision in *Bazley v Curry* involved child sexual abuse committed by an employee of a children's foundation. The foundation provided extensive care for vulnerable youth, including many of the responsibilities that a parent would typically have for a young child such as bathing and hygiene, and sleeping arrangements. The foundation employed a paedophile who abused the claimant. The claimant argued the foundation was vicariously liable for what the employee had done. A unanimous Supreme Court of Canada, in a judgment authored by McLachlin J, agreed.[17] The judgment has been extremely important for the development of the law in Canada, as well as being influential in the United Kingdom and Australian courts, so it is worthy of detailed analysis.

The Court first noted the strict liability basis of vicarious liability, that it was imposed on an employer in the absence of fault.[18] It cited the oft-used Salmond test, to the effect that an employer was liable for acts of the employee that were authorised, as well as unauthorised acts so connected with an employee's employment that they should be regarded as modes, albeit improper modes, of doing authorised acts. It noted it was often difficult to distinguish between the unauthorised modes of performing authorised acts, for which an employer would be responsible, and Salmond's other category of case, independent acts of an employee, for which an employer would not be vicariously liable.[19] The Court indicated the solution to this difficulty was either to attempt to fit a new case within the parameters of an existing precedent, or to examine the purposes that vicarious liability serves, and ask whether the imposition of vicarious liability in a particular case would serve those purposes.[20]

The Court identified three categories of case where courts had found an employer vicariously liable for unauthorised actions of an employee. They were (a) cases justified on the basis the employee was acting in furtherance of the employer's aims; (b) cases based on the employer's 'creation of a situation of friction'; and (c) cases involving dishonest employees.[21]

McLachlin J considered an underlying principle that might be said to explain each of the three disparate categories. She concluded that a common thread was

[14] ibid [63].
[15] ibid [64].
[16] ibid [75].
[17] *Bazley v Curry* [1999] 2 SCR 534.
[18] ibid 539.
[19] ibid 544.
[20] ibid 545.
[21] ibid 546.

that the employee's conduct was closely tied to a risk the employer's enterprise had placed in the community. In such cases, it was just to make the employer liable for the employee's wrong. This is commonly referred to as the theory of 'enterprise risk'.[22] It has been noted elsewhere that the enterprise risk approach to vicarious liability questions substantially differs from the Salmond 'scope of employment' approach. This is because the enterprise risk approach focuses on the employer's business, and the extent to which risk might be seen to be an inherent part of it, as opposed to the Salmond test, which focuses on the actions of the employee.[23] Australian Chief Justice Susan Kiefel noted that the close connection test was a much broader basis of liability than had been the Salmond scope or course of employment test,[24] though the Supreme Court of Canada in *Bazley* seemed to downplay the extent to which it was altering the law.

The Court said it should be acknowledged that vicarious liability was best explained as being sourced in a variety of policy considerations. It referred to Fleming's identification of two in particular in the current context—provision of a just and practical remedy for the harm, and deterrence of future harm. After referring to the fact that vicarious liability increases the chances that a victim can recover compensation from a financially sound defendant, the Court noted:

> Effective compensation must also be fair, in the sense that it must seem just to place liability for the wrong on the employer. Vicarious liability is arguably fair in this sense. The employer puts in the community an enterprise which carries with it certain risks. When those risks materialize and cause injury to a member of the public despite the employer's reasonable efforts, it is fair that the person or organisation that creates the enterprise and hence the risk should bear the loss … it is right and just that the person who creates a risk bear the loss when the risk ripens into harm.[25]

The Court noted the employer was often in the better position to spread the losses through insurance and higher prices, 'minimising the dislocative effect of the tort within the community'.[26]

The Court also noted the deterrence of future harm rationale of vicarious liability. Employers could often reduce accidents and intentional wrongs by 'efficient organisation and supervision'.[27] It again quoted Fleming to the effect that

[22] ibid 549.

[23] A Ataner, 'How Strict is Vicarious Liability? Reassessing the Enterprise Risk Theory (2006) 64(2) *University of Toronto Faculty of Law Review* 63, 84–85; A Spafford, 'The Enterprise Risk Theory: Redefining Vicarious Liability for Intentional Torts' (LLM Thesis, University of Toronto, 2000) 16.

[24] S Kiefel, 'Vicarious Liability in Tort—A Search for Policy, Principle or Justification' (New South Wales Supreme Court Judges Conference, August 2017).

[25] [1999] 2 SCR 534, 554.

[26] ibid.

[27] ibid. This reasoning was criticised as 'rather naïve and simplistic' and showing a 'lack of understanding about the actual theoretical foundation of the doctrine of vicarious liability' by Claire McIvor: C McIvor, 'The Use and Abuse of the Doctrine of Vicarious Liability' (2006) 35 *Common Law World Review* 268, 275.

by holding an employer liable 'the law furnishes an incentive to discipline servants guilty of wrongdoing'.[28]

This did not mean that an employer would be liable for every wrong committed by an employee. A wrong that was only 'coincidentally linked' to the employer's activities would not attract vicarious liability:

> To impose vicarious liability on the employer for such a wrong does not respond to common sense notions of fairness. Nor does it serve to deter future harms. Because the wrong is essentially independent of the employment situation, there is little the employer could have done to prevent it.[29]

The Court said the critical issue was the connection between the employment enterprise and the wrong committed. Where the connection was close, it was fair that the organisation that engaged in the enterprise should internalise the full cost of operation, including potential costs. It cited the works of Sykes in this regard.[30]

The Court was at pains to make clear it was not adopting a 'but-for' or 'mere opportunity' approach to vicarious liability. In other words, it was not sufficient to attract vicarious liability that the wrong would not have occurred but for the employment, or that the employment provided the mere opportunity to commit the wrong. More was required—that the employment *materially* increased the risk.[31]

The Court summarised that the following principles should apply in determining whether an employer should be vicariously liable for intentional, unauthorised actions of an employee:[32]

a. There should be an open consideration of the (policy) question whether liability should lie against the employer, as opposed to concepts such as 'scope of employment' or 'mode of conduct', which could mask the true basis of liability.
b. The question was whether a significant connection existed between the creation or enhancement of risk and the wrong that occurred, even if it is not related to the employer's desires. Time and place considerations, of themselves, did not justify the imposition of vicarious liability. However, it was fair to make an employer pay for 'generally foreseeable costs of that business'.
c. In applying the 'significant connection' test in (b) in the context of intentional torts, relevant factors might include: the opportunity that the enterprise afforded the employee to abuse their power, the extent to which the wrongful act furthered the employer's aims, the extent to which the wrongful act was related to 'friction, confrontation or intimacy' inherent in the employer's

[28] *Bazley* (n 17) 555.
[29] ibid 556.
[30] ibid 557; see also A Sykes, 'The Economics of Vicarious Liability' (1984) 93 *Yale Law Journal* 1231.
[31] ibid 559.
[32] ibid 559–60.

> enterprise, the extent of power conferred on the employee in relation to the victim, and the vulnerability of potential victims.

The question was whether the employer significantly increased the risk of the harm to the plaintiff by putting the employee in their position and requiring them to perform particular tasks.

The Court sought to distinguish cases where an institution placed children with an employee for brief periods of time, as opposed to lengthy periods of time, such as might occur in a boarding situation. The fact the employment created a position of intimacy and power over the child was also relevant. As the opportunity for abuse increased, the risk of harm increased. This in turn increased the chance that an employer would be held vicariously liable for what occurred.[33] Finally, the Court rejected the suggestion that the defendant should not be vicariously liable for what occurred because they were a non-profit organisation.[34]

On the same day, the Supreme Court of Canada by a majority of 4:3[35] found a boys' and girls' club was not vicariously liable for the actions of its project director in abusing two children members of the club.[36] The club provided recreational activities for its members but did not provide residential accommodation. The abuse incidents took place away from the club environment, in the home of the perpetrator.

The majority judgment (delivered by Binnie J) noted that a range of policy considerations underpinned vicarious liability law, however this did not diminish the importance of principle. While it adopted the approach taken by the court in *Bazley* in terms of enterprise risk, it clarified that it would be necessary in order to find vicarious liability under this concept that the enterprise materially increased the risk of the harm that occurred.[37] It observed that 'much as the court may wish to take advantage of the deeper pockets of the respondent to see the appellant compensated, we have no jurisdiction ex aequo et bono to practise distributive justice'.[38] Here it was relevant that if the club were vicariously liable for what the employee did, it would effectively mean that any organisations providing mentoring or role models for children would be financially liable in cases where their employees committed sexual abuse. This might cause such would-be providers to decline to offer such a service in future:[39]

> The imposition of no-fault liability in this case would tell non-profit recreational organizations dealing with children that even if they take all of the precautions that could

[33] ibid 561–63; 'the test for vicarious liability for an employer's sexual abuse of a client should focus on whether the employer's enterprise and empowerment of the employee materially increased the risk of the sexual assault and hence the harm' (563).

[34] ibid 565–67.

[35] Cory, Iacobucci, Major and Binnie JJ; L'Heureux-Dube, McLachlin and Bastarache JJ dissenting.

[36] *Jacobi v Griffiths* [1999] 2 SCR 570.

[37] ibid 611.

[38] ibid 589.

[39] ibid 590.

reasonably be expected of them, and despite the lack of any other direct fault for the tort that occurs, they will still be held financially responsible for what, in the negligence sense of foreseeability, are unforeseen and unforeseeable criminal assaults by their employees. It has to be recognized that the rational response of such organizations may be to exit the children's recreational field altogether.[40]

The majority considered that a range of past case law had not found an employer liable for criminal wrongdoing of employees. This was the case even though the employment provided 'privileged' access to the victim.[41] It was not possible to say that sexual abuse by an employee would further the aims of the employer.[42] It was difficult to accept that the risk that an employee would commit sexual abuse was an inherent risk of an educational enterprise. Clearly, the commission of abuse by an employee was the very antithesis of the enterprise which the defendant sought to maintain.[43]

The majority considered Fleming's two stated aims of vicarious liability in relation to the fair, just and reasonable imposition of liability, and deterrence. In relation to the first, the Court said it was relevant that the defendant was a non-profit organisation. It did not have the ability to spread losses, for example by increasing the price of its services. This did not mean it could never incur vicarious liability, but it was relevant.[44]

The majority was sceptical of the deterrence rationale for the imposition of vicarious liability. It noted that practically there might be little that an employer could do to deter criminal behaviour, if the possibility of a lengthy jail term did not do so.[45] They were also concerned that an undue emphasis on deterrence might blur the lines between vicarious liability and negligence; in so doing they concluded there were strong arguments for developing paths by which an employer could be directly liable for such behaviour committed by employees, as opposed to vicarious liability.[46]

The club was not vicariously liable for the wrongdoer's acts. The opportunity provided to the wrongdoer to commit the abuse was slight. The wrongdoer managed to manipulate the situation so that he was alone with the victims. This was far removed from the nature of his employment and interaction with the students, as envisaged by the club and the functions it conferred upon him.

McLachlin J wrote the dissenting judgment. She applied the factors that were discussed in *Bazley*. She noted that the employment provided the opportunity for the abuse:

> The first factor is the opportunity that the enterprise afforded Griffiths to perpetrate his attacks. An environment into which children are entrusted not just for adult

[40] ibid 615.
[41] ibid 600.
[42] ibid 602.
[43] ibid 603.
[44] ibid 613.
[45] ibid 614.
[46] ibid 615.

supervision, but for adult mentoring, is one highly charged with potential for an abuse of that trust.[47]

A second factor was the extent to which the wrongdoer's aims contributed to the purposes of the defendant organisation. McLachlin J seemed to suggest a one-way rather than two-way consideration of that factor:

> Clearly the club was not in the business of molesting children. But this observation is almost tautological. This suggests that whether the wrongful act furthers the employer's aims is more relevant when it points the other way ie because we assume that intentional torts do not further employers' ends, it is only remarkable when the intentional torts do, in fact, further those ends, making imposition of vicarious liability in those instances almost always appropriate.[48]

She added that although the sexual assault itself was not in furtherance of the club's aims, the securing of a position of trust, power and intimacy to provide the needed mentoring was within its objectives. For the dissenters, this meant that it was appropriate to make the employer vicariously liable for the abuse.[49] The club positively encouraged a close relationship to develop between mentor and mentee.[50] The associated risks were exacerbated by the fact that the children concerned were even more vulnerable than other children.[51] The employee here also had significant power over the children under his care.[52] The employment here materially and significantly enhanced the risk of the wrongdoing occurring.[53] It was not determinative that the abuse took place outside the operating hours of the club, and at the abuser's private premises.[54]

Somewhat paradoxically, the Supreme Court has declined to extend the vicarious liability doctrine to the Crown's possible liability for foster carers.[55] There the majority found that the relationship between the Crown and foster carers was not sufficiently close to make the Crown vicariously liable in a case where a foster carer sexually abused a child the Crown had placed within their care.

The Court there reiterated the traditional distinction between an employer's liability for employees, and liability for independent contractors. Vicarious

[47] ibid 582.

[48] ibid.

[49] ibid: 'while the intentional tort of sexual assault itself was unauthorized, its necessary predicate—cultivation of a position of trust and intimacy—was. It is this authorization of the trusting relationship that favours the attribution of vicarious liability' (583). The dissenters distinguished cases where a relationship of trust develops serendipitously between a janitor and a student, and cases where the relationship of trust is inherent in the nature of the employment, as occurred here. If the janitor commits sexual abuse, the employer might not be vicariously liable for it, because the nature of the employment was not sufficiently connected with what occurred, in contrast with a pastoral care type role, such as was concerned here.

[50] ibid 584.

[51] ibid.

[52] ibid.

[53] ibid 585–86.

[54] ibid 586.

[55] *KLB v British Columbia* [2003] 2 SCR 403; *MB v Attorney General of Canada* [2003] 2 SCR 477.

liability traditionally applied to the former, but not the latter. The majority defended this on the enterprise risk theory—it was fair that a person or organisation that created an enterprise and hence a risk should bear the loss, and such ascription would serve a deterrent purpose. Employers would be able to reduce accidents and intentional wrongs by efficient organisation and supervision. In contrast, the majority claimed that imposing vicarious liability on an independent contractor would not usually serve these policy goals. In that case, the tort could not be reasonably regarded as a materialisation of a business risk, and vicarious liability would have no deterrent effect if the wrongdoer was independent of the organisation, such that the organisation could not take measures to prevent such conduct.[56] The question here was whether the foster carers were acting 'on account' of the Crown.[57] In concluding that the Crown was not liable for the actions of a foster carer, the Court was not convinced that the deterrence rationale of vicarious liability applied in that context.[58]

More recent cases have basically applied the *Bazley* approach. A church corporation was held vicariously liable for sexual assaults committed on minors by a priest it engaged.[59] The court found the church provided the opportunity for the abuser to commit the abuse. It was part of his role as parish priest to organise a range of activities for minors. The church encouraged emotional intimacy between bishop and members of the parish. The priest had a god-like status in this particular community. This increased the risk that abuse would occur. In that particular instance, the parish was relatively isolated, which further increased the vulnerability of the young people concerned. There were limited other service outlets in the community, and a lack of policing, courts or other community leadership groups.

The Supreme Court noted in *Blackwater v Plint*[60] that five factors determined whether or not vicarious liability should be imposed. These were (a) the opportunity afforded by the employer's enterprise for the employee to abuse their power; (b) the extent to which the wrongful act furthered the employer's interests; (c) the extent to which the employment situation created intimacy or other conditions that were conducive to the wrongful act; (d) the extent of power conferred on the employee relative to the victim; and (e) the vulnerability of potential victims.[61]

Much will depend on a factual enquiry as to the precise scope of the employee's responsibilities. So, for example, the Uniting Church was found not to be liable for

[56] *KLB v British Columbia*, ibid, 418 (McLachlin CJ; Gonthier, Iacobucci, Major, Bastarache, Binnie, LeBel and Deschamps JJ; Arbour J dissenting).

[57] ibid 419.

[58] ibid, 'Given the independence of foster parents, government liability is unlikely to result in heightened deterrence. Exacting supervision cannot prevent abuse when the supervising social worker is absent ... given the nature of foster care, governments cannot regulate foster homes on a day-to-day basis. Imposition of vicarious liability can do little to deter what direct liability does not already deter': 421 (McLachlin CJ; Gonthier, Iacobucci, Major, Bastarache, Binnie, LeBel and Deschamps JJ; Arbour J dissenting).

[59] *John Doe v Bennett* [2004] 1 SCR 436.

[60] *Blackwater v Plint* [2005] 3 SCR 3.

[61] ibid 16 (McLachlin CJ, for the Court).

sexual abuse committed by a church elder. This was because he had not taken on a full-time pastoral role; his responsibilities were limited to Sunday services and Sunday school class. He was not expected to develop a close relationship with children in the community. His engagement as church elder did not create a particular opportunity for him to be alone with children.[62]

Certainly, not all criminal behaviour by an employee has been sheeted home to the employer via vicarious liability. A hospital was not held liable for the actions of a nurse in sexually assaulting a patient. The court noted that the incident took place on work premises and during work hours. The employment provided the opportunity for the abuse to occur. However, in finding the hospital not vicariously liable for the assault, it emphasised that the offender had not been assigned to this particular patient and had no care responsibilities towards them.[63] This suggests the court may have reached a different result if the offender had been assigned to the patient and did have care responsibilities towards them. A property owner was held not to be vicariously liable for a rape committed by his property manager employee upon a tenant.[64] A school authority was not vicariously liable for sexual assaults committed by a school janitor.[65] Nor was it liable for abuse committed by an employee who had a series of roles in the school, including odd-jobs, baker and boat driver. The court found that the employee's duties did not involve significant contact with students nor the kind of emotional intimacy that characterised successful claims for abuse within a school.[66]

Much of the development in Canadian case law in this area has been influenced by notions of enterprise risk, together with the objective of deterrence. Given that these theories have also underpinned developments in other jurisdictions, critical discussion of these and other theories is reserved for Part II, rather than undertaken here.

While in most instances the Canadian courts have correctly sharply distinguished between vicarious liability and direct liability for negligence,[67] this does not always occur. So, for instance, in *PD v Allen and the Roman Catholic Episcopal Corporation for the Diocese of Sault Ste. Marie*,[68] in the three paragraphs of the judgment under the heading 'vicarious liability of the diocese for the childhood abuse',[69] there appear observations about it 'defying credulity' that those in charge

[62] *LEW v United Church of Canada* [2005] BCSC 564.

[63] *JB v Jacob and Region 1 Hospital Corporation* [1998] CanLII 12231 (NBCA).

[64] *Q v Minto Management Ltd et al* [1985] CanLII 2103 (ONSC).

[65] *EDG v Board of School Trustees of School District No 44 (North Vancouver)* [2003] 2 SCR 459.

[66] *EB v Oblates of Mary Immaculate (BC)* [2005] 3 SCR 45.

[67] *John Doe v Bennett* (n 59) 444: 'the doctrine of vicarious liability imputes liability to the employer or principal of a tortfeasor, not on the basis of the fault of the employer or principal, but on the ground that as the person responsible for the activity or enterprise in question, the employer or principal should be held responsible for loss to third parties that result from that activity or enterprise' (McLachlin J, for the Court).

[68] *PD v Allen and the Roman Catholic Episcopal Corporation for the Diocese of Sault Ste* Marie [2004] CanLII 4033 (ONSC).

[69] ibid [307]–[309].

of the rectory did not know of the abuse,[70] and about the survivor of the abuse disclosing it during confession, but being told to forget about it and get on with life.[71] With respect, these observations do not relate to questions of vicarious liability, and should be discussed elsewhere in the judgment.

Another example of this occurs in the judgment of the majority in *British Columbia Ferry Corporation v Invicta Security Service Corporation*.[72] There Rowles J, with whom Donald J agreed, found an employer vicariously liable for the actions of its employee setting fire to a building he was employed to protect. Explaining why the employer (Invicta) was vicariously liable, these judges concluded that 'Invicta's greater control over the situation and greater relative fault is relevant both to the fairness of shifting the risk of loss to it, and to the deterrent rationale suggested by Fleming and others'.[73] Notions of fault also crept into the judgment of the Supreme Court in *Blackwater v Plint*, albeit in the context of determining the relative allocation of legal responsibility between defendants found to be jointly vicariously liable.[74]

These comments are noted here because they show continued confusion among some courts about the vicarious liability doctrine, and a danger of mixing discussion of a strict liability, no fault principle, with observations about fault. This observation has also been made with respect to some of the United Kingdom case law.

The Canadian courts have accepted the distinction between liability for employees, as opposed to liability for independent contractors. They have generally considered similar issues to that of United Kingdom and Australian courts in determining whether or not an employment relationship exists, such as could attract the operation of vicarious liability. Specifically, whether the worker is performing the services as part of their own business, or as part of the engaging firm will be relevant.[75] This ties in with the enterprise risk approach to vicarious liability, making individual businesses liable for risks they have created. As a result, it becomes important to consider whether the risk created by a particular worker is properly allocated to the firm that engaged them or whether, in contract, the particular worker has a business of their own, to which it is appropriate to ascribe responsibility.[76] The level of control the engaging firm has over the work will be

[70] ibid [308].

[71] ibid [309].

[72] *British Columbia Ferry Corporation v Invicta Security Service Corporation* [1998] CanLII 15029 (BC CA).

[73] ibid [54].

[74] [2005] 3 SCR 3, [69]: 'the most compelling view is that while vicarious liability is a no-fault offence in the sense that the employer need not have participated in or even authorized the employee's particular act of wrongdoing, in another sense it implies fault … the degree of fault may vary depending on the level of supervision. Parties may be more or less vicariously liable for an offence, depending on their level of supervision and direct contact' (McLachlin CJ, for the Court).

[75] *Co-Operators Insurance Association v Kerny* (1964) 48 DLR (2d) 1, 22–23 (Spence J).

[76] *671122 Ontario Limited v Sagaz Industries Canada Inc* [2001] 2 SCR. 983, 999 (Major J, for the Court).

important,[77] as will whether the worker provides their own equipment, employs their own staff, takes on financial risk and shares in the profit of the business operations.[78] This analysis has also been applied in non-profit cases, for example whether the Crown is considered to be vicariously liable for what a foster carer does.[79] An episcopal corporation that engages a priest can be liable for their actions on the basis of vicarious liability, the court accepting that the relationship between the engager and priest is often akin to that of regular employment.[80] More than one organisation may be found to be vicariously liable for given acts.[81] I will consider the relationships that should give rise to vicarious liability in more detail in chapter nine.

United States Developments

The first essential point is that any proposed summary of the 'United States position' on vicarious liability must be very carefully framed. While Canada, Australia and the United States are all federal countries, a key difference is that there is seen to be one common law in Australia,[82] rather than common law of each individual state, as occurs in the United States[83] and, to some extent, Canada. This makes it difficult to summarise anything approximating an American position.

Having said that, there is often significant commonality across jurisdictions in relation to common law principles. Further, restatements of the law issued by the American Law Institute can reflect what the law is in a significant number of states. These restatements are the result of various discussions and debates among interested parties, and can thus reflect past precedent in various jurisdictions, as well as setting the boundaries for development in other states whose laws differ from that which appears in the restatement. It should be noted that there is no obligation on states to adopt any particular restatement of the law.

Having acknowledged those limitations, there are two restatements of particular interest in this context, which the case law continues to reflect. These are the Restatement (Second) of Agency (1958) and the Restatement (Third) of Agency (2006). The latter has not necessarily superseded the former. Both continue to be

[77] *Hôpital Notre-Dame de l'Espérance* [1978] 1 SCR 605, 613.

[78] *671122 Ontario Limited v Sagaz Industries Canada Inc* (n 76) 1005 (Major J, for the Court); *Montreal v Montreal Locomotive Works Ltd* [1947] 1 DLR 161, 169 (PC) (Lord Wright).

[79] *KLB v British Columbia* (n 55).

[80] *John Doe v Bennett* (n 59) 449 (McLachlin CJ, for the Court).

[81] *Blackwater v Plint* (n 60).

[82] *Lange v Australian Broadcasting Corporation* (1997) 189 CLR 520, 563 (Brennan CJ; Dawson, Toohey, Gaudron, McHugh, Gummow and Kirby JJ).

[83] *Black and White Taxi Co v Brown and Yellow Taxi Co* (1928) 276 CLR 518, 533–34; *Erie Railroad Co v Tompkins* 304 US 64, 78–79 (1938).

widely cited and used by the courts.[84] The first point to note is the obvious one—that vicarious liability is treated in the United States as an example of agency.[85] There is not a Restatement (Vicarious Liability); rather vicarious liability is treated as being governed by the principles of agency.

Both discuss tort principles in the context of employment. Both subscribe to the theory that an employer is only vicariously liable for their employee's wrongdoing where it occurs within the scope of employment. However, they differ in how they define what is meant by 'scope of employment'. According to the Restatement (Second), conduct is within the scope of employment if, and only if:

a. It is of a kind they are employed to perform.
b. It occurs substantially within the authorised time and space limits.
c. It is actuated, at least in part, by a purpose to serve the master.
d. If force is intentionally used by the servant against another, the use of force is not unexpectable by the master.

The Restatement (Second) clarified that conduct was not considered to be within the scope of employment if it was different in kind from that authorised, far beyond authorised time or space limits, or too little actuated by a purpose to serve the master. An action of an employee was not within the scope of employment if done with no intention to perform it as part of or incident to a service on account of which they were employed.[86] An exception existed if the employee guilty of wrongdoing was 'aided in accomplishing the tort' by the existence of the agency.

The Restatement (Second) included 10 factors which were to be taken into account in determining whether or not a particular worker was to be considered an employee or an independent contractor. These included the extent to which the master may control the detail of the work to be done, whether or not the agent engaged in a distinct business, whether the work was typically done under the employer's supervision, the level of skill required, who supplied the equipment and materials and place of work, how long the person is engaged, whether a person was paid by time or per job, whether the work was part of the regular business of the employer, whether or not the parties believe they are creating an employment relationship, and whether the one who ordered the services is in business.[87] An employer would generally not be liable for actions of independent contractors, unless the activity was inherently dangerous, a non-delegable duty applied, the

[84] eg, the Restatement (Second) was applied by the United States Court of Appeals for the Ninth Circuit in *Jones et al v Royal Administration Services Inc et al* 866 F 3d 1100 (2017); the Restatement (Third) was applied by the same court in *Mavix Photographs LLC v Livejournal Inc* 853 F 3d 1020 (2017).

[85] 'Respondeat superior is a principle of agency law': *CBS Corporation v Federal Communication Commission, United States of America* 535 F 3d 167, 190 (3rd Cir, 2008) (Sirica CJ, for Rendell and Fuents JJ).

[86] s 235.

[87] s 220(2) (1958); *Nationwide Mutual Insurance Co v Darden* 503 US 318, 325 (1992).

engaging enterprise retained sufficient control, or an apparent agency situation applied.[88]

The Restatement (Third) of Agency[89] discusses tort principles in the context of employment. It reflects the general position that an employer is liable for actions of their employees that occur within the scope of the employee's employment. It further clarifies that an employee is an agent whose principal controls, or has the right to control, the manner and means of the agent's performance of work. Section 7.07 states that an employee's act is not to be considered as within the scope of employment if it occurs within an independent course of conduct not intended by the employee to serve any purpose of the employer. This is narrower than the expression of the employer's liability for the actions of an agent expressed in the Restatement (Second) of Agency.[90]

The Restatement (Third) of Agency does not use the concept of an independent contractor and does not define who is an employee. Under the Restatement (Third) either an employee or an independent contractor can be an 'agent' of the one who procures for the work to be done.[91] However, in the vast majority of cases an independent contractor will not be an agent for the purposes of vicarious liability.[92] This is due to the lack of control.[93] An agent here means one who has authority to act on the principal's behalf, and is subject to control by the principal.[94] What the courts call 'economic realities', including which party pays and deducts any taxation from payments to the worker, and who sets their working conditions, are also relevant.[95]

The Restatement (Third) of Agency defines both actual and apparent authority. Actual authority exists where the agent at the time of doing the action which has legal implications for the principal reasonably believes that the principal wishes them to act, given what the principal has indicated to them.[96] Apparent authority is the power held by an agent to effect a principal's legal relations with third

[88] D Conn, 'When Contract Should Preempt Tort Remedies: Limits on Vicarious Liability for Acts of Independent Contractors' (2009) 15 *Fordham Journal of Corporate & Financial Law* 179, 190.

[89] American Law Institute (2006).

[90] s 219(2) of the Restatement (Second) of Agency stated that a master was not liable for the torts of servants acting outside the scope of employment, unless they intended the conduct or their consequences, was negligent or reckless, breach of a non-delegable duty was involved, or the servant purported to act or speak on behalf of the principal and there was reliance upon apparent authority, or the wrongdoer's commission of the tort was aided by the existence of the agency relation.

[91] 'An independent contractor can be an agent': *1-800 Contacts Inc v Lens.Com, Inc* 722 F 3d 1229, 1251 (10th Cir, 2013) (Hartz J, for Briscoe CJ and Lucero J).

[92] *United States v Bonds* 608 F 3d 495, 505–06 (9th Cir, 2010); *Edison v United States of America and Others* 822 F 3d 510 (9th Cir, 2016); *CBS Corporation v Federal Communication Commission* (n 85).

[93] *Hollingsworth v Perry* 133 S Ct 2652, 2657–58 (2013); *Collins v United States of America* 564 F 3d 833 (7th Cir, 2009) (Posner J, for Ripple and Evans JJ).

[94] Restatement (Third) of Agency (2006) 1.01.

[95] *Muhammad v Dallas County Community Supervision and Corrections Department* 479 F 3d 377, 380 (5th Cir, 2007).

[96] Restatement (Third) of Agency (2006) 2.01.

parties, where the third party reasonably believes the actor is authorised to act on behalf of the principal due to what the principal has said or done.[97]

The American position seems to accept that where vicarious liability applies, what is imputed to the employer is liability for the acts of the agent, rather than the acts themselves.[98] This has meant that in cases where the employee is entitled to a defence, the plaintiff cannot legally claim that the employer is vicariously liable for the employee's wrongdoing.[99]

The United States Supreme Court considered the vicarious liability of an employer for sexual harassment committed by a supervisor in two decisions.[100] Before discussing these cases, it is essential to bear in mind that they were decided under the Restatement (Second) of Agency, rather than the current Restatement (Third) of Agency. There are important differences between the two. Specifically, the Restatement (Second) stated that a master is not liable for actions of the torts of their employees committed outside the scope of their employment,[101] apart from exceptional cases. Relevantly, one of the exceptional cases was when the wrongdoer 'was aided in accomplishing the tort by the existence of the agency relationship' (which I will subsequently refer to as the 'aided by the agency' concept). Neither of the two provisions of the Restatement (Third) dealing with a principal's vicarious liability for the actions of their servant, section 7.07 and section 7.08, contain such a concept.[102] Thus, the decisions are not as authoritative in terms of the current American law as would normally be expected of Supreme Court decisions.

Having said that, the Court found that an employer could be vicariously liable for the actions of one of their employees towards another that amounted to sexual harassment. This was specifically under the 'aided by the agency' concept. It determined that where the plaintiff employee had not been subject to 'tangible employment action', for example being dismissed, refused a promotion, or subject to other unpleasant treatment, the employer would have a defence to the vicarious liability claim if they could show that they had taken reasonable steps to prevent the harassing behaviour. If the employee had been subject to tangible employment

[97] ibid 2.03.

[98] *1-800 Contacts Inc v Lens.Com, Inc* (n 91) 1249.

[99] *Twila Nelson v Vince Gillette and Kidder County* 571 NW 2d 332 (1997).

[100] *Burlington Industries Inc v Kimberly Ellerth* 524 US 742 (1998); *Faragher v City of Boca Raton* 524 US 775 (1998).

[101] This was defined to mean conduct (a) of a kind the employee was employed to perform (b) occurs substantially within authorized time and space limits (c) is actuated, at least partly, by a purpose to serve the master, and (d) if the employee uses force against another, that use is not unexpectable by the master (Restatement (Second) of Agency s 228 (1958).

[102] The Reporter for the Restatement (Third) noted the omission of the 'aided in the agency' concept, stating that the purposes of the doctrine were considered satisfied by the apparent authority concept in the Restatement (Third), and the negligence standard: (Professor Deborah DeMott); noted in A Oxford, 'When Agents Attack: Judicial Misinterpretation of Vicarious Liability Under "Aided in Accomplishing the Tort by the Existence of the Agency Relation" and Restatement (3rd)'s Failure to Properly "Restate" the Ill-Fated Section 219(2)(d) Provision' (2012) 37 *Oklahoma City University Law Review* 157, 202.

action, no such defence would be available.[103] The Court stated that an employer could sometimes be vicariously liable for actions of an employee which were clearly not actuated by a purpose to serve the employer.[104]

Notions of the enterprise risk theory of vicarious liability are apparent in *Faragher*. The majority decision noted that sexual harassment in the workplace was a well-documented concern. It continued that:

> An employer can, in a general sense, reasonably anticipate the possibility of such conduct occurring in its workplace, and one might justify the assignment of the burden of the untoward behaviour to the employer as one of the costs of doing business, to be charged to the enterprise rather than the victim.[105]

The majority referred to the 'fairness of requiring the employer to bear the burden of foreseeable social behaviour'.[106] It noted that 'there is a sense in which a harassing supervisor is always assisted in (their) misconduct by the supervisory relationship',[107] in an application of the 'aided by the agency' doctrine from the Restatement (Second). (This doctrine finds no express basis in the Restatement (Third).) They also referred to the deterrence rationale, noting an employer's 'greater opportunity and incentive' to select, train and monitor supervisors.[108]

These decisions were recently applied by the United States Supreme Court in *Vance v Ball State University*.[109] There the Court reaffirmed that it would be a very rare case in which an employer would be vicariously liable for racial or sexual harassment by an employee, because those activities were unlikely to be within the scope of the agent's duties.[110]

There is significant case law from a range of American jurisdictions that have considered the possible vicarious liability of an employer for intentional, criminal wrongdoing by employees. It is fair to say that in many of these cases, the claim has been rejected. This has usually been on the basis that the employee wrongdoer is acting independently, and not seeking to further the employer's interests.[111]

[103] *Burlington Industries Inc v Kimberly Ellerth* (n 100) 761 (Kennedy J, for Rehnquist CJ, Stevens, O'Connor, Souter and Breyer JJ); *Faragher v City of Boca Raton* 524 US 742, 807 (1998) (Souter J, for Rehnquist CJ, Stevens, O'Connor, Kennedy, Ginsburg and Breyer JJ).

[104] *Burlington Industries Inc v Kimberly Ellerth*, ibid, 756 (Kennedy J, for Rehnquist CJ, Stevens, O'Connor, Souter and Breyer JJ).

[105] *Faragher v City of Boca Raton* (n 103) 798 (Souter J, for Rehnquist CJ, Stevens, O'Connor, Kennedy, Ginsburg and Breyer JJ).

[106] ibid 800.

[107] ibid 802.

[108] ibid 803.

[109] *Vance v Ball State University* 570 US—(2013).

[110] ibid 2441 (Alito J, with whom Roberts CJ, Scalia, Kennedy and Thomas JJ agreed) (noting the exception with respect to supervisors).

[111] 'An employee's conduct is not within the scope of employment if it is too little actuated by a purpose to serve the employer': *Olson v Connerly* 457 NW 2d 479, 483 (1990); *Papa John's International* 244 SW 3d 44 (2008): 'in the area of intentional torts, the focus is consistently on the purpose or motive of the employee in determining whether he or she was acting within the scope of employment'; *Osborne v Payne* 31 SW 3d 911 (2000): 'a principal is not liable under the doctrine of respondeat

Examples of this include *Webb v Jewel Companies Inc*,[112] *Rabon v Guardsmark*,[113] *Big Brother/Big Sister of Metro Atlanta, Inc v Terrell*,[114] *Doe v Village of St Joseph Inc*,[115] and *Noto v St Vincent's Hospital*.[116]

As will be seen more fully in Part II, the American courts have accepted and applied the so-called theory of enterprise risk in relation to vicarious liability. Simply, this means that the true costs of running a particular business should, for reasons of economic efficiency, be allocated to that business, and that the risk of employee wrongdoing, at least in a general sense, is one such cost. It has already been seen in chapter two that this approach and theory has in recent years found favour with the United Kingdom Supreme Court, and it was seen earlier in this chapter that this approach and theory has in recent years found favour with the Canadian Supreme Court. In other words, it is a key theory in the current discourse on vicarious liability.

However, noticeably in the country from which enterprise risk theory developed, the courts have insisted upon limits. Specifically, an employer is not liable for conduct by an employee that arises from a personal dispute.[117] So for instance an employer was not liable for an employee's involvement in a road rage incident that took place outside work hours. There was nothing to suggest the employee had the purpose and/or intent of acting for their employer's purposes.

The court forcefully rejected claims that the church was vicariously liable for sexual assaults committed by a priest, on the basis it was 'hard to imagine a more difficult argument than that (the priest's) illicit sexual pursuits were somehow related to his duties as a priest or that they in any way furthered the interests of … his employer'.[118] For similar reasons, an action against the Boy Scouts for vicarious liability for alleged abuse by one of its leaders was rejected.[119] It is not sufficient

superior unless the intentional wrongs of the agent were calculated to advance the cause of the principal or were appropriate to the normal scope of the operator's employment'.

112 *Webb v Jewel Companies Inc* 137 Ill App 3d 1004 (1985) (employer not liable for sexual assault by security guard).

113 *Rabon v Guardsmark* 571 F 2d 1277 (1978) (United States Court of Appeals, 4th Cir): 'the assault was to effect (the employee's) independent purpose, and it was not within the scope of his employment. The mere fact the tort was committed at a time when (the employee) should have been about (the employer's) business and that it occurred at the place where (he) was directed to perform (their) business does not alter these conclusions' (1279).

114 *Big Brother/Big Sister of Metro Atlanta, Inc v Terrell* 183 Ga App 496 (1987).

115 *Doe v Village of St Joseph Inc* 202 Ga App 614 (1992) (school authority not vicariously liable for a teacher's sexual assault of a child student).

116 *Noto v St Vincent's Hospital* 142 Misc 2d 292 (1988) (Supreme Court of New York).

117 *Lily Kephart et al v Genuity Inc* 136 Cal App 4th 280 (2006); *Bradley W Smith v Paul Babin and the City of Baten Rouge* 966 So 2d 1245 (2007) (Court of Appeal of Louisiana).

118 *Tichenor v Roman Catholic Church of the Archdiocese of New Orleans* 32 F 3d 953, 960 (1994) (United States Court of Appeals for the Fifth Circuit); similarly, *James O'Bryan, Donald E Poppe and Michael Turner v Holy See* 556 F 3d 361 (6th Cir, 2009) (Holy See not vicariously liable for sexual assaults by priest).

119 *Lourim v John Swensen and Cascade Pacific Council, Boy Scouts of America* 147 Ore App 425 (1997) (Court of Appeals of Oregon); see also *John R v Oakland Unified School Dist* 48 Cal 3d 438 (1989).

that the employment provided the opportunity for abuse to occur.[120] A school authority was not liable for sexual abuse committed by a janitor.[121] A hospital was not vicariously liable for sexual abuse committed by one of its technicians upon a patient.[122] A police department was not vicariously liable for sexual assault committed by one deputy sheriff upon others.[123]

It is possible that the relevant act of an employee may be considered to be within the scope of employment (as being in furtherance of their employer's interest) although the actions are criminal in nature.[124] It may also be held to be within the scope of employment although the employee deliberately committed a tortious wrong.[125]

However, a broader basis of liability has also been accepted. For example, in *Carr v Wm C Crowell Co* it was held an employer could be liable for an employee's actions although they could not be said to be in furtherance of an employer's interests.[126] The extent of this line of authority was tested in *Mary M v City of Los Angeles*.[127] In this case, the plaintiff was raped by a police officer who was on duty at the time, having pulled her over for a drink- driving test. The question was whether the employer was vicariously liable for the officer's crime. A majority of the Supreme Court of California found the employer was so liable.

The California Supreme Court articulated three rationales for the imposition of vicarious liability, to prevent recurrence of the tortious conduct, increase the likelihood a victim will be compensated, and to ensure an equitable spread of the loss to those benefiting from the enterprise giving rise to the injury.[128] It was relevant whether the risk was one that could fairly be regarded as typical or broadly incidental to the enterprise of the employer.

On the facts, the majority found imposition of vicarious liability on the police service here would encourage the employer to take preventive measures. Police had considerable power and authority over individuals. It was not 'startling or unexpected' that sometimes an officer would misuse this powerful position by engaging in assault. It was enough to attract vicarious liability, for the majority, that the risk of such an assault was reasonably foreseeable. It found the risk of sexual assaults by officers was 'broadly incidental to the enterprise of law enforcement'.[129]

Baxter J authored a sharp dissent, observing that nothing could be further from what a police officer was employed to do in protecting the public than

[120] *Boykin v District of Columbia* 484 A 2d 560, 563 (1984) (District of Columbia Court of Appeals).
[121] *Alma W v Oakland Unified School District* Cal App 3d 133 (1981).
[122] *Lisa M v Henry Mayo Newhall Memorial Hospital* 12 Cal 4th 291 (1995).
[123] *Farmers Insurance Group v County of Santa Clara* 11 Cal 4th 992 (1995).
[124] *Javier and Others v City of Milwaukee* 670 F 3d 823, 832 (7th Cir, 2012) (Sykes J, for Easterbrook CJ and Flaum J).
[125] *Cantrell v Forest City Pub Co* 419 US 245 (1974).
[126] *Carr v Wm C Crowell Co* 28 Cal 2d 652 (1946).
[127] *Mary M v City of Los Angeles* 54 Cal 3d 202 (1991) (Supreme Court of California).
[128] ibid 209.
[129] ibid 217–18.

committing a violent sexual assault. The effect of the decision was to render the public liable for virtually anything an officer did. It was wrong for the court to search for deep pockets to compensate a deserving plaintiff. A sexual assault was not an inherent or broadly incidental risk of law enforcement.[130] Baxter J noted that the majority's deterrence rationale did not support a finding of liability here—an employer could not train its staff not to commit a rape. No evidence had been provided as to how making the employer liable here would deter future assaults.[131] There was no evidence of negligence in selecting the employee. Loss spreading was not a strong argument here either—employers would likely find it very difficult to insure against an employee's criminal behaviour.[132] The fact the plaintiff deserved compensation was not enough to justify the imposition of vicarious liability on an employer—if it were, employers would be liable for everything that an employee did.

[130] ibid 230.
[131] ibid 237.
[132] ibid 239.

Conclusion to Part I

Vicarious liability has a lengthy history in the common law. Its development in the United Kingdom has inevitably been mirrored to some extent in developments in the United States, Canada and Australia. The scope of vicarious liability has vastly expanded since its inception. Its conceptual move away from notions of express command and consent inevitably broadened it. The apparent lesser importance given to issues of whether the employee was relevantly acting for the purposes of their employer and/or their benefit has broadened it. However, frustratingly and somewhat confusingly, such issues continue to be considered by courts, the same courts which had previously said that such matters were not critical. It has broadened to include relationships similar to employment relationships. The scope of employment doctrine remains important, but the 'close connection' approach has risen in prominence, particularly in Canada and the United Kingdom. Both can be difficult at the point of application.

The law of vicarious liability struggles most with cases where the employee's actions were intentionally wrong, and maybe criminal. Here notions of 'scope of employment' come close to, if not reach, breaking point. It can also create difficulties for tests based on 'close connection'. The courts' approach across jurisdictions here has been somewhat inconsistent—sometimes, a robust application of the 'frolic' principle means employers are not liable for that kind of wrongdoing; in other cases, the court seems to virtually ignore the past exception relating to frolic, and appears to have an extremely broad conception of the circumstances in which an employer is liable for what their employee has done.

It has proven to be very difficult for courts and scholars to adequately articulate the rationale for the existence of the doctrine, which is intellectually unsatisfying, not to say difficult in terms of the prediction of case outcomes. A discussion of the main competing rationales that have been suggested, and my reasons for not adopting them, appears in Part II, along with discussion of an approach that I believe would provide a better, if not perfect, approach.

Part II

Theories of Vicarious Liability

Introduction to Part II

In Part II of the book, I will consider the theoretical rationales that seek to justify or explain the doctrine of vicarious liability. Now clearly, vicarious liability is just one example of a strict liability principle. Thus, discussion of its scope, rationale and viability in the law involves the broader question of the interplay between the two great notions of civil liability, namely fault-based and no-fault, strict liability. It will be necessary to consider this broader debate to consider the underlying theoretical basis of vicarious liability, as a doctrine of strict liability.

As will be seen, the United States, Canada and the United Kingdom have all now embraced the enterprise risk basis of vicarious liability. As a result, much of this part, chapter five and chapter six of the book, are devoted to it. It is necessary to understand its historical development, and how it purports to defend and rationalise vicarious liability. Again, it is a doctrine that is part of something bigger—the law and economics movement. Thus, it will be necessary to discuss that movement to some extent, to see how well it does in explaining the common law or rationalising its doctrines, or whether the law should be influenced by that branch of legal theory. I will explain why I do not agree with the enterprise risk approach. Chapter seven is devoted to a discussion of other rationales that have been suggested, none of which I find convincing. Chapter eight develops what I consider to be the best way in which an employer's liability for actions of their employees can be explained and rationalised, imperfect as it may be.

5

Enterprise Risk Theory

Clearly vicarious liability is a form of strict liability at least to some extent, because where it applies, liability is imposed on an employer in the absence of any fault on their part. I say to some extent, because in all vicarious liability cases of which I am aware, there is fault on the part of the employee who has done wrong. Strict liability runs against the grain of most of the modern principles of tort law, which are typically heavily infused with notions of fault.

However, it should be acknowledged that our perspective depends on the time frame which we select. To the eyes of a modern tort lawyer, fault-based liability is the norm, and strict liability the anomaly. However, there is evidence that a lawyer of medieval and middle age times in England would have viewed the matter very differently. Though the historical records are scarce, one example is provided in the 1466 decision in *Thorns*. There the court stated that 'though a man doth a lawful thing, yet if any damage do thereby befall another, he shall answer for it, if he could have avoided it'.[1] Ames cites a case (not named) where a plaintiff sued a defendant for trespass to the person. The defendant argued he acted purely in self-defence. Though this was not denied, it was not a good defence. He was required to pay the plaintiff compensation.[2] He also cites a 1278 statute to the effect that 'if one kills another in defending himself, or by misadventure, he shall be held liable', subject to a pardon from the monarch.[3]

Leading English legal historians Pollock and Maitland state that 'law in its earliest days tries to make men answer for all the ills of an obvious kind that their deeds bring upon their fellows'.[4] William Holdsworth takes a similar view.[5]

[1] *Thorns*, YB 6 Ed IV, f7, pl 18 (1466).

[2] JB Ames, 'Law and Morals' (1909) 22 *Harvard Law Review* 97, 97.

[3] Statute of Gloucester, 6 Ed I, c9, 1278.

[4] F Pollock and FW Maitland, *The History of English Law Volume 2: Before the Time of Edward I* (Cambridge, Cambridge University Press, 1895) 468; see also J Wigmore, 'Responsibility for Tortious Acts: Its History' (1894) 7 *Harvard Law Review* 315 who discusses the initial strict liability approach to civil wrongs generally (319) and in the particular context of a master's liability for the acts of their servant/s (330).

[5] W Holdsworth, *The History of English Law*, 3rd edn (London, Methuen, 1923): 'the doer of a deed was responsible whether he acted innocently or inadvertently, because he was the doer; the owner of an instrument which caused harm was responsible because he was the owner … the owner of an animal, the master of a slave, was responsible because he was associated with it as owner, as master; the master was liable to his servant's relatives for the death, even accidental, of the servant, where his business had been the occasion of the evil … the popular judge was responsible for a wrong judgment, without regard to his knowledge or his good faith' (50–54).

Sayre explains that the law at this time was moving to discourage the blood feud, in favour of a more sophisticated system of compensation for victims. Pound agrees; the law at this time was seeking to encourage peace in the community.[6] As a result it tended to focus on the plaintiff's loss rather than notions of blameworthiness.[7] This was a system of strict liability.[8] *Wergild* was payable to a dead person's family for their loss; *bot* was payable to a victim for non-lethal injuries. Fault was not initially relevant. Pound said that a system of strict liability suits/suited a society that was worried about arbitrary exercise of judicial power. It is also a system featuring a strict separation between notions of morality, and legal rule.[9] Examples of such strict liability included liability for acts done by servants and slaves, harms caused by one's animals, and harm caused by one's inanimate objects, and the liability of innkeepers and common carriers.

This mirrored the situation in criminal law at the time which tended to operate in absolute terms.[10] The historical links between crime and tort are well known. However, criminal law began to distinguish between crimes depending on the circumstances in which they were committed. Bracton for instance in the thirteenth century states that the law must consider with what '*animo*' (mind) and '*voluntate*' (intent) a thing is done.[11] He stated that the person's state of mind gave meaning to their act, and a crime was not committed unless there was a proven intent. Bracton was highly influenced by ecclesiastical law, which in turn reflected Roman concepts such as *dolus*, *culpa* and *casus*, considering in effect the moral culpability of a person accused of wrongdoing. Some evidence of acceptance of the importance of intention in determining the seriousness of the defendant's wrongdoing is evident in the casebooks of the time.[12]

These views of Bracton were mirrored in the writing of later scholars. Bacon stated in his *Maxims* of the second half of the sixteenth century that 'in capital

[6] R Pound, 'The End of Law as Developed in Legal Rules and Doctrines' (1914) 27 *Harvard Law Review* 195, 199; R Leflar, 'Negligence in Name Only' (1952) 27 *New York University Law Review* 564, 565. For a case example, see *Merest v Harvey* (1814) 5 Taunt 442, 444; 128 ER 761, 761: 'It goes to prevent the practice of dualling, if juries are permitted to punish insult by exemplary damages' (Heath J).

[7] FB Sayre, 'Mens Rea' (1931–32) 45 *Harvard Law Review* 974, 977.

[8] J Smith, 'Torts and Absolute Liability—Suggested Changes in Classification' (1916) 30 *Harvard Law Review* 241, 248: 'in very early times there was no occasion to discuss the essential elements of a tort or wrong. Wrong was then no essential to liability. It was enough that the defendant's conduct, although perfectly blameless, had occasioned harm to the plaintiff'.

[9] Pound (n 6) 204.

[10] One example appears in *Leges Henrici Primi*, around 1118, which contains the statement *qui inscienter peccat scienter emended*, or that he who commits evil unknowingly must pay for it knowingly.

[11] 2 Bracton *De Legibus et Consuetudinibus Angliae* (Twiss trans, 1879) 101b.

[12] YB Mich, 6 Edw IV, f7, pl 17 (1466) ('there is no felony, for felony is of malice prepense'); YB Hil, 13 Hen VII, f14, pl 5 (1498) ('the question was whether (what happened) should be called mayhem or not … and it seems that it was, because he had a bad intent at the beginning'); YB Trin, 21 Hen VII, f28 pl 5 (1506) (Rede J, stating that a man who mistakenly shot another man while aiming at an inanimate object was not guilty of a felony 'as he had no intent to kill him'); I am grateful to Francis Bowes Sayre for these references: Sayre, 'Mens Rea' (n 7) 990–91.

cases … the law will not punish in so high a degree, except the malice of the will and intention appear'.[13] *Mens rea*, reflecting implicit notions of moral blameworthiness, became prominent in the criminal law.[14] He contrasted that with civil cases, where the damage done to the victim, rather than the wrongdoer's malice (if any) was important. Hale explained that:

> If the act that is committed be simply casual and per infortunium, regularly that act, which were it done ex animi intentione, were punishable by death, is not by the laws of England to undergo that punishment; for it is the will and intention, that regularly is required, as well as the act and event, to make the offense capital.[15]

In turn, these sentiments are echoed by Coke and Blackstone.[16]

The criminal law increased in sophistication, gradually, influenced by ecclesiastical law and notions of morality, seeking to grade wrongs, for instance by differentiating wrongs committed intentionally, and those committed unintentionally, and reducing the punishment for the latter accordingly. Inevitably this also affected how people viewed civil wrongs although, interestingly, it was the criminal law that seemed to accept defences, and to consider the moral blameworthiness of what an accused did, more quickly and readily than the civil law.[17] A specific example of this differentiation appears in the judgment in *Lambert v Bessey* where the Court notes that:

> If a man assault me and I lift up my staff to defend myself and in lifting it up hit another, an actions lies by that person, and yet I did a lawful thing. And the reason is because he that is damaged ought to be recompensed. But otherwise it is in criminal cases, for there *actus non facit reum, nisi mens sit rea.*[18]

[13] *Maxims*, Reg 7.

[14] Sayre, 'Mens Rea' (n 7).

[15] Sir Matthew Hale, *Pleas of the Crown* (Atkyns and Atkyns, London, 1682) 38; and earlier 'where there is no will to commit an offense, there can be no transgression, or just reason to incur the penalty or sanction of that law' (15); see also W Hawkins, *A Treatise of the Pleas of the Crown* (Walthow, London, 1716): 'the guilt of offending against any law whatsoever, necessarily supposing a wilful disobedience, can never justly be imputed to those who are either incapable of understanding it or of conforming themselves to it' (1).

[16] Third Institute 107; Sir William Blackstone, *Commentaries on the Laws of England 1765–1769* (Clarendon Press, Oxford, 1768) 21: 'to make a complete crime, cognizable by human laws, there must be both a will and an act … as a vicious will without a vicious act is not civil crime, so, on the other hand, an unwarrantable act without a vicious will is not crime at all. So that to constitute a crime against human laws, there must be, first, a vicious will, and secondly, an unlawful act consequent upon such vicious will'.

[17] Ames (n 2) 98: 'the criminal liability disappeared comparatively early, as in the case of killing in self-defense. But the doctrine of civil liability for accidental damage caused by a morally innocent actor was very persistent'.

[18] *Lambert v Bessey* (1681) Raym Sir T 421, 83 ER 220; similarly Lord Erskine: 'if a man rising in his sleep walks into a china shop and breaks everything about him, his being asleep is a complete answer to an indictment for trespass, but he must answer in an action for everything he has broken': *The Speeches of the Hon Thomas Erskine* 1, 362; similarly *Weaver v Ward* (1616) Hob 134, 80 ER 284, explaining that if a lunatic killed another, he would not be liable under the criminal law due to the lack of *mens rea*, but would be liable in tort.

Some of the rigidity of the common law approach was complemented by the rise of the Chancery Courts and the law of equity, where morality and the spirit of the law, rather than just its letter, was given much more prominence. In the thirteenth century, chancery courts exonerated those who had committed homicides by misadventure, rather than through intentional acts.[19] Judicial discretion increased. This loosely maps the rise of natural law as explaining the content of law. This may logically have been the time for the development of a generalised 'love thy neighbour' duty in negligence; however, it did not occur.

The strict liability concept of paying compensation for any injuries caused to another began to wane. The amount of compensation payable to the victim began to depend on whether the defendant's actions were intentional or not.[20] Pollock and Maitland state that in cases of unintentional homicide, *wer* was to be paid, but in cases of intentional homicide, both *wer* and *wite* were to be paid. Wigmore says that the negligence action, at least as such, did not exist for much of English history, and only reached prominence in the nineteenth century.[21] Winfield takes a similar position.[22] Broadly similar observations have been made by Gregory[23] and Fletcher.[24] The general move away from strict liability and towards fault-based doctrine may well have been influenced by broader social developments in the nineteenth century, specifically the industrial revolution and the need to facilitate business and enterprise.[25] Obviously, this needed to be balanced against the needs of injury victims. The result was an emphasis on a consideration of the defendant's culpability for the victim's injuries.

Examples of this in the late nineteenth century include *Holmes v Mather*, where the court found that a defendant would only be liable for injury they directly inflicted on the plaintiff if they were either wilful or negligent.[26] In *Stanley v Powell*[27] a defendant whose shot directed at a bird hit a tree and ricocheted, then striking the plaintiff was held not liable to pay the plaintiff compensation, because trespass was not available due to the defendant lacking the intention to cause the injury, and he was found not to have been negligent in firing the shot. These cases indicate the law had *at least generally* moved away from a strict liability regime for injuries caused without intention. In saying this, it is acknowledged that there were still examples of an apparently staunch application of strict liability well into the nineteenth century, perhaps the most notable being *Rylands v Fletcher*. At least

[19] Pollock and Maitland (n 4) 467.

[20] ibid.

[21] 'It seems then that the action on the case based on a mere negligent doing was of little or no consequence until the present century': J Wigmore, 'Responsibility for Tortious Acts: Its History—III' (1894) 7 *Harvard Law Review* 441, 454.

[22] P Winfield, 'The History of Negligence in the Law of Torts' (1926) 42 *Law Quarterly Review* 184.

[23] C Gregory, 'Trespass to Negligence to Absolute Liability' (1951) 37 *Virginia Law Review* 359.

[24] G Fletcher, 'Fairness and Utility in Tort Theory' (1972) 85 *Harvard Law Review* 537, 539.

[25] F James Jr, 'Tort Law in Midstream: Its Challenge to the Judicial Process' (1959) 8 *Buffalo Law Review* 315, 316–317.

[26] *Holmes v Mather* (1875) Law Rep 10 Ex 261.

[27] *Stanley v Powell* [1891] 1 QB 86.

some apparently thought it was a general (strict liability) principle of very broad application, obviating the need to consider negligence.[28]

But, somewhat confusingly, other developments away from fault and intention-based liability were also occurring at this time.[29] Legal positivism was on the rise, and concepts of natural law on the wane. Sayre notes that English criminal law began to accept so-called regulatory offences, by which a defendant could be held liable in the absence of fault. Obviously, this occurred at a time of great social and economic upheaval in the United Kingdom, with the Industrial Revolution and massive growth in enterprise and economic activity. This created greater risk of injury, sharpening concern over liability issues.

The leading case cited for this development is *Regina v Stephens*,[30] interestingly decided in the same year as *Rylands v Fletcher*. In *Stephens* a quarry owner was indicted for nuisance when some of his employees threw rubbish into a nearby river. They had done this without his knowledge, and contrary to his instructions. However, he was 'convicted' of an offence against the Act, although the court noted the proceedings were in substance civil in nature. Both the criminal law and the civil law at this time thus continued to reflect notions of strict liability, despite the growing prominence of negligence as a civil law doctrine, and the long history of a *mens rea* requirement in the criminal law.

This category of regulatory offence, or *male in prohibita* type offences, as opposed to *male in se* crimes, is usually justified on the basis of public safety, and reflects the massive increase in the size of organisations which may, in the course of their operations, cause losses to another.[31] The role of these statutory offences is really to price such behaviour, which is not necessarily morally blameworthy. Parallels between this development of regulatory type strict offences in the criminal law, and enterprise risk said to justify strict liability in tort law, are worthy of reflection. What unites them is resort to principles of economics as justification for the law recognising that a wrong has been committed, as opposed to notions of fault and moral blameworthiness of conduct. Law imposing strict liability, whether in the criminal or civil law sphere, is concerned to price behaviour appropriately, as opposed to reflecting the moral opprobrium with which society views behaviour. Principles of deterrence are not necessarily evident either in a system which seeks to price behaviour rather than prohibit it per se.

28 *Rylands v Fletcher* (1868) LR 3 HL 330, 341 where one of the two House of Lords justices hearing the case apparently put it on a very broad footing: 'in considering whether a defendant is liable to a plaintiff for damage which the plaintiff may have sustained, the question in general is not whether the defendant has acted with due care and attention, but whether his acts have occasioned the damage' (Lord Cranworth).

29 Gregory (n 23).

30 *Regina v Stephens* (1866) LR 1 QB 702; other examples include *Regina v Woodrow* 15 M & W 404 (Ex 1846); *Hobbs v Winchester Corporation* [1910] 2 KB 471; and *Provincial Motor Cab Co v Dunning* [1909] 2 KB 599.

31 FB Sayre, 'Public Welfare Offenses' (1933) 33 *Columbia Law Review* 55, 68–69.

We are usually accountable for our own actions and omissions; it is exceptional to make us liable for the actions or omissions of another.[32] If in 1881 Oliver Wendell Holmes could refer to 'blameworthiness' or fault as the general basis on which a person was liable for another's injuries,[33] and in 1914 Jeremiah Smith could call the principle that fault was requisite for liability 'the fundamental principle of the modern common law of torts',[34] the subsequent *Donoghue v Stevenson*[35] decision and explosive growth of the tort of negligence have only served to entrench the notion of fault as a basis for tort liability. The general common law move from strict liability to a fault-based liability system was noted by Lord Macmillan in *Read v J Lyons and Co Ltd*:

> The process of evolution has been from the principle that every man acts at his peril and is liable for all the consequences of his acts to the principle that a man's freedom or action is subject only to the obligation not to infringe any duty of care which he owes to others. The emphasis formerly was on the injury sustained and the question was whether the case fell within one of the accepted classes of common law actions; the emphasis now is on the conduct of the person whose act has occasioned the injury and the question is whether it can be characterised as negligent.[36]

Having said that, it is noteworthy that some examples remain where the law imposes strict liability. Lord Macmillan referred disparagingly in *Read* to the 'primitive rule' of strict liability, and its peripatetic existence.[37] Obviously the paradigm strict liability decision is *Rylands v Fletcher*.[38] Examples include liability for animals which cause injury, liability (perhaps) for so-called abnormally dangerous activity, in some jurisdictions at least product liability, liability of innkeepers, and in each of the jurisdictions studied in this book vicarious liability survives as a form of strict liability. Theorists have sought to explain and justify the survival of strict liability in some areas of the law, including in the area of vicarious liability.

Strict liability, underpinned by notions of distributive justice,[39] and fault-based liability, underpinned by notions of corrective justice and/or retributive theory, have

[32] Oliver Wendell Holmes called it 'opposed to common sense' to make one person liable for the wrongs of another: OW Holmes, 'Agency II' (1891) 5 *Harvard Law Review* 1, 14.

[33] OW Holmes, *The Common Law* (Boston, MA, Little, Brown and Company, 1881) 66.

[34] J Smith, 'Sequel to Workmen's Compensation Acts' (1914) 27 *Harvard Law Review* 235, 244.

[35] *Donoghue v Stevenson* [1932] AC 562.

[36] *Read v J Lyons and Co Ltd* [1947] AC 156, 171. Lord Simonds also addressed this point, concluding that United Kingdom law embraced both fault-based and strict liability, before concluding that the general principle was fault-based, with limited pockets of strict liability (180); see similarly *W Angliss and Co (Australia) Pty v Peninsular and Oriental Steam Navigation Co* [1927] 2 KB 456, 461 (Wright J).

[37] [1947] AC 156, 171.

[38] (1868) LR 3 HL 330.

[39] C McIvor, 'The Use and Abuse of the Doctrine of Vicarious Liability' (2006) 35 *Common Law World Review* 268, 283 stating that vicarious liability, a form of strict liability, is based on a 'very precise distributive justice theory'; see generally J Coleman, 'Moral Theories of Torts: Their Scope and Limits: Part I' (1982) 1(3) *Law and Philosophy* 371; J Coleman, 'Moral Theories of Torts: Their Scope and Limits: Part II' (1983) 2(1) *Law and Philosophy* 5.

jostled for supremacy in the law of obligations since time immemorial.[40] Coleman and Ripstein viewed the landscape as one concerning 'misfortune'.[41] They begin with two extreme views, a Hobbesian world view, and what they call the 'world of perfect community'. A Hobbesian would let losses fall where they lay. No injured person would be entitled to compensation. At the other extreme, in the world of perfect community, the entire community would share the costs of any misfortune, regardless of its nature or how it was caused.[42] Though they represent extreme environments, these two models share a common failing, in the eyes of Coleman and Ripstein. They do not embrace the concept that a person should bear the costs of their choices. A person who consciously does the wrong thing would not be personally liable under either model. They can impose externalities on others with impunity.

Coleman and Ripstein then consider two more realistic models, one they call 'libertarianism', and the other they call 'liberal egalitarian'. The libertarian model is one step removed from the Hobbesian model. It starts with a presumption that losses should lie where they fall, unless there is a reason to shift them to another. That reason could be that another person has caused that loss, deliberately or negligently.[43] They call this the idea of 'pure agency'. They explain this approach as follows:

> What I do is mine, what is mine I own; what is not mine, I do not own. The costs my conduct imposes (that is, causes) are the result of what I do and thus mine, I own them. I have to take back the costs I imposed on you, not so much to rectify your loss but to give me what is mine. In contrast, if the costs that have befallen you are not the result of what I do, then they are not mine to bear. That does not automatically mean they are yours to bear; instead, they belong to whoever's conduct caused them. If the misfortune that befalls you is your doing, you own it. If it is no one's doing, it belongs to no one; it is the result of chance, not agency … if a loss is no one's property but just the result of chance, then it must lie where it has fallen … shifting a loss to someone who did not cause it violates their agency … the libertarian view is that only the consequences of agency can be the objects of justice; mere misfortunes—the upshots of chance, are not the proper object of justice.[44]

A tort system that bases liability on fault is consistent with this libertarian philosophy. The starting point is that the plaintiff who has suffered loss is not entitled to compensation: their loss lies with them. In order to overcome this presumption, they must show why it is that the cost must be transferred to another. They do this by showing that the loss was caused by a wrong committed by another, and

40 Aristotle, *Ethics*, trans JAK Thomson (London, Penguin, 1984) 176–79.

41 J Coleman and A Ripstein, 'Mischief and Misfortune' (1995) 41 *McGill Law Journal* 91.

42 ibid 98–100.

43 eg, John Salmond: 'reason demands that a loss shall lie where it falls unless some good purpose is to be served by changing its incidence; and in general the only purpose so served is that of punishment for wrongful intent or negligence': JW Salmond, *The Law of Torts: A Treatise on the English Law of Liability for Civil Injuries*, 6th edn (London, Sweet & Maxwell, 1924) 12.

44 Coleman and Ripstein (n 41) 102.

that wrong is legally recognised as such. Perhaps they show that the defendant's actions were inherently dangerous, and so the plaintiff's loss should be transferred to the defendant. If they cannot show the justification for transferring their loss to another, the injured plaintiff wears the loss.[45]

In contrast, liberal egalitarians start with a presumption that losses should be shared among the community unless there is a reason to make only one person responsible for the loss. This approach would favour a broad social insurance scheme providing for compensation for losses, however caused. More narrowly, it might use organisations which conduct business activity and which generate these losses through their activities as the organ through which these losses should be spread, in the typical case, unless an exception applies and a particular reason why the loss should not be spread, but be borne by an individual or particular organisation only. A tort system based on strict liability is consistent with this liberal egalitarian philosophy. The enterprise risk approach is an example.

It is natural that some would want to rationalise the continued recognition of principles of strict liability in the civil law, notwithstanding the explosive growth of the fault-based negligence tort since the nineteenth century. The lack of a coherent rationale has long been noted.[46] Why does the law continue to recognise some pockets of strict liability? Is there anything that brings together the categories of case in which the common law recognises strict liability that will, at least after the event, rationally explain the existence of such pockets?[47] Or is such post-rationalisation of such categories pointless? Should strict liability be completely stricken from the law, justified when the law was trying to 'keep the peace' and

[45] This seems to have been the position of Oliver Wendell Holmes. He dismissed an argument that a defendant should be liable to a plaintiff simply because the defendant caused the plaintiff loss. He said liability would only arise in such cases if (a) a prudent man would have foreseen the possibility of harm (essentially a negligence standard), or (b) the act was of a 'nature to threaten others' (likely an early version of the special strict liability rule attached to extra-hazardous activity and/or *Rylands v Fletcher*): Holmes, *The Common Law* (n 33) 60. He also observed that 'unless my act is of a nature to threaten others, unless under the circumstances a prudent man would have foreseen the possibility of harm, it is no more justifiable to make me indemnify my neighbour against the consequences than to make me to the same thing if I had fallen upon him in a fit, or to compel me to insure him against lightning' (66).

[46] F Harper, 'Liability Without Fault and Proximate Cause' (1932) 30 *Michigan Law Review* 1001, 1013: 'current statements of the law of strict liability are extraordinarily unsatisfactory. The paucity of scientific exposition of the law in this field has made it so difficult to comprehend the appropriate scope of the principles of liability involved that courts are frequently at a loss adequately to rationalize their judgments'. Leading tort writer Salmond castigated the *Rylands* decision, lamenting 'no decision in the law of torts has done more to prevent the establishment of a simple, uniform, and intelligible system of civil responsibility': JW Salmond, *The Law of Torts: A Treatise on the English Law of Liability for Civil Injuries*, 12th edn (London, Sweet & Maxwell, 1957) 20.

[47] Viscount Simon in *Read v Lyons* (n 36) 167 suggested it was not, and criticised the judgment of Blackburn J in *Rylands* for suggesting otherwise: 'there are instances, no doubt, in our law in which liability for damage may be established apart from proof of negligence, but it appears to me logically unnecessary and historically incorrect to refer to all these instances as deduced from one common principle. The conditions under which such a liability arises are not necessarily the same in each class of case'. He agreed with a warning that if the strict liability principle of *Rylands* was extended as logic might suggest, the decision may become 'very oppressive'.

prevent resort to blood feud, but now an anachronism in the context of a generally civil society?[48]

One of the leading current theories said to underlie the imposition of (strict) vicarious liability is the notion of enterprise risk. It underpins the current iteration of vicarious liability in Canada[49] and the United Kingdom.[50] Simply, the idea is that a particular enterprise should have costs allocated to it that fairly reflect the cost of it doing business. In the simple example of an organisation that produces goods, if costs are properly allocated to it, this will ensure that an efficient level of that organisation's products will be produced. If too few costs are allocated to it—in other words costs that truly belong to it are not allocated to it—more than the efficient quantity of its goods will be produced.[51] And if too many costs are allocated to it—in other words costs that do not truly belong to it are allocated to it—less than the efficient quantity of its goods will be produced. An enterprise should be liable for the costs it causes.

As the Canadian and United Kingdom cases discussed above demonstrate, this theory is used to justify making employers liable for sexual abuse committed by their employees in care situations. Some authors strongly support such a position. For example, Bruce Feldthusen states that 'all the costs of sexual torts committed in the course of employment would (should) be allocated to a relatively sophisticated party who would take them into account rationally in pricing and output decisions'.[52] He adds that employers should be vicariously liable for intentional torts committed by employees because 'employee torts, like the bakery rats, are an unfortunate side-effect of the enterprise'.[53]

Causation is often suggested as the underlying basis of enterprise risk theory.[54] Other theorists have conditioned it on non-reciprocal risks.[55] For them, strict liability is justified when the organisation involved imposes non-reciprocal risks on others. An example of a non-reciprocal risk would be an organisation engaged in extra-dangerous activity, or a person who keeps a dangerous animal. Theorists such as Fletcher argue that in such cases imposition of strict liability is justified

[48] *Rylands v Fletcher* was subsumed into the general law of negligence by the Australian High Court in *Burnie Port Authority v General Jones Pty Ltd* (1994) 179 CLR 520, and has been progressively confined and limited, though not actually overruled, in the United Kingdom. Dean Thayer suggested that negligence law could now deal with *Rylands* type cases: ER Thayer, 'Liability Without Fault' (1916) 29 *Harvard Law Review* 801.

[49] *Bazley v Curry* [1999] 2 SCR 534.

[50] *Cox v Ministry of Justice* [2016] AC 660.

[51] G Calabresi, 'Some Thoughts on Risk Distribution and the Law of Torts' (1961) 70 *Yale Law Journal* 499, 514: 'not charging an enterprise with a cost which arises from it leads to an understatement of the true cost of producing its goods; the result is that people purchase more of those goods than they would want if their true costs were reflected in price'.

[52] B Feldthusen, 'Vicarious Liability for Sexual Torts' in N Mullany and A Linden (eds), *Torts Tomorrow: A Tribute to John Fleming* (North Ryde, NSW, LBC Information Services, 1998) 227.

[53] ibid 228.

[54] R Epstein, *A Theory of Strict Liability: Toward a Reformulation of Tort Law* (San Francisco, CA, Cato Institute, 1980).

[55] Fletcher (n 24).

on fairness grounds. In other cases, for example the risk of car accidents, because road users impose risks on each other when they use the roads, strict liability is not appropriate or justified. Under this theory causation is not regarded as being of prime significance in determining liability.

The object of chapter five and chapter six will be to explore the concept of enterprise risk in some more depth, to gauge its potential to properly theorise the imposition of vicarious liability on an organisation. There are also some legitimate questions as to whether it is appropriate legal reasoning for a court to take such matters into account, or whether their focus should be on application of legal principles to resolve the case at hand.[56]

Understandably, one does not find any reference to the theory of 'enterprise liability', at least by that moniker, in the historical English case law on vicarious liability. My reading of the cases suggests the closest the judges use a concept like this occurs where they refer to whether an employee is acting for the purpose of the employer in determining whether or not vicarious liability lies and/or the benefit of the employer. There is the reference by Lord Brougham in *Duncan v Findlater* to the point that an employer is liable for what their employee did because they 'set the whole thing in motion', which might reflect a crude notion of enterprise liability. An example of what some called the 'profit' basis of vicarious liability is *Wayland v Elkins*, where Gibbs CJ applied it to find a master liable for a servant's actions: the idea that someone who profits from a business should in fairness incur relevant costs.[57] Thus, it is fair to say that generally the English case law did not historically use the theory of enterprise risk to rationalise the imposition of vicarious liability. The idea today that vicarious liability is justified by the theory of enterprise risk can be seen by some as an example of 'retro-fitting', or an attempt to belatedly theorise and rationalise legal principle after the event, not derived from very much or any of the actual relevant decisions of earlier times.

[56] ibid 540. I would suggest the tradition of the common law judge is typically more aligned with the resolution of the case in front of them based on legal precedent, rather than the articulation of sophisticated legal theory underpinning the law, or of consideration of the broader societal context and issue of loss distribution, of which the case represents a minute part. For an example of the orthodox position, coincidentally in the strict liability context, see Lord Sumner in *Charing Cross and City Electricity Supply Co v London Hydraulic Power Co* [1914] 3 KB 772, 779: 'I am satisfied that *Rylands v Fletcher* is not limited to the case of adjacent freeholders. I shall not attempt to show how far it extends. It extends as far as this case, and that is enough for the present purpose'. There is also a question whether, given the enterprise risk theory reflects decisions about the efficient allocation and use of resources within a society and makes assumptions about loss spreading, a judge has the requisite expertise to do so. I will allude to this more fully later in the chapter. For now, note the ambivalence about the role of courts in applying principles aimed at loss spreading expressed in *Caltex Oil (Australia) Pty Ltd v The Dredge 'Willemstad'* (1976) 136 CLR 529, 580: 'the task of the courts remains that of loss fixing rather than loss spreading and if this is to be altered it is, in my view, a matter for direct legislative action rather than for the courts. It should be undertaken, if at all, openly and after adequate public inquiry and parliamentary debate and not worked towards covertly … by the adoption of policy factors which assume the desirability as a goal and to operate to further its attainment' (Stephen J).

[57] *Wayland v Elkins* (1816) Holt 227; 171 ER 222.

And still in *Lister and Others v Hesley Hall Ltd*,[58] though the House of Lords adopted a very similar position on vicarious liability principle as the Canadian Supreme Court had adopted in *Bazley v Curry*,[59] it specifically declined to accept the enterprise risk theory underlying that decision.[60] However, it subsequently apparently then accepted the enterprise risk approach.[61] It is evidenced in its most recent vicarious liability decision.[62]

Scholarly Support for Enterprise Risk Theory

Some recognition of enterprise risk theory appears in the work of Frederick Pollock. In his 1882 book *Essays in Jurisprudence and Ethics*, Pollock sets out to try to explain cases where someone is strictly liable to another; in other words, is liable although they are not shown to have been at fault. He says that what characterises situations where the law imposes such liability is that the defendant has introduced a risk:

> There seems to be this common point in all of them, that a man has for his own convenience brought about or maintained some state of things which in the ordinary course of nature may work mischief to his neighbours. Whether his property be cattle grazing in his field or water stored in a reservoir, or a structure crossing or overhanging a public road, there is a certain risk to adjoining owners or to the public which necessarily accompanies the state of things so kept up … whoever thus exposes others to risk should abide the consequences if the risk ripens into actual harm.[63]

He seeks to explain why it is that strict liability does not apply to all situations where one person causes injury to another; in other words, the existence of fault-based tort liability that was in existence when he wrote in the late nineteenth century, and which has expanded greatly since. In seeking to differentiate the two, he used a distinction between extra-hazardous activities, and things 'not dangerous in themselves'.[64] He said that in the case of things 'not dangerous in themselves', but only likely to become dangerous if reasonable care were not used, it was sufficient for the defendant to show they had used reasonable care (in other

[58] *Lister and Others v Hesley Hall Ltd* [2002] 1 AC 215.

[59] [1999] 2 SCR 534.

[60] Lord Hobhouse and Lord Steyn.

[61] *Dubai Aluminium Co Ltd v Salaam* [2003] 2 AC 366 (Lord Nichols, Lord Slynn and Lord Hutton); *Cox v Ministry of Justice* (n 50).

[62] *Armes v Nottinghamshire County Council* [2017] UKSC 60, [67]: 'a number of justifications for the imposition of vicarious liability have been advanced in the British case law … the most influential idea in modern times has been that it is just that an enterprise which takes the benefit of activities carried on by a person integrated into its organisation should also bear the cost of harm wrongfully caused by that person in the course of those activities' (Lord Reed, for Lady Hale, Lord Kerr and Lord Clarke).

[63] F Pollock, *Essays in Jurisprudence and Ethics* (London, FB Rothman, 1882) 122.

[64] The notion that the fact an activity is extra-hazardous is material in establishing a more onerous tort responsibility on a defendant is criticised by Thayer (n 48) 811.

words, that typical negligence fault principles would be applied). However, in the case of an 'undertaking dangerous in itself', strict liability would apply.[65] He cited the case of the reservoir, obviously a reference to *Rylands v Fletcher* liability,[66] as an example of an undertaking dangerous in itself. In such a case, it was strict liability, and a defence of reasonable care was not available.

He concluded that a rational foundation for the imposition of vicarious liability was that the employer was 'answerable, not for his servants as agents, or because they are his agents, but for the conduct of his undertaking with due caution'.[67] He concluded that:

> The liability of an employer to the public for injuries caused by the acts and defaults or his servants is analogous to the duties imposed with various degrees of stringency on the owner of things which are or may be sources of danger to others. The man who conducts an undertaking of any kind, or has it conducted by persons subject to his directions, is held answerable for all operations incidental to it being performed with reasonable care.[68]

Holmes posited a somewhat similar theory. He referred to some cases in which strict liability had been recognised, including liability for dangerous animals, cattle trespass, and *Rylands* liability. Holmes said that in such cases, the owner of the animals, or of the property from which the danger escaped, was 'not to blame, (but) he was bound at his peril to know that the object was a continual threat to his neighbours, and that is enough to throw the risk of the business on him'.[69]

Not everyone shared this view of *Rylands* as underpinning a broad conception of strict liability based on notions of enterprise risk.

Leflar also sought to justify the categories of case in which strict liability had been recognised. He acknowledged that the cases themselves were under-theorised, so any justification for them would need to be applied retrospectively. However, it could justify their continued existence in the law. Leflar's explanation for the recognition of some pockets of strict liability in the law was as follows:

> (The judges) agreed that some types of activity were so dangerous that ordinary care, or even higher degrees of care than ordinary, could not with any assurance guard innocent persons from harm, yet these activities were so necessary, or desirable, in a civil society … that they should not be prohibited … they were 'good' enterprises; our technology had merely failed to invent safety devices to control them. The enterpriser who satisfied society's demands by undertaking the dangerous activity could not be blamed for failing to employ uninvented safety devices, therefore negligence could not easily be charged to

65 Pollock (n 63): 'If the business be extra-hazardous as regards adjacent owners or the public, we should expect to find strict liability' (124).

66 (1866) LR 1 Ex 265; affirmed LR 3 HL 330 (1868).

67 Pollock (n 63) 126. Logically, Pollock observed the distinction between acts done for the employer's purposes and acts done for the wrongdoer's purposes alone, for which the employer would not be vicariously liable (126).

68 ibid 128.

69 Holmes, *The Common Law* (n 33) 98.

> him ... (courts) concluded generally that if an activity was so ultrahazardous that normal standards of care could not guard against normal injuries from it, and at the same time not so common in occurrence that people were accustomed to its risks in everyday life, absolute liability would be imposed for injuries caused by it ... the dangerous activity in that manner can pay its own way. If it is one worthy enough that the law will not abate it, it is by the same token worthy enough that those who benefit from it should pay what it costs not only in its mechanical operation but in incidental harms to innocent third persons as well.[70]

Even if this justification for the imposition of strict liability is accepted, it does not of course completely support the notion of strict liability via enterprise risk. The rationale only applies to 'ultra-hazardous' risks and seeks to justify the exceptional imposition of strict liability for such risks. It does not justify broader strict liability for all risks that may in some way be related to a particular business, as the enterprise risk theory suggests. Thus, at best, rationales given to support *Rylands* could only support notions of enterprise risk to a limited extent, applicable to whatever are decided to be 'ultra-hazardous' risks, not general risks.

It is noteworthy that, of other legal scholars of the time, Baty did not favour an enterprise risk approach to justifying vicarious liability. He pointed out that the theory did not explain why an individual or organisation was not generally legally (vicariously) liable for the actions of independent contractors.[71] He found it did not explain the 'unlimited nature' of the responsibility.[72] It was one of the nine rationales he noted as being put forward in an effort to justify and rationalise the doctrine, but it was not one he favoured, dismissing it as 'thoroughly opportunist and unjudicial'.[73] Holmes did not discuss the enterprise risk rationale of vicarious liability. It is not referred to in the multi-part article by Wigmore.

Laski probably comes closest to embracing the enterprise liability approach, finding that to make an employer liable for actions of their employee would provide 'least disturbance' in the social distribution of profits and losses.[74] He connects change in the law in this regard with other changes in tort law, in particular abolition of the doctrine of common employment, and the introduction of workers' compensation schemes. He reflects on this as part of society's move away from rugged nineteenth-century individualism, in recognition of the realities of modern life where large corporations do cause loss to others and act through individuals, and society's acceptance that such corporations should be financially responsible for the consequences of their activities.

Of course, even if the enterprise risk theory were accepted, it could not explain all of the dimensions of vicarious liability.[75] It heralds a shift from a traditional

[70] Leflar (n 6) 573.

[71] T Baty, *Vicarious Liability* (Oxford, Clarendon Press, 1916) 32.

[72] ibid 147.

[73] ibid 150.

[74] H Laski, 'Basis of Vicarious Liability' (1916) 26 *Yale Law Journal* 105, 112.

[75] R Stevens, *Torts and Rights* (Oxford, Oxford University Press, 2007) 271: 'vicarious liability cannot be explained in terms of an enterprise being required to internalise the risks of the activity it creates';

focus on what the employee did, and whether it is within the scope of whatever it was they were employed to do, to the nature of the employer's enterprise, and the inherent and inevitable risks it creates. There are other anomalies and lack of precise 'fit'. For example, it could not explain why the law traditionally has drawn a sharp distinction between an employer's vicarious liability for employees and the general lack of vicarious liability for acts of independent contractors.[76] Scholars discuss enterprise liability as if the orthodox distinction between employees and independent contractors is irrelevant, and enterprise liability makes the engaging organisation liable for costs and risks created by one of their independent contractors.[77] Losses caused by the actions of either would be sheeted home to the organisation that created the risk, by engaging for the work to be done, under the enterprise risk theory, or at the very least it can be said that the engaging enterprise *could* be liable for what the independent contractor did, subject to further investigation. This will be explained below.

The counter-argument might be that enterprise risk theory is consistent with the employee–independent contractor distinction, because in the case of an independent contractor, the relevant 'enterprise' is that of the independent contractor rather than the enterprise that engaged the contractor. This is not strictly correct, however, because under the enterprise risk approach, as will be seen below, where there are a range of possible enterprises involved, it would be relevant to consider which of the organisations had the better or best opportunity to prevent the loss which occurred or to insure against it, and the better or best opportunity to

R Flannigan, 'Enterprise Control: The Servant–Independent Contractor Distinction' (1987) 37 *University of Toronto Law Journal* 25, 36: 'if employer risk regulation is the correct basis for the (vicarious liability) doctrine ... there is nothing at all vicarious about vicarious liability. The liability is direct and primary. It is not the act of the servant which raises the liability; rather, it is the act or right to act of the employer, his risk contribution to the worker's activity or operation, which leads to his responsibility'.

[76] JW Neyers, 'A Theory of Vicarious Liability' (2005) 43 *Alberta Law Review* 287, 299; R Kidner, 'Vicarious Liability: For Whom Should the "Employer" be Liable?' (1995) 15 *Legal Studies* 47, 56: 'the problem is that loss distribution suggests that all losses arising directly from the operation of the enterprise ought to be borne by that enterprise but this would be manifestly too wide, meaning in effect that there would be vicarious liability for all independent contractors'; as Anne Spafford points out in her thesis, enterprise risk theory contemplates the scope of potential liability 'go(ing) beyond the employment relationship': A Spafford, 'Enterprise Risk Theory: Redefining Vicarious Liability for Intentional Torts' (LLM Thesis, University of Toronto, 2000) 16; J Steele, *Tort Law: Cases and Materials*, 2nd edn (Oxford, Oxford University Press, 2010) 574–75.

[77] D Conn, 'When Contract Should Preempt Tort Remedies: Limits on Vicarious Liability for Acts of Independent Contractors' (2009) 15 *Fordham Journal of Corporate & Financial Law* 179, 203: 'under (the theory of enterprise risk) companies are held liable for the acts of independent contractors that they hire to the same extent as employees, without regard to their status one way or another. The rationale behind enterprise liability is that the enterprise will reap the fruits and profits from the activities of those acting on their behalf, and ... should bear the burdens created by those activities ... losses that result from using contractors should be borne by the party that contracted for the work as an "externality" of doing business so that the cost of goods fully reflects the costs of production'; JD Ingram, 'Vicarious Liability of the Employer of an Apparent Servant' (2005) 41 *Tort Trial and Insurance Practice Law Journal* 1, 19.

spread that loss more broadly. It could not be said in all cases that an independent contractor was in that better or best position to do so. As such, it cannot be said that an enterprise risk approach is entirely congruent with the sharp traditional distinction between employees and independent contractors.

Nor could it explain, in the context of vicarious liability, why it is important to determine whether the employee was negligent or guilty or intentional conduct that the law regards as a wrong. No vicarious liability can arise unless it has been found that the employee has committed a 'wrong' recognised by the law. However, under an enterprise liability approach, questions of wrong and fault would not be relevant.[78] In addition, enterprise risk theory could not explain how an employer deemed vicariously liable for the wrongdoing of their employee generally has a common law right of indemnity against that employee.[79] Under an enterprise risk approach, those losses should stay with the employer. Its loss spreading assumption is questionable, to say the least, in relation to non-profit organisations.[80] Other objections have been noted.[81] In sum, at best the enterprise risk theory could only hope to *partially* explain the existing contours of the law of vicarious liability.

The early years of the twentieth century were pivotal in the debate between strict liability and negligence law. As is known, generalised duty of care doctrine would not be recognised in the English common law until 1932.[82] Loss-shifting theories could not work unless insurance was generally available, and some put that between the late nineteenth century and the early twentieth century.[83]

At the turn of the century, United Kingdom legislators introduced a no-fault workers' compensation scheme to provide appropriate compensation for workers

[78] G Williams, 'Vicarious Liability and the Master's Indemnity' (1957) 20 *Modern Law Review* 437, 442: 'in an action against the master for the negligence of the servant, it is necessary to prove the servant's negligence. This should not be the case if the underlying reason of the law is to impose upon an undertaking the social loss caused by its operation'; J Neyers and D Stevens, 'Vicarious Liability in the Charity Sector: An Examination of *Bazley v Curry* and *Re Christian Brothers of Ireland* in Canada' (2005) 42 *Canadian Business Law Journal* 371, 401; Stevens (n 75) 259; PS Atiyah, *Vicarious Liability in the Law of Torts* (London, Butterworths, 1967) 28; C Morris, 'Punitive Damages in Tort Cases' (1931) 44 *Harvard Law Review* 1173, 1202–03: 'the entrepreneur theory can not explain the difference in treatment between cases in which the servant is at fault and cases in which there is no fault. It is as desirable to distribute losses which occur accidentally as it is to distribute losses which are connected with misconduct'.

[79] *Lister v Romford Ice and Cold Storage Co Ltd* [1957] AC 555.

[80] McIvor (n 39) 285–87.

[81] Neyers (n 76) 298 points out the enterprise liability approach does not explain why charities may be vicariously liable for actions of their employees, nor why the employer's liability is not capped at the level of profit or firm assets; rather potential liability is unlimited.

[82] *Donoghue v Stevenson* (n 35).

[83] W Douglas, 'Vicarious Liability and Administration of Risk I' (1929) 38 *Yale Law Journal* 584, 591; H Klemme, 'The Enterprise Liability Theory of Torts' (1976) 47 *University of Colorado Law Review* 153, 176: 'the opportunity to develop tort rules to achieve these broader purposes (efficient use of resources and effective preventive action) came about as a result of the wider distribution among society's members of the ultimate economic burden of tort losses. This wider distribution was in turn brought about by the growth of liability and casualty insurance, and the evolution of a vast number of welfare and subsidy programs'.

injured at work. Injuries at work were seen as a 'cost of doing business' which should be internalised by the business itself.[84] Business was in a better position to spread these losses around society than was the injured worker. This seemed to give further momentum to those advocating a strict liability approach, as opposed to a fault-based system. In 1914 Roscoe Pound spoke of the

> strong and growing tendency, where there is no blame on either side, to ask, in view of the exigencies of social justice who can best bear the loss and hence to shift the loss by creating liability where there has been no fault.[85]

Other scholars at the time gave their imprimatur to notions of strict liability. In an influential article Young Smith compared developments in workers' compensation with questions about the philosophical basis of strict vicarious liability. He said what joined them together was

> the belief that it is socially more expedient to spread or distribute among a large group of the community the losses which experience has taught are inevitable in the carrying on of industry, than to cast the loss upon a few … if it is socially expedient to spread and distribute throughout the community the inevitable losses occasioned by injuries to employees engaged in industry, is it not also socially expedient to spread and distribute the losses due to injuries to third persons which are equally inevitable? Surprisingly as it might seem, by means of the doctrine of respondent superior the common law has partially accomplished in the latter case what workmen's compensation statutes have accomplished in the former.[86]

To the extent that vicarious liability is justified by an enterprise risk theory, it is clearly concerned with a distributive justice approach to tort law, as opposed to corrective justice.[87] Corrective justice implies the commission of a wrong that must be 'corrected', probably because it has caused another injury. It must embrace the concept of a wrong and define what it is. Typically, it defines a wrong as someone culpably doing something which injures another or, in other words, fault or blame, the failure to take reasonable care. As such it fits comfortably with the tort of negligence.[88] Distributive justice does not depend on identification of a wrong requiring correction; it is more concerned with the 'best' distribution of the costs of particular activities.[89] 'Best' here can involve notions of efficiency and/or justice and fairness, depending on the scholar. Strict liability is often justified by notions of distributive justice. Corrective justice in turn has obvious parallels with the libertarian approach to tort law discussed above, and distributive justice has obvious parallels with the liberal egalitarian notion discussed above.

[84] G Priest, 'The Invention of Enterprise Liability: A Critical History of the Intellectual Foundations of Modern Tort Law' (1985) 14 *Journal of Legal Studies* 461, 466.

[85] Pound (n 6).

[86] YB Smith, 'Frolic and Detour' (1923) 23 *Columbia Law Review* 444, 456–57.

[87] G Keating, 'The Theory of Enterprise Liability and Common Law Strict Liability' (2001) 54 *Vanderbilt Law Review* 1285, 1330–31; G Keating, 'Distributive and Corrective Justice in the Tort Law of Accidents' (2000) 74 *Southern California Law Review* 193.

[88] Keating, 'Distributive and Corrective Justice', ibid, 202.

[89] ibid.

Smith did not see the enterprise risk approach as antagonistic towards the 'scope of employment' approach to vicarious liability articulated by Salmond. In fact, the two were complementary. He emphasised that:

> It (did) not follow that (the employer) should be made responsible for any and every tortious act which his servant may commit. To make the entrepreneur responsible for acts of his employees in no way connected with the enterprise would be undesirable because it would result in including in the cost of production an item which economically does not belong there. Moreover, there is at present no available machinery for insuring against such losses. Consequently such a rule would likely result in a wide variance in the production costs of persons engaged in the same line of industry.[90]

Related to the nascent enterprise risk theory was the 'benefit' theory espoused by Bohlen. He equated the concept of 'benefit' in tort law with the concept of 'consideration' in contract law. Just like enforceable contractual obligations required consideration, the existence of an obligation in tort law required 'benefit' for the person alleged to owe the duty. For Bohlen, this explained why a property owner might owe a duty of care to an invitee whose presence benefits the owner (and duty holder), as compared with a trespasser whose presence does not benefit the owner and, hence, for Bohlen, means that a property owner does not owe the trespasser a duty of care.[91] Similarly Keating justified the enterprise risk basis of vicarious liability on the basis and to the extent that it 'distribute(d) the financial burdens of those accidents among those who have *benefitted* from the underlying risk impositions'.[92]

In the related context of workers' compensation, another area in which strict liability applied, and as indicated was influential in the development of the enterprise risk theory, Smith observed:

> As to considerations of justice and expediency urged in support of the statute … it is argued that a part (at least) of the damage, happening to workmen in a business without fault on the part of any one, should be borne by the owner of the business, because the latter initiated the undertaking with a view to his own benefit, and because he will reap the net profit of the business if any should accrue.[93]

Another influential writer of the time, Fleming James, criticised the fault-based system as not providing sufficient compensation for those who suffered injuries.

[90] YB Smith (n 86) 461.

[91] F Bohlen, 'The Basis of Affirmative Obligations in the Law of Torts' (1905) 53 *American Legal Register* 209.

[92] G Keating, 'The Idea of Fairness in the Law of Vicarious Liability' (1997) 95 *Michigan Law Review* 1266, 1360, and see, eg, *Fruit v Schreiner* 502 P 2d 133, 141 (1972): 'the basis of respondeat superior has been correctly stated as the desire to include in the costs of operation inevitable losses to third persons incident to carrying on an enterprise, and thus distribute the burden among those benefitted by the enterprise'; *Mary M v City of Los Angeles* 814 P 2d 1341, 1349 (Cal, 1991) (justifying imposition of enterprise risk vicarious liability on the community for police action because the community derives substantial benefit from the (proper) use of police power).

[93] J Smith (n 34) 252.

He strongly advocated a system of strict liability with the objective of risk distribution.[94]

Perhaps the other development was the realisation that some of the assumptions which underlay development of some of the nineteenth-century doctrine of civil obligations were questionable. The rugged individualism of the nineteenth century supposed that contracts were made between parties of roughly equal bargaining power, with sufficient access to information, advice and expertise, ability to negotiate contract terms and risk. It contemplated contracts as discrete transactions.

However, as the size of commerce grew, the reality of business changed. Increasingly businesses were large organisations with significant market power. They were usually in a powerful position to exercise that authority with respect to contract terms. Those with whom they dealt contractually may not in fact have much bargaining power. These trends sharpened focus on the role of the courts in protecting those who were, in reality, not able to protect themselves with well-written contract terms favourable to them. Thus, pressure for recognition of strict liability occurred in the area of product liability. Past assumptions that those purchasing products from another could 'look after themselves' with well-written balanced contract terms were challenged. The reality that in many cases the terms were not negotiated and not negotiable was realised. Prosser called the development of enterprise liability here, including strict liability for defective products, as a success in 'assaulting the citadel of privity of contract'.[95] Keating notes a shift away from a focus on the 'world of acts' in which much of tort law principle was conceived, considering wrongs as isolated, discrete instances, to a 'world of activities', where risk is endemic and inherent in particular economic activity.[96]

Priest notes[97] that the work of James and others led to acceptance of strict liability in two decisions, that of the New Jersey Supreme Court in *Henningsen v Bloomfield Motors Inc*,[98] and the California Supreme Court in *Greenman v Yuba Power Products Inc*.[99] In the first case the Court voided on the basis of public policy a purported exclusion clause in a contract dealing with the sale of a product; in the second the Court found a provider of a product was liable to someone suffering an injury through a defect in that product. The Court stated that the purpose

[94] F James, 'Last Clear Chance: A Transitional Doctrine' (1938) 47 *Yale Law Journal* 704; F James, 'Contribution Among Tortfeasors: A Pragmatic Criticism' (1941) 54 *Harvard Law Review* 1156. It has been observed that sometimes objectives of risk distribution and the enterprise risk theory are in conflict, rather than congruence. Examples given have included where neither of the parties is a large enterprise or an insurer: Priest (n 84) 481.

[95] W Prosser, 'The Assault Upon the Citadel (Strict Liability to the Consumer) (1960) 69 *Yale Law Journal* 1099.

[96] Keating, 'The Idea of Fairness' (n 92) 1332–33.

[97] Priest (n 84) 507–18.

[98] *Henningsen v Bloomfield Motors Inc* 32 N J 358 (1960).

[99] *Greenman v Yuba Power Products Inc* 59 Cal 2d 57 (1963).

of that rule of strict liability was 'to insure [*sic*] that the costs of injuries resulting from defective products are borne by the manufacturers that put such products on the market rather than by the injured persons who are powerless to protect themselves'.[100] Subsequently, strict liability for defective products was introduced into the Restatement (Second) of Torts.[101]

As interpreted by Klemme, enterprise liability considers three criteria in determining who is to bear a particular loss. The criteria are (a) which enterprise failed to meet normal expectations; (b) who is probably in the most effective position to cause preventative action to be taken within the enterprise;[102] (c) who is probably in the most effective position to cause the costs of such preventive action or in the alternative the costs of insurance to be passed on most efficiently, economically, to consumers of the services the enterprise provides.[103]

Klemme explains that the first criterion considers which enterprise an ordinary person would say went wrong or did not behave as had been expected. This will usually also be the organisation which could have best taken preventive action, if any, to avoid the loss. He says that enterprise liability theory dictates that such an organisation either takes appropriate action to prevent similar losses from arising in the future, or in addition or in the alternative, insures against such losses which will inevitably occur.[104] Klemme says that it is important to focus on the organisation which did not meet ordinary expectations because that allows an organisation to plan to utilise their resources efficiently, if they can rely on others behaving in line with expectations.[105]

Having explained the historical development of the theory of enterprise risk, and some of its claimed justification as a doctrine of strict liability, I will now consider the extensive criticism to which the theory has been subject and explain why I do not favour the theory as the best way to explain and rationalise vicarious liability in the common law.

[100] ibid 63 (Traynor CJ).

[101] s 402A.

[102] Countering this, Glanville Williams states that in many cases, the one who is in the best position to prevent the injury being caused by the employee is the employee's immediate supervisor, rather than their employer, yet no one suggests that an employee could be vicariously liable for the actions of another employee: Williams (n 78) 439.

[103] Klemme (n 83) 179.

[104] ibid 180–81.

[105] ibid 184.

6

Criticisms of Enterprise Risk Theory

Like any theory purporting to explain the law, enterprise risk theory must be carefully considered. Criteria by which it must be assessed include its utility in actually explaining the law as it is, its ability to assist in the resolution of future cases, and the extent to which any assumptions it makes are open to challenge or question. It is to a consideration of such issues that this chapter is devoted.

I first return to the work of Klemme, discussed at the end of chapter five. Klemme also notes some assumptions, and perhaps some limitations, of the model. It assumes an enterprise is better able to more realistically judge what normal expectations consumers have of how they behave than it is to determine whether a court will find it has met a 'reasonable care' standard, and it assumes the managers of an enterprise will bear in mind a broader range of possible losses and how they might come about than they would under a negligence standard. And Klemme concedes that the enterprise liability model assumes the ability of the enterprise to be able to calculate the costs of prevention, or insurance, and to cause such costs to be accurately reflected in its pricing structure.[1] He concedes that if such an organisation is not able to effect such a distribution, the enterprise liability model may introduce a market distortion. The increase in prices that the organisation imposes may be placed on consumers of other products of that organisation, or others with little or no connection to the organisation at all. This will distort the market for those services, causing the market to demand fewer of those services, and for society to allocate fewer resources to them than would be optimal.[2]

Again, Klemme sees congruence between the enterprise liability model and the scope of employment doctrine within the realm of vicarious liability. The concept of control is important because it indicates that an employer is in the most

[1] H Klemme, 'The Enterprise Liability Theory of Torts' (1976) 47 *University of Colorado Law Review* 153. See, eg, *Bazley v Curry* [1999] 2 SCR 534, 554 (McLachlin J, for the Court); B Feldthusen, 'Vicarious Liability for Sexual Torts' in N Mullany and A Linden (eds), *Torts Tomorrow: A Tribute to John Fleming* (North Ryde, NSW, LBC Information Services, 1998) 229: 'all the costs of sexual torts committed in the course of employment would be allocated to a relatively sophisticated party who would take them into account rationally in pricing and output decisions'.

[2] Klemme, ibid, 188; to like effect A Schwartz, 'The Case Against Strict Liability' (1992) 60 *Fordham Law Review* 819, 834 who claims that enterprises cannot estimate the likely losses to plaintiffs with any degree of accuracy. This compromises the ability of strict liability regimes to induce optimal safety levels. He says the imposition of strict liability may result in sub-optimal, or non-existent supply of valuable products.

effective preventive position. It also increases the likelihood that the employer can calculate the risks that are part of their enterprise and distribute those costs of prevention or insurance in an economically efficient manner.[3] Calabresi agrees that the scope of employment doctrine is congruent with enterprise risk theory, concluding that costs 'not closely associated' with an enterprise should not be allocated to it.[4] Others disagree that the scope of employment doctrine is in fact congruent with enterprise risk theory.[5]

There is one aspect of the current law of vicarious liability that Klemme says cannot be reconciled with enterprise risk theory. This is the principle that an employer who is vicariously liable for the actions of their employee has an action available against the wrongdoing employee to reclaim those costs, or an indemnity. Klemme says that under a true theory of enterprise risk vicarious liability, such recovery should not be permitted.[6] Calabresi has a similar position,[7] as does Stevens.[8]

Not everyone believes that enterprise liability is in fact congruent with vicarious liability, at least as the principle is currently interpreted and applied. Spafford says that enterprise risk theory goes beyond the employment relationship because it focuses on risk. She says that it does not depend on the degree of control the employer has or may have over the employee, rather the degree of control the employer has over the risk.[9] This leads her to conclude that the distinction between employees and independent contractors is no longer viable.[10]

Others have elaborated upon these weaknesses in the enterprise risk theory. Morris questions the loss distribution argument for the theory, as others have criticised the notion that a goal, or the main goal, of tort law is efficient loss distribution at a more general level.[11] He says it is just not possible to make generalised

[3] Klemme, ibid, 198.

[4] G Calabresi,'Some Thoughts on Risk Distribution and the Law of Torts' (1961) 70 *Yale Law Journal* 499, 514.

[5] A Ehrenzweig, 'Negligence Without Fault' (1966) 54 *California Law Review* 1422, 1466 who while discussing enterprise risk states that 'the issue is not whether the servant intended to act within his employment, but whether in view of what the servant was actually employed to do, it was probable that he would do what he did, or in other words, whether his harmful conduct was typical for the enterprise in which he was employed'.

[6] Klemme (n 1) 201.

[7] Calabresi (n 4) 544, as does Anne Spafford: A Spafford, 'The Enterprise Risk Theory: Redefining Vicarious Liability for Intentional Torts' (LLM Thesis, University of Toronto, 2000) 88.

[8] R Stevens, *Torts and Rights* (Oxford, Oxford University Press, 2007) 259.

[9] Spafford (n 7) 18.

[10] ibid 54. This is her reading of the Supreme Court of Canada's decisions in *Jacobi* and *Bazley* where the 'course of employment' test was not the focus; instead the closeness of the connection between the conduct and the risk created by the enterprise was paramount: 'the activity itself is the focus of liability' (72).

[11] E Weinrib, *The Idea of Private Law* (Oxford, Oxford University Press, 2012) 75: 'loss-spreading as a tort doctrine is incoherent'; P Cane, *The Anatomy of Tort Law* (Oxford, Hart Publishing, 1997) 231: 'it is probably true that some people see loss spreading as a function of tort law and seek to use it to that end. The real difficulty is that tort law is, by reason of its structure, not well-designed to perform this function'; R Merkin and J Steele, *Insurance and the Law of Obligations* (Oxford, Oxford University Press,

statements about the extent to which an organisation is able to distribute any or all of the costs of prevention, deterrence and insurance:

> [A]ll that can be said is that entrepreneurs probably bear part of it themselves, they spread part of it to their employees, creditors, suppliers and customers, and the members of each of these groups spread it ... to those with whom they have important economic relations.[12]

Others make the same point.[13]

The ability of an organisation to distribute these costs will depend on characteristics of the market into which it supplies services. For instance, elasticity of demand will be important.[14] Some industries are very price sensitive, or price elastic, hampering the ability of an enterprise to spread risks among customers; in contrast, in markets with inelastic demand, risk spreading will be much easier. Relatedly, one must consider whether the market into which the enterprise is supplying is highly competitive or not,[15] including matters such as number of competitors, relative market share, barriers to entry and exit, and the extent to which substitutability of products is possible.[16] It will be more difficult for an entrepreneur to spread these losses in a highly competitive market. Thus, it is dangerous to make simplistic general assumptions about the ability of any organisation to distribute losses and risks elsewhere, yet this is what enterprise liability theory relies upon. An example of this occurs in the literature, where it is boldly concluded that employers should be liable for sexual abuse committed in the course of employment because the employer 'would take them into account rationally in pricing and output decisions'.[17] With respect, how an individual employer is to actually make such a calculation is anything but clear.

Douglas has also made substantial criticisms of the enterprise risk theory. He challenges the assumption of the enterprise risk theory that entrepreneurs can price such risks and distribute them to customers or insure against them.[18] Calabresi is lukewarm about enterprise risk as a loss-spreading device, concluding it is relatively inefficient in this regard, and that a general social insurance

2013) 204: 'the job of the courts is not to seek the best loss-spreader in each case, and they are not equipped to do so'.

[12] CR Morris, 'Enterprise Liability and the Actuarial Process—The Insignificance of Foresight' (1961) 70 *Yale Law Journal* 554, 586.

[13] W Douglas, 'Vicarious Liability and Administration of Risk I' (1929) 38 *Yale Law Journal* 584, 594: 'the capacity of business individually, as well as collectively, to distribute the costs of shifting these risks or the costs of assuming them, though theoretically without limit, no doubt has bounds beyond which it does not realistically exist'.

[14] Calabresi (n 4) 523.

[15] ibid 504.

[16] ibid 523.

[17] Feldthusen (n 1) 227.

[18] Douglas (n 13) 589: 'the degrees of probability of negligent detours and negligent frolics causing damage to others are difficult to measure'.

scheme would be more efficient.[19] Williams reaches a similar position.[20] Keating has also expressed concerns about the law and economics justification for enterprise risk.[21]

Keating's work contrasts the 'world of acts' in which much of tort law principle was conceived and developed, involving a perception of wrongs as being isolated, discrete acts involving individuals or organisations. However, the industrial revolution massively changed the world, such that it became a 'world of activities' involving large-scale commercial activity, which activity inevitably created risks. The challenge for the law was to adapt principles conceived in a different context to the new context of commerce. As indicated earlier, it was around this time of change, the late nineteenth and early twentieth century, that the possibility of insurance for business risk was created. He views the availability of insurance as a possible catalyst for change in tort principle, away from its world of acts, to a world of activities, in which notions of enterprise risk, as opposed to individualised assessments of fault, find a natural home.[22]

However, he says that the potential for insurance to effect this kind of change in tort law depends on the extent to which losses are insurable.[23] He says that losses that are insurable have three characteristics—there are a large number of homogeneous exposures, losses are accidental, and losses must not be correlated in any way. He also points out that the offering of insurance for such risks including the cost of acquiring information about the risk of particular insureds, the cost of administering such insurance contracts, monitoring claims and behaviour of insureds and adjusting premiums, must be low enough to make the offer of the product viable.

[19] Calabresi (n 4) 529–30: 'though as a system of loss-spreading enterprise liability has some merits, it is still relatively inefficient. In the first place, we are not prepared to charge enterprises with losses which are not readily assignable to some specific activity … if risk spreading is really important, these general losses of living would in themselves require some kind of social insurance. Enterprise liability may be similarly inefficient where the cost of collecting the loss from the enterprise is very large—in terms of court costs or lawyers' fees … a greater misallocation is caused by incurring the avoidable costs of trying to allocate the loss than by leaving it where it falls and letting the price of the product involved understate its true costs. At best then, if risk spreading is deemed crucial, enterprise liability could only do part of the job; the other part would have to be filled in by some social insurance scheme'.

[20] G Williams, 'Vicarious Liability and Master's Indemnity' (1957) 20 *Modern Law Review* 437, 442: 'litigation is an expensive and inefficient way of administering social insurance'.

[21] G Keating, 'The Idea of Fairness in the Law of Enterprise Liability' (1997) 95 *Michigan Law Review* 1266, 1308: 'enterprise liability is out of step with optimal precaution concerns both in its definition of the boundaries of liability and in its recognition of defences to liability. It is even more out of step with optimal loss spreading concerns. For enterprise liability (or any other form of strict liability) to achieve optimal loss spreading, damages awards must be pitched at the deterrence level for negligently inflicted harms and at the insurance level for non-negligently inflicted harms. Doing this, however, converts strict liability into an echo of negligence liability'.

[22] Others say that insurance is not relevant because it introduces a foreign concept into a private relationship. For instance, Weinrib says that to take account of insurance in determining the rights and liabilities of parties under tort law amounts to the unwarranted intrusion of public law concepts into the private law realm: E Weinrib, 'The Insurance Justification and Private Law' (1985) 14 *Journal of Legal Studies* 681.

[23] Keating, 'The Idea of Fairness in the Law of Enterprise Liability' (n 21) 1336.

Others have pointed out that insurance may apply differently, according to whether the employee wrongdoing was negligent, or deliberate and wilful. Insurance policies for employers commonly contain exclusions for actions that are wilful.[24] Again, this undermines the loss-spreading rationale said to justify the enterprise risk approach.

Keating is also concerned at the possible scope of a vicarious liability doctrine premised on notions of enterprise risk:

> The claim that actors are subject to a special kind of culpability when they set in motion (or sustain) processes that are statistically certain to cause harm sweeps too broadly. Highway fatalities on Fourth of July weekends are actuarially predictable with great precision, yet no one thinks that we are, as a society, collectively culpable for failing to forbid driving on Fourth of July weekends.[25]

As a result, he favours a narrower conception of enterprise risk, focusing on cases where the defendant had direct control over the circumstances leading up to the accident, and where a defendant has done something which makes a kind of accident 'all but inevitable'.[26] For Keating it is defensible to make organisations liable for their 'characteristic risks' because the organisation can 'estimate and minimise ex ante, and to disperse ex post'.[27] Others say that risk is inherent in anything, making it an ineffective differentiator.[28]

Others have made a similar point, expressing concern that if the rationale for enterprise risk is accepted in the context of vicarious liability, it would be difficult not to extend it to a range of other cases in which liability was in issue and where it might at least theoretically be possible to distribute risk.[29] Concern by others about

[24] Spafford (n 7) 92 cites four Canadian decisions where the relevant insurance policy excluded coverage for intentional wrongdoing: *Scott v Wawanesa Mutual Insurance Co* [1989] 1 SCR 1445; *Sansalone v Wawanesa* [2000] SCJ No 27; *Bluebird Cabs v Guardian Insurance* [1999] BCJ No 694; and *University of Western Ontario v Yanush* (1988) 67 OR (2d) 525. The case *World Harvest Church v Grange Mutual Casualty Company Ohio* App Lexis 5994 (Court of Appeals of Ohio, 2013) is an example of a case involving an insurance policy excluding the insurer's liability for acts of abuse.

[25] Keating, 'The Idea of Fairness in the Law of Enterprise Liability' (n 21) 1342.

[26] ibid 1345.

[27] ibid 1354; G Keating, 'Distributive and Corrective Justice in the Tort Law of Accidents' (2000) 74 *Southern California Law Review* 193, 212.

[28] 'The real problem is that mischief is inherent in, typical of, or inevitable in human conduct, such that any time an employer hires a person to do work, the employer creates the risk that, in doing whatever it is that he or she has been hired to do, the worker will cause harm, whether randomly, deliberately or otherwise': A Ataner, 'How Strict is Vicarious Liability? Reassessing the Enterprise Risk Theory' (2006) 64(2) *University of Toronto Faculty of Law Review* 63, 91.

[29] *Wights v Staff Jennings Inc* 405 P 2d 624 (Oregon, 1965): 'substantially the same reasons for imposing strict liability upon sellers of defective chattels have been advanced in several other cases and in various texts and articles. Summarized, the thesis is that a loss resulting from the use of the defendant's defective goods is a "casualty produced by the hazards of a defendant's enterprise, so that the risk of loss is properly a risk of that enterprise", a view (known as) … the theory of enterprise liability. The reasoning would seem to apply not only in cases involving personal injuries arising from the sale of defective goods, but equally to any case where an injury results from the risk creating conduct of the seller in any stage of the production and distribution of goods … It seems to us that the enterprise liability rationale … proves too much and that if adopted would compel us to apply the principle of strict liability in all future cases where the loss could be distributed'.

the possibly open-ended scope of enterprise risk liability is shared by others.[30] This leads them to seek to find appropriate limits on the doctrine, for instance by confining it to cases where an enterprise creates an 'excessive or unacceptable level of risk', perhaps because they are involved in 'extra-hazardous activity', sourced to the original strict liability case of *Rylands v Fletcher*.[31] Obviously the Restatements (Torts) have made use of the concept of extra-hazardous in seeking to map out the limits of strict liability.[32]

Others have pointed out an apparent inconsistency at the heart of enterprise risk theory in terms of the extent to which the employer took precautions to avoid the risks created by their enterprise. Given that vicarious liability is seen as a strict liability doctrine, the fact that the employer took all reasonable precautions to avoid the risks created by their enterprise would, strictly speaking, be irrelevant. Ataner criticises this position:

> The interesting question is if, having shifted the focus to the risk-creating activity of the employer and having invited an assessment of the characteristics of the employment enterprise as a whole, the enterprise risk approach can actually sustain an absolute disregard for the level of care taken by the defendant, which is required by a doctrine of strict liability. I do not believe that it can. If the employer is to be held vicariously liable for having designed, structured and implemented an enterprise that carries the risk of employee wrongdoing, then surely the manner in which she conducts the enterprise, and whether or not she actually manages to reduce the potential risk to an acceptable minimum, should have some bearing on the courts' assessment of liability.[33]

Another justification provided by the Supreme Court of Canada in *Bazley v Curry*[34] in adopting the enterprise risk approach to vicarious liability was its potential to deter undesired conduct:

> The second major policy consideration underlying vicarious liability is deterrence of future harm. Fixing the employer with responsibility for the employee's wrongful act,

[30] 'It cannot be true that any employment enterprise, in and of itself, poses an excessive risk justifying the imposition of strict liability': Ataner (n 28) 101.

[31] ibid 101–02; see also C McIvor, 'The Use and Abuse of the Doctrine of Vicarious Liability' (2006) 35 *Common Law World Review* 268, 287 who believes it should only apply where there is a 'high degree of relevant harm' inherent in the enterprise. This might be close to the concept of extra-hazardous activity contemplated in the United States Restatements, and United States case law.

[32] Restatement (Second) of Torts s 520(f); Restatement (Third) of Torts: Liability for Physical and Emotional Harm s 20 (American Law Institute, 2010). George Fletcher would confine use of strict liability to cases of non-reciprocal risk, which has some parallels with extra-hazardous activity: G Fletcher, 'Fairness and Utility in Tort Theory' (1972) 85 *Harvard Law Review* 537.

[33] Ataner (n 28) 85. She concludes enterprise risk theory is weak because of its apparent inconsistency—its consideration of the risks created by an enterprise, but its refusal to take into account what the employer did by way of risk mitigation. This leads her to conclude that the courts adopt the German principle, allowing an employer a so-called 'exemplary defendant' defence where the employer can show they took all reasonable precautions. This is somewhat similar to a fault-based negligence doctrine. Stevens has a similar view: *Torts and Rights* (n 8) 258: 'it is commonly said that holding an employer liable for the torts of his employees will encourage the employer to be careful … however this argument fails to explain why the employer is liable even where he has taken due care in these matters. When the employer has done all that he can, what further encouragement is there in imposing liability in any event?'.

[34] [1999] 2 SCR 534.

> even where the employer is not negligent, may have a deterrent effect. Employers are often in a position to reduce accidents and intentional wrongs by efficient organisation and supervision … beyond the narrow bank of employer conduct that attracts direct liability in negligence lies a vast area where imaginative and efficient administration and supervision can reduce the risk that the employer has introduced into the community. Holding the employer vicariously liable for the wrongs of the employee may encourage the employer to take such steps, and hence, reduce the risk of future harm.[35]

With respect, this reasoning seems somewhat convoluted.[36] How can strict vicarious liability provide the required deterrent effect, and encourage 'efficient organisation and supervision', when the employer knows that, if this theory is applied, they will be held liable for the materialisation of risks connected with their enterprise regardless of the precautions they took and whether they are the most efficient organisation possible? Elsewhere, it has also been observed that in some cases, particularly deliberate employee wrongdoing, and most especially deliberate employee criminal activity, this activity is not deterrable by the employer.[37]

Thus, the deterrence rationale of vicarious liability, even if it supports the imposition of strict liability in some cases (which is not conceded, and which a recent study denies),[38] demonstrably does not apply in cases of deliberate criminal wrongdoing, yet it appears in judgments which then go on to find an employer liable for the deliberate, criminal wrongdoing of an employee. With respect, Binnie J for the majority in *Jacobi* was right to point out that care must be taken with respect to the deterrence rationale, because it can 'blur the line' between vicarious liability and negligence.[39]

The idea of deterrence does not support the imposition of strict liability upon an employer, as opposed to fault-based liability.[40] What incentive will strict liability provide to careful selection and training of staff, and efficient organisation and management, that a negligence, fault standard will not?[41] Further, practical

[35] ibid 554–55.

[36] A McPeak, 'Sharing Tort Liability in the New Sharing Economy' (2016) 49 *Connecticut Law Review* 171, 192: 'generally deterrence goals are not furthered when the actor's conduct results in liability regardless of the level of care used'.

[37] Ataner (n 28) 93.

[38] J Sevier, 'Vicarious Windfalls' (2017) 102 *Iowa Law Review* 651, 657 where an empirical test found 'no evidence that employers in our sample would meaningfully change their employee selection criteria based on their beliefs about their vicarious liability for the acts of their employees'.

[39] *Jacobi v Griffiths* [1999] 2 SCR 570, 614 (Binnie J, for Cory, Iacobucci and Major JJ); see also JW Neyers, 'A Theory of Vicarious Liability' (2005) 43 *Alberta Law Review* 287, 294: 'positive proof that the employer conducted himself without fault will not serve as a defence to the common law version of the doctrine. For these reasons … this version of the employer-focused deterrence rationale cannot explain vicarious liability'.

[40] J Neyers and D Stevens, 'Vicarious Liability in the Charity Sector: An Examination of *Bazley v Curry* and *Re Christian Brothers of Ireland in Canada*' (2005) 42 *Canadian Business Law Journal* 371, 396: 'the deterrence argument is largely incoherent because either it is based on the fault of the employer or it will not work'.

[41] GT Schwartz, 'Hidden and Fundamental Issue of Employer Vicarious Liability' (1996) 69 *Southern California Law Review* 1739, 1760: 'negligence law … seems capable of achieving all that ought to be achieved' (referring to encouraging employers to take cost-justified measures in the selection and supervision of employees, disciplining of staff and regulation of scope of activities).

constraints on the ability of employers to discipline staff, for example unfair dismissal laws, collective bargaining and other aspects of the modern workplace should be acknowledged.[42] The idea that the imposition of strict liability will provide more incentive for an employer to discipline and punish errant employees is subject to these significant practical constraints. Atiyah was unimpressed with rationales for vicarious liability based on deterrence arguments.[43]

Further, the imposition of strict liability upon an enterprise may indeed provide a deterrent effect, but the deterrence may be to operating the organisation at all, or to providing particular services, facilities and products. Consumer welfare may fall if the goods or services provided by the organisation are no longer available.

It can seem particularly perverse when applied to the non-profit sector and organisations providing essential community services. It is harder to conceive their situation in terms of an 'efficient' level, for instance, of charitable services, education, or health service provision. Is it desirable that the extent to which a school offers educational services is reduced to meet an 'efficient' level of optimal provision? After all, this is what strict liability is lauded as achieving.[44] Neyers and Stevens are particularly critical of the use of enterprise risk theory in the context of charities:

> It does not make sense to say that the existence of any particular institution increases the risk of paedophilia if we accept the assumption that there should be a sufficient number of these institutions to look after all children in need. The assumption is a solid one since the alternative to the institution is the street. Surely the children are more vulnerable and the paedophile more empowered if they are left on the street. So the policy argument supporting vicarious liability cannot apply to any particular charity … since the existence of a particular institution does not put a new risk into the community … the court (in *Bazley*) must mean that all childcare institutions that provide parent-like intervention into the lives of children are strictly liable for incidents of paedophilia that occur on their time since it is the risk of paedophilia or simply the presence of children that generates the liability. Hence the decision is an intentional and direct assault on the charity sector. It is moved by misguided and misplaced compassion, misguided because it prefers as a policy option that the children have no institution (since all institutional resources are now available to pay for the torts of paedophiles)

[42] ibid 1758.

[43] PS Atiyah, *Vicarious Liability in the Law of Torts* (London, Butterworths, 1967) 17: 'the case for imposing vicarious liability on the ground that it forwards the policy of accident prevention must … be regarded as largely not proven'. He pointed out insurance companies did not inspect the business premises of the insured to determine the extent to which they had implemented safe workplace systems, and that the accident record of an insured may be affected just as much by luck as by any accident preventive measures they took.

[44] W Landes and R Posner, 'The Positive Economic Theory of Tort Law' (1981) 15 *Georgia Law Review* 851, 904: 'strict liability is more likely to be the superior regulatory device in cases where optimal accident avoidance requires altering the defendant's activity rather than his care or the plaintiff's activity or care'.

and misplaced because it is not for judges to show compassionate bias, especially with other people's property.[45]

Of course, another option for an employer concerned with the spectre of strict liability is to engage independent contractors, rather than employees, to provide particular services on an as-needs basis since, traditionally at least, an employer is not vicariously liable for the actions or omissions of an independent contractor as they would be for an employee. As was noted above, one of the weaknesses of the enterprise liability doctrine is that it does not explain why an engaging firm is vicariously liable for acts of employees, but not independent contractors. On the basis of the existing position whereby an employer is not vicariously liable for the actions of independent contractors, the imposition of strict liability may result in some employers shifting to contract labour as needed, rather than retain employees. In economic terms, the imposition of strict liability in such circumstances has created a market distortion, where parties do not base decisions on employer/employee or employer/independent contractor on the basis of economic efficiency, but on circumventing legal liability rules. It is suggested that an aim of legal rules should be to minimise market distortion, not introduce it.

Calabresi says that the enterprise risk theory means that an employer should be liable for all injuries caused by employees that arise in the course of employment. It should not matter whether the activity was one which benefited the employer or was authorised by them. It was irrelevant whether the act was negligent or wilful. He assumes that insurance is available in each instance. He concludes that the cost of an activity is not in any way less real simply because it was deliberately caused by an employee, or the employee was not authorised to do it.[46]

In a leading United States decision, Judge Friendly considered enterprise risk theory in relation to a sailor.[47] The sailor was attached to a ship which was in dry dock for repairs. While returning from shore leave, the sailor turned a number of wheels on the side of the dry dock. As a result, the ship fell against the dry dock, causing it damage. The issue was whether the plaintiff dry dock owner could sue the sailor's employer. In his decision Judge Friendly identified further limits to the enterprise risk approach. He found that it would only lead to a more efficient allocation of resources where the result of imposing the cost on the enterprise would be that it would cause it to consider whether further steps could be taken to prevent recurrence of the accident. On the facts there, he found that imposition of liability on the United States government for the sailor's actions would not necessarily lead the government to more closely screen would-be sailors. Instead, he preferred to rest enterprise risk liability on the basis of fairness, that an enterprise should only be vicariously liable on the enterprise risk approach for 'accidents

[45] Neyers and Stevens (n 40) 402–03; similarly Stevens, *Torts and Rights* (n 8) 272: 'it stretches credibility to suggest that running a non-profit residential care home for emotionally troubled children increases the risk of children being abused'.

[46] Calabresi (n 4) 544–45.

[47] *Ira S Bushey and Sons Inc v United States* 398 F 2d 167 (2nd Cir, 1968).

which may fairly be said to be characteristic of (their) activities'.[48] The Restatement (Third) of Torts also frames strict liability in terms of the 'characteristic risks' of an activity.[49] Smith asked whether the 'conduct of the master's business was a contributing cause of the servant's act'. If the answer was no, the master was not liable. If the answer was yes, a further question should be asked: whether, in view of what the employee was employed to do, it was 'probable' that the employee would do what they did. Only if the answer to the two questions was yes would the employer be liable, in the view of Smith.[50]

Scholars are critical of the 'characteristic risks' theorem. Brodie for instance wonders how a risk can be said to be characteristic of an enterprise when the conduct is generic to society as a whole. He says it is very difficult for a court to be able to state confidently that, for example, an enterprise has increased the risk of child abuse. He notes that children who are not institutionalised are also abused, and it is not readily apparent that the risk of abuse materially increases when a child is in residential care. It is not entirely clear how much the risk caused by the enterprise needs to be higher than the risk in society generally in order to justify vicarious liability on the enterprise risk theory. Nor is it clear whether a serious risk is required in order to justify application of the doctrine. He suggests that in the absence of empirical evidence, a risk arises that unwarranted assumptions will be made.[51] Schwartz says the concept of 'characteristic risks' does not explain most cases of vicarious liability,[52] and it is not generally used in tort law.[53] Stevens likewise is sceptical of the concept of 'increased risk' as a justification for the imposition of vicarious liability, at least with respect to deliberate wrongdoing.[54]

[48] ibid 171; similarly Gregory Keating states that enterprises should only be vicariously liable for distinctive risks of an enterprise—those risks it creates which are different from those which are encountered in the community in general: Keating, 'The Idea of Fairness in the Law of Vicarious Liability' (n 21) 1360. He says the concept of 'characteristic risk' places appropriate limits and boundaries on the scope of the enterprise's strict liability for accidents. Elsewhere he talks of enterprise liability being suitable to include within the costs of business 'inevitable losses … incident to carrying on an enterprise': G Keating, 'The Theory of Enterprise Liability and Common Law Strict Liability' (2001) 54 *Vanderbilt Law Review* 1285, 1308.

[49] s 18 (Preliminary Draft No 2). Douglas Brodie is critical of the 'characteristic risk' concept. He wonders how a risk can truly be considered to be characteristic of a particular enterprise when it occurs in society generally.

[50] YB Smith, 'Frolic and Detour' (1923) 23 *Columbia Law Review* 717, 724.

[51] D Brodie, 'Enterprise Liability: Justifying Vicarious Liability' (2007) 27(3) *Oxford Journal of Legal Studies* 493; D Brodie, *Enterprise Liability and the Common Law* (Cambridge, Cambridge University Press, 2010) 43–47.

[52] GT Schwartz (n 41) 1750.

[53] ibid: 'The harms of knife cuts are in some sense "characteristic" of the distribution of knives; adverse side effects are "characteristic" of the manufacture of prescription drugs, and injuries to passengers are evidently "characteristic" of the operation of a bus system. Yet our tort system shows no interest in imposing automatic liability on the companies that produce knives and drugs and that operate buses' (1750).

[54] R Stevens, 'Non-Delegable Duties and Vicarious Liability' in J Neyers, E Chamberlain and S Pitel (eds), *Emerging Issues in Tort Law* (Oxford, Hart Publishing, 2007) 361–62: 'on the facts of Bazley it stretches credulity to suggest that running a non-profit residential care home for emotionally troubled children increases the risk of children being abused'.

Leading law and economics scholar Alan Sykes stated that whether or not vicarious liability could be justified on efficiency grounds depended on the extent to which it affected employee incentives to avoid wrongful conduct.[55] The more easily an employer could dissuade wrongdoing at little or no cost by the use of incentives, the more likely vicarious liability would be efficient.[56] He also states that it is critical to determine the extent to which the employment relation increased the probability of the wrong. The example he gives here, interestingly in light of the actual facts of the *Mohamud* decision in the Supreme Court of the United Kingdom, involves a service station attendant. He considers a situation where an attendant negligently performs repairs to a vehicle, resulting in injury to the plaintiff owner of the vehicle. He suggests that vicarious liability would apply to this loss because if the business were dissolved and the employee thrown out of work, the risk of an accident attributable to negligent repairs by the attendant would fall to zero. In contrast, in a case where the same attendant assaults his wife, the incidence of such acts bears no relation to the employee's employment. In such a case, the tort was not caused by the service station enterprise because the dissolution of the company would not reduce the probability of the tort.[57]

Sykes gives the example of a passive victim, one who either cannot or will not take cost-effective measures to protect themselves from wrongs. He takes the example of a manufacturer of a particular product. The manufacturer employs staff. However, some of the employees commit assaults. Neither the probability that an employee will commit an assault, nor the magnitude of liability that will result, depend on the employee's wealth, whether he is employed or not, or upon any characteristic of his employment. No incentive mechanism exists to enable the employer to reduce the incidence of employee assaults.

Sykes says in such a case it is inefficient to make the employer liable for the assaults. The employer could not affect the number of assaults or total amount of damages. If strict liability applies, too many costs will be placed on the employer, causing them to shrink their operations, or cease entirely. Society will lose the benefit of a profitable enterprise. Using this example, Sykes concludes that 'Vicarious liability for a given wrong is probably inefficient if (a) the enterprise does not cause the wrong, even partially, and (b) the enterprise cannot reduce the probability of the wrong through incentive contracts with its employees'.[58] Sykes says that if the given employee would likely have committed the wrong regardless of the employment relationship, vicarious liability is inefficient.[59]

It is noteworthy that the Restatement (Third) of Torts uses fault-based liability as the general rule, with strict liability the exception. One of the exceptional areas

[55] A Sykes, 'The Boundaries of Vicarious Liability: An Economic Analysis of the Scope of Employment Rule and Related Legal Doctrines' (1988) 101 *Harvard Law Review* 563.

[56] ibid 578.

[57] ibid 574.

[58] ibid 575.

[59] ibid 586; see also A Sykes, 'The Economics of Vicarious Liability' (1984) 93 *Yale Law Journal* 1231.

in which strict liability is recognised occurs in relation to 'abnormally dangerous activity'.[60] Leading law and economics scholar Richard Posner also suggests fault-based liability in negligence as the starting point. He says a fault-based system is normally workable because the hazards of activity can be avoided by being careful. In these cases, he says there is no need to recognise strict liability. He would permit the imposition of strict liability on an enterprise in cases where a particular type of accident could not be avoided by the taking of reasonable care. In such cases, the loss spreading implicit in enterprise liability is attractive.[61]

Perhaps another major criticism that can be made of law and economics theory, of which enterprise risk is a part, is that it fails the practicality test.[62] It does not in fact describe how judges, or at least the vast majority of judges, decide tort cases.[63] Judges are typically not trained economists. It might be fanciful to suggest that they do, or they have, applied economic considerations such as efficient loss distribution in deciding cases, as opposed to other sources of counsel and wisdom more familiar to legal process, such as precedent, deduction from existing principle, 'fairness' and 'reasonableness' etc. This point is necessary, in light of strident claims by some law and economics scholars that the common law is 'best (not perfectly) explained as a system for maximising the wealth of society'.[64]

For instance, some view negligence in this way, that a given defendant is, or should be deemed, negligent if the burden of taking precautions was less than the probability of the risk materialising multiplied by the gravity of the resulting loss.[65] So, applying this theory, the House of Lords must have dismissed the plaintiff's claim in *Bolton v Stone* because the probability that someone would be

[60] s 20(a) Restatement (Third) of Torts (2009).

[61] Judge Posner *Indian Harbor Bell RR v American Cyanimid* Co 916 F 2d 1174, 1177 (1990): 'the baseline common law regime of tort liability is negligence. When it is a workable regime, because the hazards of an activity can be avoided by being careful … there is no need to switch to strict liability. Sometimes, however, a particular type of accident cannot be prevented by taking care but can be avoided, or its consequences minimized, by shifting the activity in which the accident occurs to another locale, where the risk or harm of an accident will be less, or by reducing the scale of the activity in order to minimize the number of accidents caused by it … by making the actor strictly liable, by denying him … an excuse based on his inability to avoid accidents by being more careful—we give him an incentive, missing in a negligence regime, to experiment with methods of preventing accidents that involve not greater exertions of care, assumed to be futile, but instead relocating, changing or reducing … the activity giving rise to the accident'; see also Judge Posner in *Konradi v United States* 919 F 2d 1207 (7th Cir, 1990).

[62] Brodie (*Enterprise Liability and the Common Law* (n 51)), supportive of the enterprise liability approach, acknowledges the 'real difficulty in translating the concept of enterprise risk into a practically applicable test'.

[63] 'The task of the courts remains that of loss fixing rather than loss spreading': *Caltex Oil (Australia) Pty Ltd v The Dredge 'Willemstad'* (1976) 136 CLR 529, 580 (Stephen J).

[64] R Posner, *Economic Analysis of the Law*, 4th edn (Boston, MA, 1992) 23; W Landes and R Posner, *The Economic Structure of Tort Law* (Cambridge, MA, Harvard University Press, 1987) 1: 'the common law of torts is best explained as if the judges who created the law through decisions operating as precedents in later cases were trying to promote efficient resource allocation'.

[65] Landes and Posner, 'The Positive Economic Theory of Tort Law' (n 44) 884 describing the so-called Learned Hand approach to negligence in *United States v Carroll Towing Co* 159 F 2d 169 (2nd Cir, 1947).

injured by a wayward cricket ball multiplied by the likely expected loss from such activity was less than the burden of taking precautions.[66] Presumably, the same would go for *Donoghue v Stevenson*.[67] According to this view, the manufacturer was liable because the cost for them of taking reasonable precautions to prevent unsafe products was less than the probability of someone suffering an injury from an unsafe product multiplied by the likely loss that resulted.

With respect, I fundamentally disagree with Posner that economics is the best explainer of the common law principle. Economic reasoning did not underpin the reasoning in classic negligence cases like *Donoghue* and *Bolton*. There is no reference to the Learned Hand formula in either case. There seems no basis for a suggestion that the decisions were motivated by economic considerations. In the case of *Donoghue* there is a strong sense of fairness and justice evidently underpinning the decision; in the case of *Bolton* there is evident concern with the practicality of taking precautions given the very low risk of injury, and perhaps some tender fondness for the game of cricket.

In terms of the evidentiary record, there are very few occasions where judges overtly resort to economic reasoning when deciding cases, and in some torts cases, such reasoning is explicitly rejected.[68] This is not surprising. The judge will likely not be an economist, and nor will be the advocates presenting the arguments to the court. The precedents that the court will take into account will usually be decided by judges with similarly no economic background. Perhaps the most that can be said accurately is that judges *may* take a range of considerations into account when actually deciding cases. One of these *may* be economic arguments. This has rarely been express, it *may* be implicit in some of the reasoning. However, realistically this would only be, at best, one consideration for the court. Much more important considerations are likely to include relevant precedent, relevant comparative law, logical deduction from earlier premise, and in some cases arguments about justice and fairness, as subjective as those concepts admittedly are. It is disingenuous, with respect, to suggest that economics is the best explainer of the state of the common law. The suggestion is patently false.

Now, it is a materially different argument to suggest normatively that judges *should* apply economic considerations in deciding cases. It is at least intellectually honest to present law and economics as a proposal to improve legal reasoning in the future, rather than present it as a fait accompli that has been silently used by judges in the past. However, some familiar, and some different, problems arise with this suggestion. Again, we have the problem that it is very likely that

[66] *Bolton v Stone* [1951] AC 850.

[67] *Donoghue v Stevenson* [1932] AC 562.

[68] In *Modbury Triangle Shopping Centre Pty Limited v ANZIL and Another* (2000) 205 CLR 254, Gleeson CJ quoted United States torts scholar Prosser to the effect that 'the duty to take precautions against the negligence of others ... involves merely the usual process of multiplying the probability that such negligence will occur by the magnitude of the harm likely to result if it does, and weighing the result against the burden upon the defendant of exercising such care'. Gleeson CJ then added 'that does not represent an accurate statement of the common law in Australia' (267).

neither the judges, nor the advocates that present the arguments for them, have any economic training whatsoever. The utility of judges using economic notions to decide legal cases is, at the very least, highly questionable. Even if judges were economically minded and competent in this field, it presumes an ability to access relevant data in order to effect such an approach.

How could judges realistically calculate the probability that someone would be injured by a wayward cricket ball, and the likely cost of the injury? Quotes for the taking of precautions would obviously differ wildly. How could a manufacturer estimate in advance the likely loss that might be suffered by someone who used a defective product? That might depend on a range of variables, including how much of the product the plaintiff consumed, the product's interaction with other food the plaintiff was ingesting at the time, the plaintiff's general state of health, whether they actually consumed the defective product, or merely saw it affect someone else, and suffered a nervous injury as a result, for instance. There are innumerable variables making it very difficult, if not impossible, for any manufacturer to make the kind of assessment which law and economics scholars seem to suggest that would-be defendants can make, and which courts might ultimately make. In short, law and economics can make some presumptions about its practical applicability, at least in relation to tort liability, that are at the least highly questionable. Yet, this is the source from whence a doctrine like enterprise liability emanates. My doubts over the actual practicality of a law and economics approach to tort liability in general, for the reasons just explained, thus carry over to the use of enterprise liability to apparently explain one area of tort law, that of vicarious liability. Doubts over the practicality of such an approach, quite apart from whatever else may be said about it on equity/justice grounds, are substantial.

At this point it might also be convenient to point out that enterprise liability is not a principle that the common law accepts to be of general application.[69] Stevens makes the point well:

> Vicarious liability cannot be explained in terms of an enterprise being required to internalise the risks of the activity it creates. If we seek to explain vicarious liability in such terms, there is no justification for confining liability to torts by employees. If the law was that an enterprise ought to bear all of the costs associated with its activities, these limitations on when it is possible to hold the defendant liable make no sense.[70]

Of course, if it were, there would be no need for the finding in the classic case of *Donoghue v Stevenson*. Presumably, according to the enterprise risk approach, a manufacturer would be liable for the costs of defective products, since that was a cost that was characteristic of their activity. It was a cost of doing business, and should be internalised to that business, to allow it to make good economic

[69] Neyers and Stevens, 'Vicarious Liability in the Charity Sector (n 40) 400: 'the theory (of enterprise risk) has never been applied in a principled way in the common law'; Stevens, 'Non-Delegable Duties and Vicarious Liability' (n 54) 343: 'there is general strict liability for harm caused by enterprises'.

[70] Stevens, ibid, 361.

decisions about resource allocation. Demonstrably then, the common law does not apply an enterprise risk approach to a manufacturer's product liability generally.

In fact, in relation to other harms that a business might cause, again there is a lack of evidence of a strict liability enterprise risk approach. Certainly, a business is liable for negligence and for nuisances that it might create. However, plaintiffs seeking to sue an organisation for these torts must prove the elements of the relevant tort. The business is not seen as strictly liable for every loss to another that might be related to the business in some way. The law of tort has special rules carefully outlining the circumstances in which a business will be liable, for instance that it owed and breached a duty of care it owed to the plaintiff. This makes it all the more anomalous to seek to justify one principle of the law of tort, namely vicarious liability, on the basis of enterprise risk, when evidently, most of the law of tort, as it applies to business organisation defendants, demonstrably does not adopt an enterprise risk approach to determining whether or not the defendant business is liable.

Above I have alluded to a number of weaknesses of the enterprise risk theory as an explanation underpinning the imposition of vicarious liability upon a defendant employer. Given the length of the chapter, it might be helpful to summarise these weaknesses here.

Summary of Weaknesses in Relation to Enterprise Risk as a Species of Strict Liability to Justify the Imposition of Vicarious Liability

Historical Weaknesses

— There is very little evidence of notions of enterprise risk in the vast majority of the case law in which principles of vicarious liability developed.

— It probably derives most support from the *Rylands* principle of the late nineteenth century and development of statutory offences, created in response to the Industrial Revolution, but again is little articulated in the way we would now recognise it, and *Rylands* itself was not expressly decided on such a basis.

— Later cases have persistently denied that *Rylands* is authority for a general strictness of liability principle; to the contrary, most of the effort has subsequently been to minimise and confine it, explain it in terms of another tort, or abolish it altogether.

— There is very little use of the enterprise risk theory among scholarly writing about vicarious liability in the late nineteenth and early twentieth century, times when legal scholarly writing gained in prominence.

— There is long evidence of strict liability, of which family enterprise risk is a member, in the law, but this can be explained in terms of the development of a legal system out of a system of blood feud and vengeance. Understandably, the law was particularly concerned at this time with providing compensation to those who had been injured, regardless of the cause or the circumstances.
— The law of wrongs, including what we would now regard as criminal law and tort law, began to take into account the culpability of the defendant, in particular whether their actions were intentional or not. This started in the criminal law but became increasingly evident in tort law, and was well established by the nineteenth century, before negligence principle grew exponentially in the twentieth century.

The Theory Does Not Explain the Existing Contours of Vicarious Liability

It can be difficult to support a theory that demonstrably does not explain key concepts of existing vicarious liability principles. Specifically, notions of enterprise risk theory do not explain the traditionally sharp distinction between liability for employees and for independent contractors, does not explain why vicarious liability is dependent upon proof that the employee committed a tort, and does not explain why the common law permits an employer who was vicariously liable to claim an indemnity from the employee who caused them loss. There is also doubt as to whether it fits the concept of 'scope of employment', which has traditionally been a fundamental part of the law of vicarious liability.

One wonders how a theory can effectively purport to underpin and explain a legal principle when, demonstrably, it does not explain many aspects of that principle.

The Theory Seems Applicable as a General Principle by which an Organisation is Liable to Others for Harms Caused, but is Not So Applied

The theory of enterprise risk could, if taken to its logical conclusion, provide a general all-encompassing explanation of the circumstances in which a business enterprise will or should be liable to others for injuries or losses caused to them. If the theory were accepted in the common law, there would have been no need for the *Donoghue v Stevenson* decision, since production of a defective good was a 'cost of doing business' which the manufacturer should bear internally. Demonstrably then, the doctrine does not apply generally to an organisation's liability to others for the materialisation of 'business risks'. Courts in the United Kingdom have continually rejected suggestions that *Rylands* strict liability is a general principle of tort law, and it has been entirely abandoned in Australia.

Its ambit seems to be confined to pockets of liability of a business, for instance vicarious liability, and in some jurisdictions, liability for 'extra-hazardous' activity and liability for defective goods. If the enterprise risk theory is sound, it should be applied comprehensively to explain the liability of a business, not to a select few categories of case. It is difficult to justify its use to support strict liability of a business in some categories of case, but not others, if the rationale really is about allocating costs where they belong. Surely, either the law of obligations needs to embrace the theory and make businesses liable accordingly or not. It should not retrofit it to try to explain existing common law principle in the area of vicarious liability, but not generally in relation to the liability of a business, without justification as to why it apparently applies to vicarious liability, but not the general principles by which the liability of an organisation is assessed in all other contexts.

It Makes 'Brave' Assumptions about Loss Spreading and Insurance

Enterprise risk seeks to allocate costs to the organisation that is (assumed to be) in a better position to spread the costs of such risks materialising. However, it makes sweeping assumptions about the ability of an organisation to spread such costs through pricing and/or insurance. These assumptions simply cannot be made at such a level of generality. It assumes that a business organisation is able to spread the cost of risks, for instance to its customers and clients. However, the extent to which an organisation practically can do so would depend on important features of the market(s) in which it operates, including the level of competition, the market share of the defendant, the extent of barriers to entry, the elasticity of demand, exit costs etc. So an organisation may be able to spread losses in some cases but sweeping assumptions that they can fully do so in all cases are heroic. The judges do not have the expertise to make the necessary enquiry in a particular case to see whether the assumption is actually valid in the particular case before them and should not do so. However, this difficulty must not be overcome by simply ignoring these practical difficulties and making the highly questionable assumption anyway.

Similarly, it tends to assume the availability of insurance for particular risks. However, again this assumption may be heroic. While in most cases insurance may be available, there will often be exclusions in the fine print, whereby an insurer denies coverage. This seems particularly likely in the realm of deliberate employee wrongdoing. It is relatively common for insurers to deny coverage in cases where insureds or their representatives are guilty of deliberate wrongdoing.

And again, if loss spreading is considered important, its acceptance and application in tort law again seems selective and piecemeal. Judges may be surprised that their role is not to do justice between the parties before them according to law, but to 'spread losses efficiently'. This is highly contested; certainly many judges would not conceive of their role in this way. There are many adherents of a corrective justice approach to tort law, as opposed to distributive justice. And why is it only in the realm of vicarious liability that the law of tort is asked to consider loss spreading? One does not find much mention of it in tort law generally, and in particular in negligence. If a court does not decide a negligence case against an organisation on the basis of loss spreading, why is it apparently justified when the action is against an employer on the basis of vicarious liability?

The other point is that to the extent that enterprise risk assumes that the risks of a particular activity will be borne by the enterprise that creates them, this does not appear to hold true in the likely case where the enterprise is insured for such risks. An individual firm's premiums will probably not reflect individualised assessments of their particular risks. There is evidence that when insurance companies determine the premium that a particular organisation would-be insured is to pay, they base their calculations on the rate of claims within that particular industry, as opposed to that particular organisation's claims history.[71] Atiyah concluded that premiums are likely to be affected only very marginally, if at all, by the claims history of a particular insured.[72] This counters the assumption of the enterprise risk theory that the costs of an enterprise will be internalised to it, either directly or through the insurance premiums it will pay.

Further, the orthodox position is that the common law does not take into account when determining liability issues the fact that a defendant has insurance. As Viscount Simonds put it in *Lister v Romford Ice and Cold Storage Co Ltd*: 'as a general proposition it has not, I think, been questioned for nearly 200 years that in determining the rights inter se of A and B the fact that one or other of them is insured is to be disregarded'.[73] Courts should apply this position consistently, not occasionally take into account (or, more accurately, make assumptions about) whether the defendant has appropriate insurance.[74] Recently in *Woodland v Swimming Teachers Association* several members of the United Kingdom Supreme Court appeared to attempt to justify their finding of liability partly on the basis of insurance considerations,[75] a suggestion with which I respectfully disagree. As Atiyah puts it, in terms with which the United Kingdom Supreme Court

[71] Atiyah (n 43) 16–17: 'premiums are fixed by reference to the type of business carried on, and there is little scope for variation by reason of the record of the particular insured' (the word 'insurer' appears rather than 'insured' in the original text, but the word 'insured' is surely what the learned author meant); Morris (n 12) 565.

[72] Atiyah, ibid, 17.

[73] *Lister v Romford Ice and Cold Storage Co Ltd* [1957] AC 555, 576–77; to like effect *Hollis v Vabu Pty Ltd* (2001) 207 CLR 21, 68 (Callinan J); and *Dobson (Litigation Guardian Of) v Dobson* [1999] 2 SCR 753, [74]; see also *Davie v New Merton Board Mills Ltd* [1959] AC 604, 626–27 (Viscount Simonds).

[74] J Stapleton, 'Tort, Insurance and Ideology' (1995) 58(6) *Modern Law Review* 820, 829: 'That there is no broad formulation of where and why liability insurance or insurability should be a factor relevant to the imposition and shape of liability, suggests that commentators deploy it selectively, and therefore unconvincingly, in the normative debate just as they do in the descriptive debate'; for a contrary view see Merkin and Steele (n 11) 203–05.

[75] *Woodland v Swimming Teachers Association* [2014] AC 537, 590 where Baroness Hale (with whom Lord Clarke, Lord Wilson and Lord Toulson agreed) referred to the situation of 'poorer and

agreed,[76] the law should determine the extent of insurance, not the other way around.[77] Clearly, an argument justifying vicarious liability via enterprise liability on the basis of assumptions about insurance involves a high degree of retrofitting, whatever else may be said about it. The bulk of the cases establishing the doctrine of vicarious liability were decided well before insurance became generally available in the late nineteenth century.[78] Some might have a logical difficulty with attempting to justify a doctrine in the present day based on concepts that clearly did not exist when the doctrine was in its critical formative years, and which largely retains the same shape today as it did then, notwithstanding its expansion.

It Does Not Describe How Judges Actually Decide Tort Cases, and Does Not Describe How Judges Should Decide Tort Cases

As noted above, enterprise risk theory is sourced in the law and economics movement and is characterised by the same kinds of assumptions that that branch of legal thought typically makes. Again, some of these can be sweeping. I discussed above law and economics expert Richard Posner, and his sweeping assumption that the rules of the common law are best explained by efficiency considerations. As I indicated above, I respectfully suggest that this would be news to the great majority of judges through history and today. Simply, it is not accurate to make this type of claim. If it were true, *Donoghue v Stevenson* was pointless, because a manufacturer should already have been strictly liable for the risks that the organisation created, and the cost of defective products should be allocated to that organisation. In fact, in the vast majority of cases, judges decide based on precedent.

Further, the theory does not describe how judges should decide tort cases. This is because in the vast majority of cases judges are not economics experts, and nor are the advocates presenting them with arguments. One cannot realistically expect judges to be making decisions based on expertise they clearly do not have. Further, even if it were acceptable legal reasoning to do so, judges would have to be presented with accurate and comprehensive economic information about a particular enterprise, its practical ability to spread the cost of risks, the availability of insurance etc. This is on the assumption that this is even legitimate

un-or-under-insured contractors' in seeking to justify the imposition of a non-delegable duty on a (presumably better insured) defendant.

[76] *Cox v Ministry of Justice* [2016] AC 660, 669: 'employers insure themselves because they are liable; they are not liable because they have insured themselves'.

[77] Atiyah (n 43) 27; *cf* P Giliker, *Vicarious Liability in Tort: A Comparative Perspective* (Cambridge, Cambridge University Press, 2010) 193–94: '(The employer's) ability to act and implement greater accident prevention measures and to distribute loss via the mechanism of liability insurance justifies the imposition of liability'.

[78] Merkin and Steele (n 11) 302.

legal reasoning, which is also highly questionable. I have read many cases, and it is very rare that this kind of evidence is apparently provided by the advocates. One cannot expect a judge to make their decisions on the basis of scant evidence. If they do so, they will be forced to rely on generalisations that may not reflect the reality of the situation.

It Relies on Inherently Ambiguous Concepts

Some advocates of strict liability, including enterprise risk, confine it to limited types of case, including where the enterprise creates an 'extra-hazardous risk'. The precise meaning of this, and when a risk crosses the line between 'normal' or even 'hazardous' to 'extra-hazardous', is not clear.[79] This was noted, in concluding that such a special rule should not exist for such activities, by the Law Commission of England and Wales.[80] Lord Atkin made the same point in his celebrated *Donoghue v Stevenson* decision.[81] And what conceptually should change the legal approach to extra-hazardous activity, as compared with normal or hazardous activity? The law of negligence would already accommodate such facts; obviously the standard of care that would be expected from an organisation engaged in dangerous activity would be higher than the standard of care expected from an organisation engaged in non-dangerous activity. So it is hard to discern a rationale for an assertion that while ordinary negligence principles apply to most organisations, different, strict liability, rules apply to organisations engaged in extra-hazardous activity.

It is true that some have attempted to demonstrate why the law should distinguish between ordinary business risks, and so-called extra-hazardous risks.[82] However, with respect, they can seem like a retrospective attempt to rationalise

[79] AJ Waite, 'Deconstructing the Rule in *Rylands v Fletcher* (2006) 18 *Journal of Environmental Law* 423; K Stanton, 'The Legacy of *Rylands v Fletcher*' in N Mullany and A Linden (eds), *Torts Tomorrow: A Tribute to John Fleming* (North Ryde, NSW, LBC Information Services, 1998) 91; Stevens, 'Non-Delegable Duties and Vicarious Liability' (n 54) 341: 'a rule based solely upon the degree of risk the activity involves has few attractions ... why should the mere fact that the risk run is very hazardous entail strict liability even where the decision to undertake the activity was reasonable and all reasonable care was taken to carry it out?'.

[80] *Civil Liability for Dangerous Things and Activities* (1970) No 32, [12]–[14], noted by Lord Goff for the House of Lords in *Cambridge Water Co Ltd v Eastern Counties Leather Co* [1994] 2 AC 264.

[81] [1932] AC 560, 595–96: 'I do not find it necessary to discuss at length the cases dealing with duties where the thing is dangerous, or, in the narrower category, belongs to a class of things which are dangerous in themselves. I regard the distinction as an unnatural one so far as it is used to serve as a logical differentiation by which to distinguish the existence or non-existence of a legal right'.

[82] eg, Richard Posner stated that strict liability was justified for extra-hazardous activity where the taking of reasonable care would not avoid accidents from occurring: *Indian Harbor Bell RR v American Cyanimid Co* (n 61) 1177; F Pollock, 'Duties of Insuring Safety: The Rule in *Rylands v Fletcher* (1886) 2 *Law Quarterly Review* 52.

and incorporate the *Rylands v Fletcher* precedent into the law of obligations.[83] The utility of such attempts can be seriously questioned. The United Kingdom House of Lords apparently rejected a more general doctrine of liability for extra-hazardous activity, beyond the specific situation in *Rylands*,[84] when it was asked to so extend that precedent. Several members of the House of Lords in *Read v J Lyons and Co Ltd* specifically rejected a suggestion of special rules of liability applying where a business defendant was engaged in 'dangerous' or 'extra-hazardous' activity.[85] Again in *Cambridge Water Co Ltd v Eastern Counties Leather Co* the House of Lords refused to formulate a general legal principle regarding liability for extra-hazardous activity out of *Rylands*.[86]

It is not surprising that in Australia the supposed exception for extra-hazardous activity was eventually doubted,[87] and then subsequently the *Rylands* rule itself[88] was interred. The *Rylands* principle has been progressively narrowed and effectively reinterpreted as a rule of private nuisance in the United Kingdom,[89] and progressively narrowed in scope.[90] Calls continue for the United Kingdom Supreme

[83] For some attempts to rationalise and explain the doctrine see F Bohlen, 'Rule in *Rylands v Fletcher*' (1911) 59 *University of Pennsylvania Law Review* 298, 373, 423; R Molloy, '*Fletcher v Rylands*—A Reexamination of Juristic Origins (1942) 9 *University of Chicago Law Review* 266; AWB Simpson, 'Legal Liability for Bursting Reservoirs: The Historical Context of *Rylands v Fletcher*' (1984) 13 *Journal of Legal Studies* 209; WTS Stallybrass, 'Dangerous Things and the Non-Natural User of Land' (1929) 3 *Cambridge Law Journal* 376.

[84] The relevant references from *Rylands* itself are Blackburn J's references to liability for a thing 'likely to do mischief if it escapes': *Fletcher v Rylands* (1866) LR 3 Ex 265, 279 (Blackburn J for the Court); expressly accepted by Lord Cairns in *Rylands v Fletcher* (1868) LR 3 AC 330, 340.

[85] *Read v J Lyons and Co Ltd* [1947] AC 156, 165–66: 'the fact that the work that was being carried on was of a kind which requires special care is a reason why the standard of care should be high, but it is no reason for saying that the occupier is liable for resulting damage to an invitee without any proof of negligence' (Viscount Simon); 'in my opinion it would be impracticable to frame a legal classification of things as things dangerous and things not dangerous, attaching absolute liability in the case of the former but not in the case of the latter' (172, Lord Macmillan); 'there is no rule which imposes on him who carries on the business of making explosives, though the activity may be "ultra-hazardous", and an explosive a "dangerous thing" a strict liability to those who are lawfully on his premises' (182, Lord Simonds); 'I do not think that the invitee, any more than the occupier, would assume that, by reason only of the dangerous nature of the business carried on, the occupier guaranteed him freedom from harm' (186, Lord Uthwatt). The other Law Lord in the case, Lord Porter, did not address the matter.

[86] [1994] 2 AC 264, 305 (Lord Goff, for the Court); in *Transco Plc v Stockport Metropolitan Borough Council* [2004] 2 AC 1, 16 Lord Hoffmann noted that while it was tempting to see *Rylands* as an enterprise risk strict liability principle of broad application, the common law took a different course, declining to view it as a general principle of liability, and instead favouring the general principle of no liability in the absence of fault.

[87] *Stoneman v Lyons* (1975) 133 CLR 550, 563–65 (Stephen J) and 575 (Mason); *Stevens v Brodribb* (1986) 160 CLR 16, 29 (Mason J) and 41–42 (Wilson and Dawson JJ).

[88] *Burnie Port Authority v General Jones Pty Ltd* (1994) 179 CLR 520.

[89] *Cambridge Water Co Ltd v Eastern Counties Leather Co* (n 80).

[90] eg, it does not apply to claims for personal injury; and it does not apply to functions governed by statute. Its requirement that the defendant be engaged in a non-natural use of the land has been interpreted narrowly, the court has insisted that the thing complained of 'escaped' from premises, and the interference complained of must to a proprietary interest in land.

Court to finally deliver the *coup de grace* to it.[91] The Canadian courts, while still recognising *Rylands* as a head of tort liability separate from nuisance,[92] have also refused to find that it underpins a general strict liability principle for extra-hazardous activity, as opposed to other types of activity.[93]

It lives on in the Restatement (Third) of Torts,[94] but perhaps it is time for the common law to abandon the use of this concept as a basis for justifying the imposition of strict liability, given difficulties in defining precisely what is meant, as well as convincingly explaining why the mere fact that an activity is deemed extra-hazardous justifies a large leap out of the realm of fault-based liability and into strict liability, when fault-based doctrine will already take that fact into account in determining liability.

It should also be noted that legislatures are increasingly willing to regulate particular industries. If there is thought to be a need for specific regulation to deal with the risks of particular activities, including what might be strict liability, it might be thought that a legislature might be a more suitable body to provide such regulation, permitting appropriate specificity and detail with respect to a particular activity, as opposed to piecemeal development by the courts through a common law principle of uncertain scope.[95] One would hope that legislatures would have undertaken appropriate research about the impacts of such regulation prior to introducing it. This type of policy assessment seems much easier and more appropriate within the non-judicial branches of government where particular industries can be effectively studied and modelled, as opposed to the judicial branch.

Similar difficulties attend the argument that strict liability applies to 'characteristic risks' of the enterprise. How does one go about determining what these are? Is the risk that a teacher or boarding master/mistress will commit sexual abuse against students a 'characteristic risk' of providing education? Should the law differentiate between a residential teaching facility, such as a boarding school, and a teacher in a non-boarding environment? Is abuse more likely to be a 'characteristic risk' of a boarding activity, than an ordinary school environment. Why? And again, what is it about a characteristic risk, however defined, that justifies the leap out of fault-based liability and into strict liability? It escapes this author. Again, incoherence of principle is evident. Surely, the risk that a defective product will be

[91] S Tofaris, '*Rylands v Fletcher* Restricted Further' (2013) 72 *Cambridge Law Journal* 11, 14 wondered 'whether it would not be better to put it out of its misery by abolishing it altogether', and Robert Stevens said it should be put out of its misery because it was so 'enfeebled': Stevens, 'Non-Delegable Duties and Vicarious Liability' (n 54) 342.

[92] *Tock v St John's Metropolitan Area Board* [1989] 2 SCR 1181.

[93] *Smith v Inco Ltd* (2011) ONCA 628, [78] (Ontario Court of Appeal).

[94] (2009) s 20.

[95] This point was noted, in the course of refusing to ground a general strict liability in the common law for extra-hazardous activity, by Lord Goff for the House in *Cambridge Water Co Ltd v Eastern Counties Leather Co* (n 80); see also *Transco Plc v Stockport Metropolitan Borough Council* (n 86) 9 (Lord Bingham).

produced would be a 'characteristic risk' of a manufacturing business. Evidently, that has not been sufficient in the common law to justify the imposition of strict liability upon a manufacturer. And the risk that a cricket ball will be struck out of a cricket stadium is a 'characteristic risk' of owning or managing such a stadium, yet no one suggests *Bolton v Stone* should have been decided on strict liability grounds. The incoherence is hard to accept and cannot be justified.

Deterrence

Confusion worsens when advocates of enterprise liability seek to justify its imposition on a supposed deterrence rationale. The best exemplar of this appears in the classic enterprise risk decision of *Bazley v Curry*, where the Supreme Court of Canada stated that one of the two rationales for the imposition of vicarious liability under its preferred enterprise risk theory was deterrence. The unanimous Court found that employers were often in a position to reduce accidents and intentional wrongs by 'efficient organisation and supervision', so that 'imaginative and efficient administration and supervision' could reduce the risk that the employer has introduced into the community.[96] It should be noted that though the United Kingdom Supreme Court has eventually accepted and applied the enterprise risk approach, it continues to decline to embrace the deterrence rationale.[97]

There are many difficulties with this reasoning. It does not in fact justify the imposition of strict liability. The same reasoning and logic would apply to a duty of care that an employer owes in the selection, management and supervision of staff. It would equally have been open to the Supreme Court to find that a robust application of the negligence standard to employers in relation to their staff would provide the necessary incentive and inducement for them in relation to good staff selection, management and supervision.

But in an important respect this reasoning actually supports the imposition of a duty of care negligence standard on employers in this regard, as opposed to a strict liability standard. It is a sound argument that if an employer knows they will held to account under negligence principles in relation to the selection, supervision and management of staff, this certainly could lead to the desirable outcome that they will take more care with each of these tasks, reducing the likelihood they will harm others by their behaviour. So while the deterrence potential of tort law is acknowledged, it leads to a conclusion that negligence law should be applied to such enterprise decisions and practices. It is not easy to see why the Supreme Court thought such reasoning justified the imposition of strict liability.

96 [1999] 2 SCR 534, 554–55.

97 *Armes v Nottinghamshire County Council* [2017] UKSC 60, [67] (Lord Reed, with whom Lady Hale, Lord Kerr and Lord Clarke agreed).

If an organisation knows that it is subject to a strict liability regime, and that regardless of what level of care it takes to select, train and supervise staff, it will be liable for what that employee does, it is hard to argue that this provides the needed incentive for the enterprise to put resources into doing so. The organisation will know it will be liable regardless of what it does in this regard. So rationally it might decide not to provide those services or might try to obtain insurance which will adequately cover it for such risks. I referred to difficulties with the insurance argument above. So if the aim really is to get employers to take more care in the selection, management and supervision of staff, a laudable objective which really could work to reduce the level of injuries to others, which is of course something we all want, surely imposition of the negligence standard provides the appropriate motivation and deterrent? An employer subject to this regime would know that if it put the appropriate resources and care into these decisions, it would not automatically be liable, and would have a chance to defend itself by showing it took reasonable care. But an employer who knew that regardless of what it did in this regard, it would be liable nonetheless, would rationally respond surely in many cases by either discontinuing the activity or just insuring against it, if possible.

Therefore, where the organisation cannot obtain insurance for the activity on terms suitable to them, or at all, they may discontinue the activity, or at the very least, scale it back.[98] Now of course there are numerous societal implications of an organisation no longer conducting an activity. They have been providing a very useful service upon which many individuals relied. They were probably employing individuals. As a company they were presumably creating wealth which would be given back to shareholders, who in turn would spend that money and stimulate the economy (known as the 'multiplier effect' of economic activity). A principle by which that activity is shut down due to an injury that could not have been avoided by the taking of reasonable precautions is questionable, to say the least. These implications are worsened when the organisation was providing an essential public service, such as providing education, health or charity service. The result of the imposition of strict liability upon them might be a reduction of the level at which these services are provided. The public benefits thus to be gained by the imposition of strict liability are not immediately obvious to me. Thomas Baty presciently noted this almost a century earlier when the contours of vicarious liability were much narrower than they are today: 'Unknown to the classical jurisprudence of Rome, unfamiliar to the medieval jurisprudence of England, it has attained its luxuriant growth through carelessness and false analogy, and it cannot but operate to check enterprise and to penalise commerce'.[99] The United Kingdom Supreme Court has recently expressed great ambivalence about the use

[98] This point is made by Lord Hughes (dissenting) in *Armes v Nottinghamshire County Council*, ibid, [89].

[99] T Baty, *Vicarious Liability* (Oxford, Clarendon Press, 1916) 7.

of deterrence to justify the imposition of vicarious liability. They pointed out that deterrence rationales had not been prominent in much of the British case law, and added that, in the factual context of whether the imposition of vicarious liability upon a council for the actions of foster carers, any conclusions about the deterrence effect of imposing vicarious liability were essentially speculative.[100] So, however else the enterprise risk theory might be justified, its justification on the basis of deterrence is considered to be very weak.

One of the Achilles heels of the law of vicarious liability has been the great difficulty in articulating a rationale for the existence of such a strict liability doctrine in today's tort world. Many rationales have been tried and discarded in the past. Three jurisdictions studied in this book have now adopted an enterprise risk approach. However, the theory is open to serious criticisms and is conceptually very weak, as this chapter has sought to show.

The numerous weaknesses and difficulties with the enterprise risk theory are sufficient to convince me that the theory is not helpful as a rationalisation or justification for the current state of vicarious liability. A theory that demonstrably does not explain all, or even many, of the current aspects of the doctrine is unhelpful. A theory that makes assumptions about insurance and loss spreading that will often not be correct, or entirely correct, it not helpful. A theory based on a category of legal thought that assumes that the common law is directed to economic efficiency, and which clearly flies in the face of how judges have been deciding cases for centuries, and how they continue to do so, is not helpful. Judges and courts lack the kind of economic expertise that would be needed to actually apply this theory in practice, even assuming that economic efficiency was the best 'explainer' of common law rules, or perhaps more accurately, that it should be the basis of common law rules, both of which are highly contestable, and not accepted here. A theory based on concepts such as extra-hazardous activity, a concept very difficult to define and which courts have consistently rejected as a basis for the imposition of general strict liability in common law jurisdictions, apart from the United States, is not helpful. The concept of 'characteristic risk' is no more helpful as an explanation for the imposition of strict liability on an enterprise.

And it is circular to laud enterprise risk theory as delivering a kind of deterrence to undesired behaviour when it is admitted that even a defendant who had taken every conceivable precaution would still be liable under it. The only deterrence likely to be delivered is to a business offering the service at all. This is not beneficial for society in most cases, and it is particularly troubling when the organisation would otherwise deliver essential social services such as education, health or

[100] *Armes v Nottinghamshire County Council* (n 97) [67]–[69]; in particular, its concession that claims about the effect of the structure of vicarious liability principle in motivating desired changes in practice was 'empirically untested' [69] (Lord Reed, with whom Lady Hale, Lord Kerr and Lord Clarke agreed).

charity work. The Canadian Supreme Court was wrong to embrace notions of enterprise risk in *Bazley*. The hesitation of some members of the House of Lords in *Lister* to accept that theory as an explanation of vicarious liability was prescient and justified. The subsequent acceptance of that principle, without a full consideration of what it involved and the implications, exemplified in cases such as *Dubai Aluminium*, and evidenced most recently in *Cox v Ministry of Justice* and *Armes*, represents a wrong turn. The fact that the High Court accepted it in *Hollis* and just a couple of members of the High Court of Australia flirted with the theory in *Lepore*, but that it did not gain general acceptance, and was all but ignored by the High Court of Australia in its recent *Prince Alfred* decision, is a good thing. The Australian Court must not take the lead from Canada and the United Kingdom here. United Kingdom and Canadian courts should reconsider their use of the theory.

7

Other Theories

If enterprise liability is discredited and wanting as an explainer and rationaliser of vicarious liability in our law, we must search to see if there is an adequate alternative. Other options will now be considered. Before doing so, it should be acknowledged that many sources decry the possibility of articulating a rationale that fully explains the current state of the principles of law in this area. Glanville Williams laments that the case law reflects various creations of judges, some of whom had conflicting ideas of policy or justification, or no idea at all.[1] Oliver Wendell Holmes dismissed it as an 'irrational fiction'.[2] Baty called attempts to justify or rationalise it 'hopeless groping'.[3] The High Court of Australia, with masterly understatement, reflected recently that a satisfactory rationale and justification had been 'slow to appear'.[4] And in *Lister and Others v Hesley Hall Ltd* Lord Clyde had apparently given up, concluding 'I am not persuaded there is any reason of principle or policy which can be of substantial guidance in the resolution of the problem of applying the rule in any particular case'.[5] This is considered to be a most unsatisfactory state of affairs. If enterprise risk theory cannot be used, let us consider other possible rationales for the doctrine. However, the possibility that it will be a fruitless or unsatisfying search should be acknowledged upfront.

Evidentiary Considerations

Occasionally it is sought to justify the imposition of strict liability upon a defendant, as opposed to a negligence standard, on the basis that it may be difficult for a plaintiff to garner the evidence they need to successfully make a claim.[6] This is

1 G Williams, 'Vicarious Liability and the Master's Indemnity' (1957) 20 *Modern Law Review* 220, 231.

2 OW Holmes, 'Agency II' (1891) 5 *Harvard Law Review* 1, 22–23.

3 T Baty, *Vicarious Liability* (Oxford, Clarendon Press, 1916) 148.

4 *Prince Alfred College Inc v ADC* (2016) 258 CLR 134, 148 (French CJ; Kiefel, Bell, Keane and Nettle JJ).

5 *Lister and Others v Hesley Hall Ltd* [2002] 1 AC 215, 232, citing Lord Pearce in *Imperial Chemical Industries Ltd v Shatwell* [1965] AC 656 to the effect that vicarious liability had not grown from clear, logical principles, but from social convenience and 'rough justice'.

6 J Murphy, 'The Merits of *Rylands v Fletcher*' (2004) 24 *Oxford Journal of Legal Studies* 643: 'to allow the rule in *Rylands v Fletcher* to be swallowed up by the law of negligence would mean that in

reminiscent of justifications for a reverse onus of proof in some criminal cases, on the basis that it is difficult for a prosecution to obtain appropriate evidence, and/or it is easier for a person accused to provide evidence that they are innocent, rather than for the prosecutor to prove they are guilty. This idea appears in numerous criminal law decisions in the United Kingdom[7] and Canada,[8] and to some extent in Australia.[9] I have written about these supposed justifications for such exceptional rules elsewhere.[10] Suffice to say that I am opposed philosophically to a reverse onus provision in the criminal law context on the basis of 'evidentiary ease'. Consistently, I am also opposed to the imposition of strict liability upon a defendant for similar reasons in a civil context. It is fundamental that a person who accuses another of wrongdoing must prove their allegations. The default is that the legal system should do nothing, if allegations cannot be proven. This principle has been part of the legal fabric for a very long time. It should not lightly be disturbed, and possibly unintended consequences of so doing must be carefully considered. It is not and should not be incumbent on a person accused of wrongdoing to prove their innocence.

As a last resort, if the law really did perceive an issue with problems of proof in such cases, it would be better to impose a reverse onus with respect to such cases than to use issues with proof to justify a strict liability approach.[11] To be clear, I am not personally advocating for a reverse onus approach; rather the point is that difficulties with evidence and proof can be better dealt with in other ways that are much less violative of the structure of tort law than recognising a species of strict liability in tort law with ill-defined parameters, justifications and rationale.

some cases claimants would face insurmountable evidentiary burdens; indeed, that may be thought inappropriate as a matter of policy and justice'. He said it would be 'daunting and unmanageable to a relative man of straw' to prove negligence against an organisation'; PS Atiyah, *Vicarious Liability in the Law of Torts* (London, Butterworths, 1967) 20; C Morris, 'Punitive Damages in Tort Cases' (1931) 44 *Harvard Law Review* 1173, 1205: 'it is hard to prove the fault of masters, and easy for them to present a case which indicates they are blameless when they actually are not. In order that all of the guilty may be admonished, a few innocent must suffer'. With respect, this kind of reasoning seems inverted, and certainly inconsistent with fundamental legal maxims like the presumption of innocence, and that it is for the one alleging wrongdoing to prove their allegations, not for anyone to prove they are innocent of wrongdoing. Difficulties with proof have always existed, but for centuries the common law, knowing this, has insisted upon a presumption of innocence. It is a presumption for which I have argued elsewhere: A Gray, *Presumption of Innocence in Peril: A Comparative Critical Perspective* (Lanham, MD, Lexington Books, 2017).

[7] *R v Director of Public Prosecutions; Ex Parte Kebilene* [2000] 2 AC 326, 386 (Lord Hope); *R v Lambert* [2002] 2 AC 545, 608–09 (Lord Clyde); *R v Johnstone* [2003] 1 WLR 1736, 1750 (Lord Nicholls, for Lord Hope, Lord Hutton and Lord Rodger); *Sheldrake v Director of Public Prosecutions* [2005] 1 AC 264, 309 (Lord Bingham).

[8] *Whyte v The Queen* [1988] 2 SCR 3, 26; *The Queen v St Onge-Lamoureux* [2012] 3 SCR 187, 213.

[9] *International Finance Trust v New South Wales Crime Commission* (2011) 240 CLR 319, 366–67 (Gummow and Bell JJ).

[10] Gray (n 6).

[11] R Townshend-Smith, 'Vicarious Liability for Sexual (And Other) Assaults (2000) 8 *Tort Law Review* 108, 128.

Deep Pockets

On occasion, courts have been quite open about the fact that at least one major reason for their finding that a defendant employer is vicariously liable for losses one of their employees caused a third party was that the defendant had, or was assumed to have, 'deep pockets'. In other words, that they had the financial resources to honour any judgment made against them. This was quite openly expressed in *Various Claimants v Catholic Child Welfare Society*, where Lord Phillips for the Court stated that

> the policy objective underlying vicarious liability is to ensure … that liability for tortious wrongs is borne by a defendant with a means to compensate the victim … the employer is more likely to have the means to compensate the victim than the employee.[12]

This is considered to be deeply unprincipled reasoning.[13] Elsewhere in the law we do not find defendants liable to pay compensation because they are better resourced. Rightly, we only require a defendant to pay compensation when the plaintiff has made out a legal claim, that they have proven, in the case of an alleged tort, that the elements of that tort have been proven on the facts. If they cannot do so, the defendant is usually entitled to a judgment in their favour, no matter that they had substantial resources to honour any judgment made against them. It is highly anomalous to suggest that legal decisions should be based on whether a defendant has 'deep pockets'.

Glanville Williams spoke strongly against such an argument:

> There is the purely cynical theory that the master is liable because he has a purse worth opening. The master is frequently rich, and he is usually insured—two arguments that might be used by any burglar, if he ever troubled to justify his thefts. The strange thing is to find them put forward by judges of eminence (citing Lord Lyndhurst and Willes J) … whatever … can have put this extraordinary idea into judges' heads, that the mere possession of wealth is enough to justify the imposition of legal liability for a wrong.[14]

Of the nine rationales Baty cited for the imposition of vicarious liability, all of which he dismissed as 'hopeless groping',[15] he stated that the deep pockets rationale was the most likely explanation, though he clearly disagreed with it:

> The real reason for employers' liability is the ninth: that damages are taken from a deep pocket. The present is not a very propitious time for withstanding a dogma based on

[12] *Various Claimants v Catholic Child Welfare Society* [2013] 2 AC 1, 15; see likewise *Limpus v London General Omnibus Company* (1862) 1 H & C 526, 539; 158 ER 993, 998: 'there ought to be a remedy against some person capable of paying damages to those injured' (Willes J).

[13] I respectfully agree with the acknowledgement of that point by the Supreme Court in *Cox v Ministry of Justice* [2016] AC 660, 669 (Lord Reed, for the Court): 'the mere possession of wealth is not in itself any ground for imposing liability'.

[14] Williams (n 1) 232.

[15] Baty (n 3) 148.

> such a principle. But a return to simpler manners will probably bring with it a return to saner views of liability, even if it is not sooner recognized that to injure capital is to injure industry.[16]

It may be added to the comments of Baty that to 'injure capital' is to also potentially injure those whom they employ, their shareholders, their customers and others in the industry. It may also injure the economy more broadly, depending on scale.

Atiyah was also unconvinced about the deep pockets rationale for vicarious liability. After conceding that the doctrine would never have existed if employers were not generally wealthier than their employees, he added:

> But it does not follow that this fact can itself be treated as justifying the imposition of vicarious liability. After all there will always be plenty of people in the world better able to pay damages than any particular defendant who may be unfortunate enough to be sued for a tort, but mere wealth, however good a ground it may be for imposing taxation, could never by itself be treated as a ground for imposing liability in tort ... and even if it were, why should the employer out of all the wealth people in the world be singled out for liability? Clearly this justification is no justification at all, when taken by itself.[17]

Further, of course the common law is a precedent based decision. Decisions rendered today influence cases decided tomorrow. If the 'deep pockets' theory were accepted, that would seek to justify the imposition of vicarious liability on an employer today. But what about tomorrow, in a case involving very similar facts, but a case in which, as it happens, the employer was in a very financially difficult situation? Does the decision of today, premised on the deep pockets of the employer, apply tomorrow, to an employer whose pockets are much shallower? And precisely when are an employer's pockets deep enough that the doctrine applies? The law would get itself into terrible difficulties if it started deciding cases based on whether or not a defendant had deep pockets, or was in a class of individuals or organisations, about which assumptions about the depth of their pockets might be made. Rightly, it is not a consideration elsewhere in the law in terms of applying principle. We do not run a Robin Hood-style system of justice. If wealth redistribution is to be pursued as a social policy objective, the government is well

[16] ibid 154.

[17] Atiyah (n 6) 22. However, Atiyah went on to distinguish what he called 'contractors, (which) tend to conjure up an image of a large and wealthy organisation doing some work for a person perhaps much less able to meet any liabilities than they are', with a 'round the corner' contractor running a small business (334). He seemed to be justifying the imposition of liability upon the former but not the latter, in terms which can suggest an underlying redistributive, deep pockets philosophy. Frederick Pollock in *Essays in Jurisprudence and Ethics* (London, FB Rothman, 1882) refers to the deep pockets rationale but dismisses it as 'too crude and formless to be a starting point' (119), preferring a notion of enterprise risk to explain vicarious liability. It should be conceded that four pages later, Atiyah, ibid, added that: 'in general the policy of placing the liability for the torts of servants on their employees is broadly a sound one. It is sound simply because, by and large, it is the most convenient and efficient way of ensuring that persons injured in the course of business enterprises do not go uncompensated' (26).

placed to do this through the imposition of taxation. The role of a court is much different and should remain so.

Basically, it is illegitimate legal reasoning for a court to render a decision in a disputed case based on assumptions about the relative wealth of the parties, or the fact that the defendant is, or might be, in a position to pay. Often, the financial position of a defendant, particularly a private company, would not be a matter of public knowledge anyway. A defendant should not be required to divulge its financial position in order for a court to assess whether it is 'wealthy enough' to bear a judgment against it. The reputation of courts as courts of justice is liable to be imperilled if the public perceives that the courts are making decisions on grounds other than legal principle and are presuming to operate as agencies of social welfare.

Fair, Just and Reasonable

In Canada and the United Kingdom in particular, the courts have sought to rationalise the imposition of vicarious liability on an employer on the basis it is fair, just and reasonable to do so. This reasoning appears in *Bazley v Curry*,[18] where McLachlin J for the Canadian Supreme Court explained the need to provide a 'just and practical' remedy to someone who suffered due to a wrong committed by an employee.[19] She said it was fair that a person who or organisation that creates enterprise should bear the associated losses.[20] In the United Kingdom Lord Phillips used the phrase in *Various Claimants* in determining whether vicarious liability applied on the facts.[21] It was referred to in *Cox v Ministry of Justice*, Lord Reed for the Court simply stating it was 'not always necessary' to ask that question in determining whether vicarious liability applied.[22] The joint reasons in the companion case of *Mohamud v Wm Morrison Supermarkets Plc* included consideration of whether it was 'just' to make the defendant vicariously liable.[23] It can be said that the United Kingdom courts generally do take such considerations into account in the vicarious liability space.

It is not entirely clear when the concept of 'fair, just and reasonable' entered the law of vicarious liability in the United Kingdom, though *Various Claimants* in 2013 is clearly an example of its use.[24] Of course, the same concept is used elsewhere in tort law, and in particular as one of the three elements used in the United Kingdom

[18] *Bazley v Curry* [1999] 2 SCR 534.
[19] ibid 553.
[20] ibid 554.
[21] [2013] 2 AC 1, 15, 18 (for the Court).
[22] [2016] AC 660, 675.
[23] *Mohamud v Wm Morrison Supermarkets Plc* [2016] AC 677, 681 (Lord Toulson, for Lord Neuberger, Baroness Hale, Lord Dyson and Lord Reed).
[24] Certainly, in the classic strict liability case of *Fletcher v Rylands* (1866) LR 3 Ex 265, Blackburn J sought to justify the 'true rule of law' he espoused by reference to its 'justness' (280).

to determine whether or not a defendant owes a duty of care to the plaintiff to avoid negligence.[25] A similar approach is taken by the Canadian Supreme Court to duty of care questions. That country takes a modified *Anns* approach,[26] with fairness, justness and reasonableness considered as part of the second stage of the test.[27] Interestingly, the High Court of Australia did not embrace the three-stage *Caparo* approach to establishing a duty of care, including the concept of 'fairness, justice and reasonableness'. In *Sullivan v Moody* it explained why:

> There is … a danger that the matter of foreseeability … having been determined, the succeeding questions will be reduced to a discretionary judgment based upon a sense of what is fair, and just and reasonable as an outcome in the particular case … the question is what is fair, and just and reasonable is capable of being misunderstood as an invitation to formulate policy rather than to search for principle. The concept of policy, in this context, is often ill-defined. There are policies at work in the law which can be identified and applied to novel problems, but the law of tort develops by reference to principles, which must be capable of general application, not discretionary decision making in individual cases.[28]

Most recently in its vicarious liability decision of *Prince Alfred College v ADC* the High Court of Australia again rejected use of the 'fair, just and reasonable' criterion on the basis that the concept(s) depended on policy choices and the allocation of risks, about which reasonable minds might differ.[29] Criticism of its use in the context of vicarious liability is also apparent in some United Kingdom decisions.[30]

There is no necessary logic apparent to me as to why a principle used to determine whether a duty of care is owed in terms of negligence law should be applied in the context of vicarious liability, where typically the defendant is not actually accused of any wrongdoing. Perhaps the explanation for its use is that it is effectively a label for the use of policy reasons in determining whether or not liability exists, or at least, in the case of negligence, whether legal liability could exist because a duty of care is owed. Some might find it anomalous that courts in some jurisdictions are considering both (a) whether it is fair, just and reasonable to impose fault-based liability upon a defendant; and (b) whether it is fair, just and reasonable to impose strict liability upon a defendant, and exacerbated by the lack

[25] *Caparo Industries Plc v Dickman* [1990] 2 AC 605, 617–18 (Lord Bridge).

[26] *Anns v Merton London Borough Council* [1978] AC 728, 751–52 (Lord Wilberforce).

[27] *Cooper v Hobart* [2001] 3 SCR 537, [14].

[28] *Sullivan v Moody* (2001) 207 CLR 562, 579 (the Court); see also Callinan J in *State of New South Wales v Lepore* (2003) 212 CLR 511, 626: 'cases would, as a practical matter, be deciding according to whether the judge or jury thought it "fair and just" to hold the employer liable. Perceptions of fairness vary greatly. The law in consequence would be thrown into a state of uncertainty'.

[29] (2016) 258 CLR 134, 150 (French CJ; Kiefel, Bell, Keane and Nettle JJ).

[30] *Bernard v Attorney General of Jamaica* [2005] IRLR 398, [23]: 'the Board is firmly of the view that the policy rationale on which vicarious liability is founded is not a vague notion of justice between man and man. It has clear limits … the principle of vicarious liability is not infinitely extendable'; *E v English Province of Our Lady of Charity* [2013] QB 722, 780 (Tomlinson J, dissenting).

of clear articulation of precisely when it is that the law should impose strict liability, and when it should impose fault-based liability.

That being acknowledged, it is preferred that the judges actually articulate the basis/bases upon which they will determine whether or not it is 'fair, just and reasonable' to impose vicarious liability upon an employer. In that vein, it is considered laudable that Lord Phillips in *Various Claimants* at least articulated the factors he was considering in determining whether or not it was fair, just and reasonable to impose vicarious liability.[31] The debate is surely most insightful when those particular factors are discussed and analysed. Obviously, fairness, justice and reasonableness are in the eye of the beholder, acknowledging that the law of tort makes extensive use of the concept of 'reasonableness', in particular, elsewhere. To be clear, I do not agree that all of the factors espoused by Lord Phillips are important in determining whether vicarious liability should apply, sharing seeming ambivalence towards them with the United Kingdom Supreme Court,[32] but I applaud the actual articulation of the real basis or bases behind generic phrases like fair, just and reasonable and would prefer that the debate be about the substantive issues underlying that pithy label, rather than about the label itself.

In terms of Lord Phillips' five factors, I have dealt with the first, involving assumptions about deep pockets and insurance, elsewhere. The second, third and fourth all deal essentially with the enterprise risk theory, which I have substantially dealt with above. And the fifth refers to notions of control. As chapter one indicates, this harks back to the 'command and control' theory of vicarious liability which sought to explain some of the early vicarious liability cases, but which has fallen into disfavour.[33]

Control is generally used now in determining whether or not an employment relationship exists, rather than in determining whether or not vicarious liability applies. There is the possibility that the traditional two-stage test in terms of vicarious liability, asking first whether (a) a relationship between the employer and the wrongdoer is such as to attract vicarious liability; and (b) the extent to which an employer is liable for actions of their employees, is effectively being merged into one test. This is considered further in chapter nine.

[31] [2013] 2 AC 1, 15: 'there is no difficulty in identifying a number of policy reasons that usually make it fair, just and reasonable to impose vicarious liability on the employer when these criteria are satisfied: (i) the employer is more likely to have the means to compensate the victim than the employee and can be expected to have insured against that liability, (ii) the tort will have been committed as a result of activity being taken by the employee on behalf of the employer, (iii) the employee's activity is likely to be part of the business activity of the employer, (iv) the employer, by employing the employee to carry on the activity, will have created the risk of the tort committed by the employee, and (v) the employee will to a greater or lesser degree have been under the control of the employer (Lord Phillips, for the Court).

[32] *Cox v Ministry of Justice* (n 13) 669: 'the five factors which Lord Phillips mentioned … are not all equally significant', before criticising particularly the first and fifth.

[33] ibid 669 (Lord Reed).

The concept of fairness and justice is considered to be inherently subjective. Is it fair and just to impose strict liability on an employer for what their employees do? Most especially, is it fair and just to do so when an employee has engaged in criminal action, or otherwise ignored specific instructions from an employer? This is surely a matter on which reasonable minds might differ. Some might consider the unfairness of an injured plaintiff going uncompensated. Others might consider the unfairness of imposing liability, perhaps large, on an employer not shown to be at fault. Who is right? Will it still be fair if the employer cannot afford to pay the damages, or their insurer finds some small print in the policy so they are not liable to indemnify the employer for their loss? Is it still fair if the employer shuts down, causing unemployment and poverty to ex-employees, because it cannot financially honour the judgment against it? A utilitarian might deny the fairness of this, if not others.

There is no easy answer to these questions. This fact suggests to me that the concept of 'fair, just and reasonable' is not likely to be of strong assistance in shedding light on the law of vicarious liability or assisting in the resolution of difficult cases. Cases must be decided on principle, and the result of law disputes should be reasonably predictable and certain. We risk dissolving the law of tort into idiosyncratic, subjective and arbitrary judgements when we make decisions about vicarious liability based on one judge's idea of fairness and justice in a particular case. Fairness and justice are in the eye of the beholder.

Conclusion

Having explained why I do not find any of the main current rationales for the imposition of vicarious liability to be convincing or defensible, it is incumbent upon me to suggest a workable alternative. It is easy to criticise what is, and what others have tried to do. It is much more difficult to construct a workable alternative. I will attempt to do so in the next chapter. First, I must acknowledge that the model I will propose cannot explain every aspect of the current doctrine as it is interpreted and applied in the case law. I doubt that any theory could do so. So this much is readily conceded. Now, in order to be fair and consistent I must acknowledge that one of the criticisms that I made of the enterprise risk theory above was that it demonstrably did not explain many of the existing principles within vicarious liability. Therefore I am acutely aware of the possibility that the same criticism can be levelled at the model that I will proceed to explain and hopefully defend. Am I not criticising another model for precisely the same defect that my model will admittedly have?

Now, if the only criticism that I levelled against the enterprise risk theory was that it did not explain all of the current doctrine, I can understand the difficulty with my proposing an alternative doctrine that will suffer from exactly the same defect. However, I hope I have demonstrated above that the enterprise risk theory suffers from many significant defects, of which its inability to explain current doctrine is merely one. I hope that the model I propose in the next chapter will not suffer from these other defects. In other words, I acknowledge that what I propose will not be perfect, in the sense of explaining all of the existing precedents and principles, a defect it would share with enterprise risk; but I believe it will be an improvement, because it will not suffer from the other defects of that model.

Now it is my hope that, if judges or legislators were to accept my model, we would reform the law in this area in a way that would better reflect my model. So unlike some models or theories that are suggested, it is not my argument that the model I will suggest does explain all existing precedent and principle in this area. Evidently, it will not. Rather, it is hoped to provide a catalyst for reform in this area, to effect rationalisation of principle, and so that the case law will come to reflect the model that I prefer. In essence, the model is not designed, as many academic theories are, to explain what has occurred. Rather, it is future focused, suggesting a better theoretical model for the resolution of such disputes in future, accepting that not everything that has been decided will fit the proposed new regime.

8

Agency Theory

Introduction to Agency Theory of Vicarious Liability

Having criticised the leading theory currently used to justify and defend the imposition of vicarious liability, namely enterprise risk, it is now necessary to suggest what should take its place. It will now be argued that an 'agency' approach to be applied to vicarious liability cases should be taken. This is consistent with the implied command theory of vicarious liability, considering whether it truly can be said that the employee is acting on behalf of their employer and for their purposes. As indicated above, this is still a factor to which courts have regard in determining whether or not vicarious liability exists, whether or not they have expressly adopted an enterprise risk approach to vicarious liability.

In other words, it will ask whether the worker concerned had actual or apparent authority to do the thing for which the engager is now argued to be (vicariously) liable. Here, questions of whether the employee was acting for the employer's purposes and benefit will be crucial—specifically, it will be argued that it is only in such cases that the engager will or should be vicariously liable for the actions or omissions of the relevant worker. Only in such cases can morally blameworthy behaviour be attributed to the employer so as to justify liability.

Several preliminary points must be made about the possible use of agency in the context of an explanation of vicarious liability. First, it is clear that the word 'agency' has been used in the context of many cases dealing with vicarious liability. This includes use by Sir Owen Dixon, perhaps the most revered jurist Australia has produced.[1] Secondly, it is clear that the judges have used that word to mean a range of concepts, such that confusion can easily arise as to precisely what a

[1] *Colonial Mutual Life Assurance Society Limited v Producers and Citizens Co-Operative Assurance Company of Australia Limited* (1931) 46 CLR 31, 49: 'the rule which imposes liability upon a master for the wrongs of his servant committed in the course of his employment is commonly regarded as part of the law of agency: indeed, in our case law the terms principal and agent are employed more often than not although the matter in hand arises upon the relation of master and servant' (Dixon J, as he then was); PS Atiyah, *Vicarious Liability in the Law of Torts* (London, Butterworths, 1967) 102.

particular court means when it uses the concept in this context.[2] Obviously, the concept of 'agency' is also associated with a range of legal principles in its own right. Specifically, the concept of 'agency' can be used to mean:

a. That one person has the authority to enter into legally binding contractual transactions on behalf of another (narrow sense of agency);[3] or
b. That one person is authorised to act on behalf of another (broad sense of agency).[4]

Having acknowledged that, there is extensive reference to notions of 'agency' (concededly, meaning different things and in different contexts) in cases involving vicarious liability. So, for example, in *Barwick v English Joint Stock Bank* Willes J for the court noted:

> The general rule is that the master is answerable for every such wrong of the servant or agent as is committed in the course of the service *and for the master's benefit* (emphasis added), though no express command or privity of the master be proved … it is true, he has not authorised the particular act, but he has put the agent in his place to do that class of acts, and he must be answerable for the manner in which the agent has conducted himself in doing the business which it was the act of his master to place him in.[5]

Members of the Privy Council endorsed these comments.[6] In *Houldsworth v City of Glasgow Bank*, Lord Selborne, referring to the judgment of Willes J noted above,

[2] P Giliker, *Vicarious Liability in Tort: A Comparative Perspective* (Cambridge, Cambridge University Press, 2010) 132: 'it is commonly recognised that a precise definition of the term 'agent' is elusive, if not impossible'.

[3] GE Dal Pont, *Law of Agency*, 2nd edn (Chatswood, NSW, LexisNexis Butterworths, 2008) 5 calls this the narrowest legal definition; eg, Giliker, ibid, 109–10: 'agency renders the principle primarily liable for the actions of his agent within the scope of his authority. It determines the ability of the agent to enter legal transactions on the principal's behalf … as such, agency as a concept is distinct from that of vicarious liability'; C Beuermann, 'Dissociating the Two Forms of So-Called Vicarious Liability' in S Pitel, J Neyers and E Chamberlain (eds), *Tort Law: Challenging Orthodoxy* (Oxford, Hart Publishing, 2013) 468, who defines 'agency' for the purposes of her discussion as someone with the authority to effect *transactional* (my emphasis) legal relations on behalf of another, though she conceded that some courts have used the concept in a broader way.

[4] This is the definition which appears in PG Watts (ed), *Bowstead and Reynolds on Agency*, 19th edn (London, Sweet & Maxwell, 2010): 'Agency is the fiduciary relationship which exists between two persons, one of whom expressly or impliedly manifests assent that the other should act on his behalf so as to affect his relations with third parties, and the other of whom similarly manifests assent so to act'; Dal Pont (n 3) refers to broader definitions of agency, including a person able to create or affect legal rights and duties between a principal and a third party, or has authority to act on behalf of a principal.

[5] *Barwick v English Joint Stock Bank* (1867) LR 2 Ex 259, 265–66 (Willes J, for Blackburn, Keating, Mellor, Montague, Smith and Lush JJ); noted as the 'best definition' by the Privy Council in *Mackay v Commercial Bank of New Brunswick* (1874) LR 5 (PC) 394, 411.

[6] *Mackay v Commercial Bank of New Brunswick*, ibid; *Swire v Francis* (1877) 3 AC 106: 'the master is liable for every such wrong of his servant or agent as is committed in the course of his service, and for the master's benefit … he has put the agent in his place to do that class of acts, and he must be answerable for the manner in which the agent has conducted himself in doing the business which it was the act of his master to place himself in'; *The National Exchange Company v Drew* (1855) 2 Macq 102, 103; *New Brunswick Railway Company v Conybeare* 10 WR 305, 9 HLC 711.

and its subsequent application in later cases, stated that 'it is a principle, not of the law of torts, or of fraud or deceit, but of the law of agency'.[7]

Similar sentiments are evident in *Laugher v Pointer*.[8] There Littledale J noted that 'if a man for his benefit or pleasure employs an agent to conduct any business, such agent is to be looked upon in the same light as if he was the immediate servant of the employer'.[9] Abbott CJ noted that 'whatever is done by his authority is to be considered as done by him'.[10] In *McGowan v Dyer* the court found a company should not be liable for the actions of their managing director 'any more than an ordinary employer would be answerable for the act of his agent not acting within the scope of his authority'.[11]

Further, in *Coleman v Riches* the court considered the possible liability of a master for the acts of their servant.[12] All members of the court expressed these principles in terms of concepts of agency. Jervis CJ stated 'when we find no actual authority in the agent to do the act complained of, we must see whether the facts warrant the inference that in doing it he was acting within the scope of the authority conferred upon him by his general employment'.[13] Cresswell J noted the employee lacked express or implied authority to do what he did, so the employer should not be held liable.[14] Williams J referred to *Story on Agency* to answer the question.[15] Crowder J concluded that the relevant man 'has no right to bind his employer' because he was not acting within the scope of his authority.[16]

All members of the House of Lords referred to notions of agency in the context of vicarious liability in *Lloyd v Grace, Smith and Co*.[17] Specifically, Lord Macnaghten refers to the idea that a 'principal must be liable for the fraud of his agent committed in the course of his agent's employment and not beyond the scope of his agency'.[18] Lord Shaw considered whether the employee agent's authority included within its scope transactions of a particular character.[19]

[7] *Houldsworth v City of Glasgow Bank and Liquidators* (1880) 5 AC 317, 326 (with whom Lord Hatherley agreed).

[8] *Laugher v Pointer* (1826) 5 B & C 547, 553; 108 ER 204.

[9] 108 ER 204, 207.

[10] ibid 215.

[11] *McGowan v Dyer* (1873) LR 8 QB 141, 145 (Blackburn J, for Cockburn CJ, Mellor and Lush JJ). Earlier on the same page, Blackburn J for the Court had quoted *Story on Agency* that 'the general rule is that the principal is liable to third persons in a civil suit for the frauds, deceits, concealements, misrepresentations, torts, negligences and other malfeasances or misfeasances and omissions of duty of his agent in the course of his employment'.

[12] *Coleman v Riches* (1855) 16 CB 104; 139 ER 694.

[13] ibid 118.

[14] ibid 120.

[15] ibid.

[16] ibid 122–23.

[17] *Lloyd v Grace, Smith and Co* [1912] AC 716.

[18] ibid 731 (with whom Lord Atkinson agreed).

[19] ibid 740–41; see similarly Earl Loreburn (724) and Earl of Halsbury (726): 'the principal is liable for the act of his agent in the course of his master's business'.

Other examples of this in non-motor vehicle contexts can be readily cited,[20] and legal historian Ibbetson notes the historical link between agency and vicarious liability.[21]

Bowstead and Reynolds on Agency acknowledges that in the *Lloyd* case the clerk could be more appropriately described as an agent.[22] They reflect more generally on the relation between vicarious liability and agency thus:

> There are various ways in which considerable interrelation with the law of agency exists and these prevent a total separation between agency in contract and vicarious liability in tort … terminologies of master and servant and principal and agent have been and still are readily interchanged: the same applies to the phrases 'course of employment' and 'scope of authority' … there is a further group of tort cases where agency principles seem especially relevant, because it is sought to hold a principal liable for the torts of one who could be called an agent where the normal rules of master and servant and as to independent contractors, might not easily permit of such a result being achieved. In this area, agency reasoning may arguably extend the principal's tort liability.[23]

Dal Pont, referring to the similarities between agency law and vicarious liability, notes:

> These similarities make it unsurprising that courts refer to the vicarious liability of a principal for the wrongful acts or omissions of an agent, and speak in the language of principal and agent in referring to the master–servant relationship. Though in an agency relationship the principal is liable directly as principal as opposed to vicariously, this distinction has been treated as of little practical significance by the case law, being evident from judges' reference to principals as vicariously liable for their agents' acts.[24]

Dal Pont notes, with evident approval, the convergence in the law of agency and law of vicarious liability evidenced in cases such as *Lloyd*, in terms of consistency of principle.[25]

Bowstead and Reynolds on Agency also refers to motor vehicle cases as another category in which agency principles have been utilised in vicarious liability cases.[26] The agency nature of vicarious liability is regularly seen in the so-called 'motor

[20] eg, the question whether the defendant owner of goods was liable for the deceitful actions of the captain of the ship upon which the goods were being transported. The case describes the captain as the 'servant and agent' of the defendant. The court found the defendant was not liable because it was beyond the scope of the captain's authority to sign a bill of lading when the goods had not arrived on the ship: *Grant v Norway* (1851) 10 CB 665; 138 ER 263.

[21] D Ibbetson, *A Historical Introduction to the Law of Obligations* (Oxford, Oxford University Press, 1999), discussing vicarious liability in the earlier common law: 'in so far as lawyers put their minds to it, it could be explained by a theory of identification, treating X's acts as Y's in law, or by a notion of agency' (181).

[22] *Bowstead and Reynolds on Agency* (n 4) 487.

[23] ibid 486–88.

[24] Dal Pont (n 3) 595–96.

[25] ibid 602: 'Consistency in the law, in view of the practical similarities between principal-agent and employer-employee relationships, and the courts' frequent tendency to assimilate the two, can be seen to justify such a convergence'.

[26] *Bowstead and Reynolds on Agency* (n 4) 488.

vehicle' cases where an owner of a vehicle permits another to use their vehicle for the purposes of the owner. So, for example, in *Morgans v Launchbury* Lord Wilberforce noted that:

> In order to fix vicarious liability upon the owner of a car in such a case as the present it must be shown that the driver was using it for the owner's purposes, under delegation of a task or duty … I accept entirely that 'agency' in contexts such as these is merely a concept, the meaning and purpose of which is to say 'is vicariously liable' … the owner ought to pay … because he has authorised the act, or requested it, or because the actor is carrying out a task or duty delegated, or because he is in control of the actor's conduct. He ought not to pay … if he has no control over the actor, has not authorised or requested the act, or if the actor is acting wholly for his own purposes.[27]

Without wishing to place too much emphasis on the word 'ought' above, it can suggest a justification for the imposition of liability like the one suggested here—a person who is in control of the actions of the person doing the wrong is considered sufficiently 'morally blameworthy' to be responsible for the wrong; similarly if the employer authorised or requested that act or delegated its performance to the other.

Some may see in the so-called motor vehicle cases a policy of seeking to find a defendant with appropriate insurance, available to practically fund any compensation ordered. This is evident, for example, in judgments of Lord Denning in this space.[28] However, members of the House of Lords were at pains to reject this reasoning in *Launchbury*, including Lord Pearson who accused Lord Denning of a departure from the agency principle,[29] Lord Cross who said that all questions of insurance should be put 'out of mind',[30] and Lord Salmon who held that such question was 'irrelevant'.[31] I agree with the view of Atiyah that the extent of insurance is determined by the law, not the other way around.[32]

It is often pointed out that the so-called first limb of Salmond's classic statement on vicarious liability, where it is said that an employer is liable for wrongful acts authorised by their master, is not in fact an example of vicarious liability, but rather direct liability.[33] It is probably best seen as an example of agency.

[27] *Morgans v Launchbury* [1973] AC 127, 135; see also *Samson v Aitchison* [1912] AC 844, 850 (Lord Atkinson, for the Privy Council); *Ormrod v Crosville Motor Services Ltd* [1953] 2 All ER 753, 755 (Lord Denning).

[28] [1971] 2 QB 245, 255: 'the reason behind this principle is at bottom the principle which lies behind all vicarious liability … it is to put the responsibility on to the person who ought in justice bear it. Now the owner of the vehicle is in most cases the person who ought to bear the responsibility … he is the one who is, or ought to be, insured in respect of it' (*Launchbury*, CA).

[29] [1973] AC 127, 141–42.

[30] ibid 145.

[31] ibid 150 (five Law Lords decided the case).

[32] Atiyah (n 1) 27.

[33] *Lister and Others v Hesley Hall Ltd* [2002] 1 AC 215, 244 (Lord Millett); M Roberts, 'Tortious Statements, Vicarious Liability and the 'Authority Test'' [2013] *New Zealand Law Review* 625, 647–48.

(Lord Denning appeared to view the *Lloyd* precedent as an example of the operation of agency principles.)[34]

In a series of judgments Lord Wilberforce appeared to draw parallels between agency law and the scope of employment doctrine in terms of vicarious liability. In *Heatons Transport (St Helens) Ltd v Transport and General Workers' Union* he stated:

> No new development is involved in the law relating to the responsibility of a master or principal for the act of a servant or agent. In each case the test to be applied is the same: was the servant or agent acting on behalf of, and within the scope of the authority conferred by, the master or principal.[35]

In *Kooragang Ltd v Richardson and Wrench*, an Australian case heard by the Privy Council, Lord Wilberforce again linked vicarious liability with agency notions.[36]

Kooragang was a fraud case, and this area is one where the courts have recognised significant overlap between notions of vicarious liability and agency.[37] In the leading case of *Armagas Ltd v Mundogas SA*,[38] all members of the Court of Appeal referred to comments by Holt CJ in *Hern v Nichols* that 'seeing somebody must be a loser by this deceit, it is more reason that he that employs and puts a trust and confidence in the deceiver should be a loser than a stranger'.[39] Each of them agreed that the comments were too broadly expressed.[40]

The judges in the Court of Appeal and in the House of Lords made more general observations regarding the interplay between notions of agency and vicarious liability. Goff LJ stated that:

> In cases of fraud at least, involving as they do a representation by the servant in reliance upon which the third party has acted to his detriment, the master can only be vicariously liable for the servant's fraud where he has acted within his ostensible authority (he referred to numerous authorities) ... in other cases the reasoning of the court is consistent only with the proposition that the criterion for the master's vicarious liability is that the servant acted within his ostensible authority.[41]

[34] *Rooke v Viscount Chelmsford* [1965] 1 QB 248, 261 (CA).

[35] *Heatons Transport (St Helens) Ltd v Transport and General Workers' Union* [1973] AC 15, 99; *Kooragang Investments Pty Ltd v Richardson and Wrench Ltd* [1982] AC 462.

[36] *Kooragang Ltd*, ibid, 475 who, concluding that an employer was not liable for their employee's fraudulent valuations, stated that to make the employer, who was completely unaware of the employee's actions, liable for what they did 'would strain the doctrine of vicarious liability beyond the breaking point and in effect introduce into the law of agency a new principle equivalent to one of strict liability'.

[37] eg, *George Whitechurch Ltd v Cavanagh* [1902] AC 117 was decided on the basis of agency principles, although it involved conduct of two individuals, at least one of whom was an employee of the company. In *Uxbridge Permanent Benefit Building Society v Pickard* [1939] 2 KB 248, 254–55 Greene MR referred to the case of 'the servant who goes off on a frolic of his own (where) no question arises of any actual or ostensible authority upon the faith of which some third person is going to change his position'.

[38] *Armagas Ltd v Mundogas SA* [1986] 1 AC 717.

[39] *Hern v Nichols* (1709) 1 Salk 289.

[40] Robert Goff LJ (735); Dunn J (752); and Stephenson J (768).

[41] *Armagas Ltd v Mundogas SA* (n 38) 738.

Other members of the Court of Appeal expressed a similar view.[42] On appeal, Lord Keith for the House of Lords expressed similar views. Lord Keith noted:

> In the present case, so it was maintained, Mr Magelssen was acting in the course of his employment, though not within the scope of his actual or ostensible authority, so Mundogas was liable. In my opinion, the attempted distinction has no validity in this category of case. Lord Macnaghten in *Lloyd v Grace Smith and Co* regarded the two expressions as meaning one and the same thing.[43]

It should be conceded that the decision was in the context of a fraud case. Some judges appear to believe that different rules apply to vicarious liability in the context of fraud cases, compared with vicarious liability in other cases.[44] Some courts have attempted to argue that the tests used in these two types of case, the former involving 'authority' and the other involving close connection, are effectively the same.[45] These suggestions have been rightly criticised by commentators.[46] They are different tests.

On the other hand, the Privy Council in *United Africa Co Ltd v Saka Owoade* stated that no distinction should be drawn in vicarious liability cases between circumstances of fraud and other factual scenarios.[47] Lord Wilberforce's statements connecting agency concepts with scope of employment concepts were not expressly confined to cases of fraud. Atiyah read the judgment of Lord Selborne in *Houldsworth* as denying there was any special rule applicable to cases of fraud.[48] *Bowstead and Reynolds on Agency* argues that, at least in respect of cases of negligent misstatement by the employee, an authority approach, rather than a close connection approach, might be more appropriate in the context of possible vicarious liability for the misstatement.[49]

[42] 'The scope of the ostensible authority defines the course of the employment' (Dunn LJ, 751), and Stephenson LJ agreed with the trial judge that, at least on the facts of that case, the phrases ostensible authority and in the course of employment had the same meaning (768). Stephenson LJ expressly rejected (766) a suggestion by Denning LJ that the existence of actual or ostensible authority indicated that the wrongdoer's actions were within the course of their employment, but that the absence of such authority did not mean the wrongdoer's actions were necessarily outside the course of their employment (*Navarro v Moregrand Ltd* [1951] 2 TLR 674, 677).

[43] *Armagas Ltd v Mundogas SA* (n 38) 781; see, to like effect, *Credit Lyonnais Bank Nederland v Export Credits Guarantee Department* [2000] 1 AC 486, 494.

[44] *Armagas Ltd v Mundogas SA* (n 38) 780; *Bowstead and Reynolds on Agency* (n 4) 493; more recently both an agency and 'scope of employment' approach were taken to considering an employer's liability for their employee's fraud in *Quinn v CC Automotive Group Ltd* [2010] EWCA Civ 1412. For discussion see Roberts (n 33).

[45] *Quinn v CC Automotive Group Ltd*, ibid, [21] and [25] (Gross LJ, with whom Sullivan LJ and Mummery LJ agreed).

[46] P Watt, 'Principals' Tort Liability for Agents' Negligent Statements—Is 'Authority' Necessary?' (2012) 128 *Law Quarterly Review* 260, 274; Roberts (n 33) 634–36.

[47] *United Africa Co Ltd v Saka Owoade* [1955] AC 130, 144: 'there is in their Lordships' opinion no difference in the liability of a master for wrongs whether for fraud or any other wrong committed by a servant in the course of his employment. It is a question of fact in each case whether the wrong was committed in the course of the servant's employment'. The matter was expressly left open in *Frederick & Ors v Positive Solutions (Financial Services) Ltd* [2018] EWCA Civ 431 [77].

[48] Atiyah (n 1) 103.

[49] *Bowstead and Reynolds on Agency* (n 4) 492; such a suggestion finds support in the judgment of Goff LJ in *Armagas Ltd v Mundogas SA* (n 38) 738.

Similarly, in *Credit Lyonnais Nederland v Export Credits Guarantee Department*[50] the House of Lords noted, after referring to a statement on vicarious liability by Blackburn J in *McGowan v Dyer* where he referred to vicarious liability discussion in *Story on Agency*, that:

> This statement makes clear the principle on which vicarious liability depends. It is that the wrong of the servant or agent for which the master or principal is liable is one committed in the case of a servant in the course of his employment, and in the case of an agent in the course of his authority. It is fundamental to the whole approach to vicarious liability that an employer or principal should not be liable for acts of the servant or agent which are not performed within this limitation.[51]

Robert Stevens has suggested that the House of Lords decision in *Lister* may not be consistent with its earlier decision in *Armagas*.[52] He discussed that case in terms again combining vicarious liability with agency concepts.[53]

Similarly, we find liberal use of the concept of 'agency' in the Australian case law. So in *Colonial Mutual Life Assurance*[54] it is conceded that use of the concept of 'agency' is slightly ambiguous in terms of the two meanings above, because the person who committed the wrong (Ridley) for which it was sought to make the insurance company which engaged him liable, was a door-to-door salesman charged with soliciting insurance proposals and accepting premiums, if not making contracts on behalf of the insurance company.[55] Gavan Duffy CJ and Starke J concluded that a principal was liable for acts of their agents within the scope of their authority.[56] Dixon J, with whom Rich J agreed, noted the agent did not have authority to enter into binding contracts on behalf of the company. This would have taken him outside the narrow definition of 'agent' to which reference was made above. Notwithstanding this, Dixon J found the employer liable for Ridley's actions because

> he does not act independently, but as a representative of the company, which accordingly must be considered as itself conducting the negotiation in his person. The rule which

50 [2000] 1 AC 486.

51 ibid 494 (Lord Woolf MR, for the House).

52 R Stevens, *Torts and Rights* (Oxford, Oxford University Pres, 2007) 273, discussing the facts of *Armagas*, explaining that 'whether the statement could be attributed to the company is determined by whether the director had actual or ostensible authority to make it. Whether the company should be vicariously liable for its vice president's deceit should be determined by whether he was acting in the course of his employment' (clearly notions of actual and ostensible authority are agency notions). He refers to the *Armagas* decision as the *Ocean Frost* decision because that was the name of the ship the subject of the dispute; R Stevens, 'Non-Delegable Duties and Vicarious Liability' in J Neyers, E Chamberlain and S Pitel (eds), *Emerging Issues in Tort Law* (Oxford, Hart Publishing, 2007) 363.

53 Finally, a recent example of a United Kingdom judge applying agency concepts in discussing vicarious liability appears in the judgment of Smith LJ in *Maga v Trustees of the Birmingham Archdiocese of the Roman Catholic Church* [2010] EWCA Civ 256, [94]–[95]; P Morgan, 'Recasting Vicarious Liability' (2012) 71 *Cambridge Law Journal* 615, 626–28 notes other decisions in which principals have been found vicariously liable for actions of their agents, other than in the context of fraud and motor vehicles.

54 (1931) 46 CLR 41.

55 ibid 49 (Dixon J).

56 ibid 46.

> imposes liability upon a master for the wrongs of his servant committed in the course of his employment is commonly regarded as part of the law of agency.[57]

In *Deaton Proprietary Ltd v Flew*[58] there is limited support for notions of agency in relation to vicarious liability. The case involved the question of liability of a hotelier for the actions of a barmaid who threw a glass of beer into a customer's face. There Dixon J did not use the word 'agency' but considered whether the barmaid's actions occurred in pursuance of 'the authority the servant is held out as possessing or of the position in which he is placed as a representative of his master'.[59] He repeatedly considered whether the employee's actions were done in purported pursuit of their master's interests.[60] McTiernan J considered the 'authority' and 'implied authority' of hotel employees, in language often associated with agency.[61]

Agency concepts again appear in the context of vicarious liability in the classic motor vehicle liability case of *Soblusky v Egan* where Dixon CJ, Kitto and Windeyer JJ stated:

> The owner or bailee being in possession of the vehicle and with full legal authority to direct what is done with it appoints another to do the manual work of managing it and to do this on his behalf in circumstances where he can always assert his power of control. Thus it means in point of law that he is driving by his agent.[62]

In more modern times in Australia, McHugh J has been a strong advocate of the agency foundation of vicarious liability; other advocates have included Kirby J.[63] In *Lepore* Gaudron J expressly used agency concepts, and other judges perhaps indicated implicit support for their use here.[64] In *Scott v Davis* McHugh J found:

> A principal is also liable for the wrongful acts of an agent where the agent is performing a task which the principal has agreed to perform or a duty which the principal is obliged to perform and the principal has delegated that task or duty to the agent, provided that the agent is not an independent contractor. The principal is also liable for the wrongful acts of a person who is acting on the principal's behalf as a representative and not as an independent principal and within the scope of authority conferred by the principal.[65]

[57] ibid 49.

[58] *Deaton Proprietary Ltd v Flew* (1949) 79 CLR 370.

[59] ibid 381.

[60] ibid 380–81.

[61] ibid 382.

[62] *Soblusky v Egan* (1960) 103 CLR 215, 231.

[63] *Sweeney v Boylan Nominees Pty Ltd* (2006) 226 CLR 161, 186–87.

[64] *State of New South Wales v Lepore* (2003) 212 CLR 511, 560–61; elsewhere in that case, Gummow and Hayne JJ did not expressly support the use of agency concepts, but used language often used in the context of agency—ostensible and apparent authority (594).

[65] *Scott v Davis* (2000) 204 CLR 333, 346; 'a principal is liable for the wrongful act of an agent causing damage to a third party when that act occurred while the agent was carrying out some activity as the principal's authorised representative in a dealing with a third party': *Hollis v Vabu Pty Limited* (2001) 207 CLR 21, 59 (McHugh J). No member of the High Court referred to agency principles in the most recent vicarious liability pronouncement in *Prince Alfred College v ADC* [2016] HCA 37.

Agency notions have also underpinned New Zealand decisions on the liability of government and religious providers for abuse committed on children by other organisations entrusted with their care.[66]

Notions of vicarious liability as being agency based may be implicit in cases which have found that an employer was not vicariously liable for actions of the employee that the employer lacked legal power to do. For example, the court in *Poulton v London and South Western Railway Company* found that an employer could not be vicariously liable for what their employee did, because the employer lacked the legal power to do it.[67] This has obvious parallels with a principle of agency law, that the agent's powers are co-extensive with those of the principal.

I also derive support for an agency-based approach from the numerous references in the vicarious liability case law, which exist from the earliest times and which continue to be made in the 2016 decision in *Cox v Ministry of Justice* and the 2017 decision in *Armes v Nottinghamshire County Council*,[68] to questions of whether the relevant worker was doing work for the benefit of, or for the purposes of, their employer. This fit makes sense for at least two reasons. First, if *Bowstead and Reynolds on Agency* refer to an agent as someone who acts 'on behalf' of another, this is considered to be equivalent to saying that the person is working for the benefit of the other, and for their purposes. It would be much more difficult to say that someone was acting on behalf of another when they were not working to further the purposes of the employer and/or were acting for personal advantage, and not for the benefit of the employer. Thus, for example, in the important decision of *Turberville v Stampe* Holt CJ, often seen as the leading developer of vicarious liability in that period, notes that 'it shall be intended that the servant had authority from his master, it being for his master's benefit'.[69]

I read this as an affirmation that *because* the actions were for the master's benefit, the servant had the required authority. As discussed in chapter one, the notion of whether the worker was acting for the master's purposes and for their benefit has been repeatedly considered in case law, such as *William v Jones*,[70] *Stone v Cartwright*,[71] *Laugher v Pointer*,[72] *Duncan v Findlater*,[73] *Limpus v London General Omnibus Company*,[74] *British Mutual Banking Company Limited*,[75]

[66] *S v Attorney-General* [2003] NZCA 149; *A v Roman Catholic Archdiocese of Wellington* [2008] NZCA 49.

[67] *Poulton v London and South Western Railway Company* (1867) 2 QB 534.

[68] *Cox v Ministry of Justice* [2016] AC 660; *Armes v Nottinghamshire County Council* [2017] 3 WLR 1000.

[69] *Turberville v Stampe* (1698) 1 Ld Raym 264; 91 ER 1072.

[70] *Williams v Jones* (1865) 3 H & C 602, 612; 159 ER 668, 672.

[71] *Stone v Cartwright* (1795) 6 TR 411, 413; 101 ER 622, 623.

[72] (1826) 5 B & C 546, 554; 108 ER 204, 207.

[73] *Duncan v Findlater* (1839) 6 Cl & F 894, 910; 7 ER 934, 940.

[74] *Limpus v London General Omnibus Company* (1862) 1 H & C 526, 537, 540, 541 and 543; 158 ER 993, 997–99.

[75] *British Mutual Banking Company Limited v Charnwood Forest Railway Company* (1887) 18 QBD 714 (CA).

Dyer v Munday,[76] *Croft v Alison*,[77] *Wheatley v Patrick*,[78] *Cheshire v Bailey*[79] and *Ruben v Great Fingall Consolidated*.[80] It appeared in a Privy Council decision in 1988.[81] It was referred to again in 2016 in *Cox v Ministry of Justice*[82] and in 2017 in *Armes v Nottinghamshire County Council*.[83] As has been acknowledged above, the House of Lords decision in *Lloyd v Grace, Smith and Co* apparently jettisoned such a requirement in order that vicarious liability could apply,[84] a decision which I have criticised above. And clearly in *Cox*, 104 years later, the United Kingdom Supreme Court is still referring to it as being relevant.

Atiyah reaches a position similar to the one I favour in this passage:

> ((A)s to) whether the master's authority can be implied for an act which is done solely in the servant's own interests the answer is likely to be, in most cases, no. But the reason for this is not that a permitted act is not an authorised act for the law of vicarious liability, but that, in the nature of things, the master's permission for the servant to perform acts entirely for his own purposes is not lightly to be implied.[85]

Some theoretical support for conditioning liability on evidence that the employee was acting for the purposes of the employer appears in the work of Ernest Weinrib. Weinrib favours a system of corrective, rather than distributive, justice. Relatedly, at least in my mind, he favours a fault-based negligence system of liability rather than a system of strict liability. One of the reasons he favours the fault-based system is that it recognises and respects what he calls an individual's (in this context, the employer's) 'capacity for purposiveness':

> The injurer can be liable only for action that flows from the capacity for purposiveness. Such action characterizes the injurer's status as an agent, and differentiates the injurer from an irresponsible force of nature … because the standing of the plaintiff is a reflection of the agency that both litigants embody, the complaint cannot demand a judgment on action that renders action illegitimate. Liability implies that what the defendant did was inconsistent with the plaintiff's equal status as an agent. The point of an award of damages is to vindicate the moral dimensions of agency by undoing those acts that cannot coexist with the agency of others. An agent therefore ought not to be held liable merely for being active. Strict liability however implies that the very production of external effects—an indispensable part of agency—can itself be a violation of the equality of

[76] *Dyer v Munday* [1895] 1 QB 742, 747.
[77] *Croft v Alison* (1821) 4 B & Ald 589; 106 ER 1052.
[78] *Wheatley v Patrick* (1837) 2 M & W 649; 150 ER 917.
[79] *Cheshire v Bailey* [1905] 1 KB 237, 245.
[80] *Ruben v Great Fingall Consolidated* [1906] AC 439, 446.
[81] *General Engineering Services v Kingston Corp* [1988] 3 All ER 867, 870 (Lord Ackner, for the Council).
[82] [2016] AC 660, 672 (Lord Reed, for the Court).
[83] [2017] 3 WLR 1000, 1018 (Lord Reed) (with whom Baroness Hale, Lord Kerr and Lord Clarke agreed) (quoting with evident approval an extract from *Cox* in which the benefit principle is discussed).
[84] [1912] AC 716.
[85] Atiyah (n 1) 195, adding that 'permission will be much more readily implied for an act which is performed in the master's interests or supposed interests than for an act which is solely in the servant's interests'.

> agents. The difficulty with this is that precisely because action has effects, those effects cannot in themselves constitute the plaintiff's case. Effects are merely the fruition of activity. To ascribe liability to an action, regardless of culpability, for whatever harmful effects it has had simply because they are its effects, is to hold the agent liable for being active. In judging action by its effects, strict liability treats the defendant's agency as an incoherent normative phenomenon. On the one hand, strict liability regards the effect as integral to the defendant's action (otherwise, the defendant would not be held liable); on the other hand, because the effect is not the outcome of culpability, its link to the defendant's action consists solely in its being an effect. Thus the act turns out to be wrongful … because of the effect that completes the action. The agent is conceded a capacity for purposiveness that, when harm occurs, turns out to have been morally incapable of being exercised and therefore to have been no capacity at all.[86]

It is acknowledged that on occasion it can be difficult to discern whose interests or purposes the employee's actions were designed to further. It is submitted that the test could only be applied in an objective way—what does the objective evidence suggest as to the purposes of the employee in the particular case? It would not be a matter of the employee stating what their purpose was. So, to argue from the extreme, say that an employee shot a customer who was being particularly difficult and holding other customers up. The employer could not be held vicariously liable for this violence on the basis that the employee bizarrely believed that he or she was acting for the benefit of the employer in getting the waiting line moving by resorting to such extreme measures. This is a simple example, but in my mind it reaffirms that an objective, rather than a subjective, assessment must be made as to whether the employee was relevantly acting for the purposes and benefit of the employer in order to determine whether or not the latter is liable for the actions of the former.

Consideration of the purposes of the employee and whether they were acting for the benefit of their employer fits nicely into another principle relevant to vicarious liability, namely 'frolic'. The concept of frolic appeared originally in the vicarious liability context in the decision of *Joel v Morison*.[87] There the question arose of the liability of the owner of a horse and cart. Their servant had driven the horse and cart in such a manner as to collide with and injure the plaintiff. There was evidence that the course of the employee's employment required travel only between two particular areas; but the accident occurred in a different area. Baron Parke stated that 'if (the employee) was going on a frolic of his own, without being at all on his master's business, the master will not be liable'.[88] This approach was applied to various journey cases where the worker was deemed to have abandoned their employer's business and embarked on business of their own.[89] For instance

[86] E Weinrib, *The Idea of Private Law* (Oxford, Oxford University Press, 2012) 181–82.

[87] *Joel v Morison* (1834) 6 C & P 501; 172 ER 1338.

[88] ibid 504; 1339.

[89] *Storey v Ashton* (1869) LR 4 QB 476; *Chester v Bailey* [1905] 1 KB 237 (two members of the Court of Appeal in *Morris v CW Martin and Sons Ltd* [1966] 1 QB 716 doubted whether *Chester* remained good law after Lloyd (735 (Lord Diplock) and 739 (Lord Salmon)).

in *Storey v Ashton* Cockburn CJ noted that the employee 'started on an entirely new and independent journey which had nothing at all to do with his employment'.[90] This removed the possibility that their employer could be vicariously liable for what they did. This position was adopted by the United States courts.[91]

While the concept of 'frolic' has typically been applied to cases where the employee physically deviates from a journey for the purposes of the employer, it can and should also be applied in a more abstract way to cases where the employee deviates from the purposes of the employer, to a purpose of their own. This explains sentiments expressed in cases like *Limpus v London General Omnibus Company*,[92] where for instance Blackburn J explains that the employer would not be liable for actions of an employee committed as a result of private spite, rather than for the employer's purposes.[93] Though Blackburn J does not use the word 'frolic' to explain such a situation, it is similar to the journey cases in that it is a departure from the confines of the employment, and the furtherance of the purposes of the employer.

The concept of frolic continues to be applied in assessing whether or not vicarious liability applies in a given case.[94] On the other hand, some say the fact that an employee was motivated by personal spite is irrelevant in determining vicarious liability issues.[95] There is certainly potential for the 'frolic' doctrine to play a much more pivotal role in the law of vicarious liability than it has to date. Specifically, for instance, it might be argued that where the employee is acting out of anger and not for any purpose of their employer, they are, in essence, on a 'frolic'. The fact they are on a frolic means their employer is not generally legally responsible for what they have done. In other words, notions of 'frolic' can and should be used in contradistinction to a situation where an employee is acting for their employer's benefit and for their purposes.

Now of course, it is possible to link these notions of 'benefit of the employer' and 'purposes of the employer' to enterprise risk theory. This appears most recently in the United Kingdom Supreme Court in *Armes v Nottinghamshire County Council*:

> The most influential idea in modern times has been that it is just that an enterprise which takes the benefit of activities carried on by a person integrated into its organisation

[90] *Storey v Ashton*, ibid, 478.

[91] *Standard Oil Co v Anderson* 212 US 215, 221 (1909): 'the master's responsibility cannot be extended beyond the limitations of the master's work. If the servant is doing his own work or that of some other, the master is not answerable for his negligence in the performance of it'; see YB Smith, 'Frolic and Detour' (1923) 23 *Columbia Law Review* 444.

[92] (1862) 1 H & C 526; 158 ER 993.

[93] ibid 543; 1000; see similarly *Power v Central SMT Co Ltd* [1949] SLT 302, 302 (Lord President).

[94] *Graham v Commercial Bodyworks Ltd* [2015] EWCA Civ 47.

[95] Atiyah (n 1), criticising a Scottish decision which found an employer would not be liable for actions of an employee which were motivated by personal spite (199), and claiming that 'common sense and common experience suggest that ... the deviating or frolicsome servant should always render his master liable' (255); *Daniels v Whetstone Entertainments Ltd* [1962] 2 Lloyd's Rep 1, 10: 'the fact that an act is a private act of vengeance by itself is insufficient to protect the employer from liability if the act is one which takes place in the course of the employee's employment. The fact that the act may be the

should also bear the cost of harm wrongfully caused by that person in the course of those activities.[96]

On the other hand, it may be argued that the employer only obtains the benefit of activities carried on by a person integrated into the organisation to the extent that the person carries on activities in furtherance of the employer's interests. In no sensible way could it be argued that an employee's assault of a customer (*Mohamud*) or an employee's sexual abuse of a child (*Various Claimants, Lister*) is for the benefit of the employer and in furtherance of their interests. In my view, this type of behaviour fits much better within the description of a frolic. The employee is acting for their own personal ends. They do not have the employer's interests in mind when they are committing assault and/or abuse. This is purely for their own personal gratification. On this view, the employer should not be vicariously liable for such activity. Yet, in applying the enterprise risk approach, the United Kingdom Supreme Court found that it was.

We currently have the unsatisfactory situation where the courts seem to continue to refer to the issue of whether the employee was acting for the purposes of their employer and for their benefit in considering vicarious liability cases. However, even when the employee is demonstrably not acting for the purposes of the employer, for instance assaulting customers or abusing children, they are still being held vicariously liable for such conduct.

The other type of case where one would expect the question of whether the employee was relevantly acting for the purposes and the benefit of the employer would be in cases involving specific employer instructions that were not complied with. An early example of this scenario is *Limpus v London General Omnibus Company*,[97] which is worthy of more detailed consideration.

The case involved a defendant omnibus company. The company had specifically directed its drivers not to obstruct another omnibus. Contrary to these instructions, an employee driver deliberately drove across the road in front of an omnibus owned by a rival company, thereby causing damage to the plaintiff. The plaintiff sued the defendant company, arguing they were vicariously liable for the driver's actions. The defendant argued it was not liable because the driver had ignored specific instructions not to do what they did. A jury had found in favour of the plaintiff, and the court dismissed an appeal from the jury's finding. I will not consider some of the reasoning of the majority which is open to critique—for instance, the observation of Willes J that 'there ought to be a remedy against some person capable of paying damages to those injured by improper driving',[98] because I have criticised such deep pockets reasoning elsewhere.

result of a desire for vengeance or is an act of spite on the part of the employee is, I think, irrelevant if on the true view of the facts the act is done in the course of the employer's employment' (Harman LJ).

[96] [2017] UKSC 60, [67].

[97] (1862) 1 H & C 526; 158 ER 993.

[98] ibid 539; 998 (Willes J).

Issue may also be taken with the statement by Willes J that 'the law is not so futile as to allow a master, by giving secret instructions to his servant, to discharge himself from liability'. In the immediate sentence that followed, Willes J concluded that 'therefore I consider it immaterial that the defendants directed their servant not to do the act'.[99] It seems with respect that Willes J would view dimly an attempt by an employer to limit their liability to third parties by appropriately wording the employee's terms of engagement. But it is not entirely clear why. Elsewhere, the law allows disclaimers and exclusion clauses. The law recognises the concept of limited liability in companies, permitting entrepreneurs to limit their liability to shareholders, creditors and other third parties. Individuals might well deal with shelf companies, or shell companies, so that if the individual had a legal claim against such company, it may in reality be of little use because of the company structure. The individual may not have known of all details of the company structure when they contracted with them. Would Willes J view company law as futile in permitting this structuring of affairs?

Now in *Limpus*, the court accepted the finding of the jury that the driver was acting for their master's purposes and for their benefit. Blackburn J for instance, as explained above, indicated that if the jury had found the employee had been acting out of personal spite, it would have found for the defendant. The majority seemed to dismiss as irrelevant the fact that the employer had specifically told the employee not to do what he did, Willes J claiming that fact was immaterial.[100]

The dissentient, Wightman J, considered the matter more fully. He noted the employee's actions were not in prosecution of the master's business. It was not part of the employment to obstruct or hinder competitors' omnibuses—Wightman J stated, 'on the contrary, he was directed not to do so'. For Wightman J, the fact that an employee wilfully disobeyed directions from an employer took the employee's actions beyond the scope of employment. Wightman J departed from the majority by stating he

> cannot consider the express prohibition to the coachman to do what he did as immaterial in considering what was the course of his service in that respect ... this cannot ... be considered as an act done in the course of his service, even though the coachman might think that it was for his master's interest by such wrongful means to obstruct the business of the other omnibus.[101]

Obviously, Wightman J's comments support the point made above, that the issue of whether the employee's conduct was in their master's interest and for their purposes must be applied in an objective, rather than subjective, sense.

While Wightman J was the sole dissentient, Crompton J confessed he was first inclined to the position of Wightman J and had he heard the matter afresh rather

[99] ibid.

[100] ibid; to like effect Byles J (541; 999) and Blackburn J (543; 1000). Crompton J agreed with the trial judge though he expressed considerable doubt and opined that if the matter had come to the court afresh, rather than from a jury trial, he may have sided with the dissentient Wightman J (538; 998).

[101] (1862) 1 H & C 526, 536; 158 ER 993, 997.

than hearing an appeal from a jury finding, he may have found as Wightman J had. With respect, I find the reasoning of Wightman J much more cogent. I have criticised aspects of the reasoning of the majority.

The precedent having been set, it was followed by a majority of the Court of Appeal in *Rose v Plenty*.[102] There the employer had specifically forbidden an employee from using children to assist with their duties. Contrary to that express prohibition, an employee engaged a 13-year-old child to assist with milk deliveries. In the course of doing that work, the 13-year-old was injured due to the employee's negligent driving. The question was whether the employer was vicariously liable for their employee's negligence. By a majority of 2:1, the Court found that it was.

Lord Denning MR in the majority relied on the *Limpus* precedent, explaining that case as one where

> the employers were held liable because the injury resulted from an act done by the driver in the course of his service and for his masters' purposes. The definitive point was that it was not done by the servant for his own purposes, but for his masters' purposes.[103]

With respect, it is difficult to accept that an act which was specifically forbidden by the employer could be held to be for the employer's purposes. Similarly, Scarman LJ was satisfied the employee here was acting for the master's purposes. He distinguished between limits on the sphere of employment, and prohibitions dealing only with conduct within the sphere of employment.[104] He concluded the prohibition here was of the latter kind. He concluded the sphere of employment was not affected by the express instructions not to sub-contract the work out. He also appeared to channel the conception of Lord Brougham in *Duncan v Findlater* of an employer being liable because they 'set something in motion'.[105]

The law elsewhere permits individuals to manage and minimise their risk. The whole notion of contracts involves parties' decisions about the allocation of risks. Thus, the law generally permits parties to bargain about liability. It allows parties to limit risk. Specifically, for centuries entrepreneurs have been aided and abetted by the law, company law, in limiting risk. That is the whole purpose of a company structure. The obvious question is why does the law permit parties to manage risk through contracts, and to limit or remove risk through company structures, but baulks at such efforts in relation to vicarious liability? Why is an employer not free to bargain with their employee, by in effect saying to them that these are the parameters of our contractual working arrangement? These are the limits. If you go outside those limits, you may well be personally liable

[102] *Rose v Plenty* [1976] 1 WLR 141.

[103] ibid 143.

[104] ibid 149.

[105] (1839) 6 Cl & F 894, 910; *Rose v Plenty* (n 102) 147: 'it is a case in which the employer, having put matters into motion, should be liable if the motion that he has originated leads to damage to another' (Scarman LJ).

for what you have done, but I will not be. Why is such a bargain wrong in policy or principle?

Pragmatism and Principle

Crucially, this distinguishes the agency approach from the 'enterprise risk' approach or the 'close connection' approach. Employers have been found vicariously liable for intentional criminal actions of employees on the basis of the enterprise risk theory and its association with distributive justice (*Mohamud*); they have also been found liable for such actions on the basis that they are 'closely connected' with what the employee was engaged to do (*Bazley*, *Various Claimants*). In contrast, an approach focusing on whether the actions or omissions of the employee were committed for the employer's benefit and for their purposes, applied objectively, is expected to significantly narrow the scope for such liability, it being confined to cases where there is a need for corrective justice.

How can such an approach be intellectually justified, quite apart from its historical basis, and its support in the case law? We start with the fundamental legal premise that one person is generally not liable for actions or omissions of another. Individuals are generally personally responsible for their own actions or omissions, but not those of others. Any exceptions to this principle must be thoroughly justified. In my mind, A should only be liable for the actions or omissions of B where it is justified to impute their consequences to A. When is it so justified?

It might be justified to impute them to A when legally it is *their* act, not the act of B, or in circumstances where the law should treat B's act for liability purposes as if it were A's act. It might be legally their act (A's act), or it might be that the law should treat it liability-wise as if it were, where they have authorised it, in a broad sense. In such circumstances, the law can coherently call it their action, and not B's action, or can treat it for the purposes of liability as if it were their action.

Here we might draw on concepts of delegation of responsibility—that A is liable where they have delegated responsibility to do a particular thing to B, and in the course of that delegation, a third party suffers injury. But the delegation must be carefully limited so that it can reasonably be said that B's actions or omissions are legally those of A, or that they ought to be liable for them as if they were, because A has authorised them. Just as A would be legally liable if they committed the actions themselves, so they are liable for actions of B that they have authorised (in a general, broad sense) to be done on their behalf and in their name.

One is tempted to resort to notions of fairness, that A is only liable for the actions or omissions of B where it is fair to do so. But what does 'fairness' mean in this context? It is a fraught concept, given its inherent subjectivity. Clearly, broader imposition of vicarious liability in recent decisions is said to be based on principles of 'fairness'. It is clear that the concept of fairness could be used to justify a range of views as to the scope of vicarious liability principles. I have explained above in chapter seven my disagreement with the 'fair, just and reasonable' approach to a finding of vicarious liability.

Perhaps, rather than fairness, it is more accurate to say that the law of tort should not impose liability on a person or organisation that is not morally blameworthy for the injury caused to the plaintiff. The view might be that an employer is only *morally blameworthy* for actions or omissions they have *authorised*. And authorised here is used in the broad 'implied command' sense of the eighteenth century—that an action does not need to be expressly authorised by the master. It is sufficient that the act was (objectively) considered as being done by the employee for the employer's benefit and purposes and is within the scope of activity that the employee was engaged to perform. Now, notions of moral blameworthiness here connect vicarious liability with its original conception in the criminal law and reflect the historical links more broadly between crime and tort. Of course, morality plays a pivotal part in tort law, most clearly shown by the centrality of the 'neighbour' principle underpinning the vast terrain of the law of negligence, and its description by Lord Atkin in the *Donoghue* decision.

Comparisons with crime and tort will bear a little more analysis. I have written elsewhere on the issue of whether a substantive view ought to be taken of the criminal law, suggesting limits on the types of behaviour which a legislature might make criminal, or whether a procedural view should be taken, such that the legislature could in theory make anything it wished criminal. Specifically, I canvassed the suggestion that the legislature could only criminalise activity that reached a certain minimum level of 'moral blameworthiness': in other words, that criminal law had a substantial inherent content, and was not just an empty vessel in which legislatures might 'pour' anything it wished. This analysis drew on decisions such as *R v Director of Public Prosecutions; Ex Parte Kebilene*.[106] I noted concern there with legislatures criminalising conduct that was not 'sufficiently morally blameworthy'.[107]

The same concern, though at a lesser level, might exist in the law of tort, given their shared history and partly shared current goals. The law of tort should not make liable someone who is not morally blameworthy. An employer who employs someone to do something and tells them not to do it in a particular way, should not be liable if the employee in fact does it in that way, causing injury to another. They are not morally blameworthy. Responsibility for the action of the wrongdoer should not be attributed to them. They have done nothing that the law of tort needs to correct. This clearly does, in turn, raise the question of the proper role of the law of tort itself, and the comparison between corrective justice and distributive justice/efficient loss distribution, and the place of strict liability in the law of tort.

[106] *R v Director of Public Prosecutions; Ex Parte Kebilene* [2000] 2 AC 326.

[107] A Gray, *Presumption of Innocence in Peril: A Comparative Critical Perspective* (Lanham, MD, Lexington Books, 2017) 111–16.

In my view this is the sense of vicarious liability espoused by Willes J for all members of the Court in *Barwick* to which reference was made above. In particular, that judgment emphasised the liability of an engager for the wrongs of agents committed for the benefit of the engager, because the engager 'put the agent in his place to do the acts'. It is neatly reflected in the maxim *qui facit per alium facit per se* (he who acts through another does the act himself).[108] This *perhaps* should be rephrased as 'treated by the law as if they did the act themselves, rather than that they did the act themselves. This debate will be elaborated upon further below. It derives some support also from the so-called 'motor vehicle' cases where findings that an owner of a vehicle is in some circumstances liable for the driving of someone to whom they delegated responsibility are based on notions of agency.[109] These notions have proven to be quite workable.[110]

Adoption of this approach should mean that A is no longer responsible for criminal actions of B that they did not authorise and would never have authorised if asked. In other words, cases where clearly B was not acting for the benefit or purposes of A. A (an employer) would not be liable for tortious acts of an employee (B) which they had specifically prohibited, for instance. In such cases, in no coherent sense is B acting in an authorised way. B's actions are not those of A, and A should not be liable for them as if they were. A is not morally blameworthy. Yet, according to current vicarious liability law as applied in jurisdictions such as the United Kingdom and Canada, at least, employers are routinely being found responsible for such actions. This means (to me) that notions of enterprise risk and close connection test, or 'fair and reasonable', are not leading to outcomes that

[108] Atiyah (n 1) discusses this theory of vicarious liability in the context of the nine rationales for vicarious liability referred to (disparagingly) by Baty. Atiyah notes: 'the master and servant are identified: the act of the servant is the act of his master: *qui facit per alium facit per se*. These are all ways of saying the same thing, and they have all been put forward at one time or another in justification of vicarious liability. Baty dismissed the whole argument as an "inane fiction" and most modern writers follow suit. Nevertheless, it might be unwise to dismiss this out of hand as Baty did': Atiyah, ibid, 19. Atiyah noted that the law, including corporate law, was prepared to treat an association of persons as one whole, including those operating through a corporate structure. He expressed apparent agreement with the conclusion reached by Glanville Williams that 'the notion of group unity is a powerful reason for the general acceptance of vicarious liability' (G Williams, 'Vicarious Liability and the Master's Indemnity' (1957) 20 *Modern Law Review* 220, 234).

[109] Atiyah (n 1) 128: 'it is now clear that the true question in all these cases is whether the driver is driving as the agent of the owner at the time when the negligence occurs'.

[110] Giliker (n 2) criticises the use of the concept of 'representative agent', which McHugh J used to describe situations where an engager would be liable for the actions of an agent. He appeared to use this as a third concept of worker, apart from an employee or independent contractor. Giliker says that this concept 'is incapable of providing greater clarity than the composite test'. I don't use the concept of agency as a third category in contrast with employees and independent contractors, as McHugh J does. This partly meets Giliker's criticism that McHugh J's concept of representative agent relies on concepts such as direction, control and resources which overlap the existing distinction between employees and independent contractors (133). This criticism cannot apply here, because I am not proposing a 'third category', so the criticism of overlap cannot be made. And I must respectfully disagree with Giliker's suggestion that agency concepts will add to the confusion (132–33), though I concede that clear exposition of what agency means in this context is essential, and that it is important to be careful in phrasing to avoid confusion.

are intellectually defensible. They are wrongly focused on distributive justice, as opposed to corrective justice, and even if a goal of distributive justice is intellectually defensible, the ability of vicarious liability to achieve or assist to achieve such goals is questionable anyway, for the reasons indicated in chapter six.

Now, some will argue that if the actions of B are really considered to be those of A, because B is carrying out authorised tasks for the benefit of A, that this is really not vicarious liability at all, but direct liability.[111] The response is that I would not object to a change in terms. It may mean that what we currently think of as a principle of tort law, namely vicarious liability, is in future thought of as a branch of the law of agency, as indeed it once was, and sometimes still is. It will be necessary to clarify a position regarding whether the master's tort theory or the servant's tort theory is the preferable conceptual approach to this area, or whether neither should be adopted. There is clearly some case law support for both, though most courts accept the latter is correct. Often the outcome will be the same.

This would also counter the objection of some that the concept of 'morally blameworthy' is inapt in relation to vicarious liability, because demonstrably it is a notion of strict liability, explaining the imposition of liability on an organisation that is demonstrably not at fault. Such adherents might argue it is incongruent to use a concept of 'moral blameworthiness' upon a doctrine that is unabashedly strict and no-fault in nature. They might ask why the concept of moral blameworthiness matters at all, when the liability is not fault based.

My answer is simply that the law should not impose liability upon a person or an organisation that is not at fault. I did not believe that the criminal law should impose liability upon someone who is not guilty of wrongdoing. Similarly, I do not believe that the civil law should impose liability upon someone who is not guilty of wrongdoing. In my view liability, whether criminal or civil, should only be visited upon a person or organisation that is proven to have done something that the law requires be addressed—punished, rehabilitated, compensated. A no-fault, strict liability doctrine of vicarious liability demonstrably does not do this, casting the net of liability far wider to capture employers who are entirely innocent of wrongdoing. The law risks losing its moral force when it ensnares the innocent.

I do believe that there are some actions of employees that should make their employers legally liable and accountable. However, the range of such actions at present is much too broad in the law. It must be narrowed substantially to ensnare only employers who are themselves morally blameworthy. They are morally blameworthy because they authorised, expressly or implicitly, the employee to commit a wrong. They are liable to that extent, and only to that extent. They are not liable for unauthorised employee actions. In such cases, they are not morally blameworthy. There is nothing for the law to correct.

[111] Atiyah (n 1) 105: 'liability for authorised conduct is not, of course, vicarious liability at all'; Giliker (n 2) 132: 'a true agency relationship imposes primary, not vicarious, liability on the principal for the actions of his agent'.

When an employer's liability for the actions of their employees is posited in such a way, arguments that it is incoherent to consider issues such as 'moral blameworthiness' in the context of a strict liability doctrine melt away. This is because employers are only liable where they are at fault, because they have authorised an action that is recognised by the law as a tort. I have no difficulty with the argument that this is not 'true vicarious liability'—so much may be conceded. The employer's liability for the actions of their employees should be reconceptualised as an instance of the law of agency, of direct liability, rather than vicarious liability.

There is another important matter to be resolved. Specifically, it must be determined whether (a) the *actual actions* of the agent are imputed to the employer, or whether (b) it is *responsibility* for the actions of the agent that is imputed to the employer. There is also debate as to whether only (a) is compatible with notions of agency, or whether (b) can be as well. In other words, is it inevitable that in the case of a person described as an agent, that their actions are imputed to their principal? Or is it possible that in the circumstances of a person described as an agent, it is not their actions per se that are imputed to the principal, but (merely) liability for them?

This distinction may be important in the context of insurance and the possibility of punitive damages, an issue considered separately in chapter eleven. As previously stated, this is not to suggest that the law should be dictated to by mandates of insurance. I do not believe that the law should be determined by questions of insurance, as already stated.[112] Specifically, what is meant here is that the existence of insurance means this issue must be resolved. As Merkin and Steele point out, the employer is likely to have an insurance policy. It is likely to contain exclusion clauses, circumstances in which the insurer is not liable to indemnify the insured. Such a clause may well include wrongdoing on the part of the insured.

Thus, it can become important as to whether, under the theory proposed here, (a) the actual employer is deemed to have committed the wrong or, in the alternative, (b) whether they simply assume the responsibility for the act of the agent as if it were their own, as Kitto J put it in *Darling Island Stevedoring and Lighterage Co Ltd v Long*.[113] As has been noted, in many cases it will make no difference to the result in that the employer will be liable either way. However, it will or may make a difference in terms of matters peripheral to vicarious liability.

For instance, it is likely that the employer has an insurance policy which indemnifies them for various losses, including losses caused by their employees. However, it might create an exception for wrongs committed by the insured. Thus, the question of whether the employee's wrongful act is itself deemed to be the act

[112] J Stapleton, 'Tort, Insurance and Ideology' (1995) 58 *Modern Law Review* 820; for a contrasting view see R Merkin and J Steele, *Insurance and the Law of Obligations* (Oxford, Oxford University Press, 2013) 204–05.

[113] *Darling Island Stevedoring and Lighterage Co Ltd v Long* (1957) 97 CLR 36, 61 (with whom Taylor J agreed).

of the employer, the insured, becomes important. A position that the employer is deemed to have committed the wrongful act may preclude the employer from relying on their insurance policy, given the exclusion. Further, the distinction may impact on the question whether an employer is liable for aggravated or exemplary damages for the actions of their agent, and the extent to which the insurance policy excludes payment for such. This is further considered in chapter eleven. To clarify, it is not considered that adoption of the moral blameworthiness rationale is necessarily inconsistent with either option (a) or (b) above.

(a) Argument that the Act of the Agent (Employee) is in Effect the Act of the Principal (Employer)

First, it should be noted that there is support from agency scholars for the view that, where an agency relationship exists, acts of the agent (at least, those within authority) are deemed to be the acts of the principal. *Bowstead and Reynolds on Agency* takes this position. It refers to an agency relationship involving the power of one person to effect legal relations of another person with a third person through authorised acts. These acts are 'in some respects treated as the principal's acts'.[114] Dal Pont makes this observation strongly. In referring to various definitions of agency, after noting the narrow definition involving a person empowered to create legal relations between principal and third parties, he continues:

> A broader conception covers 'a person who is able, by virtue of the authority conferred upon him, to create or affect legal rights and duties as between another person, who is called his principal, and third parties'. Wider again is the characterisation of an agent as a 'person who has authority to act on behalf of a principal, either generally or in respect of some particular act or matter'. Each of these definitions recognise agency as giving effect to the maxim qui facit per alium facit per se—a person who acts through another is deemed to act in person.[115]

There is substantial historical support for the view that where vicarious liability applies, the act of the wrongdoing employee is deemed to be the act of the employer.[116] Pollock and Maitland succinctly state that 'the man who commands a trespass, which is committed in obedience to his command, is himself a trespasser'.[117] It is apparent in the decision of Holt CJ in *Middleton v Fowler*, and its reference to the act of the servant being considered as the act of the master.[118] It is apparent in other cases such as *Lane v Cotton*,[119] *Ackworth v Kempe*,

[114] *Bowstead and Reynolds on Agency* (n 4) 1-003; 1-005.
[115] Dal Pont (n 3) 5.
[116] M Bacon, *A New Abridgement of the Law: Volume I*, 5th edn (London, A Strahan, 1798) 583.
[117] F Pollock and FW Maitland, *The History of English Law Volume 2 Before the Time of Edward I* (Cambridge, Cambridge University Press, 1895) 470.
[118] *Middleton v Fowler* (1699) 1 Salk 282; 91 ER 247.
[119] *Lane v Cotton* (1701) 1 Salk 17, 18; 91 ER 17 (Holt CJ).

Laugher v Pointer[120] and *Williams v Jones*.[121] It is encapsulated in the Latin phrase often used to describe vicarious liability, *qui facit per alium facit per se* (the direct act of one is treated as if it were the direct act of another). It is apparent in the decision in *Twine v Bean's Express Ltd*.[122] Glanville Williams took the view that the acts of the wrongdoer were attributed to the employer such that they were the employer's acts.[123] Such an approach is evident in the judgment of Dixon J in *Colonial Mutual Life Assurance* where he refers to the fact that the agent there 'does not act independently, but as a representative of the company, which accordingly must be considered as itself conducting the negotiation in his person'.[124]

In current debate, Robert Stevens takes a similar view.[125] In *Torts and Rights* he claims that 'the area of law traditionally labelled vicarious liability is not concerned with the attribution of liability for loss, but is rather based upon rules for the attribution of one's words or actions to another'.[126]

There is a still current line of cases which appears to adopt this approach. Some decisions suggest that actions of a key person within a corporation, for instance in the case of a one-person company,[127] or the managing director or member of the board of directors, may be imputed to the company, as if those actions were of the company itself.[128]

There is debate as to whether this approach is tied to the master's tort theory of vicarious liability, a theory which enjoyed some adherents for a time,[129] but which was eventually discarded.[130] The better view is that it is,[131] with the consequence that it would be difficult to maintain, given the general abandonment of the master's tort theory.

This view is probably most congruent with the corrective justice view of tort liability. As Weinrib put it, 'respondeat superior fits into corrective justice only if the employer can, in some sense, be regarded as a doer of the harm'.[132]

It may be that this view is more congruent with earlier manifestations of vicarious liability, involving notions or express command or consent. In such cases,

[120] *Ackworth v Kempe* (1778) 1 Doug 41; *Laugher v Pointer* (1826) 5 B & C 547, 108 ER 204 (Littledale J, 554 and 207 respectively; Abbott CJ, 576 and 215 respectively).

[121] (1865) 3 H & C 602, 609; 159 ER 668, 671 (Blackburn J).

[122] *Twine v Bean's Express Ltd* [1946] 1 All ER 202, 204 (Uthwatt J).

[123] G Williams, 'Vicarious Liability: Tort of the Master or of the Servant?' (1956) 72 *Law Quarterly Review* 522.

[124] (1931) 46 CLR 41, 49 (it should be conceded that the 'agent' in this case was an agent in the narrow sense, in that they had power to enter into contracts on behalf of the principal).

[125] Stevens, *Torts and Rights* (n 52) 262–63; R Stevens, 'Vicarious Liability or Vicarious Action?' (2007) 123 *Law Quarterly Review* 30; Stevens, 'Non-Delegable Duties and Vicarious Liability' (n 52).

[126] Stevens, *Torts and Rights* (n 52) 267.

[127] *Stone and Rolls Ltd (In Liquidation) v Moore Stephens* [2009] 1 AC 1391.

[128] *Lennard's Carrying Co Ltd v Asiatic Petroleum Co Ltd* [1915] AC 705.

[129] *Broom v Morgan* [1953] 1 QB 597; *Darling Island Stevedoring and Lighterage Co Ltd v Long* (n 113) 61 (Kitto J) and 66 (Taylor J).

[130] *Majrowski v Guy's and St Thomas's NHS Trust* [2007] 1 AC 224, 230 (Lord Nicholls).

[131] Merkin and Steele (n 112) 301.

[132] Weinrib (n 86) 186.

it may be argued more strongly that where the principal has specifically commanded the specific act in issue, the person (agent) who acted in response was really acting on behalf of the principal, such that the agent's acts could more easily be seen to be those of the principal. In contrast, as vicarious liability moved away from express command or consent notions to implicit commands and eventually enterprise risk (for some), it became more difficult to argue that the agent's acts were really those of the principal. This became clear when the forms of action were critical. So in *McManus v Crickett* it was found that an employer could not be sued in trespass for the acts of their employee unless they had specifically ordered it.[133] It is acknowledged that principles of implied and/or ostensible and/or usual authority could be utilised, but the case law in those areas is typically concerned with contractual disputes rather than tortious ones.

There are at least two issues which are affected by a determination of whether position (a) or position (b) is taken. If position (a) is taken and the employee's actions are deemed to be those of the employer, an employer could justifiably be held liable for any punitive damages that the court orders in relation to the relevant employee's wrong. This is because it is deemed to be their wrongful action, so that the rationale for punitive damages would be applicable and would favour the employer being held liable for punitive damages awarded in the case.[134] On the other hand, if it is merely the liability that is transferred to the employer, the efficacy of making the employer liable for any punitive damages awarded is less clear.[135] Employers in such circumstances who have been ordered to pay punitive damages have been permitted to claim their payment of punitive damages from their insurance company.[136] This issue will be explored in more detail in chapter eleven.

The second issue affected is insurance. Whatever else may be said about approach (a), this could potentially create significant difficulties with insurance and vicarious liability. The reality is that many insurance policies contain specific exclusions preventing an insured from bringing a claim where they are a wrongdoer. This would be a simple application of the ancient legal doctrine of *ex turpi causa*.[137] For example, the insurance policy considered in the case of

[133] *McManus v Crickett* (1800) 1 East 106; see for discussion H Glass, M McHugh and F Douglas, *The Liability of Employers in Damages for Personal Injury* (Sydney, Law Book Co, 1979) 89.

[134] Stevens, *Torts and Rights* (n 52) 266: 'once we accept that the law is concerned with the attribution of action, the employer should be held liable on the same basis as if he had personally committed the wrong'. He notes the Law Commission recommended that punitive damages be available against an employer for vicarious liability: Law Commission, *Aggravated, Exemplary and Restitutionary Damages* (Law Com No 247,1997) paras 1.213–1.227.

[135] In fact, in *Kuddus v Chief Constable of Leicestershire* [2002] 2 AC 122 Lord Scott suggested punitive damages should not be payable by an employer due to vicarious liability. He adopted a position that the employer was liable for the actions of the employee, but the actions themselves were not to be imputed to the employer.

[136] *Lancashire County Council v Municipal Mutual Insurance Ltd* [1997] QB 897.

[137] *Holman v Johnson* (1775) 1 Cowp 341, 343; 98 ER 1120, 1121 that a court will not assist a person who founds their action on an immoral or illegal act (Lord Mansfield).

KR and Ors v Royal and Sun Alliance Plc[138] contained an exclusion clause preventing the insured from claiming with respect to loss resulting from 'deliberate acts or omissions' of the insured. If the act of the wrongdoer is deemed to be the act of the insured, this may effectively preclude the insured from being able to access their insurance policy to indemnify them for their vicarious liability. Again, to so point out is not to say that the law should be influenced by insurance. However, when many argue that vicarious liability is best seen as a principle of loss spreading or loss distribution, it can be difficult to reconcile that goal with adoption of an approach that may effectively preclude any loss spreading from occurring, at least through the mechanism of insurance.

Acceptance of this position would presumably mean that at least in most cases if the employee had a defence to any claim against them, given that their acts were viewed as acts of the employer, the employer would be entitled to the same defence(s). It would clearly be inconsistent with the decision in *Broom v Morgan*,[139] where the Court of Appeal specifically found that a defence available to the employee was not available to the employer. On the other hand, cases where the availability of an immunity or defence available to the employee was held to be also available to the employer through vicarious liability doctrine, such as *Staveley Iron and Chemical Co Ltd v Jones*[140] and *Imperial Chemical Industries Ltd v Shatwell*[141] would be consistent with this approach.

(b) Argument that the Law of Vicarious Liability Imposes Liability on the Principal (Employer) for the Acts of the Agent (Employee), but Does Not Consider them the Employer's Acts

An early case that apparently appreciated the distinction between (a) and (b) is *Sharrod v London and North Western Railway Co.*[142] There Baron Parke for the Court explained that vicarious liability meant not that the employee's actions were the act of the employer, but merely that the principal was liable for them. Esteemed legal historians Pollock and Maitland, having just acknowledged that one who commanded a trespass was themselves a trespasser, then added that 'what is done by a man's command may be imputed to him as though it were his own act'.[143] Thus, it is not entirely clear whether they favoured position (a)

[138] *KR and Ors v Royal and Sun Alliance Plc* [2006] EWCA Civ 1454.
[139] [1953] 1 QB 597.
[140] *Staveley Iron and Chemical Co Ltd v Jones* [1956] AC 627.
[141] *Imperial Chemical Industries Ltd v Shatwell* [1965] AC 656.
[142] *Sharrod v London and North Western Railway Co* (1849) 4 Ex 579, 586; 154 ER 1345, 1347–48 (Baron Parke, for the Court).
[143] Pollock and Maitland (n 117) 526–27.

or position (b) here. With great respect, the learned authors may not have appreciated the significance of the distinction.

More recent decisions appear to confirm that vicarious liability means that the employer is liable for the employee's wrongdoing, but the act is not deemed to be the act of the employer themselves. This is apparently the position taken by the House of Lords in *Majrowski v Guy's and St Thomas's NHS Trust.*[144] Its decision in *Dubai Aluminium Co Ltd v Salaam* reflects similar sentiments.[145] The recent vicarious liability decision of the High Court of Australia also apparently takes this view.[146] It is a view strongly endorsed by Merkin and Steele.[147]

As discussed above, one practical advantage of an approach whereby an employer is vicariously responsible for the wrongdoing of their employee but is not considered to have committed the wrong themselves, is that the insurance difficulty discussed above that would otherwise arise, will not arise. Clauses voiding insurance if the insured was guilty of wrongdoing will generally not then apply to prevent the kind of loss distribution for which vicarious liability is often lauded. As also discussed above, acceptance of approach (b) does raise questions regarding whether it is appropriate that the employer could be vicariously liable for paying punitive damages as part of the payout. I will consider this issue further in chapter eleven.

The Law of Agency

When any change to the law is considered, possible impacts, including unintended impacts, on other legal principles must be considered. So here, if an employer's liability for the actions of their employee were better seen as an example of agency, how, if at all, does this affect other dimensions of the law of what we currently call 'vicarious liability'? Specifically, how would an 'agency' approach to 'the second question' impact, if at all, on 'the first question'? Specifically, should the agency approach be applied to both employees and independent contractors, and should that distinction therefore effectively be abolished? Or should it only be applied to employees, leaving untouched the position of liability of an engager for the acts or omissions of an independent contractor, which itself has a long history in the law of tort, and its own controversial doctrines such as non-delegable duties? Now

144 [2007] 1 AC 224, 230 (Lord Nicholls); 242 (Lord Hope); 245 (Baroness Hale); and 248 (Lord Brown).

145 *Dubai Aluminium Co Ltd v Salaam* [2003] 2 AC 366, 379 (where the employee does an authorised act, 'it may well be appropriate to attribute responsibility for his act to the employer' (Lord Nicholls, with whom Lord Slynn (386) and Lord Hutton (386) agreed); 388: ('the law attributes the responsibility of the employer to the employee' (Lord Hobhouse)).

146 *Prince Alfred College Inc v ADC* (n 65) 148 ('vicarious liability is imposed despite the employer not itself being at fault' (French CJ; Kiefel, Bell, Keane and Nettle JJ)).

147 Merkin and Steele (n 112) 322.

the distinction between employees and independent contractors is often criticised for its formality, and difficulty in application in practice, given changes in work practices, growing flexibility in the labour market etc.[148] The author has much sympathy with these arguments.

However, upon reflection, it is believed that the 'agency' approach to the second question, in other words that an engager of services should be liable for actions or omissions of the person engaged that were in furtherance of the employer's interests and done for their benefit, should not be applied to cases where an independent contractor is engaged. If that were to happen, a defendant would be liable (for example) for the actions of the taxi or uber driver whom they engaged to take me to the airport. Such a defendant should not be liable. If the question is why I should not be, we fall back on traditional arguments around employee versus independent contractor, namely concepts of control, whose resources are being utilised etc. In essence, my answer is that I am not liable because they are not my employee. I do not control their actions. As such, I have committed no morally blameworthy act for which I should legally be held responsible.

On the other hand, the answer might be different if the driver were my personal chauffeur. Say that I paid them on a weekly basis to ferry me around town. The driver did not work for anyone else. I provided this driver with the car, and with uniforms. I trained them. In such a case, their reckless driving could much more readily be brought to bear upon me. I was in a position to control their behaviour. They acted in furtherance of my interests and for my benefit. They were an employee, and I am morally accountable for what they do under my direction and control. The liability for independent contractors has obviously been dealt with in some legal systems under the auspices of a non-delegable duty concept, and this is subject to extended consideration in chapter ten.

Atiyah wrote a masterly book on vicarious liability. He cited cases which had apparently recognised that a principal was vicariously liable for agents, and cases where the opposite conclusion was reached. He concludes that the 'strongest argument against any theory of general (vicarious) liability for agents is undoubtedly the great difficulty which arises if there is any such liability, in explaining why some independent contractors can be treated as agents and others cannot'.[149]

Now there are (at least) two possible responses to this very important point. The first response is to say that agency concepts can be used to explain why in some cases an engager is liable for actions of an independent contractor. Atiyah attempts this himself in the following passage. It is a lengthy one, but pivotal to the current proposal:

> If there is any general principle of liability for agents there must be some explanation of why every independent contractor is not an agent … for instance, in *Sharpe v ET Sweeting and Son Ltd*, Nield J held that a building contractor did not act as agent of a

[148] Giliker (n 2) 60.
[149] Atiyah (n 1) 106.

> local authority in constructing houses for the authority … then again it has been said that stevedores in unloading a ship are in a sense acting as agents of the shipowner and yet are independent contractors for whom he is not liable … obviously a solicitor in private practice is an independent contractor of his clients yet he is for some purposes at least treated as an agent. Again, a carrier is normally treated as an independent contractor though in some cases he may be treated … as the agent of the consignor or even the consignee … it is clearly extremely difficult if not impossible to produce an explanation of the distinction between an independent contractor and an agent which will explain all these relationships with consistency. If there is any distinction it seems that the key must lie in the fact that, in some sense, some independent contractors may, in doing certain acts, be said to be acting on their own behalf, in carrying on their own business, while in other respects they may be said to be doing something on behalf of the client. In this way it may be possible to assert that, for example, the ordinary building contractor in building a house for a client is carrying on his own business, and not building on behalf of the client, whereas a solicitor in issuing a writ is acting in the name of, and on behalf of the client. It may well be that some such idea plays its part in the law because there is undoubtedly a much greater tendency to hold a person vicariously liable for the acts of an individual engaged by him to do a particular act on his behalf, than there is where the person engaged is a large organisation carrying on an independent business on its own behalf. As a matter of policy this distinction is clearly to be encouraged, but although it does seem to influence decisions it has never been expressly countenanced, and in any case recognition of the distinction normally takes the form of holding a person to be a servant in one case and an independent contractor in the other, rather than in relation to vicarious liability for agents.[150]

The distinction that Atiyah drew between cases in which a person acts on behalf of another (agent) and when they are really acting on their own account (independent contractor) is supported here. Though I was for a time considering the argument that the old distinction between employees and independent contractors should be abolished given changes in the nature of work and working arrangements, I have reached the conclusion that there is merit in retaining the distinction. The law should distinguish, in terms of liability, between cases where one person is acting on behalf of another, and cases when they are not. That should make a difference in terms of liability. If the distinction between agents and independent contractors is retained, it will. As such, Atiyah's concern with agency theory would disappear, since his expressed concern was with the use of agency theory to explain the liability for independent contractors, rather than its use in the context of liability for employees.

[150] ibid 107.

Conclusion to Part II

Part II has considered the leading theory currently said to support vicarious liability in three distinctions, that of enterprise risk. This theory has been rejected, on the basis it has little historical support in the case law, demonstrably does not explain significant features of vicarious liability, relies on ambiguous concepts, is difficult to apply to the non-profit sector, and is just not the way in which the common law typically deals generally with the legal liability of a business organisation. It becomes incoherent when it simultaneously claims both a deterrent effect and a loss distribution effect. Other claimed rationales, including loss distribution, evidentiary considerations, and 'fair, just and reasonable' rationales have also been found wanting.

It has been concluded that the best way to think of an employer's liability for the actions of their employees is via concepts of agency. This idea enjoys far greater historical case law support than models of enterprise risk. It is a much better descriptor of how judges have actually decided cases involving the possible liability of an employer for actions of their employees. It has strong connections with the implied command theory that underpinned vicarious liability for many years, in that it embraces consideration of whether the employee is acting in the interests of their employer and for their benefit, assessed in an objective sense. It also embraces the 'frolic' concept which is often sidelined in current discussions. In effect, they are two sides of the same coin. An employee who, objectively speaking, is acting in the interests of their employer and for their benefit is not engaged in a frolic; an employee who is not acting in the interests of their employer and for their benefit is engaged in a frolic. Vicarious liability should attach to the former, but not the latter.

The philosophical basis of a finding that an employer is only liable for these kinds of actions is that individuals should only be civilly liable for acts that are morally blameworthy and deserving of punishment. It is sound to make an employer liable for what an employee did for their purposes and benefit because the actions were authorised, expressly or implicitly, by the employer. The law either sees that the employee's actions are those of the employer, or, what is preferred given other developments in the law of vicarious liability and other factors, the law says that the employer is liable for the actions of the employee as if they were the employer's actions. This is because the employer has authorised that type of action. In other words, it is within the employee's scope of employment. It is within the terms of the employment contract to which the parties have agreed. If it is more accurately described as 'direct' rather than 'vicarious liability', I have no objection to the change in label.

One of the main advantages of adopting this approach is that employers would no longer be liable for actions of a kind they did not authorise, and never would have authorised. As such, they would not, except in relation to a very unusual organisation, be liable for intentional and possibly criminal wrongdoing by an employee. Such actions would be a 'frolic'. They were not objectively done for the benefit or the purposes of the employer. The employer should not be legally liable for them.

Another advantage would be the end of case law where an employer was liable for things which they specifically forbade the employee from doing. Again, such an employee would be engaged in a frolic. They were not acting for the employer's purposes or their benefit. The law is not usually shy about allowing individuals, as rational actors, to make arrangements about risk. It should not be shy about allowing employers to manage risk, by setting out very clearly to employees what the scope of their obligations, responsibilities and parameters of authority are, on the clear understanding that if an employee goes beyond those parameters, the employer will not legally pick up the tab for the financial consequences.

It is not a valid criticism of this conclusion to point out that, if it were accepted, 'vicarious liability' in the true sense of that phrase would no longer feature in the law, because the employer's liability would be direct, rather than vicarious. As indicated, my answer is that I have no difficulty with this recasting of the appropriate words. It is certainly not without precedent for the word 'agency' to be liberally used in vicarious liability cases. But the law should only intervene when there is something that requires correction. It should leave the innocent alone. An employer who has not authorised, expressly or implicitly, the wrongful behaviour should be left alone.

Part III

Miscellaneous Issues

Introduction to Part III

In Part III, a range of other issues pertaining to vicarious liability are considered. They include a discussion of the kinds of relationships to which vicarious liability should apply (chapter nine), the question of an employer's liability for actions of independent contractors, including the spectre of non-delegable duties (chapter ten), and the question whether an employer who is liable for the actions of their employees should be required to pay punitive damages (chapter eleven).

9

The Relationships to Which Vicarious Liability Might Attach

Traditionally, as has been seen the law of vicarious liability focused on two discrete questions. The first question was whether the relationship between the defendant and the wrongdoer was such that the defendant could, at least in some cases, be vicariously liable for what the wrongdoer had done. Some might call this the threshold issue. It considers whether vicarious liability could possibly exist for a given factual scenario. If the threshold issue were satisfied, a second question was considered, whether responsibility for the acts or omissions of the wrongdoer could in fact be sheeted home to the employer. In other words, whether vicarious liability does in fact exist for a given factual scenario. Here, the issue of scope of employment, as articulated by Salmond, and more recently, issues of closeness of connection have been important.

There is some suggestion in recent case law that these formerly two discrete questions have to some extent collapsed into a single all-encompassing approach, which I will discuss later. Even if this is indeed the case, the new approach will still draw on many of the concepts utilised when the law considered two discrete questions. As such, it remains important to understand the legal principles so applied. This chapter will particularly focus on the first of those questions, the threshold question of whether the relationship between the employer and wrongdoer is such that vicarious liability could potentially exist in the former for the acts of the latter.

Establishing that an Employment Relationship Exists

From early times, the concept of vicarious liability relied on a supposed strict distinction between workers who were employees, and workers who were independent contractors. While vicarious liability could be applied in the former case, it could not be applied in the latter case. Logically, it became necessary to try to articulate the substantive difference between a worker who should be considered an employee, and one who was a mere independent contractor. This is putting aside for now real questions regarding the compatibility of this distinction in light of possible enterprise risk theory. Others have pointed out, as discussed in chapter six, that the logic of enterprise risk theory would undermine the traditional distinction between employees and independent contractors.[1] Specifically, the distinction would be redundant if enterprise risk theory were truly applied.

This distinction would also be utilised in other areas of law apart from vicarious liability, raising the subsidiary question of whether the law should take a consistent position on the issue, or whether different areas of law could make this assessment using rules and principles applicable only in a particular context. In other words, could a worker be considered an employee for the purposes of some areas of law and not others? Or should a consistent approach be taken across all fields of law to this question?

The earliest English cases distinguished an employment relationship from other kinds of relationship such as an independent contractor in terms of the extent to which the engager had a right to direct the worker not only in what to do, but how it was to be done.[2] This has been referred to as the 'control' test. In the words of Crompton J in *Sadler v Henlock*, the question was whether the engager 'retained the power of controlling the work',[3] or in other words whether the worker was 'under the control (of) and bound to obey the orders of the master'.[4] This has been referred to as the 'final test' and the test that is generally to be applied.[5] The court indicated in *Performing Right Society Ltd v Mitchell and Booker*[6] *Ltd* that other factors, such as the nature of the task undertaken, freedom of action of the worker, magnitude of the contract amount, manner of payment, and the right of the engager to withhold payment were all relevant. The engager's power to select and dismiss the worker has also been emphasised.[7]

The House of Lords in *Mersey Docks and Harbour Board v Coggins and Griffith (Liverpool) Ltd*[8] emphasised the importance of the extent to which the engager *could* control the manner in which the work was to be done, not what actually occurs.[9] Significant potential control would suggest that an employment

[1] D Brodie, *Enterprise Liability and the Common Law* (Cambridge, Cambridge University Press, 2010) 159.

[2] *R v Walker* (1858) 27 LJMC 207, 208 (Bramwell B); *Yewens v Noakes* (1880) 6 QBD 530, 532 (Bramwell LJ) (CA); *Bain v Central Vermont Railway Company* [1921] 2 AC 412.

[3] *Sadler v Henlock* (1855) 4 E & B 570; 119 ER 209, 212.

[4] *R v Negus* (1873) LR 2 CC 34, 37 (Blackburn J).

[5] *Performing Right Society Ltd v Mitchell and Booker Ltd* [1924] 1 KB 762, 767.

[6] ibid 767 (McCardle J).

[7] *Short v J & W Henderson Ltd* (1946) 62 TLR 427, 429 (Lord Thankerton).

[8] *Mersey Docks and Harbour Board v Coggins and Griffith (Liverpool) Ltd* [1947] AC 1.

[9] ibid: 'the ultimate question is not what specific orders … were given but who is entitled to give the orders as to how the work should be done' (17, Lord Porter); see subsequently *Viasystems (Tyneside) Ltd v Thermal Transfer (Northern) Ltd* [2006] QB 510, [16] (May LJ) and *E v English Province of Our Lady of Charity* [2013] QB 722, 768: 'an employee is one who is paid a wage or salary to work under some, if only slight, control of his employer in his employer's business for his employer's business' (Ward LJ); 779 ('nature and extent of the control exercised or capable of being exercised'); 784 ('(whether the engager) is capable of having some control of (the worker's) activities') (Davis LJ).

relationship existed.[10] Lord Uthwatt explained that the reason why the engager's ability to control the manner in which the worker does the work was important was that 'it is the manner in which a particular operation ... is carried out that determines its lawful or wrongful character'.[11]

The Privy Council has acknowledged that control will usually be a relevant, important factor, but other factors are also important, such as whether the worker is using their own equipment, whether they engage their own workers, the degree of financial risk (if any) the worker takes, whether they have responsibility for investment and management, and whether the worker stands to profit from performance of the task.[12]

As with many of the issues around vicarious liability, difficulties have subsequently arisen. Questions have been raised over the utility of a control approach to determining a worker's employment status. Sometimes this has been on the basis that the world of work has changed vastly. Many enterprises are large scale. While it might have made sense in a very small, household business to refer to the control that the head of household had over workers, it becomes more difficult as the size of enterprise has grown substantially. Further, workers are often applying high levels of skill to their work, such that it will be difficult to say that the organisation engaging them is effectively controlling how they do the work, yet nevertheless the law would regard them as an employee.[13] To some extent, the response was to refine the control test, so that it focused on the right of the employer to exercise control, rather than the extent to which they actually did so. Even if this modification were accepted, pressure remained for a different, or at least more sophisticated, approach that would accurately capture the realities of work, while providing a workable rule of liability.

This has led some judges to a search for a materially different approach. The so-called 'organisation test' has gained some support.[14] It may have derived from Douglas' scholarly work.[15] It focuses attention away from control issues and asks whether the one engaged has a business of their own. In two decisions the Privy Council apparently provided support for the so-called organisational test approach. In *Montreal v Montreal Locomotive Works Ltd* Lord Wright said that in some cases it could be useful, in determining whether or not an employment relationship

[10] *Mersey Docks and Harbour Board v Coggins and Griffith (Liverpool) Ltd* (n 8) 12 (Lord Simon); 17 (Lord Porter); 18 (Lord Simonds); and 21 (Lord Uthwatt).

[11] ibid 21 (Lord Uthwatt).

[12] *Lee Ting Sang v Chung Chi-Keung* [1990] 2 AC 374, 382.

[13] *E v English Province of our Lady of Charity* (n 9) 766 (Ward LJ).

[14] Sometimes it is referred to as the entrepreneurial test, though others say they are materially different: A Spafford, 'The Enterprise Risk Theory: Redefining Vicarious Liability for Intentional Torts' (LLM Thesis, University of Toronto, 2000) 61–62. I am not convinced there is such a material difference between the organisational test approach and the entrepreneurial test as is sometimes suggested.

[15] W Douglas, 'Vicarious Liability and Administration of Risk I' (1929) 38 *Yale Law Journal* 584, 595–96 where Douglas referred to an 'entrepreneur test', including issues such as control, ownership of property used in the work, and the extent to which the one engaged might profit from the transaction or loss from its failure.

existed, to ask 'whose business is it, or in other words by asking whether the party is carrying on the business, in the sense of carrying it on for himself or on his own behalf and not merely for a superior'.[16] In *Lee Ting Sang v Chung Chi-Keung* the Council said that factors such as whether the worker takes financial risk or could earn financial profit and the extent to which they were responsible for investment and management could be relevant, alongside notions of control, whose equipment was being used and whether the worker engages workers of their own.[17]

The organisational approach is often associated with the judgment of Denning LJ in *Stevenson Jordan & Harrison Ltd v Macdonald and Evans*,[18] and in *Bank Voor Handel en Scheepvaart NV v Slatford (No 2)*.[19] In *Stevenson Jordan* Denning LJ stated that:

> One feature which seems to run through the instances is that, under a contract of service, a man is employed as part of the business, and the work is done as an integral part of the business; whereas, under a contract for services, his work, although done for the business, is not integrated into it but is only accessory to it.[20]

In *Market Investigations Ltd v Minister of Social Security* Cooke J stated the distinction was whether the worker was performing them as a business in their own account or not.[21] Others have been critical of the organisational approach.[22] Little guidance to the issue is found in cases such as *Lister* and *Mohamud*, since in those cases it was clear that the relevant wrongdoer was an employee. The issue was discussed at some length in *Viasystems (Tyneside) Ltd v Thermal Transfer (Northern) Ltd*.[23] The issue there was primarily whether dual vicarious liability was possible. In the course of that discussion, the first question of whether vicarious liability could potentially apply to a given relationship was considered. In that case there was little clarity in terms of a control or organisation test, because May LJ seemed to apply a control test,[24] while Rix LJ seemed to apply an organisation test.[25]

Another challenge for the principles in this area was the question of whether the principles of vicarious liability could apply not merely to true employment relationships, but to relationships that were 'sufficiently akin' to employment.

[16] *Montreal v Montreal Locomotive Works Ltd* [1947] 1 DLR 161, 169.

[17] [1990] 2 AC 374, 382.

[18] *Stevenson Jordan & Harrison Ltd v Macdonald and Evans* [1952] 1 TLR 101.

[19] *Bank Voor Handel en Scheepvaart NV v Slatford (No 2)* [1953] 1 QB 248, 295: 'the test of being a servant does not rest nowadays on submission to orders. It depends on whether the person is part and parcel of the organisation'.

[20] [1952] 1 TLR 101, 111.

[21] *Market Investigations Ltd v Minister of Social Security* [1969] 2 QB 173, 184–85.

[22] *Ready Mixed Concrete (South East) Ltd v Minister of Pensions* [1968] 2 QB 497, 524 (Mackenna J).

[23] [2006] QB 510.

[24] 'Who was entitled, and perhaps, theoretically obliged, to give orders as to how the work should or should not be done … entire and absolute control is not … a necessary precondition of vicarious liability': [16].

[25] '[W]hat one is looking for is a situation where the employee in question … is so much a part of the work, business or organisation … that it is just to make (the employer) answer for his negligence': [79].

This challenge was probably primed by the growing discovery of child sexual abuse within institutions, and the very difficult questions around the legal liability of institutions for such abuse. Thus, difficult questions arose as to the extent to which vicarious liability could apply in the religious setting, where relationships between religious adviser and religious institution may be difficult to fit within traditional conceptions of employment. Questions arose as to whether vicarious liability could apply in the case of a foster care situation—could the institution which placed the victim in the foster care environment be held vicariously liable for abuse committed by that carer? Obviously, a foster carer is not an employee in the traditional meaning of that concept. Again, the parameters of vicarious liability principle were being stretched and strained by the reality of the matters with which it was asked to deal, far removed from the original context in which such principle developed.

These very difficult matters were considered by the Court of Appeal again in *E v English Province of Our Lady of Charity*.[26] After an exhaustive discussion of the authorities, Ward LJ seemed to suggest an amalgamation of the control and organisation test:

> [A]n employee is one who is paid a wage or salary to work under some, if only slight, control of his employer in his employer's business for his employer's business. The independent contractor works in and for his own business at his risk of profit or loss.[27]

Tomlinson LJ, dissenting in the result, seemed to prefer the control test, stating that an employment relationship contained 'assumptions … as to the nature and extent of the control exercised or capable of being exercised'.[28] Davis LJ agreed with use of the control test,[29] adding that it would also be important that the activities concerned were performed on behalf of the engager or designed to further their aims, interests or purposes.[30]

In *Various Claimants v Catholic Child Welfare Society*[31] Lord Phillips discussed five factors that made it 'fair, just and reasonable' to impose vicarious liability on an employer. He did not specifically distinguish between the first question and the second question in relation to vicarious liability. However, he cited the fact of control by the employer of the worker's actions, as well as whether the employee's activity was seen as part of the business activity of the employer, as relevant.[32] He emphasised the evolution of the control test, to one based on the extent to which an employer can direct what an employee does, not how they do it, in recognition of the fact that the worker may be involved in a highly specialised

[26] [2013] QB 722.

[27] ibid 768.

[28] ibid 779.

[29] 'That an appropriate level of control is ordinarily required for vicarious liability to be capable of arising is, I think, borne out by the authorities', ibid (784).

[30] ibid.

[31] *Various Claimants v Catholic Child Welfare Society* [2013] 2 AC 1 (for the Court).

[32] ibid 15.

task in which the employer may not have particular expertise.[33] Lord Phillips also discussed whether the activity was part of the employer's 'business activity' such that the employer created the risk, in shades of the 'organisational' test. The court accepted that vicarious liability could be applied to relationships that were sufficiently akin, or analogous to, employment relationships.[34] The control and organisation test could be applied to determine whether a relationship was either an employment one, or sufficiently akin to an employment one, to justify the possible imposition of vicarious liability principle.

Thus, United Kingdom law has appeared to settle upon an amalgam of the control and organisation test approaches to determine whether or not a relationship is sufficiently akin to an employment relationship so that vicarious liability principles could apply.[35] And the reference in the five factors to issues like whether the worker was acting on behalf of the engager and part of their business activity, and whether the employer created or increased the risk of wrongdoing, suggests a merging of the formerly two discrete tests or stages into one test. In saying that, I must acknowledge that after discussing and applying the five-factor test, Lord Phillips then went on to separately consider the question of the closeness of connection. However, when factors relevant to that clearly include the extent to which the defendant used the wrongdoer to carry on its business or further their interests are considered, and the extent to which the defendant has materially increased the risk of wrongdoing are being considered, these are surely matters traditionally relevant to the second of the questions, namely the extent to which an employer is liable for the wrongdoer's actions, not whether the employer is potentially liable for the wrongdoer's actions because they are an employee.

These comments were essentially mirrored in the Supreme Court decision in *Cox v Ministry of Justice*.[36] Lord Reed for the Court referred with evident approval to the comments of Lord Phillips regarding use of the control test.[37] He elaborated some more on the organisational test, though not using that expression, in determining whether a relationship was of a type to which vicarious liability might relate:

> A relationship other than one of employment is in principle capable of giving rise to vicarious liability where harm is wrongfully done by an individual who carries on activities as an integral part of the business activities carried on by a defendant and for its benefit (rather than his activities being entirely attributable to the conduct of a recognisably independent business of his own or of a third party), and where the commission

[33] ibid 15–16.

[34] ibid 18.

[35] R Merkin and J Steele, *Insurance and the Law of Obligations* (Oxford, Oxford University Press, 2013) 307: 'courts will increasingly consider the issues relevant to the "close connection" or "course of employment" criterion to be relevant also to definition of a relationship as one effectively of employment'.

[36] *Cox v Ministry of Justice* [2016] AC 660.

[37] ibid 669.

of the wrongful act is a risk created by the defendant by assigning those activities to the individual in question.[38]

Lord Phillips' five-factor test was recently applied in *Various Claimants v Barclays Bank Plc* to make a bank vicariously liable for sexual abuse committed by a doctor who was clearly an independent contractor. The bank had required potential new employees to undergo a physical examination by a doctor. That doctor sexually abused a number of victims. While the doctor was not an employee of Barclays Bank, ran his own business and saw a range of patients, many of whom were not related to Barclays Bank, nevertheless the Court found Barclays Bank vicariously liable for the abuse. The Court found the doctor was furthering the business interests of the bank and was part of its business activity. The medical examinations were undertaken at the request of the bank. They paid for the examinations. The activity was for the benefit of the bank and on its behalf. By requiring staff to undergo a medical examination with the doctor, they created the risk of possible abuse. It found the doctor was an integral part of the business activity of the bank. The bank significantly controlled aspects of the medical examination, including the questions to be asked.[39]

Most recently in *Armes v Nottinghamshire County Council*[40] members of the United Kingdom Supreme Court again referred to aspects of both the organisation test[41] and the control test,[42] in determining that a relationship between council and foster parents was sufficiently akin to an employment relationship that the council could be vicariously liable for actions of the foster parents.

The distinction between employees and independent contractors has long been recognised in Australian law.[43] In Australia numerous authorities have endorsed the control test, in the sense of whether the engager has the right to control the worker's actions.[44] As Dixon J put it in *Humberstone*, the question is whether 'the contract placed the supposed servant subject to the command of the employer in the course of executing the work not only as to what he shall do

[38] ibid 670.

[39] *Various Claimants v Barclays Bank Plc* [2017] EWHC 1929 (QB).

[40] *Armes v Nottinghamshire County Council* [2017] UKSC 60.

[41] Lord Reed, with whom Lady Hale, Lord Kerr and Lord Clarke agreed, concluding that 'the foster parents … cannot be regarded as carrying on an independent business of their own' (para 59); 'the foster parents provided care to the child as an integral part of the local authority's organisation of its child care services' (para 60); as did Lord Hughes (dissenting): 'the essential minimum for vicarious liability is that the tortfeasor is acting as an integral part of the defendant's enterprise, which need not only be a commercial enterprise' (para 76).

[42] Lord Reed, with whom Lady Hale, Lord Kerr and Lord Clarke agreed, concluding that 'the local authority exercised a significant degree of control over both what the foster parents did and how they did it, in order to ensure that the children's needs were met' (para 62); Lord Hughes (dissenting) (para 77).

[43] *Leighton Contractors Pty Ltd v Fox* (2009) 240 CLR 1, 13 (French CJ; Gummow, Hayne, Heydon and Bell JJ).

[44] *Federal Commissioner of Taxation v J Walter Thompson (Aust) Pty Ltd* (1944) 69 CLR 227, 233 (Latham CJ); *Queensland Stations Pty Ltd v Federal Commissioner of Taxation* (1945) 70 CLR 539, 545 (Latham CJ), 549 (Rich J), 553 (Dixon J); *Humberstone v Northern Timber Mills* (1949) 79 CLR 389, 396 (Latham CJ), 399 (Rich J), 404 (Dixon J).

but to how he shall do it'.[45] It is the potential for the engager to provide 'direction or command … what matters is lawful authority to command so far as there is scope for it'.[46] In this way the court countered arguments that given workers were highly skilled, it could not be said that the employer had the relevant control over the manner in which the employees conducted work activities (acrobatics, in that case). The fact that the worker provides their own equipment and workers is relevant.[47]

Relatedly, these issues of control have also been articulated in the context of assessing the extent to which an engager has an action for loss of the services of a 'servant'.[48] In that case Webb J stated that notions of 'control' of a servant harked back to the days involving slaves and were explicable on that basis.[49] Subsequently the notion of control was adapted in response to the move of master–servant relationships away from a proprietary interest to a mere contractual one.

One judge in that case said that care must be taken in making any argument about equivalence in terms of 'servants' for the purposes of vicarious liability, and servants for the loss of service action, stating they were 'radically' different.[50] Fullagar J there explained why control was important in the vicarious liability context:

> The theory is that he who has the control should carry the responsibility, and the right to control in the actual execution of the work is said to be the test to be applied in determining whether the relationship which involves responsibility exists or not. When control ceases, responsibility ceases, and a master is not liable for wrongs committed by his servants outside the course of his employment.[51]

Kitto J got to this issue in a slightly different way. His definition of a servant for the purposes of vicarious liability included that the relationship involve obedience to orders in doing work, and that the work be for the benefit of the master, relating to his affairs.[52]

Some suggestion of the organisational test approach appears in the judgment of Dixon J in *Colonial Mutual Life Assurance Society Limited v Producers and*

[45] (1949) 79 CLR 389, 404.

[46] *Zuijs v Wirth Brothers Pty Ltd* (1955) 93 CLR 561, 571 (Dixon CJ; Williams, Webb and Taylor JJ); *Marshall v Whittaker's Building Supply Co* (1963) 109 CLR 210, 218 (Windeyer J), concluding that the matter depended on 'whether the supposed servant was subject to the commands of his employer, not only as to what he should do but as to how he should do it. Lawful authority to command, so far as the work to be done gives scope for it, is still the important test'.

[47] *Marshall v Whittaker's Building Supply Co*, ibid, 215 (Kitto, Taylor, Menzies and Owen JJ).

[48] *Attorney-General for NSW v Perpetual Trustee Co (Ltd)* (1952) 85 CLR 237.

[49] ibid 272: 'the action (for loss of services) originated at a time when the relationship of master and servant … to which it has always been confined was based on status and not on contract … when the legal right or interest of the master in the services lost was of a proprietary nature, and the master, *therefore*, had complete control of those services' (emphasis added).

[50] ibid 284.

[51] ibid 285.

[52] ibid 299.

Citizens Co-Operative Assurance Company of Australia Limited.[53] Dixon J spoke of an independent contractor as engaged in

> (w)ork, although done at (the engager's) request and for his benefit … considered as the independent function of the person who undertakes it, and not as something which the person obtaining the benefit does by his representative standing in his place, and therefore identified with him for the purpose of liability arising in the course of its performance. The independent contractor carries out his work, not as a representative but as a principal.[54]

It is also reflected in the judgment of Windeyer J in *Marshall v Whittaker's Building Supply Co*.[55]

In *Stevens v Brodribb*[56] Mason J reasserted that the right of an employer to potentially control an employee was important, but other factors, such as the mode of remuneration, whether the worker provided equipment, the obligation to work, hours of work and holiday arrangements and deduction of tax, and the ability of the worker to delegate tasks was also important. He acknowledged that the control test could be criticised on the basis that it spoke to a different era of working arrangements, but argued it could adapt; for instance that it now was not the sole determinant of the existence of an employment relationship, but merely one important consideration.

Mason J addressed the so-called 'organisation test', stating that the legal authority to control was the more cogent approach.[57] The organisation test would not justify a finding as to the existence of an employment relationship one way or the other if the issue of control and other relevant factors suggested the opposite conclusion.[58] He doubted the organisation test would be of material assistance in determining vicarious liability issues.[59] Similarly, Wilson and Dawson JJ concluded the so-called organisation test was just a means of redefining the relevant questions, rather than providing much by way of clarity.[60] They agreed that notions of potential control remained important, as well as the extent to which the worker can delegate the work, the right to dismiss the worker, the right to exclusive service from the worker, the right to dictate work, hours of work, whether the worker uses their own place of work or equipment, whether the worker is paid substantial business expenses, and whether taxation is deducted from their payments.[61]

[53] *Colonial Mutual Life Assurance Society Limited v Producers and Citizens Co-Operative Assurance Company of Australia Limited* (1931) 46 CLR 41.

[54] ibid 48.

[55] (1963) 109 CLR 210, 217, stating the distinction between an employee and an independent contractor was 'rooted fundamentally in the difference between a person who serves his employer in his, the employer's, business, and a person who carries on a trade or business of his own'.

[56] *Stevens v Brodribb* (1986) 160 CLR 16.

[57] ibid 27.

[58] ibid.

[59] ibid 28.

[60] ibid 36.

[61] ibid 36–37.

This position was broadly maintained by the High Court in *Hollis v Vabu Pty Limited*,[62] the joint reasons reasserting that control was an important consideration, along with others, in determining whether an employment relationship existed. Interestingly, the joint reasons quoted a textbook which criticised the control test on the basis it spoke to a different era of work, and the manner in which it was conducted.[63] The joint reasons did not specifically discuss the organisation test as such, but quoted with evident approval earlier (effective) iterations of it in the judgment of Dixon J in *Colonial Mutual Life Assurance Society* and Windeyer J in *Marshall*. They considered whether the worker was 'running his own enterprise',[64] as well as notions of control, outward appearances (ie, wearing of uniforms), financial arrangements, equipment issues, and even deterrence considerations.[65] Interestingly, also apparent in the joint reasons is apparent acceptance of the 'enterprise risk' theory to the second question in vicarious liability, namely the scope of behaviours of an employee for which an employer will be liable.[66] As has been pointed out above, the High Court subsequently appeared to move away from the enterprise risk theory,[67] with only two judges referring to it in the subsequent *Lepore* decision,[68] and it not being discussed at all in the most recent *Prince Alfred* decision.[69]

The organisational test approach is clearly evident in the High Court decision in *Sweeney v Boylan Nominees Pty Ltd*.[70] In concluding that the worker was an independent contractor, the joint reasons noted:

> He conducted his own business … that the mechanic was engaged in a business other than that of the respondent was demonstrated by a number of circumstances but chief among them were his invoicing the respondent for each job he did and the respondent's concern to verify that the worker had the proper workers' compensation and public liability insurance … he was engaged in a business other than that of the respondent.[71]

Writing extrajudicially, Chief Justice of the High Court of Australia, Susan Kiefel, noted that 'a test which places emphasis on control speaks of other times when control may have been a reality', before conceding that in the current approach involving a question of the totality of the relationship between the parties, the ability to exercise control may be important.[72]

[62] *Hollis v Vabu Pty Limited* (2001) 207 CLR 21.
[63] ibid 40–41 (Gleeson CJ; Gaudron, Gummow, Kirby and Hayne JJ).
[64] ibid 42.
[65] ibid 42–45.
[66] ibid 40.
[67] *State of New South Wales v Lepore* (2003) 212 CLR 511, 543 (Gleeson CJ); 586–88 (Gummow and Hayne JJ).
[68] ibid (Gaudron and Kirby JJ).
[69] *Prince Alfred College Inc v ADC* (2016) 258 CLR 134.
[70] *Sweeney v Boylan Nominees Pty Ltd* (2006) 226 CLR 161.
[71] ibid 173 (Gleeson CJ; Gummow, Hayne, Heydon and Crennan JJ).
[72] S Kiefel, 'Vicarious Liability in Tort—A Search for Policy, Principle or Justification' (New South Wales Supreme Court Judges Conference, August 2017) 9–10.

Like the other jurisdictions, Canadian law seemed to commence with a control approach to determining whether or not an employment relationship existed such as might attract vicarious liability.[73] Control over the location and the timing of the work was important.[74] In a Canadian appeal the Privy Council began suggesting that factors beyond control could be important, such as ownership of the equipment used, as well as profit/loss risk.[75] In more recent cases the Canadian courts have apparently embraced the organisational test approach, considering whether the contractor was an inherent part of the engager's business, or was operating a business on their own account, at least with respect to the particular function in issue.[76] Issues such as control will be relevant in answering this question, together with issues such as whose assets were being used, whether the one engaged engages their own workers, and risk and return issues.[77] The right of the engager to hire and fire the employee, and to control their budget and finances, will also be relevant to issues of control.[78]

In *KLB v British Columbia* it was the lack of control by the state over the conduct of foster parents that convinced the Supreme Court of Canada that the state should not be vicariously liable for the wrongdoing of foster carers.[79] Care was provided in carers' own homes using their own 'equipment'. Imposition of vicarious liability on the government for the actions of foster carers would not further deterrence goals.

In a useful contribution to the debate, Kidner suggests five factors are to be considered in the context of determining who is an employee for the purposes of vicarious liability:

a. Control by the employer by the employee—Kidner says this should consider the degree of managerial control exercised over the activity and the extent to which an individual is integrated into the organisation's enterprise, and the extent to which the worker is accountable to the employer.
b. Control by the contractor of himself—issues such as use by the worker of their own assets, their own staff, payment issues.
c. The organisation test—how central the activity is to the enterprise in terms of its objectives, on the basis that the more relevant the activity is to the fundamental objectives of the business, the more appropriate it is to apply the risk associated with the activity to the business.

[73] *Sisters of St Joseph of the Diocese of London v Fleming* [1938] SCR 172; *Hôpital Notre-Dame de l'Espérance v Laurent* [1978] 1 SCR 605, [128].

[74] *Kennedy v CAN Assurance Co* (1978) 6 CCLT 201; *Lapensee v Ottawa Day Nursery* (1986) 35 CCLT 129, 153–54.

[75] *Montreal v Montreal Locomotive Works Ltd* (n 16) 169 (Lord Wright).

[76] *671122 Ontario Ltd v Sagaz Industries Canada Inc* [2001] 2 SCR 983, 1005 (Major J, for the Court); *KLB v British Columbia* [2003] 2 SCR 403, 419–20.

[77] *671122 Ontario Ltd v Sagaz Industries Canada Inc*, ibid, 1005 (Major J for the Court); *KLB v British Columbia*, ibid, 419–20 (McLachlin CJ, for Gonthier, Iacobucci, Major, Bastarache, Binnie, LeBel and Deschamps JJ).

[78] *Blackwater v Plint* [2005] 3 SCR 3, 17 (McLachlin CJ, for the Court).

[79] [2003] 2 SCR 403.

d. The integration test—whether the activity is integrated into the organisational structure of the enterprise, whether the function is provided for the business or by the business.
e. Whether the person is in business on their own account; whether they are acting as an entrepreneur, taking appropriate risks, and has the chance to make profit.[80]

Another useful contribution is made by Phillip Morgan, who suggests a flexible approach considering a two axes scale, with levels of control on one axis, and discretion in role on the other. Consideration of both elements would determine whether or not vicarious liability applied to the particular relationship, regardless of how it was formally structured.[81]

The United States Restatement (Second) of Agency (1958) adopted a multi-factor approach to determining whether a worker was an employee or an independent contractor.[82] However, the Restatement (Third) of Agency (2006) takes a simplified approach, merely stating that an employee is an agent whose principal controls or has the right to control the manner and means of the agent's performance.[83]

Thus, in summary the United Kingdom and Canada seem to have settled upon an approach which incorporates both the control and organisation tests to determine whether or not a particular relationship is sufficiently akin to an employment relationship to justify the imposition of vicarious liability. In Australia, there is some use of the organisation test, though control is typically seen as being important in many cases. In contrast, the United States seems to be committed to a control-based approach, the United States Restatement (Agency) having apparently moved away from a multi-factor approach, and back to a test which focuses on control or the right to control, in so far as the Restatement can be taken to be evidence of the United States position with respect to a particular legal issue.

I must express some concern with the way in which the amalgamated control and organisation tests are being applied in the United Kingdom courts. In particular, I express concern with Lord Phillips' five-factor approach and the way it has

[80] R Kidner, 'Vicarious Liability: For Whom Should the "Employer" be Liable?' (1995) 15 *Legal Studies* 47, 63–64; Kidner's approach was favourably referred to by Ward LJ in *E v English Province of Our Lady of Charity* (n 9) 768–69. Risk is emphasised by Robert Flannigan: R Flannigan, 'Enterprise Control: The Servant–Independent Contractor Distinction' (1987) 37 *University of Toronto Law Journal* 25, 46.

[81] P Morgan, 'Recasting Vicarious Liability' (2012) 71 *Cambridge Law Journal* 615, 641–43.

[82] These factors included (a) the extent of control which the master may exercise over details of the work; (b) whether the one employed is engaged in a distinct occupation or business; (c) the kind of occupation and whether the work is usually done under the employer's direction or by a specialist without supervision; (d) the extent of skill required; (e) whether the worker supplies the equipment and the location where the work is done; (f) the length of time for which the person is employed; (g) how they are paid, whether by time or job; (h) whether the work is part of the employer's regular business; (i) whether the parties believed they were creating a master–servant relationship; and (j) whether the principal is 'in the business'; see *Nationwide Mutual Insurance Co v Darden* 503 US 318 (1992).

[83] s 7.07.

been applied. I express significant concern with the outcome of the application of this five-factor approach to the facts in *Various Claimants v Barclays Bank Plc*.[84]

It seems that the so-called organisation test has evolved in meaning in the years since it was first utilised. Initially it appeared to concern whether the worker was conducting a business themselves or was part of the engager's business. This is evident in decisions such as *Montreal*, *Stevenson Jordan* and *Market Investigations*. It is also evident in the exhaustively reasoned judgment of Ward LJ in *E v English Province*. Such an approach appears workable. Applying this approach to the facts in *Barclays Bank Plc*, it is suggested that a doctor who conducts medical examinations, albeit at the direction of a bank, is doing so as part of their own business—their medical practice. They are using their own equipment, own premises and employ their own staff.

With respect, it is possible that Lord Phillips' five-factor approach has created uncertainty in this area. As has earlier been noted, Lord Phillips arguably effectively merged the traditionally two-stage process of determining whether or not vicarious liability should exist on particular facts to a five-factor approach. Lord Phillips identified these as five indicia whose existence would usually make it fair, just and reasonable to impose vicarious liability. He referred to consideration of whether the activity concerned was likely to be conducted by the worker on the part of the employer (second factor), whether they were part of the business activity of the employer (third factor), and whether the employer, by employing the worker to carry out the activity, created the risk of the tort occurring (fourth factor). He did also consider the close connection issue, but given his discussion of that matter concerns matters such as whether the defendant engaged the wrongdoer to carry on its business or further its interests in a manner which created or significantly enhanced the risk of wrongdoing, clear overlap can be seen between Lord Phillips' five-factor approach, and the subsequent application of the close connection test, such that it may be that in future cases the courts simply refer to and apply the five-factor approach.

This is different from, and broader than, the terms in which the organisation test was originally crafted. It is submitted that in many cases, the work done by an independent contractor is done by the contractor on the part of the employer (in terms of the second factor). In terms of the fourth factor, again the independent contractor only did the work because they were requested to do so by the engaging organisation. This suggests a conflict between the traditional distinction between employees and independent contractors and the tests Lord Phillips now proposes we use to determine whether or not vicarious liability exists. The conflict exists because two of the five indicia he espouses as determining whether or not vicarious liability should exist do not work with a distinction between an employee and an independent contractor. Both an employee and an independent contractor could easily meet the two indicia. So either the traditional distinction between

[84] [2017] EWHC 1929.

employee and independent contractor must be abandoned, or Lord Phillips' tests must be modified or discarded. Both cannot continue to be correct.

There is also some issue with Lord Phillips' third indicia—whether the worker's activity is likely to be part of the business activity of the engaging organisation. Now this may simply be a reflection of the original roots of the organisation test noted above, asking whether the worker is running their own business or is part of the engaging firm's business. If this is all it is, it is considered workable. However, there is the risk that it is applied incorrectly. I do not believe it can reasonably be argued that a doctor who has their own medical practice, who conducts medical examinations on behalf of a bank, is not running their own business. Clearly they are. A medical practice is very far removed from the business of running a bank. So I would prefer the original formulation of this requirement, asking whether the person concerned is running their own business or not, rather than a question of whether the person is part of the business activity of the organisation. Expression of this test is apt to mislead, which has arguably occurred in *Barclays Bank Plc*, where a judge is led to conclude that a doctor performing medical services is part of the business activity of a bank. On this reasoning, many, if not all, independent contractors performing services for an organisation may be considered to be employees for the purposes of vicarious liability law. If it is not sufficient to avoid being considered an employee that the worker clearly has their own business enterprise and works with a range of different engagers, we have some serious questions to ask. I suggest the problem is with Lord Phillips' five indicia of vicarious liability.

The Exceptionality of Making One Person Liable for the Actions of Another

It is considered important to reflect on the primary rule within the law of tort that, as a corollary of the fact that one person is generally legally responsible for their own actions and omissions, they are generally not legally responsible for the actions or omissions of another. It is proper to regard vicarious liability as an outlier, an exceptional case, in sharp contrast to general principles of tort liability.

This position is reflected in the judgment of Dixon J in *Smith v Leurs* where he indicated that:

> (A)part from vicarious responsibility, one man may be responsible to another for the harm done to the latter by a third person; he may be responsible on the ground that the act of the third person could not have taken place but for his own fault or breach of duty. There is more than one description of duty the breach of which may produce this consequence (for example, cases of special danger) … It may even be a duty of care with reference to the control of actions or conduct of the third person. It is, however, exceptional to find in the law a duty to control another's actions to prevent harm to strangers. The general rule is that one man is under no duty of controlling another man to prevent

> his doing damage to a third. There are, however, special relations which are the source of the duty of this nature. It appears now to be recognised as incumbent upon a parent to maintain control over a young child to take reasonable care so as to exercise that control as to avoid conduct on his part exposing the person or property of others to unreasonable danger. Parental control, where it exists, must be exercised with due care to prevent the child inflicting intentional damage on others or causing damage by conduct involving unreasonable risk or injury to others.[85]

Members of the House of Lords referred to these comments with evident approval in *Home Office v Dorset Yacht Co Ltd*,[86] a well-known case involving government liability for the actions of at-risk youth who were under their care. While the context was different, the judges who found that the government owed a duty of care to third parties for the actions of the escaped youths emphasised the control that the government had over the youths, and that it was the government's control over them that made it effectively responsible for their actions.[87] Now of course the government was not vicariously liable for the actions of the youths, but the case reflects the strength of the starting presumption that one person is not liable for the actions of another, unless some kind of special circumstance applies. The ability of the defendant to control the wrongdoer's activities was critical in *Dorset Yacht* to establishing the legal liability of the defendant.

It is interesting to reflect upon what, if anything, this tells us about the law of vicarious liability. Again, it is conceded that the government was not vicariously liable for the actions of the youths. Vicarious liability was only relevant in that case in the sense of making the government responsible for what their officers did or failed to do. However, the case still has some pertinent messages for the current context.

Obviously vicarious liability was originally conceived of in terms of 'command and consent' theory, that an employer was only liable for actions they had commanded or later ratified. This obviously reflects notions of control; if I command something to be done, it is within my control. If I ratify something later, I am exerting control. And obviously notions of control traditionally assist in determining whether or not an employment relationship exists, such that vicarious liability can potentially apply, as opposed to an independent contractor relationship, where vicarious liability is not typically applicable. As acknowledged above, my actual control of, or perhaps my ability to control a worker, suggests that the worker is my employee, rather than an independent contractor. The question is what is it about notions of 'control' that attracts liability, as it did in *Dorset Yacht*, which it traditionally does in terms of creating an employment relationship to which vicarious liability might apply?

[85] *Smith v Leurs* (1945) 70 CLR 256, 261–62.

[86] *Home Office v Dorset Yacht Co Ltd* [1970] AC 1004, 1027 (Lord Reid); 1038 (Lord Morris); 1046 (Viscount Dilhorne); 1055 (Lord Pearson); and 1063 (Lord Diplock).

[87] ibid Lord Morris (1038) and Lord Pearson (1055).

Why Has the Law Fixated on 'Control' in Relation to Liability for What Another Did?

It is considered important to consider why the law has apparently fixated on control in determining whether or not a person is liable for what another has done. The leading cases in which 'control' is discussed as a factor in determining whether or not an employment relationship exists do not provide much by way of explanation. So in *Yewens v Noakes*[88] Lord Bramwell states simply that a servant is a person subject to the *command* of their master as to the manner in which they will do their work. This is referred to with evident approval by McCardle J in *Performing Right Society Ltd v Mitchell and Booker Ltd.*[89] That judgment also emphasises the power of the employer to control the work.[90] In *Mersey Docks and Harbour Board*[91] it is asked who is entitled to give the orders as to how the work is to be done.[92] Lord Uthwatt agreed it was the power of the engager to control the manner in which the work was to be done that determined the existence of an employment relationship, because 'it is the manner in which a particular operation … is carried out that determines its lawful or wrongful character'.[93] In *E v English Province* Ward LJ said an employee was someone who was under some control of the employer, 'in his employer's business for his employer's business'.[94] Davis LJ asked whether the employer was capable of having some control over the worker's activities and whether the activities were 'performed on behalf of or are designed to further the aims or interests or purposes' of the employer.[95]

One answer might be, consistently with observations made in the previous chapter, that when the employer is deemed to have controlled the wrongful behaviour, or to have been in such a position, they may be considered to be 'morally blameworthy' in a way that justifies the law requiring them to compensate the party injured by the wrongful behaviour. The fact, or at least the potential, of control makes it justified to attribute the wrongful acts, or at least liability for the wrongful acts (the preferred approach, as seen in chapter eight) to the employer.

There are clear links between the concept of 'control', which helps determine whether or not there is an employment relationship from which vicarious liability will flow; in other words it *grounds the possibility* of vicarious liability (the first issue) and concepts of 'command and consent' which initially *determined the scope* of vicarious liability (the second issue). Initially an employer was only vicariously

[88] (1880) 6 QBD 530, 532.
[89] [1924] 1 KB 762, 768.
[90] ibid 767–68.
[91] [1947] AC 1.
[92] ibid 17 (Lord Porter).
[93] ibid 21.
[94] [2013] QB 722, 768.
[95] ibid 784.

liable for actions they had specifically expressly commanded and/or consented to. Later a theory of 'implied consent' emerged.

The question is whether there is any necessity of linking the two. As will be shown below, not everyone believes that control is the key, or an important, determinant of whether or not an employment relationship exists (ie, the first issue). The law in relation to the second issue has evolved from notions of command, express or implied, and/or consent to scope of employment and then enterprise risk theory (in some jurisdictions). The question is the extent to which resolution of problems of interpretation with the first or second issue depend on resolution of the other issue. Atiyah canvasses this point, stating that there are two approaches in determining who is an employee: one which simply applies a discrete test or tests (which would indicate the first issue is not or should not be influenced by the second issue), and one which determines whether or not a particular worker is an employee in light of the purpose for which the classification is being made. Even if he is making a slightly different point from the one made here, he at least identified that the question of who is an employee and who is not may or may not be answered in isolation from other questions pertaining to liability. He declines to favour one approach over the other.[96]

For example, if we apply the control theory to the first issue, to determine whether or not an employment relationship exists, does this have consequences for how we resolve the second issue, namely the scope of vicarious liability? Specifically, if we accept 'control' is the best test to apply to determining whether an employment relationship exists, does this suggest a return to a 'command and consent' approach to the second issue? Is the traditional scope of employment concept for the second limb consistent with consideration of control in relation to the first? Another test that has been considered in relation to establishing whether an employment relationship exists is the so-called enterprise test, asking whether the worker is a part of the business of the engaging firm, or really has their own business. Now, does that approach to the first question suggest embrace of the enterprise risk approach to the second question?

And the reverse question may also be asked. Does the acceptance by some courts of the enterprise risk approach to the 'second question'—in other words the scope of vicarious liability—impact on issues relevant to the 'first question', of the types of relationship capable of giving rise to vicarious liability. At least some scholars believe that it does. Writing in the context of Canadian law Anne Spafford states:

> By endorsing the enterprise risk theory and rendering the enterprise as a whole liable for employee torts, the Supreme Court (of Canada) has adopted an approach which will no longer require that a distinction between servants and independent contractors be made for the purposes of attributing vicarious liability.[97]

[96] PS Atiyah, *Vicarious Liability in the Law of Torts* (London, Butterworths, 1967).
[97] Spafford (n 14) 54.

Later she adds that

> [i]f one views the scope of vicarious liability as defined by the risks created or exacerbated by the enterprise, one realizes that control is no longer determinative. Clearly the ambit of risk cast by enterprise is broader than situations where management exercises control over the manner of doing work.[98]

However, despite what some may see as the logic of Spafford's position, it has not been the direction of Canadian case law. While embracing the enterprise risk theory in cases like *Jacobi* and *Bazley*, the Canadian Supreme Court at the same time in other contemporary cases expressly re-endorsed the distinction between employees and independent contractors as being of continuing use.[99]

There is some evidence of a crossover of the issues in the judgment of Ward LJ in *E v English Province*.[100] There Ward LJ, in articulating the control test which is relevant to the first question of whether or not an employment relationship existed, stated that control should be interpreted

> [m]ore in terms of whether the employee is accountable to his superior for the way he does the work so as to enable the employer to supervise and effect improvements in performance and eliminate risks of harm to others (the notions relied on by McLachlin J in *Bazley v Curry*).[101]

Ward LJ also suggested the close connection test should be applied to determine the first question of whether an 'employment relationship', or relationship sufficiently like employment, existed so that the potential of vicarious liability arose.[102]

Davis LJ, clearly discussing the 'first issue' of whether an employment relationship existed or not, said:

> (P)ointers at the first stage are, if D can be vicariously liable for the torts of A: (1) that D has caused A to be placed in a position, or where D and A are otherwise in a relationship, whereby D is capable of having some control of A's activities and (2) that the

[98] ibid 60; and 'whether the relationship between the operator and the cleaner can broadly be characterised as one in which control exists should have no bearing on the issue of whether the employer should be held vicariously liable' (64); 'the designation of the wrongdoer as an employee or independent contractor therefore seems to be losing importance. In fact I would suggest that given recent developments, the distinction should be abolished when it comes to deciding whether vicarious liability should be imposed. The scope of the liability should not be determined according to whether the employer had control over the wrongdoer, or whether the wrongdoer can be characterized as an employee. Rather, the scope should be circumscribed by the risk-creating activities of the enterprise. A test such as organisation test is helpful in identifying the boundaries of the enterprise. Whose liability is it? Whose risk is this?' (69).

[99] *671122 Ontario Ltd v Sagaz Industries Canada Inc* (n 76) 999 (Major J for the Court); *KLB v British Columbia* (n 76) 418 (McLachlin CJ, for Gonthier, Iacobucci, Major, Bastarache, Binnie, LeBel and Deschamps JJ).

[100] [2013] QB 722.

[101] ibid 770–71.

[102] ibid 765.

activities are performed on behalf of or are designed to further the aims or interests or purposes ... of D.[103]

This resembles the approach taken by MacDuff J, the trial judge in the case. MacDuff J concluded that the 'close connection test', which most thought to be applicable to the second question of the scope of vicarious liability, was also applicable to the first question,[104] of whether the relationship between the employer and the tortfeasor was such that vicarious liability could be applicable. MacDuff also thought that the concept of 'fair, just and reasonable' was relevant in determining the first question.[105] Of all the judges in *E v English Province*, MacDuff J was clearest about the mixing of issues across the two questions: 'the two stages of the test are not to be determined in isolation; the overall test is a synthesis of the two stages'.[106]

I have indicated above that my reading of Lord Phillips' five-factor approach in *Various Claimants* effectively suggests a merger of the two-stage approach formerly taken to vicarious liability questions to a one stage approach. It may be that the courts' eventual acceptance of the organisational test approach (at least, as a test to be applied with the control test) to what is traditionally regarded as the first question has helped usher in a new phase where the two issues are merged.

The question is whether it is correct, or beneficial, to take into account matters typically relevant to the other of the two issues when deciding the issues. Specifically, the question of whether the worker's activities were designed to further the aims, interests or purposes has, as we have seen in chapter one, traditionally been used to answer the second question—namely the scope of vicarious liability in a particular situation. And similarly, the ability of the employer to supervise and effect improvements in performance was discussed by the Canadian Court in *Bazley* as part of its enterprise risk theory applicable to the second question, again of the scope of vicarious liability. Yet, here in *E v English Province*, the majority justices both use these concepts to help determine the first issue, namely whether an employment relationship exists. Further, consideration of the concept of 'fair, just and reasonable' has typically been applied to the second question, of the scope of vicarious liability, as opposed to threshold question one. The question is whether it is a good legal approach to consider these two questions holistically, in which case considerations relevant to one of them maybe should inform the other, or whether they should remain discrete questions, with separate principles and issues to address.

This apparent merging or crossover of the two issues is not unique to the law of the United Kingdom. Another instance of a 'crossover' occurs in the Australian

[103] ibid 784; Davis LJ also indicated that whether it was 'fair, just and reasonable' to treat a worker as an employee would also be relevant (784), as did Ward LJ ('fair and just', 769) also a doctrine typically applied to the second question, in the context of whether it was fair, just and reasonable to make the employer liable for what the employee did.

[104] ibid 733.

[105] ibid 735.

[106] ibid.

High Court decision in *Attorney-General for NSW v Perpetual Trustee Co (Ltd)*.[107] The context there was an action for loss of services. Fullagar J sought to explain how the loss of services action differed from vicarious liability:

> The theory is that he who has the control should carry the responsibility, and the right of control in the actual execution of the work is said to be the test to be applied in determining whether the relationship which involves responsibility exists or not. When control ceases, responsibility ceases, and a master is not liable for wrongs committed by his servant outside the course of his employment.[108]

Another example appears in the same case in the judgment of Kitto J. There, in the course of explaining who was a 'servant' for the purposes of establishing an employment relationship, Kitto J referred to three elements: the relationship involved obedience to orders; the orders related to doing work; and the doing of the work was for the benefit of the master, or in other words, for the master's own affairs.[109] Kitto J emphasised that the power of direction must belong to the engager 'for the purpose of enabling him to conduct his own affairs'.[110]

It is also apparent in the High Court of Australia decision in *Hollis v Vabu Pty Limited*.[111] This was the decision in which the High Court apparently affirmed the enterprise risk theory of vicarious liability,[112] which is usually associated with the second question in terms of vicarious liability, ie, the scope of activity for which an employer will be liable for an employee's actions/omissions. Was it a coincidence that the joint reasons, in embracing the enterprise risk theory, also came closest to adopting the 'organisational test' approach to determining whether or not a worker was an employee, citing Dixon J in *Colonial Mutual Life Assurance Society*[113] and Windeyer J in *Marshall*,[114] both decisions seen as examples of the organisation test to determine whether or not a worker is an employee, as opposed to the traditional control test? And further, that in *Hollis* the court quotes a textbook entry which criticises the alternative control test as an anachronism suited to earlier ways of working, but out of date in a modern industrialised world.[115] The joint reasons also asked whether the worker 'was running their own enterprise'[116] and referred to deterrence theory[117] in determining whether or not the worker was an employee.

It makes logical sense that, if one is to adopt an enterprise risk approach to the second question, one would adopt an organisational test to the first question.

[107] (1952) 85 CLR 237.
[108] ibid 285.
[109] ibid 299.
[110] ibid 300.
[111] (2001) 207 CLR 21.
[112] ibid 40 (Gleeson CJ; Gaudron, Gummow, Kirby and Hayne JJ).
[113] (1931) 46 CLR 41, 48.
[114] (1963) 109 CLR 210, 217.
[115] *Hollis v Vabu Pty Limited* (n 62) 40–41.
[116] ibid 42.
[117] ibid 43.

Broadly, this is what has occurred in Canada, and to some extent in the United Kingdom, though there is less authority there for the organisational test approach, and a majority of the Court of Appeal in *E v English Province* seems to apply only the control approach. This may be problematic in light of the United Kingdom Supreme Court's eventual acceptance of the enterprise risk approach to answering the second question. However, the most recent United Kingdom decisions such as *Various Claimants* and *Cox* seem to embrace an amalgamated test, where issues of both control and organisation are canvassed, perhaps lessening any potential conflict.

So at least in that way, if one accepts the logic of aligning the enterprise risk approach to question two with the organisational test approach to question one, one cannot fault the logic of the High Court's position in *Hollis v Vabu Pty Limited*. They applied both. The same can be said in respect of the Canadian jurisprudence—their acceptance of the enterprise risk approach to question two has been mirrored by their acceptance of the organisational test approach to question one. The logic is not as strong with the United Kingdom position, with respect, because there the Supreme Court has eventually accepted and applied the enterprise risk approach to question two, courts (including the Court of Appeal in *E v English Province*), have applied the control approach to question one. Recent decisions in *Various Claimants* and *Cox* where the Court takes an amalgamated approach involving both control and organisation lessen the force of this criticism.

The issue though is that in subsequent decisions the High Court of Australia appears to have 'gone cold' over the enterprise risk approach, with only two of seven justices accepting and applying it in *Lepore*,[118] and it being totally ignored in the most recent *Prince Alfred*.[119] So of course the question arises, if the High Court of Australia has effectively abandoned the enterprise risk approach to the 'second question', does this mean that the 'organisational test' approach to the first question is also to be abandoned? In neither *Lepore* nor *Prince Alfred* was the status of the worker as an employee in question, so this question was not answered, but logic suggests that the High Court's apparent rejection of enterprise risk should be accompanied by a step away from the organisation test approach to questions of identifying an employment relationship. Having said that, it is not entirely clear what would replace it, if this were to occur.

Yet paradoxically, in *Sweeney v Boylan Nominees*, decided years after the *Lepore* decision, we see a prime example of the organisational test approach to determining whether or not an employment relationship exists.[120] If the approaches are or should be congruent, in that the enterprise risk approach couples with the organisational test approach, logically the High Court's rejection of the enterprise risk approach in *Lepore* to the second question ought to have precluded their

[118] (2003) 212 CLR 511 (Gaudron and Kirby JJ).
[119] (2016) 258 CLR 134.
[120] (2006) 226 CLR 161, 173 (Gleeson CJ; Gummow, Hayne, Heydon and Crennan JJ).

subsequent use of the organisational test approach to the first question. But this is not what in fact occurred.

Borrowed Employees and the Possibility of Dual Vicarious Liability

It should be noted for the purposes of completeness that at one time the law seemed to be that only one employer could be held vicariously liable for the actions of an employee.[121] Subsequent case law would assume the correctness of this position, rather than consider it in depth.[122] In *Viasystems (Tyneside) Ltd v Thermal Transfer (Northern) Ltd*[123] the Court of Appeal found that, upon an application of either or both the control and enterprise tests, it might be possible for dual vicarious liability, or that more than one employer could be vicariously liable for given wrongdoing. This position was accepted by the United Kingdom Supreme Court in *Various Claimants v Catholic Child Welfare Society*.[124] It has also been accepted in Canada.[125] The matter has not been determined authoritatively in Australia as yet. I have no objection to this development, and there is no need for me to discuss it further.[126]

Conclusion

Traditionally the law applied two discrete tests in relation to vicarious liability issues, considering first whether or not the relationship between the parties was such as to attract the possible application of vicarious liability, and secondly whether or not the wrongdoer's actions were within the scope of their employment such that the employer was vicariously liable for what they did.

The case law—particularly the United Kingdom case law—suggests that a merger of the traditionally two discrete tests has occurred, with a joint discussion of these issues, applying similar principles to both. In that light, given that courts

[121] *Laugher v Pointer* (1826) 5 B & C 547, 558 (Littledale J).

[122] *Mersey Docks and Harbour Board v Coggins and Griffith (Liverpool) Ltd* (n 8); *Esso Petroleum Co Ltd v Hall Russell and Co Ltd* [1989] AC 643.

[123] [2006] QB 510 (May and Rix LJ).

[124] [2013] 2 AC 1.

[125] *Blackwater v Plint* (n 78).

[126] See for further discussion P Giliker, *Vicarious Liability in Tort: A Comparative Perspective* (Cambridge, Cambridge University Press, 2010) 81–98; Atiyah (n 96) said the law's past reluctance to embrace the possibility of joint vicarious liability was 'strange' (156) and found American decisions permitting the possibility were 'sensible' (157).

of many jurisdictions have applied the so-called enterprise risk approach to what would traditionally be considered the 'second test' of the scope of employment, it is not surprising they have become more comfortable applying the 'enterprise' or 'organisation' test to what traditionally was considered to be the 'first test' of whether the relationship was one in which vicarious liability obligations should be recognised. There is a certain logic to this. However, I do not favour the enterprise risk approach to the second question, for the reasons elaborated upon in chapter six and chapter seven. Thus, according to that logic, there is no essentiality about applying an 'enterprise' or 'organisation' test to the threshold, first question. On this logic, it may be better to stick with an adapted control test.

The other factor favouring the control test approach is that it is coherent with a view that an employer should only be liable for actions of their employee that they have authorised, expressly or implicitly, and where the employee is acting for the purposes and benefit of their employer. An employee so acting is acting under the control of their employer. However, an employee who is on a 'frolic' is not so acting. They are no longer under the control of their employer. The law should not make the employer liable for what they do. As is implicit in this argument, I have no essential objection to the collapse of the two formerly discrete tests in relation to vicarious liability to essentially one test, considering a range of factors. And the 'control' test can be adapted to consider not just whether a person is generically to be considered an employee, but whether specific actions committed by the employee should be sheeted home (or liability for them should be sheeted home) to the employer. Thus, perhaps it is better to ask this question about the relation between the employer and employee in relation to specific acts in question, rather than in the abstract, as the law traditionally does here.

Whichever test is applied, however, it is submitted that the law has taken a wrong turn when it makes employers such as banks vicariously liable for doctors performing medicals on their behalf. As discussed above, in the *Barclays Bank* case, applying the 'enterprise risk' and 'organisational tests', a bank was found so liable. The law has gone too far. In no sensible way is a doctor part of the enterprise of a bank.

The bank had little control over how a doctor performs a medical. The doctor, in doing what he did, was not acting for the bank's purposes and for their benefit. He was acting on a 'frolic' on his own. The bank should not have been liable for what he did on the basis of vicarious liability. An argument that they should be held liable in negligence because they selected a doctor inappropriately to conduct such medicals is a separate question that is beyond the scope of this book. However, they should not be vicariously liable for the actions of an independent contractor over whom they had little control and direction and where that person substantially deviated from the purposes for which they were engaged. When the law reaches these conclusions, it risks its moral authority, by effectively punishing the innocent.

10

Non-Delegable Duties

Relationship with Vicarious Liability

Another way in which the law has sought to make an enterprise legally liable in the civil law is through the device of the non-delegable duty. Non-delegable duties are duties that cannot be legally delegated to another;[1] in other words they are personal duties imposed on the relevant person or organisation. They may be described not as a duty to take care, as would be typical in fault-based regimes, but as a duty to ensure that care is taken.[2] Readers of a book on vicarious liability may be wondering why it is considered necessary to devote a chapter to the position of so-called non-delegable duties.

The answer is that the doctrines are closely linked.[3] Both principles involve a defendant being held liable for the actions of another. Some judges have referred to a non-delegable duty as an example of vicarious liability,[4] though this is considered to be incorrect. In some cases, both claims have been run together, or in the alternative.[5] In some cases, limitations in the scope of vicarious liability, for example a traditional past reluctance to find hospitals vicariously liable for actions of employees,[6] and the general inapplicability of vicarious liability for actions of independent contractors, has fed recognition of a non-delegable duty in such context.[7] Some say that non-delegable duties were only created in order to avoid

[1] *Armes v Nottinghamshire County Council* [2017] 3 WLR 1000, 1011 (Lord Reed, with whom Baroness Hale, Lord Kerr and Lord Clarke agreed).

[2] *Kondis v State Transport Authority* (1984) 154 CLR 672, 681 (Mason J, with whom Deane J agreed).

[3] Robert Stevens observes that 'most textbooks include them (non-delegable duties) as an embarrassing coda to vicarious liability': R Stevens, 'Non-Delegable Duties and Vicarious Liability' in J Neyers, E Chamberlain and S Pitel (eds), *Emerging Issues in Tort Law* (Oxford, Hart Publishing, 2007) 368.

[4] *Honeywill and Stein Ltd v Larkin Brothers Ltd* [1934] 1 KB 191, 197 (Slesser LJ, for Hewart CJ and Lord Wright).

[5] *Davie v New Merton Board Mills Ltd* [1959] AC 604.

[6] *Hillyer v Governors of St Bartholomew's Hospital* [1909] 2 KB 820.

[7] *Cassidy v Ministry of Health* [1951] 2 KB 343, 363–64 (Denning LJ). The other justices in the Court of Appeal (Somervell and Singleton LLJ) were content to revisit the limit on vicarious liability for hospital staff, revisiting the earlier decision of *Hillyer v Governors of St Bartholomew's Hospital*, ibid, which apparently denied that a hospital could be vicariously liable for actions of doctors, and did not find it necessary to base liability upon a non-delegable duty. The view of Denning LJ would subsequently be accepted: *Woodland v Swimming Teachers Association* [2014] AC 537, 583 (Lord Sumption, for Lord Clarke, Lord Wilson and Lord Toulson).

the limitations on vicarious liability, or those limitations, together with the doctrine of common employment, as will be discussed below. Thus, the concept of non-delegable duties is considered to be inextricably woven into the concept of vicarious liability, justifying their extended treatment here.

The doctrines share a common weakness—a lack of agreement on any single rationale for their imposition. This has been noted earlier in the case of vicarious liability; the same point has been made repeatedly about the concept of a non-delegable duty, by scholars and judges. There are sometimes suggestions that, as with vicarious liability, notions of deep pockets and/or presumptions about who is insured underlie the doctrine.[8]

Leading torts writer Fleming went so far as to suggest that the concept of a non-delegable duty was a 'disguised form of vicarious liability'.[9] Gummow and Hayne JJ suggested in *New South Wales v Lepore* that a non-delegable duty was a 'species of vicarious responsibility',[10] which is surely not correct with respect, but which demonstrates confusion at the highest levels.

The concept of 'danger' either has been used, or is still currently used, to justify the imposition of vicarious liability and/or the imposition of a non-delegable duty. In the context of vicarious liability, the notion of being liable because the employer 'set the whole thing in motion', according to *Duncan v Findlater*, contemplates the concept of danger. Pollock sought to justify vicarious liability on the basis of a concept of dangerousness.[11] As was discussed in chapter five, concepts of dangerousness or extra-hazardous activity have been used to try to justify the imposition of strict liability, and still in 2014 the United Kingdom Supreme Court in *Woodland* stated that one of the two categories of case in which a non-delegable duty had been held to be owed was in relation to 'dangerous' activity.

On the other hand, there are key differences. The liability, if any, for breach of non-delegable duty is really direct, and personal upon the employer.[12] They are liable for breach of a duty *they* owed. This is in contrast to true vicarious liability, where an employer is liable not for *their* breach of duty or wrongdoing, but that of someone for whom they are legally responsible, such as an employee or agent. In addition, while traditionally an employer was only vicariously liable

[8] *Woodland v Swimming Teachers Association*, ibid, 590 (Baroness Hale, with whom Lord Clarke, Lord Wilson and Lord Toulson agreed); *Kondis v State Transport Authority* (n 2), 690 (Murphy J); *Burnie Port Authority v General Jones Pty Ltd* (1994) 179 CLR 520, 552 (Mason CJ; Deane, Dawson, Toohey and Gaudron JJ) (referring to the fact the defendant upon whom the non-delegable duty was cast was 'probably financially responsible', in the words of Thayer).

[9] JG Fleming, *The Law of Torts*, 9th edn (Sydney, Law Book Co, 1998) 434; PS Atiyah, *Vicarious Liability in the Law of Torts* (London, Butterworths, 1967) said that liability for actions of an independent contractor (typically rationalised on non-delegable duty grounds) was sometimes vicarious (338), and he calls non-delegable duties an 'extended form of vicarious liability' (349); for criticism see Stevens (n 3) 363.

[10] *New South Wales v Lepore* (2003) 212 CLR 511, 599.

[11] F Pollock, *Essays in Jurisprudence and Ethics* (London, FB Rothman, 1882) 114.

[12] *Armes v Nottinghamshire County Council* (n 1) 1010 (Lord Reed, with whom Baroness Hale, Lord Kerr and Lord Clarke agreed); *Stevens v Brodribb* (1986) 160 CLR 16, 29 (Mason J).

for employees and agents, and not for independent contractors, an employer who owed a non-delegable duty could be held liable for actions or omissions of others who were employees, agents or independent contractors. The United Kingdom Supreme Court has recently confirmed the independence of the two actions, and specifically the fact that the Court finds that no vicarious liability exists in a particular situation does not necessarily mean that a non-delegable duty is not applicable.[13]

Development of the Non-Delegable Duty Concept in the United Kingdom

Prior to considering the development of what today we call a non-delegable duty, at least four preliminary points should be made. First, developments in this line of cases are inextricably connected with developments elsewhere in tort law. It must be kept firmly in mind once again that until 1932 the United Kingdom common law of tort did not recognise a generalised duty of care. The law of negligence did not remotely resemble its current breadth. Thus, discussion in these cases of 'duties' must be considered in light of the lack of a generalised duty of care for much of this time. It will also be interesting to note the change in the legal precedents in this area following the House of Lords decision in *Donoghue v Stevenson*. It can be wondered whether, if the generalised duty of care had existed at the relevant time, the courts would have created the non-delegable duty concept. And the obvious corollary will be that, given the generalised duty is now well enshrined and has grown exponentially within a relatively short space of time, questions arise as to whether there is a continuing need for the non-delegable duty concept.[14] This matter will be considered at the end of this chapter.

Secondly, for a long time the doctrine of common employment,[15] together with contributory negligence and *volenti* (the so-called 'unholy trinity'), precluded an injured employee from being able to claim compensation from their employer. While this situation was eventually remedied by statute in the United Kingdom and elsewhere,[16] the existence of those doctrines inevitably led some courts to find other ways in which employers could be legally liable for injured employees.[17]

[13] *Armes v Nottinghamshire County Council*, ibid, 1015 (Lord Reed, with whom Baroness Hale, Lord Kerr and Lord Clarke agreed).

[14] Atiyah (n 9) 333: 'to give the plaintiff a direct right of action against the employer of the contractor is merely to give an unnecessary remedy against a person who is in no way to blame for the damage or injury caused'.

[15] *Priestley v Fowler* (1837) 3 M & W 1.

[16] Law Reform (Personal Injuries) Act 1948 (UK).

[17] Viscount Simonds noted in *Davie v New Merton Board Mills Ltd* (n 5) 618 that the shadow of *Priestley v Fowler* has remained in the law, well after the formal removal of the decision.

The idea that an employer might owe a non-delegable duty of care to their employees to provide safe premises, and thus be liable in cases where their employees were injured, and at a time prior to general workers' compensation schemes, can thus be attributed at least in part to the 'unholy trinity'.[18] However, the disappearance of part of the unholy trinity, and the significant retraction of contributory negligence and *volenti*, has not correspondingly led to the law abandoning the non-delegable duty concept, though a substantial reason for its original creation has effectively been removed or at least largely neutered.[19]

Thirdly, the courts did not use the term 'non-delegable duty' in their attempts to articulate the precise circumstances in which a defendant who had engaged the services of a contractor would be liable for their acts. And fourthly, *Rylands v Fletcher* belongs in this discussion, although it clearly did not involve the question of liability for the acts or omissions of a contractor. It belongs because it is another demonstration of the general thinking of the courts in the mid-nineteenth century, still influenced by old notions of strict liability, but attempting to limit it appropriately, and not realising the potential of the negligence behemoth.

An early case considering the liability of one person for the actions or omissions of another was *Bush v Steinman*.[20] A contracted with B for B to work on his house. B sub-contracted some of the work to C, who sub-contracted some of it to D. D left some lime at the side of the roadway near A's premises. As a result, the plaintiff suffered injury. The court held that A could be liable for D's actions.

The court was clearly somewhat ambivalent about the result in the case and the kind of precedent it would set for other cases. Eyre CJ observed that the 'general proposition that a person shall be liable for any injury which arises in carrying into execution that which he has employed another to do, seems to be too large and loose'.[21] However, he sought to explain the principle to be derived from another

[18] 'That rule (doctrine of common employment) made it necessary to find another basis for the employer's liability, and this was found in the idea of duties personal to the employer': *Davie v New Merton Board Mills Ltd* (n 5) 637 (Lord Reid); *Woodland v Swimming Teachers Association* (n 7) 588 (Baroness Hale, with whom Lord Clarke, Lord Wilson and Lord Toulson agreed); *Kondis v State Transport Authority* (n 2) 678: 'one legacy of the doctrine (of common employment) is the concept of the personal or non-delegable duty, a concept which was designed to circumvent the doctrine of common employment' (Mason J, with whom Deane J agreed); G Williams, 'Liability for Independent Contractors' (1956) 14 *Cambridge Law Journal* 180, 190: 'in the days of the doctrine of common employment, the judges for reasons of policy carved an exception out of that doctrine in respect of the duty to provide proper staff etc. In order to give a semblance of consistency to the law, it was said that the master's responsibility in such a case was not vicarious … but personal. He was under a personal duty to his servants to provide proper staff (and) premises and this duty was non-delegable … this was a typical piece of judicial legislation, designed to mitigate the mischief of the doctrine of common employment'.

[19] Williams, ibid, 191: 'with the abolition of the doctrine of common employment, the special rule in *Wilsons and Clyde Coal Co v English* (non-delegable duty with respect to contractors) is no longer needed in the circumstance that gave it birth'.

[20] *Bush v Steinman* (1799) 1 B & P 404; 126 ER 978. It is said that this case was overruled by the court in *Reedle v London and North West Railway Co* [1949] 4 Ex. 256.

[21] *Bush v Steinman*, ibid, 404; 979.

case he found was analogous to the current one, *Littledale v Lord Lonsdale*.[22] He explained the case as involving a colliery operated for Lord Lonsdale by his agents and servants. He added that it could have been operated by his contractors, 'for that would have made no difference'. As a result of the work the plaintiff's premises were damaged. The court found Lord Lonsdale liable for the damaged premises. This was because the damage was caused in the course of working the defendant's colliery. Although another person might have been contracted for the management of the work, 'yet the work is still carried on for his benefit', and thus he was legally responsible.[23]

Eyre CJ said that *Lonsdale* had empowered the contractor to appoint such contractors as they should think fit. The business was carried on either by the express direction of Lord Lonsdale or under a presumed authority from him. He comes closest to an analogy with vicarious liability, given its history in family home-based businesses, by adding that 'according to the doctrine cited from *Blackstone's Commentaries*, if one member of a family "layeth or casteth" a thing out of the home which amounts to a nuisance, the owner of the home was liable'.[24] Practical considerations seemed to justify this outcome, Eyre CJ suggesting it was 'highly convenient and beneficial to the public'. The person injured should only have to discover the owner of the house which was the occasion of the mischief, not be concerned with the contractual arrangements between the owner and others.[25]

Heath J apparently took a similarly broad position. In one example, he suggested that if a person hires a coach, and a coachman was sent with the coach, the person who hired the coach would be liable for any mischief done by the coachman while in his engagement, though the coachman was not the employee of the defendant.[26] Rooke J took a similarly broad position:

> [H]e who has work going on for his benefit, and on his own premises, must be civilly answerable for the acts of those whom he employs ... he has a control over all those persons who work on his premises and he shall not be allowed to discharge himself from the intendment of law by any act or contract of his own ... he ought to reserve such control, and if he deprive himself of it, the law will not permit him to take advantage of that circumstance in order to screen himself from an action.

Rooke J concluded that 'the person from whom the whole authority is originally derived is the person who ought to be answerable and great inconvenience would follow if it were otherwise'.[27]

Thus, *Bush v Steinman* seems to suggest a kind of vicarious liability for the actions of employees, agents and sub-contractors. The traditional distinction between employees on the one hand and contractors on the other is not discussed.

[22] *Littledale v Lord Lonsdale* 2 H Bl 267.
[23] *Bush v Steinman* (n 20) 406; 979.
[24] ibid 408; 980.
[25] ibid.
[26] ibid.
[27] ibid 410; 981.

Some of the rationale for liability, including who obtains the benefit of the work and issues of control, are analogous to that which has traditionally justified the imposition of vicarious liability.

By the mid-nineteenth century the common law had recognised that different rules should apply in relation to liability for employees, and that of independent contractors. Specifically, the rule that at least generally an employer was not liable for actions of independent contractors.[28]

In the next important decision of *Quarman v Burnett*,[29] involving precisely the factual situation posited by Heath J in *Bush v Steinman*, a different approach is evident compared with that decision. There the plaintiff was injured due to the negligent driving of a coachman engaged by the defendants. The defendants hired the horses and coachman from a third party. The third party paid the coachman's wages. This particular coachman had been regularly engaged by the defendants.

Baron Parke P for the court explained the concept of vicarious liability, and the fact that it applied in cases of employer and employee. The suggestion that a defendant could be liable for the actions of another merely because the defendant contracted them to act for their benefit was 'too large a position'. It would require the overturning of precedents and lead to results that would shock the conscience. In seeking to explain the precedents, Baron Parke P seemed to suggest a difference for cases involving fixed property, where the possessor would be required to take care to ensure their property was managed well so that others would not be injured. It would not matter whether the property was managed by employees, agents or contractors. He suggested the result might be different if what was involved was, like in this case, personal movable chattels. In such cases a person engaging with contractors for work to be done involving the personal movable chattels would not necessarily be liable for those actions.

The distinction made by Baron Parke P between cases involving fixed property, and those involving movable chattels, was likely to have been an attempt to rationalise and explain existing disparate precedents. Baron Parke P did not explain conceptually why apparently a responsibility might exist with respect to real property, but not with respect to personal chattels. Nor did he specifically use the concept of 'non-delegable duty', but his attempted justification for the imposition of liability upon a property owner for work done by contractors with respect to it can, in hindsight, be seen as the real beginning of the common law's recognition of a non-delegable duty of care, at least with respect to some activities. However, a satisfactory elucidation of its rationale and scope would remain elusive.

A different justification for the imposition of what we might now call a non-delegable duty appeared in *Pickard v Smith* in 1861.[30] There the case involved the

[28] *Laugher v Pointer* (1826) 5 B & C 547; *Reedie v London and North Western Railway Co* (1849) 4 Ex 244.

[29] *Quarman v Burnett* (1840) 6 M & W 499; 151 ER 509.

[30] *Pickard v Smith* (1861) 10 CB (NS) 470; 142 ER 535.

possible liability of the lessee of a railway station. The station contained a cellar in which coal was stored. The lessee engaged a coal merchant to supply coal to them. In the course of delivering the coal, the merchant negligently left the cellar door open. The plaintiff was walking along the railway platform at night and suffered injuries when they fell into the cellar. A jury awarded the plaintiff damages. On appeal it was argued the plaintiff should have been non-suited. The appeal was dismissed.

Williams J, for Willes and Keating JJ, noted the merchant was an independent contractor, rather than an employee, of the defendant. He acknowledged that generally if an independent contractor was employed to do a lawful act and, in the course of the work they or their servants committed a wrong, the employer was not legally responsible. However, he opined that:

> That rule is, however, inapplicable to cases in which the act which occasions the injury is one which the contractor was employed to do; nor, by parity of reasoning, to cases in which the contractor is intrusted with the performance of a duty incumbent upon his employer, and neglects its fulfilment, whereby an injury is occasioned.[31]

Willes J added that the defendant, 'having thereby caused danger' by opening the cellar through their agent, 'was bound to take reasonable steps to prevent mischief'. The engagement of an agent to perform the duty was no defence. *Pickard v Smith*, like others in this line, also reflects the master's tort theory of liability,[32] a theory which as has been discussed earlier in this book, is now thoroughly discredited. *Pickard v Smith* contains new notions of duties that are incumbent on the defendant, and a nascent idea that these duties, however defined, cannot be legally delegated to others.[33] It also refers to liability being based on a defendant having 'created a danger'.

This concept of liability being based on the defendant creating a danger is clearly critical in the classic *Fletcher v Rylands*[34] case of this period, and Blackburn J's statement articulating a defendant landowner's legal responsibility for things that 'though harmless whilst it remains (on the defendant's premises), will naturally do mischief it is escapes',[35] liable for things the property owner 'knows to be mischievous' if it were to escape.[36] Though clearly not a case involving liability

[31] ibid 480; 539. Around the same time the court found that a statutory duty imposed upon an employer was personal in nature to the employer and could not legally be delegated to another: *Hole v Sittingbourne and Sheerness Railway Co* (1861) 6 H & N 488; 158 ER 201. Atiyah suggests that while indeed the nature of statutory duties is often non-delegable, involving a positive obligation to act, it should not have necessarily been assumed that such concept could be applied as readily to cases of common law obligation: (n 9) 332.

[32] (1861) 10 CB (NS) 470, 480; 142 ER 535, 539: 'the act of opening it was the act of the employer, though done through the agency of the coal-merchant' (Williams J, for Willes and Keating JJ).

[33] Atiyah (n 9) says that the court simply assumed the duty was non-delegable, without elaboration, explanation or justification (329).

[34] *Fletcher v Rylands* (1866) 1 LR Ex 265.

[35] ibid 279.

[36] ibid 280.

for contractors or sub-contractors, the concept of 'dangerousness' in this case, and liability being based on 'having created a danger' or 'creating a mischief', would be influential in subsequent cases. The Supreme Court has observed that the concept of a non-delegable duty was implicit in *Rylands*.[37]

Another important case of this period where the concept of dangerousness was used to establish liability, again in the context of a contractor relationship, was *Bower v Peate*.[38] There the defendant property owner engaged a builder to build a new house on his property, which adjoined that of the plaintiff. Under the terms of engagement, the builder agreed to do what was necessary to support buildings adjoining the defendant's premises, and to make good any damage that may be caused to those surrounding buildings as a result of the works. Due to insufficient support given to the plaintiff's premises during the construction work, the plaintiff's premises were damaged. The legal question was whether the defendant was liable for the builder's negligent work.

Cockburn CJ, with whom Mellor and Field JJ agreed, stated:

> A man who orders a work to be executed, from which, in the natural course of things, injurious consequences to his neighbour must be expected to arise, unless means are adopted by which such consequences may be prevented, is bound to see to the doing of that which is necessary to prevent the mischief, and cannot relieve himself of his responsibility by employing someone else.[39]

The court claimed there was an

> [o]bvious difference between committing work to a contractor to be executed from which, if properly done, no injurious consequences can arise, and handing over to him work to be done from which mischievous consequences will arise unless preventive measures are adopted. While it may be just to hold the party authorizing the work in the former case exempt from liability for injury, resulting from negligence which he had no reason to anticipate, there is, on the other hand, good ground for holding him liable for injury caused by an act certain to be attended with injurious consequences if such consequences are not in fact prevented.[40]

Similar principles were discussed and applied in *Tarry v Ashton*,[41] where a defendant landowner was found guilty when a lamp on their premises fell on to a plaintiff walking by. The defendant had previously engaged a contractor to repair the lamp,

[37] *Woodland v Swimming Teachers Association* (n 7) 574–75 (Lord Sumption, with whom Lord Clarke, Lord Wilson and Lord Toulson agreed): 'it is clear from Lord Blackburn's observations that the essential point about them was that there was an antecedent relationship between the parties as neighbouring landowners, from which a positive duty independent of the wrongful act itself could be derived. The duty was personal to the defendant, because it attached to him in his capacity as the occupier of the neighbouring land from which the hazard originated'.

[38] *Bower v Peate* (1876) 1 QBD 321.

[39] ibid 326.

[40] ibid 326–27. Again, there is evidence of the master's tort theory: 'the act of removal was an act done by the order and authority of the defendant—in other words, was the act of the defendant' (327).

[41] *Tarry v Ashton* (1876) 1 QBD 314.

and it was said that in the course of doing so that contractor had loosened the lamp, contributing to the accident. The contractor was admitted to be such, and not an employee. Nevertheless, the defendant was held to be liable on the basis it was their duty to make the lamp reasonably safe.[42] Lush J said the defendant had 'put the public safety in peril', and the defendant could not rid themselves of liability by claiming they engaged a contractor to fix it.[43] The principles were also applied when the duty to repair was statutory in nature.[44]

This idea of liability being based loosely on the creation of a danger, evidenced in *Pickard*, *Fletcher*, and *Bower*, was continued in further pre-*Donoghue* decisions. So in 1881 in *Dalton v Angus*[45] a defendant homeowner was held liable for the actions of a sub-contractor which undermined the foundations of the neighbouring premises. The House of Lords adopted the 'creation of a danger' line evidenced in the earlier decisions. Lord Watson for instance stated that:

> When an employer contracts for the performance of work, which properly conducted can occasion no risk to his neighbour's house which he is under obligation to support, he is not liable for damage arising from the negligence of the contractor. But in cases where the work is necessarily attended with risk, he cannot free himself from liability by binding the contractor to take effectual precautions.[46]

Lord Blackburn agreed that generally a person engaging a contractor to do work was not liable for the negligence of that contractor or their servants. However, it would be otherwise if the person engaging the other to do the work 'had a duty'. In such cases they could not avoid responsibility by delegating that task to a contractor. He did not specifically call this duty 'non-delegable' as a judge today would. Nor did he precisely articulate the circumstances in which a person might owe such a duty. However, given his express agreement with *Bower*, and his classic judgment in *Rylands*, it can be reasonably concluded that in the view of Blackburn J, a person would owe such a duty while they were engaged in dangerous activity of some kind.

In 1883 in *Hughes v Percival* Lord Blackburn referred to a non-delegable duty in framing the defendant's duty as one requiring that reasonable care and skill be exercised, and that the duty could not be negated by the engagement of an independent contractor.[47] There was discussion in *Hughes* on the nature of the non-delegable duty said to be owed in some circumstances. Specifically, the issue arises as to whether it is strict in nature, or whether it requires proof of some kind of fault on the person said to be so liable.

[42] ibid 319 (Blackburn J).
[43] ibid 320; to like effect Quain J (320). Atiyah notes the case could be explained on the basis of simple nuisance principles: (n 9) 330–31.
[44] *Gray v Pullen* (1864) 5 B & S 970; 122 ER 1091.
[45] *Dalton v Angus* [1881] 6 AC 740.
[46] ibid 831.
[47] *Hughes v Percival* (1883) 8 AC 443, 446.

In *Hughes* different positions are evident on this point. Lord Blackburn seemed to believe that the duty was simply to 'see that reasonable skill and care were exercised'.[48] He stated that it was *not* an absolute obligation to ensure the plaintiff suffered no damage from particular works. However, other judges seemed to have a wider ambit in mind for the scope of the non-delegable duty. Lord Watson said that one who owed a non-delegable duty would be liable for an independent contractor's negligent act unless the defendant could show they could not have reasonably foreseen a contractor who was 'neither insane nor dishonest' would commit the wrong.[49] Lord FitzGerald was most explicit on this, noting the law had been 'verging somewhat in the direction of treating parties engaged in (operations like the defendant's) as insurers of their neighbours'. However, he said the law had not quite reached that point, and adopted an approach close to a negligence type standard.[50] The case of *Smith v Baker and Sons* is further evidence of the concept of dangerousness being used to justify the imposition of a duty of care upon an employer, not to impose strict liability upon them.[51]

A further example of this 'dangerousness' doctrine appears shortly afterwards in *Black v Christchurch Finance Co* where Lord Shand for the Privy Council noted:

> The lighting of a fire on open bush land, where it may readily spread to adjoining property and cause serious damage, is an operation necessarily attended with great danger, and a proprietor who executes such an operation is bound to use all reasonable precautions to prevent the fire extending to his neighbour's property. And if he authorises another to act for him he is bound, not only to stipulate that such precautions shall be taken, but also to see that these are observed, otherwise he will be responsible for the consequences.[52]

Again, it assists in understanding these precedents to appreciate they were developed at a time when a generalised duty of care had not been recognised; rather the existence of a duty of care depended on whether the relationship could be held to fit within existing categories of relationship. Thus, these cases can be read as a finding by the court that one category of relationship where a duty will be recognised will be one where the defendant has created a danger, or is involved in dangerous activity. In this light, it is somewhat unfortunate that the concept of dangerousness got caught up in the *Rylands* discussion, because that gave rise to the notion that the inherent dangerousness of an activity could give rise to the kind of *Rylands* strict liability, whereas my reading of the other cases in this field suggests that the court was mainly using the concept of dangerousness to justify

[48] ibid 446.

[49] ibid 451.

[50] He concluded the defendant 'must be vigilant and careful, for he is liable for injuries to his neighbour caused by any want of prudence or precaution', ibid (455).

[51] *Smith v Baker and Sons* [1891] AC 325, 353: 'at common law a master who employs a servant in work of a dangerous character is bound to take all reasonable precautions for the workman's safety' (Lord Watson). Of course, if the employee was aware of the dangerousness, the *volenti* defence may apply.

[52] *Black v Christchurch Finance Co* [1893] AC 48, 54.

the imposition of a duty of care upon a defendant, rather than to impose strict liability upon them. Thus, *Rylands* muddied the waters in relation to the utility of the concept of dangerousness.

Just after *Donoghue v Stevenson*, the Court of Appeal continued to apply this 'dangerous activity' line of cases, specifically noting the 'special rules that apply to extra-hazardous or dangerous operations'.[53]

The House of Lords in *Wilsons and Clyde Coal Co Ltd v English*[54] seemed to accept that an employer's responsibility to provide a safe system of work was non-delegable in nature.[55] Several of the speeches seem to confirm that the nature of this non-delegable duty is not absolute or strict in nature.[56] It is necessary to show that the defendant has breached the duty, by not taking reasonable care, *or not ensuring that reasonable care is taken*. This is broader than the traditional negligence doctrine, but is not strict liability, in the sense that liability is imposed without fault. The fault could be in failing to ensure that reasonable care was taken. It is appreciated that, depending on how such a doctrine was interpreted and applied by judges, this could be something *close* to strict liability. For instance, in *Wilsons*, Lord Maugham concluded the defendant could be liable to the plaintiff 'unless the agent has himself used due care and skill in carrying out the employer's duty'.[57] Presumably it would not be sufficient to avoid liability to show that the wrongdoer had been chosen carefully, and there was no other evidence that the defendant themselves were guilty of wrongdoing. Lord Wright seemed to be of like mind when he said:

> The duty of the invitor towards the invitee is, in my opinion, a duty personal to the former, in the sense that he does not get rid of the obligation by entrusting the performance to independent contractors. It is true that the invitor is not an insurer; he warrants, however, that due care and skill to make the premises reasonably safe for the invitee have been exercised, whether by himself, his servants, or agents, or by independent contractors whom he employs to perform his duty. He does not fulfil the warranty merely by leaving the work to contractors however reputable or generally competent. His warranty is broken if they fail to exercise the proper care and skill.[58]

[53] *Honeywill and Stein Ltd v Larkin Brothers Ltd* (n 4) 200 (Slesser LJ, for Hewart CJ and Lord Wright).

[54] *Wilsons and Clyde Coal Co Ltd v English* [1938] AC 57.

[55] 'The defendants cannot divest (themselves) of this duty, though (they) may—and, if it involves technical management and he is not himself technically qualified, must—perform it through the agency of an employee. It remains the employer's obligation' (75) (Lord Macmillan); 'I think the whole course of authority consistently recognises a duty which rests on the employer and which is personal to the employer, to take reasonable care for the safety of his workmen, whether the employee be an individual, a firm, or a company and whether or not the employer takes any share in the conduct of the operations' (83–84) (Lord Wright).

[56] 'The master, being under a duty to take due care in the provision of a reasonably safe system of work' (65) (Lord Thankerton); 75 (Lord Macmillan); 78 (Lord Wright: 'when I use the word absolutely, I do not mean that employers warrant the adequacy of plant, or the competence of fellow employees, or the propriety of the system of work. The obligation is fulfilled by the exercise of due care and skill'; 87 (Lord Maugham).

[57] *Wilsons and Clyde Coal Co Ltd v English* (n 54) 88.

[58] *Thomson v Cremin* [1956] 1 WLR 103, 110.

However, this 'dangerousness' doctrine, and the system of strict liability which it eventually was said to support, at least as a result of *Rylands*, was seriously undermined in *Read v Lyons and Company Limited.*[59] My reading of the case suggests that the court was very much influenced by the decision of *Donoghue v Stevenson* a decade earlier, and the ushering in of the negligence era as opposed to strict liability doctrine, yet in fact *Donoghue* attracts a mere passing reference by one of the judges in *Read*. If not the influence of *Donoghue*, how else can one explain the court's apparent rejection of dangerousness as a foundation for the imposition of strict liability, a doctrine the courts had been propounding for more than 80 years until *Read*?

Lord Macmillan led the rejection of the so-called dangerousness doctrine as the basis for the imposition of strict liability:

> (The appellant) sought to convince your Lordships that there is a category of things and operations dangerous in themselves and that those who harbour such things or carry on such operations in their premises are liable apart from negligence for any personal injuries occasioned by these dangerous things or operations … I do not think that it has ever been laid down that there is absolute liability apart from negligence where persons are injured in consequence of the use of such things or the conduct of such operations … every activity in which man engages is fraught with some possible element of danger to others … it (is) impracticable to frame a legal classification of things as things dangerous and things not dangerous, attaching absolute liability in the case of the former but not in the case of the latter.[60]

Lord Macmillan, together with other Law Lords,[61] was at pains to emphasise that *Rylands* should not be read as setting down a general principle of strict, or absolute, liability for dangerous activity. He and other justices sought to limit *Rylands* to cases involving neighbouring property owners,[62] denying that it applied to cases of personal injuries,[63] and recasting it as truly a nuisance case,[64] rather than presaging a strong independent principle of strict liability. He suggested that the fact that an activity was relatively dangerous or relatively safe would be taken into account in determining the content of the duty of care that the defendant owed with respect to such activity; it should not be used to determine whether a strict liability or fault-based liability principle should be applied. Other Law Lords similarly rejected the use of a concept of dangerousness to differentiate the application of strict liability and a negligence standard.[65]

59 *Read v Lyons and Co Limited* [1947] AC 136.
60 ibid 172.
61 ibid 167 (Viscount Simon); 178 (Lord Porter).
62 ibid 174 (Lord Macmillan); 186 (Lord Uthwatt).
63 ibid 173.
64 ibid 183 (Lord Simonds).
65 ibid 180 (Lord Simonds); Lord Uthwatt: 'I do not think that by reason only of the dangerous nature of the business carried on, the occupier guaranteed (the invitee) freedom from harm. If that be so, it is against reason that the law, whose function is to give effect to reasonable expectations, should impose such a guarantee. A measure of care determined by the degree of danger is in my

The issue as to whether an employer owed a non-delegable duty to employees to provide safe premises was considered in *Davie v New Merton Board Mills Ltd.*[66] The question there involved an employee injured due to a defective work implement. These had been supplied to his employer by a third party and manufactured by another. It was common ground that the implement had been manufactured negligently. There was no negligence by the employer in relation to their inspection and maintenance of work tools. The question was the extent of the employer's legal responsibility, if any, for the injuries to the employee that resulted. The injured employee's case seemed to be run on two arguments, though they often seemed to overlap. First, that the employer was vicariously liable for the negligent manufacture,[67] and secondly that the employer owed a non-delegable duty to provide a safe working environment, including safe tools and implements.[68]

The House of Lords rejected both arguments, the first because the employer could not be vicariously liable for what the manufacturer did. The manufacturer was not known to them, and they did not engage them. In no sense was the manufacturer the employee, agent or even the independent contractor of the employer.[69] It rejected the second argument that an employer had breached a non-delegable duty to provide safe tools and premises.[70] This was a significant finding, because although some earlier cases had reached the same conclusion,[71] other cases seemed to suggest that an employer did owe a non-delegable duty to employees around workplace safety issues.[72] In saying this, some members of the

opinion the utmost that either party would envisage and, in my opinion, the law demands that and no other standard of duty' (186), and 'a claim based only on the dangerous nature of the business is not admissible' (188).

66 [1959] AC 604.

67 ibid 'The respondents are liable (if they are liable) for the accident to the appellant because the manufacturers were careless, and for that carelessness they must assume vicarious responsibility' (619, Viscount Simonds).

68 ibid 'The appellant (says) here the employer was under an absolute personal obligation to supply proper tools to the workman which he could not fulfil by purchasing defective tools in the market' (623, Viscount Simonds).

69 ibid 624–25 (Viscount Simonds); 629 (Lord Morton).

70 ibid 625 (Viscount Simonds); 629 (Lord Morton). Lord Reid agreed, though he conceded that in some cases the law imposed a 'personal duty' on a defendant with respect to work done by a contractor on the defendant's own premises, but said that this applied 'at least' if the negligent workmanship were discoverable by reasonable inspection (646). With respect, this appears to combine a doctrine of strict liability with a fault-based concept. Lord Tucker appeared to agree that in some cases at least an employer would remain liable although they had delegated the task to an independent contractor with respect to cases involving the employer's 'personal duty' but he declined to elaborate the scope of such duty/duties (647); Lord Keith (653).

71 *Weems v Mathieson* (1861) 4 Macq HL 215; *Ovington v M'Vicar* (1864) 2 M 1066, 1072–73 (Inglis LJC).

72 *Baird v Addie* (1854) 16 D 490, 493n: 'the primary obligation being imposed on the coalmaster, it is clear that if he employs another to fulfil it, he is liable for any failure or neglect in its fulfilment'; *Macdonald v Andrew Wyllie and Sons* (1898) 1 F 339, 345: 'if a master buys a machine ... necessary for the execution of his work, and gives it to his workman, it is the master's machine, not the workman's or manufacturer's. If the machine turns out to be faulty, defective or otherwise insufficient, the master must answer for it' (Lord Trayner); *Donnelly v Glasgow Corporation* [1958] SC 107, 122: 'it is admitted

Court suggested that a category of case did exist where an employer's obligations, being personal in nature, could not be delegated,[73] but all members of the Court agreed that this was not such a case, and the judges were (perhaps understandably) reluctant to explain in what circumstances such a personal duty might arise, other than to reject that it applied to the facts at hand.

The other noteworthy feature of *Davie* is the discussion by several members of the Court of the fact that any non-delegable duty owed was not strict in nature. That, in other words, the one owing such a duty would only be legally responsible if there was some kind of negligence on their part. A majority of judges took this position.[74] There are conclusions by the judges that the one owing the non-delegable duty is not an effective insurer of the work of the independent contractor, and that the one owing the non-delegable duty does not effectively provide some kind of guarantee or warranty as to the quality of the work or service provided by the independent contractor.[75] In other words, that the non-delegable duty is not considered to be strict liability or absolute liability.[76]

by the corporation that the omnibus was defective and they aver that their suppliers were responsible for the defective condition. But on this branch of the law a master cannot escape liability to his servant for defective plant by blaming his agents. The personal responsibility which the law lays on the master in respect of the plant covers the activities of any person whom the master employs to provide that plant. The supplier and the master are as one. If then the supplier erred, the master is saddled with that error' (Lord Justice-Clerk, for Lord Mackay and Lord Patrick).

[73] *Davie v New Merton Board Mills Ltd* (n 5) 625 (Viscount Simonds) (referred to an exception involving duties that were for the employer to perform); 646 (Lord Reid) (who believed the exception applied to 'personal duties' owed by the employer with respect to work done on their own premises by an independent contractor where the work might normally be done by an employee, at least if the defective work was reasonably discoverable); 647 (Lord Tucker) (who believed in the exception relating to cases involving the employer's 'personal duty'); and 653 Lord Keith agreed that an employer could be held liable in a case of 'delegated performance', but this was not such a case.

[74] eg, Lord Reid held that the one owing a non-delegable duty would be liable for the work of the independent contractor if the negligent work would have been discovered if the duty holder had made a reasonable inspection of the work done (646), but would not be liable if they had made such an inspection, and had been competent in their choice of contractor (646). Lord Tucker said the one owing the non-delegable duty could be liable if they had created faulty specifications or failed to reasonably inspect the product supplied (648). Lord Keith said that the duty of a master in supplying an employee with equipment 'cannot be placed higher than a duty to exercise reasonable care to see that (it) is safe for the purpose for which it is intended' (653). On the other hand, Glanville Williams suggested the one owing the non-delegable duty should be considered to have met their obligation if they engaged competent contractors: Williams (n 18) 191. Williams rejected the suggestion that the duty should encompass inspecting the work of the independent contractor on the basis that the contractor was the expert and the owner of the duty may not have the requisite expertise (188).

[75] Lord Keith explained that although a Scottish Lord President had used the word 'guarantee' to describe the obligations of the one who owed a non-delegable duty, 'I am not satisfied that he meant more than that the employer was under a duty to take reasonable means to satisfy himself as far as possible by inspection or otherwise that (work or services provided) safe for his workplace' (650). Lord Keith referred to the statements of Lord Wright in *Angliss* as to the indeterminacy involved in the holder of the obligation being an effective insurer of all contractors and sub-contractors with whom they might engage (652). He rejected the argument of the appellant in that case that the employer was effectively required to warrant the safety of tools used by their employees.

[76] Lord Reid said 'no one has ever supported' an argument that the one owing the non-delegable duty had obligations that were absolute in nature (638).

By the time of *McDermid v Nash Dredging and Reclamation Co Ltd* the House of Lords had apparently accepted that an employer owed a non-delegable duty to provide a safe system of work.[77]

The House of Lords rejected a suggestion that an owner of premises generally owed a non-delegable duty of care with respect to work that an independent sub-contractor had done on their behalf.[78] As a result of the work, the plaintiff's adjoining premises were damaged. The Court unanimously rejected the plaintiff's argument that the defendant owed them a non-delegable duty of care with respect to the building work.

Lord Bridge, with whom all other Law Lords agreed, stated:

> If (the defendants) are to be held liable for the negligent workmanship of their sub-contractors ... it must first be shown that in the circumstances they had assumed a personal duty to all the world to ensure that (their premises) should be free of dangerous defects ... whence does this non-delegable duty arise? (The plaintiff) submits that it is a duty undertaken by a main contractor in the building industry who contracts to erect an entire building. I cannot agree because I cannot recognise any legal principle to which such an assumption of duty can be related. Just as I may employ a building contractor to build me a house, so may the building contractor, subject to the terms of my contract with him, in turn employ another to undertake part of the work. If the mere fact of employing a contractor to undertake building work automatically involved the assumption by the employer of a duty of care to any person who may be injured by a dangerous defect in the work caused by the negligence of the contractor, this would obviously lead to absurd results.[79]

Lord Bridge referred to a decision of the New Zealand Court of Appeal in *Mount Albert Borough Council v Johnson*,[80] where a plaintiff successfully claimed compensation from a property developer for defects in the premises. The defects were caused by the negligent work of a contractor whom the developer had engaged. The Court of Appeal found that the developer's duty was to ensure that proper care and skill were exercised during construction, and that this responsibility could not (legally) be delegated to an independent contractor.[81]

Commenting on the outcome, Lord Bridge pithily observed that 'as a matter of social policy this conclusion may be entirely admirable'. However, it was a decision better left to the legislature. It was dangerous for the common law to 'adopt ... novel policies which it sees as instruments of social justice but, to which, unlike the legislature, it is unable to set carefully defined limitations'.[82]

[77] *McDermid v Nash Dredging and Reclamation Co Ltd* [1987] 1 AC 906, 910 (Lord Hailsham) and 919 (Lord Brandon) (Lord Bridge, Lord Mackay and Lord Ackner agreed with both judgments).

[78] *D and F Estates Ltd v Church Commissioners for England* [1988] 1 AC 177.

[79] ibid 209 (Lord Bridge, with whom Lord Templeman, Lord Ackner, Lord Oliver and Lord Jauncey agreed).

[80] *Mount Albert Borough Council v Johnson* [1979] 2 NZLR 234.

[81] ibid, Cooke J, with whom Somers J agreed, 240–41.

[82] *D and F Estates Ltd v Church Commissioners for England* (n 78) 210.

The concept of a non-delegable duty was considered in more detail in the recent decision of *Woodland v Swimming Teachers Association*.[83] There the plaintiff was a student at a school. The school arranged for the students to travel to a swimming pool managed by a different authority. The plaintiff suffered severe brain injuries in the course of swimming at the pool. One of her claims was against her school. She argued that it owed her a non-delegable duty of care, such that it could not legally delegate responsibility for her wellbeing to the organisation which managed the swimming pool, its contractors and/or its staff. All members of the Supreme Court agreed that the school authority owed the plaintiff a non-delegable duty of care.

Lord Sumption, with whom Lord Clarke, Lord Wilson and Lord Toulson agreed, noted that while the common law exceptionally recognised that non-delegable duties existed, it did not have a single theory to explain why that was so.[84] However, the judgment recognised two particular categories of case in which such duties had been held to exist. The first was a somewhat loose category of cases in which the defendant was involved in activity which was inherently hazardous or likely to become so. Lord Sumption candidly admitted this category of cases was blighted by arbitrary distinctions between ordinary and extraordinary hazards, and that it might be ripe for re-examination. He observed that this category might be seen as one grounded in 'special public policy' involving the creation of exceptional dangers.

However, this case involved the second category of non-delegable duty case. He said that cases in this category were characterised by three aspects:

1. The duty arose not from the negligent character of the defendant's act, but because of an antecedent relationship between plaintiff and defendant.
2. The duty is a positive or affirmative duty to protect a particular class of persons against a particular class of risks, not simply a duty to refrain from acting in a way which might foreseeably cause injury.
3. The duty is by virtue of that relationship personal to the defendant. While the defendant might practically be able to, and may well have, delegated its performance to another, due to its non-delegable nature, the defendant retained legal responsibility for compliance with the duty.[85]

Lord Sumption used the concept of an 'assumption of responsibility' that could be imputed to the defendant, by virtue of their relationship with the plaintiff.[86]

[83] [2014] AC 537.

[84] ibid 573.

[85] ibid 575.

[86] ibid (for Lord Clarke, Lord Wilson and Lord Toulson); similarly Baroness Hale (with whom Lord Clarke, Lord Wilson and Lord Toulson also agreed) 588. Some see this 'assumption of responsibility' notion as the corollary of the old 'extra-hazardous activity' which at one time was said to justify the recognition of a non-delegable duty. John Murphy makes this argument: 'the creation of an exceptional risk can be invoked to justify the imputation to the defendant of an assumed responsibility': J Murphy, 'Juridical Foundations of Common Law Non-Delegable Duties' in J Neyers, E Chamberlain and S Pitel (eds), *Emerging Issues in Tort Law* (Oxford, Hart Publishing, 2007) 386.

Where such an assumption of responsibility arose, a non-delegable duty could be recognised. He noted that such an assumption had been found in cases involving employees, hospitals, schools, invitees and independent contractors engaged by the defendant. He attempted to characterise these cases as where (a) the danger emanated from the defendant's premises and (b) cases involving the vulnerability of the claimant, involving existence of a relationship between plaintiff and defendant such that the latter has a degree of protective custody over the former, where that custody had been delegated elsewhere.[87] The plaintiff would have no control over how the defendant chose to perform their operations. What had been delegated would need to have been an integral part of the positive duty assumed towards the plaintiff, and the negligence of the person to whom the task had been delegated would need to concern the very act(s) delegated, not something peripheral. It was not necessary that the defendant control the immediate environment in which the plaintiff's injury or loss occurred.[88] A non-delegable duty would only be imposed where it was 'fair, just and reasonable' to do so.[89]

Lord Sumption claimed the extent of liability was limited. For example, a school's non-delegable duties would generally be confined to activities within school hours and on school premises, though he then included other times or places 'where the school may carry out its educational functions'.[90] The non-delegable duty would not extend to extra-curricular activities or school trips in school holidays. A school would not be liable 'for the negligence of those to whom no control over the child has been delegated, such as bus drivers or theatres, zoos or museums to which children may be taken by school staff in school hours'.[91]

Lord Sumption explained that the law regarding non-delegable duties had assumed a greater significance today given the growing trend for organisations to outsource activities that formerly would have been undertaken in-house.[92]

Whereas a majority of the judges in *Davie* had seemed to require some negligence on the part of the holder of the non-delegable duty, for instance in the selection of contractor, or the failure to inspect the goods or test the services supplied, Lord Sumption in *Woodland* sought to sharply distinguish the non-delegable duty from anything resembling negligence on the part of the one who owed it. He said that a non-delegable duty was a 'markedly more onerous obligation' than the general negligence standard.[93] They were 'inconsistent with the fault-based principles' on which the law of negligence was based.[94] It was an assumption of responsibility for the exercise of due care by the one to whom the work was delegated.

[87] *Woodland v Swimming Teachers Association* (n 7) 576; Baroness Hale (with whom Lord Clarke, Lord Wilson and Lord Toulson agreed) concurred (589).
[88] ibid 583.
[89] ibid 584.
[90] ibid 585.
[91] ibid.
[92] ibid.
[93] ibid 576.
[94] ibid 582.

Though Lord Sumption did not use the word, the one owing the non-delegable duty would be an effective insurer of the work of the independent contractor.

Lord Sumption made it clear that the defendant who owed a non-delegable duty would be strictly liable for the negligence of an independent contractor to the extent the contractor performed obligations that the defendant had assumed a responsibility to perform.[95] They would not be strictly liable for the negligence of an independent contractor that related to something for which they merely had a duty to arrange performance, as opposed to their personal duty. They could also be liable in negligence, for example if they did not apply diligence in selecting a contractor.[96]

Most recently in *Armes v Nottinghamshire County Council*[97] the Supreme Court reaffirmed Lord Sumption's judgment in *Woodland* regarding the characteristics of a non-delegable duty: nothing that the duty, where it existed, involved a positive or affirmative duty to protect a class of persons including the plaintiff from a particular class of risks. It was not simply a duty to refrain from acting in a particular way that might foreseeably cause injury, as would be the case in a standard negligence case.[98] The Court interpreted foster care legislation there to not impose a non-delegable duty on the state with respect to the placement of children in foster care.[99] The Court also confirmed that in principle a defendant could be liable for breach of a non-delegable duty although the relevant action(s) were deliberate, rather than merely negligent.[100]

Australian Developments

Prior to explaining developments in Australian law in this area, one point should be repeated. It is that until 1963 the Australian High Court considered itself to be bound by decisions of the House of Lords.[101] Further, until 1975 appeals from decisions of the High Court of Australia lay with the Privy Council. This partly explains the kind of deference to the United Kingdom decisions evident in some of the earlier High Court decisions referred to below. However, later High Court decisions show an increasing willingness to depart from United Kingdom legal principle, such that today, the position of non-delegable duties is far different in Australian law compared with what was been discussed above. Today, the relationship between the two legal systems should be seen as an equal one, with

[95] ibid 585.
[96] ibid.
[97] [2017] 3 WLR 1000.
[98] ibid 1011 (Lord Reed, with whom Baroness Hale, Lord Kerr and Lord Clarke agreed) (Lord Hughes J concurring).
[99] ibid 1015.
[100] ibid.
[101] *Parker v The Queen* (1963) 111 CLR 610.

extensive reference to the case law of the other,[102] and of course a mutual deference. However, the days of unthinking acceptance and application of United Kingdom precedent in developing Australian common law are long gone.

The initial United Kingdom influence on Australian legal principle in this area is obvious in the first case where the matter was considered by the High Court, *McInnes v Wardle*.[103] There the defendant had engaged an independent contractor to destroy some rabbits on his property. Pursuant to this task the contractor lit fires on the defendant's land. The fire escaped onto the plaintiff's neighbouring property, and he sustained damage. The question was the liability of the defendant for the actions of the independent contractor he engaged. All members of the Court found the defendant was liable. Four of them used the concept of 'dangerousness' which had appealed to the House of Lords in cases such as *Black v Christchurch Finance*,[104] citing it and cases such as *Bower v Peate* and *Dalton v Angus* to justify their conclusions.

A similar question arose as to the liability of a defendant for the work of an independent contractor in *Torette House Proprietary Limited v Berkman*.[105] The contractor had negligently rendered a water pipe operational, unknown to the defendant. As a result, water leaked from the defendant's premises onto the neighbouring premises of the plaintiff. Again, the question arose as to the defendant's liability for the negligence of their independent contractor which caused a third party damage. Despite what some might have expected after the *McInnes* decision, here the court found the plaintiff had no case against the defendant.

Latham CJ found the case did not fall within the parameters of *Rylands* since the use of the land was 'natural' and did not bring with it increased risk to others.[106] Latham CJ cited the general rule that an employer was not liable for the actions of their independent contractors. Exceptions existed in relation to contractors engaged to do illegal acts, cases where the employer was personally bound to perform a particular duty, and where the employer specifically engaged the contractor to do the specific act which caused the damage. None of them applied to the facts.[107] He discussed the alleged special rule with respect to dangerous or extra-hazardous activity but appeared to leave open the extent to which it should be held applicable in Australia.[108] Starke J seemed to accept the existence of such a rule but found it did not apply to the facts.[109]

[102] eg, in *Woodland v Swimming Teachers Association* (n 7) 579–82 there is substantial discussion of the Australian case law concerning non-delegable duties.

[103] *McInnes v Wardle* (1931) 45 CLR 548.

[104] [1894] AC 48; Gavan Duffy CJ and Starke J (550); Dixon J (552); Evatt J (553).

[105] *Torette House Proprietary Limited v Berkman* (1939) 62 CLR 637.

[106] ibid 646; to like effect Starke J (650) and Dixon J (655).

[107] ibid 647; to like effect Dixon J (655–56).

[108] ibid 648.

[109] ibid 652. The matter was considered briefly by Windeyer J in *Voli v Inglewood Shire Council* (1963) 110 CLR 74, 95 who noted that it had become 'fashionable' to speak of delegable and non-delegable duties, but doubted the distinction was anything more than the adoption of headings for cases in which an employer had been found liable for the actions of an independent contractor, and

The matter was considered again in *Stoneman v Lyons*[110] where the High Court reiterated the general rule that an employer was not generally liable for the negligence of an independent contractor. Exceptions existed in relation to conduct that the employer specifically authorised, or was necessarily inherent in what they authorised. Stephen J doubted the existence of an exception for so-called extra-hazardous activity, noting its eventual rejection by the House of Lords in *Read v Lyons*.[111] Mason J expressed similar doubts, concluding that the decision in *Read v Lyons*, 'by accepting the principle that in the case of dangerous things and operations there is a special responsibility to take care proportioned to the danger, discarded the notion of strict liability and preserved the concept of fault'.[112]

The contours of the supposed non-delegable duty were considered at some length by Mason J in *Kondis v State Transport Authority*.[113] He observed that the concept of non-delegable duties had been criticised for the failure of its proponents to provide a convincing rationale for the doctrine, and why in some cases it was appropriate for the law to fix essentially a strict liability upon a defendant, as opposed to the ordinary duty of care negligence standard.[114]

Having acknowledged that, Mason J surveyed the English and Australian case law in which such a duty had been posited, involving employer–employee, hospitals, schools, adjoining property owners, and invitor–invitee type relationships. He attempted to provide a rationalisation, or at least an explanation of what united these categories. Essentially, he described an 'assumption of responsibility' rationale:

> When we look to the classes of case in which the existence of a non-delegable duty has been recognised it appears that there is some element in the relationship between the parties that makes it appropriate to impose on the defendant a duty to ensure that reasonable care and skill is taken for the safety of the persons to whom the duty is owed … the element in the relationship between the parties which generates a special responsibility or duty to see that care is taken may be found in one or more of several circumstances. The hospital undertakes the care, supervision and control of patients who are in special need of care. The school authority undertakes like special responsibilities in relation to the children whom it accepts into its care. If the invitor be subject to a special duty, it is because he assumes a particular responsibility in relation to the safety of premises and the safety of his invitee by inviting him to enter them … and the … undertaking of the landlord to renew the roof of the house was seen as impliedly carrying with it an undertaking to exercise reasonable care to prevent damage to the tenant's property. In these situations the special duty arises because the person on whom it is imposed has

cases in which they had not. In contrast, in *Ramsay v Larsen* (1964) 111 CLR 16, some members of the Court (28, Kitto J) and (38, Taylor J) appeared to accept a rationale for non-delegable duties.

110 *Stoneman v Lyons* (1975) 133 CLR 550.

111 ibid 563.

112 ibid 575 (with whom Barwick CJ and Gibbs J agreed).

113 (1984) 154 CLR 672. Deane J agreed with the judgment of Mason J (694). All members of the Court in *Commonwealth v Introvigne* (1982) 150 CLR 258 had accepted that school authorities owed a non-delegable duty to provide a safe environment for students.

114 *Kondis v State Transport Authority*, ibid, 686–87.

> undertaken the care, supervision or control of the person or property of another or is so placed in relation to that person or his property as to assume a particular responsibility for his or her safety, in circumstances where the person affected might reasonably expect that due care will be exercised.[115]

Mason J held that this rationale strongly supported imposing upon an employer a non-delegable duty regarding a safe system of work. The employee had no choice but to accept the employer's systems and processes. The employee's safety was in the hands of the employer. He expressed some reservations as to whether the rationale held as strongly in cases involving invitor–invitee.[116] Murphy J took a similar position, concluding there were 'sound policy reasons' for attaching to employers liability for independent contractors, referring to the fact that contractors or sub-contractors may not be financially strong and/or insured.[117]

In *Stevens v Brodribb* Mason J concluded that the idea of strict liability being based on dangerous or extra-hazardous activity 'had no place in Australian law'.[118] Likewise Wilson and Dawson JJ observed that the trend in Australian law had been away from the imposition of strict liability, and specifically found that the principle that an employer should be strictly liable for extra-hazardous activities in which an independent contractor whom they engaged should not be accepted as part of Australian law.[119]

The High Court next considered the matter in the important decision of *Burnie Port Authority v General Jones Pty Ltd*.[120] In this case, a majority of the High Court subsumed the existing *Rylands v Fletcher* strict liability principles into the general law of negligence in Australia.[121] Aspects of the Court's reasoning are important in the current context.

A majority of the Court rejected the concept of 'dangerousness' as a basis for the imposition of strict liability, as had occurred in *Rylands* (and other cases discussed above). The High Court noted that if it had been determined, as it had in *Rylands*, that water was a dangerous substance, it was difficult to identify anything which, depending on the circumstances, could not be viewed as 'dangerous'.[122]

The majority sought to overcome arguments that the *Rylands* strict liability principle should be maintained, because it provided a remedy in cases where ordinary negligence principles would not. In rejecting such an argument, the High Court pointed out that many of the factors said to be relevant in a *Rylands* analysis, including the precise nature of the defendant's activity and its reasonableness, would be relevant in determining the extent to which they owed the plaintiff

[115] ibid 687.
[116] ibid 688.
[117] ibid 690.
[118] (1986) 160 CLR 16, 30 (with whom Brennan J agreed).
[119] ibid 43.
[120] (1994) 179 CLR 520.
[121] ibid 556 (Mason CJ; Deane, Dawson, Toohey and Gaudron JJ; Brennan and McHugh JJ dissenting).
[122] ibid 538.

a duty of care, and whether they had breached it.[123] Another way in which the majority sought to convince their audience that a subsumption of *Rylands* liability into the law of negligence would not represent a major change to the law or the results of cases was to reaffirm the existence of a non-delegable duty of care, in limited cases.

The judgment in *Rylands* represents a reaffirmation of the explanation of the kinds of cases in which a non-delegable duty will be owed that was provided by Mason J in *Kondis*. Again, it was emphasised that such duties exist in situations where the person held to owe the duty has undertaken care, supervision or control of the person or property of another, or had assumed a responsibility for their safety, such that the plaintiff could reasonably expect that due care would be exercised. The special vulnerability or dependence of that person was critical. The court held that such a description applied to the duties owed to others by a property owner. A property owner was in control of their premises. They could choose to engage in particular activities or not, including the use of dangerous substances and the commission of dangerous acts. The other person, nominally the plaintiff, was vulnerable if reasonable precautions were not taken. This meant the defendant could be taken to have assumed responsibility for the safety of the plaintiff, a responsibility which in law could not be delegated elsewhere.[124] The majority also fortified their reassertion of the non-delegable duty by recourse to financial considerations.[125]

The court noted that the fact that a particular activity was dangerous would be relevant to establishing whether the particular duty of care the defendant owed had been met—in other words, to the standard of care expected.[126] Obviously, the more dangerous an activity, the more the defendant would need to do by way of precautions and preventive measures, in order to meet that duty.

It is sometimes said that the decision in *Northern Sandblasting Pty Ltd v Harris*[127] represents the high-water mark of the non-delegable duty concept in Australian tort law. The case involved the question of the liability of a property owner to their tenants. Due to negligent electrical work performed by an independent contractor engaged by the property owner, one of the tenants on the property was electrocuted. A majority of the court found that the property owner had a non-delegable duty to provide safe premises, a duty that had been breached on the facts.

Brennan CJ referred to the explanation of non-delegable duties by Mason J in *Kondis*, and agreed that a defendant could owe a non-delegable duty with respect

123 ibid 539, 545, 547.

124 ibid 551–52 (Mason CJ; Dean,e Dawson, Toohey and Gaudron JJ). They later reserved judgment as to whether this rationale would apply in respect of a visitor to premises (557).

125 ibid 552, quoting Thayer on the practical advantages of imposing liability on a defendant who was 'easily discoverable and probably financially responsible').

126 ibid 555.

127 *Northern Sandblasting Pty Ltd v Harris* (1997) 188 CLR 313.

to 'inherent risks' associated with work delegated to a contractor.[128] Dawson, Toohey, Gaudron and McHugh JJ also referred with approval to Mason J's explanation of the concept in *Kondis*,[129] noting the touchstones of control and assumption of responsibility, vulnerability and special dependence. In contrast neither Gummow nor Kirby JJ found that the concept of a non-delegable duty was applicable to the facts, Gummow J on the basis that the relevant renting legislation did not indicate an intention to make property owners effective insurers of the property,[130] and Kirby J on the ground that the relationship between property owner and tenant did not contain the kinds of characteristics which Mason J had outlined in *Kondis* as suggestive of a non-delegable duty context.[131] Kirby J also referred more broadly to criticism of the non-delegable duty concept for its lack of precision.[132]

While the *Northern Sandblasting* decision reflects that a majority of judges at that time accepted the place of non-delegable duties in the law of tort, based on the kinds of factors identified by Mason J in *Kondis*, developments elsewhere in the Australian law of tort would soon undermine this majority view. As discussed above, the existence of a non-delegable duty of care had been premised on concepts such as assumption of responsibility, control, and special vulnerability. These developments had occurred at a time when, elsewhere in the law of tort, the High Court was enamoured with the concept of 'proximity' as the touchstone of negligence liability.[133]

However, the proximity doctrine fell out of favour, and was rejected by the High Court.[134] This left a vacuum. How else could establishment of a duty of care be rationalised, apart from concepts of reasonable foreseeability? The High Court then settled upon a 'salient features' approach to establishment of a duty of care. There was no magic bullet in establishing whether a duty of care should exist; rather a case-by-case approach should be taken. However, the High Court did provide a list of 'salient features' which would often be important in determining whether or not a duty of care should be recognised in a particular case. The problem for adherents of the non-delegable duty concept was the factors which the High Court indicated as being relevant to this 'salient features' enquiry in the context of ordinary negligence—they were concepts like assumption of responsibility, control, dependence and special vulnerability.[135] In other words, the very factors

[128] ibid 332.
[129] ibid 344–45, 350, 361 and 368 respectively.
[130] ibid 385.
[131] ibid 401.
[132] ibid 395.
[133] *Gala v Preston* (1991) 172 CLR 243.
[134] *Hill v Van Earp* (1997) 188 CLR 159; *Perre v Apand Pty Ltd* (1999) 198 CLR 180.
[135] *Hill v Van Earp*, ibid 184–85 (Dawson J), 188 (Toohey J), 198–99 (Gaudron J) and 229 and 234 (Gummow J); *Perre v Apand Pty Ltd*, ibid, 194 (Gleeson CJ), 201 (Gaudron J), 220 (McHugh J), 259 (Gummow J), 326–28 (Callinan J); *Graham Barclay Oysters Pty Ltd v Ryan* (2002) 211 CLR 540, 559 (Gleeson CJ), 577 (McHugh J), 597–98 (Gummow and Hayne JJ) (with whom Gaudron J agreed at 570), 630 (Kirby J) and 664 (Callinan J).

which earlier High Courts had used to map out the circumstances in which a non-delegable duty of care would be owed were now being used to map out the circumstances in which an ordinary, delegable duty of care would be owed. Obviously, this state of affairs could not continue, and the rationalisations for non-delegable duties, such as they were, themselves became 'vulnerable'.

Dissatisfaction with the non-delegable duty concept became more pronounced in *New South Wales v Lepore*,[136] which it will be recalled involved a conjoined appeals case involving deliberate sexual and physical abuse of children within a school environment. Obviously, the school authority student relationship had been recognised by earlier United Kingdom decisions as one of the relationships in which a non-delegable duty would be owed. Regarding non-delegable duties, Gleeson CJ stated:

> The proposition that, because a school authority's duty of care to a pupil is non-delegable, the authority is liable for any injury, accidental or intentional, inflicted at school upon a pupil by a teacher, is too broad, and the responsibility with which it fixes school authorities is too demanding … in cases where the care of children or other vulnerable people is involved, it is difficult to see what kind of relationship would not give rise to a non-delegable duty of care.[137]

The sharpest criticism of the non-delegable duty concept appeared in the judgment of Gummow and Hayne JJ:

> The early English cases, which first identified non-delegable duties to ensure that reasonable care was taken, offered no reason for departing from the generally accepted rule that a person was not liable for an accident that occurred without the fault either of that person or a servant in the course of employment. Lord Blackburn's often quoted proposition, about not escaping responsibility by engagement of a contractor, if applied to cases of duties to act carefully as distinct from duties to achieve a particular result, proffers no basis for what appears to be the resulting conflation of two distinct propositions—one about personal responsibility to see that a duty is performed and the other about vicarious responsibility for the negligent performance of the task. At best, when applied in the context of duties to act carefully, the proposition appears to be an assertion of a conclusion about responsibility, rather than any demonstration of a reason for reaching that conclusion. That being so, its citation offers no certain basis for defining the breadth of the proposition that it is intended to state.[138]
>
> To hold that a non-delegable duty of care requires the party concerned to ensure that there is no default of any kind committed by those to whom care of the plaintiff is entrusted would remove the duty altogether from any connection with the law of negligence. No longer would the duty of the employer, the hospital, the school authority, be in any sense a duty to take reasonable care for the safety of the employee, the patient, the pupil. It would be a duty to bring about a result that no person (employee or independent contractor) who was engaged to take steps connected with the care of the plaintiff

[136] (2003) 212 CLR 511.
[137] ibid 533–34.
[138] ibid 599–600.

> did anything to harm the plaintiff. This would introduce a new and wider form of strict liability to prevent harm, a step sharply at odds with the trend of decisions in this Court rejecting the expansion of strict liabilities. It would sever the duty from its roots in the law of negligence. It would make the employer (the hospital, the school authority) an insurer of the employee (the patient, the pupil) against any harm done by any person engaged by the former to care for the latter.[139]

Gummow and Hayne JJ also concluded that a non-delegable duty was a species of vicarious liability, which appears with respect to confuse personal duty with true vicarious liability. Further, they were adamant that where a non-delegable duty existed, it was a form of strict liability.[140] This mirrors the position apparently taken by the United Kingdom Supreme Court in *Woodland*, though the Court did not explicitly use the phrase 'strict liability', but seems inconsistent with earlier cases such as *Davie*, where the Court seemed to believe that a non-delegable duty contemplated something akin to a negligence standard.

Of the other judges, Kirby J maintained his indifference towards the suggestion of a non-delegable duty,[141] and Callinan J expressly rejected it.[142] Only Gaudron[143] and McHugh JJ continued to embrace and apply the concept.[144] The previous majority view favouring and applying the non-delegable duty concept had effectively disappeared.

In *Leichhardt Municipal Council v Montgomery* the High Court considered the possible application of non-delegable duties in the context of highway liability, again a category of case in which non-delegable duties had been recognised in the United Kingdom. Again, ambivalence towards the non-delegable duty concept was evident.

Gleeson CJ stated that the case

> [r]aises a more general question concerning non-delegable duties. A 'special responsibility' or a duty to 'see' or 'ensure' that care is taken by an independent contractor and the contractor's employees goes beyond a duty to act reasonably in exercising prudent oversight of what the contractor does. In many circumstances it is a duty that could not be fulfilled. How can a hospital ensure that a surgeon is never careless? If the answer is that it cannot, what does the law mean when it speaks of a duty to ensure that care is taken? It may mean something different. It may mean that there should be an exception to the general rule that a defendant is not vicariously responsible for the negligence of an independent contractor. The present case illustrates the artificiality of attributing to the appellant a duty to ensure that care was taken. The failure to take care consisted of a workman in the employment of (a construction company) placing a carpet over a

[139] ibid 601–02; this was consistent with Gummow J's apparent non-acceptance of the non-delegable duty concept in *Scott v Davis* (2000) 204 CLR 333, 316–17. Kirby J also rejected the suggestion that a 'superior party which is in the best position to accept such liability' should effectively become an insurer.

[140] *New South Wales v Lepore* (n 10) 599.

[141] ibid 608.

[142] ibid 624.

[143] ibid 551–53.

[144] ibid 568.

> telecommunications pit that had a defective cover, in circumstances where the workman should have noticed the defect. Thus a trap was created and the respondent fell into it. To speak of a local council having a duty to ensure that such an apparently low-level and singular act of carelessness does not occur is implausible.[145]

Gleeson CJ lauded the more flexible reasonable care standard, which would permit the court to consider all of the circumstances of such a delegation of responsibility, as opposed to an inflexible supposed duty to ensure care was taken.[146] So while the non-delegable duty concept has not been technically overruled, sufficient justices have spoken negatively about it in the most recent decisions to suggest it is no longer part of Australian law. It is no doubt this view of the existing law that has led to the Royal Commission into Institutional Responses to Child Sexual Abuse recommending that a statutory non-delegable duty of care be imposed on some institutions responsible for the welfare of children.[147] Logic would suggest there would be no need for the introduction of a comprehensive statutory non-delegable duty if a common law equivalent duty were currently accepted and applied as part of Australian law.

Notwithstanding this, members of the High Court suggested in *Leighton Contractors Pty Ltd v Fox* suggested that an employer may be subject to a non-delegable duty with respect to a safe workplace.[148]

Criticisms of the Concept of a Non-Delegable Duty

There has been substantial criticism of the concept of a non-delegable duty.[149] The most serious weakness with the doctrine is the failure of those who articulate it to advance a satisfactory reason for its existence. Obviously, this is also a criticism regularly levelled at the notion of vicarious liability.

[145] *Leichhardt Municipal Council v Montgomery* (2007) 230 CLR 22, 34–35.

[146] ibid 36; other justices remained negative about the possibility of non-delegable duties: Kirby J (64–65); Hayne J (75); Callinan J (86–87). Crennan J agreed with both Gleeson CJ and Callinan J (88). By this stage Gaudron and McHugh JJ had retired.

[147] *Commonwealth of Australia Royal Commission into Institutional Responses to Child Sexual Abuse: Redress and Civil Litigation Report* (2015) 77. The posited non-delegable duty would be owed in respect of (a) residential facilities for children, including out of home care facilities and juvenile detention centres; (b) day and boarding schools and early childhood facilities, and outside school hours services; (c) disability services for children; (d) health services for children; (e) any other for-profit facility providing care, supervision or control of children (excluding foster or kinship care); and (f) any facilities or services provided by religious organisations (Recommendation 90).

[148] *Leighton Contractors Pty Ltd v Fox* (2009) 240 CLR 1, 12 (French CJ; Gummow, Hayne, Heydon and Bell JJ).

[149] Williams (n 18) 181 dismissed it as one of the 'leading sophistries in the law of tort', complaining that 'the truth seems to be that the cases are decided on no rational grounds, but depend merely on whether the judge is attracted by the language of non-delegable duty' (186).

As indicated above, the doctrine was created at a time when the doctrine of common employment operated to preclude an injured employee in some circumstances from successfully claiming against their employer. Rather than criticise or overrule that doctrine, some courts sought to circumvent it by resorting to other arguments, including the idea that the employer owed a non-delegable duty in relation to a safe workplace.[150] This was also at a time when general schemes of workers' compensation did not exist. Obviously, workers' compensation schemes do now exist, and statute has interred the past doctrine of common employment.

Thus, it is perhaps not altogether surprising that a doctrine designed to overcome a problem which no longer exists should be difficult to justify in today's tort landscape, which features the exponential growth of a fault-based doctrine such as negligence. Though the doctrine was originally interpreted to be a duty to take reasonable care, as evidenced in cases like *Davie*, subsequent decisions, in particular *Woodland*, have pushed it to the stage where it basically operates as a doctrine of strict liability.[151] This creates an awkward situation, where Australian tort law has moved well away from strict liability, subsuming *Rylands* into the law of negligence, and where United Kingdom tort law has effectively marginalised, restricted and limited the *Rylands* doctrine so that many respected commentators effectively have called last rites upon it. In this landscape, the development of a doctrine of strict liability in another guise in the law of tort is puzzling.

Further, the doctrine was created at a time when the generalised duty of care was not recognised. It has perhaps not been sufficiently realised, apart from in cases like *Read v Lyons*, that development of a generalised duty of care obviates the need for a non-delegable duty. Focus on 'creating a danger' might have made sense when it was necessary to try to align one's case with *Rylands*, or to ask the court to recognise the relationship as a category of case in which a duty of care ought to be recognised. It is much less defensible now when a generalised duty of care exists, when that doctrine is quite flexible and able to take into account the dangerousness or otherwise of a particular activity, in giving appropriate content to the relevant duty.

I have in chapter six criticised the notion that the concept of 'hazardous' or 'extra-hazardous' activity should be used as a basis for the imposition of strict liability.[152] What was said there was in the context of the imposition of vicarious

[150] Murphy, 'Juridical Foundations of Common Law Non-Delegable Duties' (n 86) 379.

[151] [2014] AC 537, 573 (Lord Sumption); *New South Wales v Lepore* (n 10) 599 (Gummow and Hayne JJ); J Morgan, 'Liability for Independent Contractors in Contract and Tort: Duties to Ensure That Care is Taken' (2015) 74 *Cambridge Law Journal* 109: 'the defendant (in a non-delegable duty case) must exceptionally ensure that they take reasonable care (or rather, since it is impossible to ensure that contractors are never careless, he must answer for any harm negligently caused'; C Witting, 'Breach of the Non-Delegable Duty: Defending Limited Strict Liability in Tort' (2006) 29 *University of New South Wales Law Journal* 33; J Murphy, 'The Liability Bases of Common Law Non-Delegable Duties: A Reply to Christian Witting' (2007) 30 *University of New South Wales Law Journal* 86.

[152] Williams (n 18) 181–82; 'the concept of extra-hazardous acts is not a suitable one for legal rules (192); Stevens (n 3) 341; Atiyah (n 9) 372: 'the whole doctrine ("dangerousness" or "extra-hazardous

liability; however, the same arguments can be made against their use to justify one of the two categories of case in which a non-delegable duty of care should be owed, according to the judgment of Lord Sumption in *Woodland*. It will be recalled that Lord Sumption gave two categories of case in which a non-delegable duty had been recognised. The first of them was in the context of hazardous or extra-hazardous activity. For the reasons given in chapter six, these doctrines must not be used to justify the imposition of strict liability. They are uncertain, arbitrary and subjective, and thus unsuitable foundations for a fundamental distinction between fault and no-fault based liability. The doctrine cannot bear the weight that the law currently puts upon it, at least in the context of non-delegable duties.

The other category of case in which Lord Sumption claimed that a non-delegable duty had been recognised was in cases of an 'assumption of responsibility', citing cases involving school authorities,[153] hospitals, employer and employee, invitor and invitee and neighbouring property owners. With respect, it is one thing to round up the anomalous circumstances in which such a duty has been found in disparate cases and try to put a label on them that will post-the-event justify them; it is quite another to make such a label stick.[154] And labels like assumption of responsibility, control and vulnerability are, with respect, poor choices.[155] These are exactly the same concepts that the courts have come to use to ascertain the circumstances in which a duty of care will be owed in ordinary cases of negligence.[156] And even more unfortunately, given the ease with which vicarious liability and

activity") is so manifestly unsatisfactory that one may be permitted to hope that if the House of Lords is ever called upon to consider it the House will reject it altogether ... (given) ... the sheer impossibility of producing any satisfactory criteria for deciding ... whether any particular operation can be called "extra-hazardous"'.

[153] Christine Beuermann's work supports the notion of 'conferred authority strict liability' in the context of a non-delegable duty imposed on school authorities: C Beuermann, 'Conferred Authority, Strict Liability and Institutional Child Sexual Abuse' (2015) 37 *Sydney Law Review* 113; C Beuermann, 'Tort Law in the Employment Relationship: A Response to the Potential Abuse of an Employer's Authority' (2014) 21 *Torts Law Journal* 169; C Beuermann, 'Vicarious Liability and Conferred Authority Strict Liability' (2013) 20 *Torts Law Journal* 265; C Beuermann, 'Dissociating the Two Forms of So-Called Vicarious Liability' in S Pitel, J Neyers and E Chamberlain (eds), *Tort Law: Challenging Orthodoxy* (Oxford, Hart Publishing, 2013).

[154] Stevens (n 3) 367: 'the search for a single factor which links all of the cases commonly grouped together as non-delegable duties is a mistake'.

[155] For criticism of use of the assumption of responsibility principle in this context see Morgan (n 151).

[156] Murphy, 'Juridical Foundations of Common Law Non-Delegable Duties' (n 86) 387: 'the assumption of responsibility criterion also functions, however inadequately, to ground an ordinary duty of care in negligence cases—especially those falling within ... the extended *Hedley v Byrne* category. It therefore follows that if the special, non-delegable duty is to be distinguished from the ordinary duty of care, some further criterion must be found to be working in tandem with an assumption of responsibility in order to ground such a special duty'. Unfortunately, identifying precisely what that extra thing is, is with respect difficult, and arguably it begs the question to simply assert that it exists when there is an affirmative duty to act. This does not get us any further in rationalising and articulating when and why such affirmative duty exists or, more precisely, ought to exist.

non-delegable duties can be confused, used by Lord Hobhouse in *Lister* as a reason for imposing *vicarious* liability upon the school.[157]

We come back to the same problem, which is the failure of those who advocate a non-delegable duty of care, which has come in the United Kingdom cases to amount effectively to making the owner of such a duty an effective insurer, to justify it. An explanation of why these particular relationships warrant the imposition of effective insurer obligations is elusive. An explanation of why ordinary negligence principles are demonstrably insufficient to deal with these situations is elusive. And for the reasons explained earlier at some length, it does not do to make assumptions about who has appropriate insurance, as some members of the United Kingdom Supreme Court sought to do in *Woodland*.[158] Again, I do not accept the assumptions about who has, or may have access to, insurance should justify in any way a legal principle, or the imposition of liability. Insurance follows the law; it should not lead the law.

At least one of these instances, that of the liability of a hospital to its patients, may be explained by a past reluctance of courts to find that a hospital was vicariously liable for its medical staff. However, again that reluctance has been overcome in the law of vicarious liability. To the extent that Lord Denning's judgment in *Cassidy v Ministry of Health*, and his development of a non-delegable duty in that context, was premised on the lack of vicarious liability, a further rationale for recognition of a non-delegable duty has disappeared. Perhaps this is evidence of a pathology sometimes seen in the common law, with the gradual accretion of precedents, and following of doctrine developed in past similar cases, without sufficient thought about the rationale and reasons for such developments, and thought about whether the issue animating such developments remains. Doctrines that once were defensible must be discarded if their reason for being no longer exists, and in particular where they are at odds with the structure of that area of law, as a strict liability doctrine in the law of tort today is.

Others have made the practical point that one of the reasons for the engagement of a contractor may be that they have expertise which the engager does not possess, either themselves or in the workplace. Thus, they rely upon the contractor's expertise, and would be entitled to do so. It may not be reasonable to expect the engager to check that the work or the services performed by the contractor were of the required quality.[159] If the engager is practically unable to vouch for the quality of the work done, it does seem onerous to impose an effective insurer obligation on the engager for the work of the contractor. They are being asked to

[157] 'Where the defendant has assumed a relationship to the plaintiff which carries with it a specific duty towards the plaintiff, the defendant is vicariously liable in tort if his servant to whom the performance of that duty has been entrusted breaches that duty': *Lister and Others v Hesley Hall Ltd* [2002] 1 AC 215, 239.

[158] [2014] AC 537, 590 (Baroness Hale, with whom Lord Clarke, Lord Wilson and Lord Toulson agreed).

[159] Williams (n 18) 183.

insure work when they may not be in a position to assess risk. It is not clear that the law should impose such an obligation on them.

Another practical issue is that the engager may employ many different contractors, who might then engage many different sub-contractors, and the delegations could go on and on. It seems ridiculous to make the engager an effective insurer of all these possible contractors and subcontractors.[160] Indeed, this is one of the reasons why the law distinguishes between employees on the one hand, and independent contractors on the other, as was seen in chapter nine. The employer is thought to have control over an employee, in a way that they do not in the case of an independent contractor. Control is defensible as a concept which limits the liability of an employer. It justifies making the employer liable for the actions of the employee—the employee's actions are authorised, the employer is morally blameworthy if they are carried out contrary to legal obligations. In sharp contrast are the actions of an independent contractor; by definition, these are actions of an individual that the law recognises that the employer cannot effectively control. Thus, serious questions arise as to the efficacy of making an employer liable for what the independent contractor may have done wrong. The employer may be blameless; again, the law should not impose liability upon the blameless.

More recently, as has been discussed, the control test has been supplemented by the organisation or enterprise test. An employer is considered liable for workers that may be considered to be part of their organisation and enterprise, while they are not similarly liable for independent contractors, who have their own organisations and enterprises.[161] This is on the theory that the employee is part of the employer's organisation, and that an organisation should be required to internalise the costs it generates. If the costs are generated by an independent contractor, presumably those costs should be assigned to that independent business. They cannot be double assigned; thus they should not be assigned also to the firm that engaged the independent contractor.

If an engager is held to be an effective insurer for independent contractors they engage to perform tasks through a doctrine of non-delegable duties, this dichotomy disappears. Still the engager lacks the control over the contractor, still the contractor is not part of the engager's organisation or enterprise, but now, under the non-delegable duty concept, the engager is liable for such contractors. The legal principles of vicarious liability and the principles, if any, relating to

[160] This is noted in Pollock (n 11) 129 who said that if liability did not stop at employees, and extended to contractors, 'liability would be endless, and we should be involved in a multiplicity of unknown risks. Besides, it (would) … be overharsh to make men liable not only for acts which they cannot practically control in detail, but for the acts of persons over whom they have no control at all'.

[161] Leading proponent of the enterprise risk theory which currently underpins vicarious liability in the United States, Canada and the United Kingdom, Young Smith, agreed that an engager should not be legally liable for the actions of a contractor, because in that case the contractor was the entrepreneur, such that the risk should be with them, not the one who engaged them: YB Smith, 'Frolic and Detour' (1923) 23 *Columbia Law Review* 444, 461.

non-delegable duties should work together harmoniously, not contradict each other. The law risks incoherence.

If the logic of enterprise risk is accepted, as it has been by courts in the United Kingdom, United States and Canada, then surely the notion of non-delegable duties by which a defendant enterprise is deemed strictly liable for actions of an independent contractor, who by definition runs their own business and is not part of the business of the defendant enterprise, becomes untenable. With respect, the United Kingdom Supreme Court should not uphold and apply enterprise risk notions to justify the imposition of vicarious liability upon an employer, on the basis they must internalise the cost of risks they generate (*Mohamud*), and then at the same time, through another legal principle within the house of torts, make an employer liable for costs that another organisation has generated (*Woodland*).

Another argument sometimes made in support of a non-delegable duty is the notion that it is justified because the one who owes the duty chose the relevant contractor. For example, Clarence Morris stated:

> The most popular argument for insulation (of a defendant from the action or omissions of an independent contractor) is that since the employer of an independent contractor has no control over him in the prosecution of his work and since it is unjust to hold a man liable for the torts of another whom he cannot direct, the employer of an independent contractor should not be liable for the latter's torts. Those who make this argument overlook the fact that while the contractor does not bargain for and usually does not want control of the contractor, he nevertheless makes the selection of the contractor.[162]

Respectfully, the fact that the engager chose the independent contractor does not justify making the former the effective insurer of the latter. If the engager has negligently chosen an incompetent contractor, they may be held to have breached their ordinary duty of care in negligence. No special imposition of non-delegable duties in such an instance is warranted or justified. Other justifications for non-delegable duties have also been suggested, but since they have not garnered much support,[163] I do not dwell upon them here.

Conclusion

The law traditionally distinguishes between employees and independent contractors for the purposes of vicarious liability. An employer was not liable for the actions of the latter but could be vicariously liable for the actions of the former. Some courts sought to obviate this sharp distinction by finding in some cases that

[162] C Morris, 'The Torts of an Independent Contractor' (1935) 29 *Illinois Law Review* 339, 343.

[163] Christian Witting advances the theory of 'bodily integrity': C Witting, 'Case Note: *Leichhardt Municipal Council v Montgomery*: Non-Delegable Duties and Road Authorities' (2008) 32 *Melbourne University Law Review* 332, 348; Witting 'Breach of the Non-Delegable Duty (n 151) 49.

an employer is liable for the actions of an independent contractor, through the concept of a non-delegable duty.

Developments elsewhere in the law of tort strongly suggest that the concept of a non-delegable duty should no longer have a place within it. It suffers from the same problems that other doctrines of strict liability in the law currently face, which have been documented earlier in the book. And the acceptance in the United Kingdom, United States and Canada of the concept of 'enterprise risk' in an attempt to rationalise its sister doctrine 'vicarious liability' causes serious further difficulties with the concept of a non-delegable duty. It is considered incoherent for the law simultaneously to find that an organisation must be liable vicariously in order to internalise the costs it generates, as enterprise risk theory would have it, but then at the same time force the business to 'internalise' the cost of risks generated by another independent enterprise, as the non-delegable duty concept requires. Simply, either the law expects businesses to internalise their own costs or not. Whatever else may be said about the enterprise risk theory, and I have criticised it above, we must not add to the dysfunction by applying doctrines elsewhere in tort law which are demonstrably at complete odds with it.

11

Punitive Damages

Punitive or Exemplary Damages

It is one thing to make an employer vicariously liable to pay compensatory damages to a person injured by the wrongdoing of an employee. It is another thing to order that an employer pay punitive or exemplary damages to the injured person.[1] As will be discussed more fully below, as their name suggests punitive damages are designed to punish a wrongdoer for their bad deeds and to deter such wrongful behaviour in future. They are quite separate and distinct from compensatory damages. Compensatory damages include aggravated damages, and as a kind of compensatory damages, these must also be distinguished from punitive damages.[2] It can be somewhat challenging to apply these in the context of vicarious liability, a doctrine of strict liability in which, by definition, the employer being held legally responsible is not guilty of any wrongdoing. Further difficulties arise to the extent that the imposition of vicarious liability is said to be justified by the defendant's deep pockets. As indicated in chapter seven, I do not agree with such a rationale, but many others have given this as a prime justification and/or explanation for the imposition of vicarious liability. Even if it does explain the imposition of vicarious liability, it is even more difficult to use it to explain the imposition of punitive damages via vicarious liability, given that their purpose is not in fact compensatory.[3]

Some scholars[4] and courts[5] have apparently endorsed the position that an employer deemed to be vicariously liable for the actions of their employee may be liable to pay the injured plaintiff punitive damages. The Law Commission found

[1] For ease of reference, I will for the remainder of this chapter refer to such damages as 'punitive damages'. The word 'exemplary' is taken from the Latin for example, suggesting that in awarding such damages, an example is being made of the defendant, presumably with the purpose of deterring other would-be wrongdoers.

[2] J Murphy, 'The Nature and Domain of Aggravated Damages' (2010) 69 *Cambridge Law Journal* 353.

[3] J Reingold Katz, 'Finding Fault: Implications of Importing the Title VII Standard for Vicarious Punitive Liability to the Fair Housing Act' (2008) 29 *Cardozo Law Review* 2749, 2761.

[4] P Giliker, *Vicarious Liability in Tort: A Comparative Perspective* (Cambridge, Cambridge University Press, 2010) 39–43.

[5] *Rowlands v Chief Constable of Merseyside Police* [2007] 1 WLR 1065.

that punitive damages could be included as part of vicarious liability.[6] In order to reach a position on this matter, it is necessary to consider the nature of punitive damages in some more detail.

Nature of Punitive Damages

The concept of punitive damages has enjoyed a long history in the law. They are apparent in the Code of Hammurabi in 2000 BC. The Twelve Tables of 450 BC provide for double, treble, quadruple or some other multiplier in damages ('multiplied damages'),[7] and the Bible contains several references to the notion of multiplied damages.[8] An English Act of 1275 provided for the payment of 'double' damages.[9]

At a time when English juries were comprised of local townsfolk who were thought to have a strong understanding of the facts surrounding a dispute, juries awarded damages that some might consider to have been excessive in relation to the plaintiff's loss.[10] This was rationalised as being based on their superior factual knowledge, and reviewing judges were reluctant to disturb the findings of the jury in this regard.[11] This was at a pivotal time in the development of the law of wrongs. As noted above, the law wished to encourage the settlement of conflicts in a peaceful, state-sanctioned manner, rather than have individuals believing they had been wronged resorting to the blood feud or other types of vengeance.[12] The making of a 'generous' damages award could certainly assist in reducing the plaintiff's angst and make it less likely they would resort to self-help.

[6] Law Commission, *Aggravated, Exemplary and Restitutionary Damages* (Law Com No 247, 1997), which found that punitive damages could justifiably be imposed vicariously 'where employers are unlikely to be able to satisfy a punitive damages award of any significant size; and secondly, where a claimant has problems identifying the culpable member of the employer's workforce': para 5.221.

[7] WW Buckland, *A Textbook of Roman Law* (Cambridge, Cambridge University Press, 1966) 581–84; D Owen, 'A Punitive Damages Overview: Functions, Problems and Reform' (1994) 39 *Villanova Law Review* 363, 368.

[8] eg, Exodus 22.1: 'if a man shall steal an ox, or a sheep, and kill it, or sell it, he shall restore five oxen for an ox, and four sheep for a sheep'; Exodus 22.9: 'for all manner of trespass, whether it be for ox, for ass, for sheep, for raiment, or any manner of lost thing … the judge … (shall) pay double unto his neighbour'.

[9] Statute of Westminster I, 3 Edw, ch.1 (Eng); F Pollock and FW Maitland *The History of English Law Volume 2 Before the Time of Edward I* (Cambridge, Cambridge University Press, 1895) 521: 'under Edward I a favourite device of our legislators is that of giving double or treble damages to the party grieved'.

[10] D Ellis, 'Fairness and Efficiency in the Law of Punitive Damages' (1982) 56 *Southern California Law Review* 1, 12.

[11] J Sales and K Cole, 'Punitive Damages: A Relic That Has Outlived its Origins' (1984) 37 *Vanderbilt Law Review* 1117.

[12] An example of this appears in the writing of Coke who in *De Libellis Famosis*, 5 Co Rep f125a (1607) who stated that libel 'deserves a serious *punishment*, for although the libel be made against one, yet it incites all those of the same family, kindred or society to revenge, and so tends *per consequens* to

In addition, this was a time prior to the introduction of a formal criminal law system. Punitive damages incentivised plaintiffs to bring alleged wrongs to the attention of the court, in the likely absence of the state doing the same. Pollock and Maitland note that legislators:

> Have little faith in communal accusation or in any procedure that expects either royal officials or people in general to be active in bringing malefactors to justice. More was to be hoped from the (victim) who had suffered. He would move if they made it worth his while. And so in a characteristically English fashion punishment was to be inflicted in the course of civil actions: it took the form of manyfold reparation, of penal and exemplary damages.[13]

Thus, the practice of awarding damages in excess of the plaintiff's loss became established in the common law.

In two cases in 1763 English courts recognised the possibility of damages being awarded in excess of the plaintiff's actual loss. In *Huckle v Money* the court upheld a jury award of £1000 in damages, though conceding the plaintiff's personal injuries in the matter could be compensated for approximately £20.[14] In *Wilkes v Wood* Lord Chief Justice Pratt stated that:

> A jury have it in their power to give damages for more than the injury received. Damages are designed, not only as a satisfaction to the injured person, but likewise as a punishment to the guilty, to deter from any such proceeding for the future, and as a proof of the detestation of the jury to the action itself.[15]

Their position in the common law remains contentious. Many frown upon them, on the basis that they unacceptably mix criminal law purposes such as punishment and retribution in with a civil law context, but without the ordinary safeguards that would apply to a criminal process. Calls continue for punitive damages to be abandoned.[16] It is not necessary for present purposes to enter into that debate.

Subsequently numerous cases confirmed the possibility of awarding punitive damages against a range of defendants, including both private organisations and individuals, and government bodies. What seems to unite such cases appears to be particularly grievous behaviour on the part of the defendant, including being

quarrels and breach of the peace, and it may be the cause of shedding of blood, and of great inconvenience'; see also *Merest v Harvey* (1814) 5 Taunt 442, 444; 128 ER 761, 761: 'it goes to prevent the practice of duelling if juries are permitted to punish insult by exemplary damages' (Heath J).

[13] Pollock and Maitland (n 9) 521. Issue may be taken with the use by the learned authors of the word 'reparation' to describe the punitive damages payout. Today at least, a clear separation is made between compensatory damages (which I would describe as reparation), and punitive or exemplary damages (which I would not describe as reparation).

[14] *Huckle v Money* (1763) 2 Wils, KB 205; 95 ER 768. Other examples during this time include *Grey v Grant* (1764) 2 Wils, KB 252; 95 ER 794, *Benson v Frederick* (1766) 3 Burr 1845; 97 ER 1130 and *Tullidge v Wade* (1769) 3 Wils, KB 18; 95 ER 909.

[15] *Wilkes v Wood* (1763) Lofft 3; 98 ER 489.

[16] A Beever, 'The Structure of Aggravated and Exemplary Damages' (2003) 23(1) *Oxford Journal of Legal Studies* 87, 105–09; A Beever, 'The Future of Exemplary Damages in New Zealand' (2010) 24 *New Zealand Universities Law Review* 197, 219.

found to have acted in a 'high-handed manner',[17] actuated by malice or ill-will towards the plaintiff,[18] abusive behaviour,[19] wilful wrongdoing,[20] and contempt for the plaintiff's rights.[21] The Privy Council discussed the award of punitive damages in the context of behaviour that was unlawful, wilful, persistent and definite.[22]

Subsequently the House of Lords would move to limit the range of cases in which punitive damages would be available.[23] It confirmed that the object of punitive damages was to punish and deter wrongful behaviour.[24] Such damages should be reserved for cases where it was necessary to award them to punish the defendant's outrageous conduct, mark their disapproval of such conduct, and/or deter the wrongdoer from further wrongdoing.[25] The House of Lords stated that one relevant factor in assessing such damages would be the means of the defendant.[26] About 20 years ago the Law Commission proposed significant reform to the law related to punitive damages.[27] Specifically, it recommended that such damages be available for any tort or equitable wrong involving deliberate and outrageous behaviour by the defendant, rather than the narrow categories of case favoured in *Rookes*.[28] To some extent the categories of case in which punitive damages might be available has been frozen, with the Court of Appeal finding that such damages were limited to causes of action in which punitive damages had been previously recognised as being available at the time of the decision in *Rookes*.[29] However, a broader view was taken in *Kuddus v Chief Constable of Leicestershire*, and it now seems that in the United Kingdom the categories of case in which punitive damages might be payable are not so limited.[30]

The Australian law has to a large extent followed the English precedents. From early days the High Court accepted that punitive damages could be awarded in cases of 'conscious wrongdoing in contumelious disregard of another's rights',[31]

[17] *Bell v Midland Railway Co* (1861) 10 CB (NS) 287, 307; 142 ER 462, 470 (Willes J); *Emblem v Myers* (1860) 6 H & N 54, 60 (Wilde B).

[18] *Bell v Midland Railway Co*, ibid.

[19] ibid 309; 471 (Byles J).

[20] *Emblem v Myers* (n 17) 58–59 (Pollock CB) and 59 (Bramwell B); 158 ER 23, 25.

[21] ibid 58 (Pollock CB).

[22] *McArthur and Co v Cornwall* [1891] AC 75, 88 (Lord Hobhouse, for the Court).

[23] *Rookes v Barnard* [1964] AC 1129. The limited categories of case in which Lord Devlin, with whom all other Lords agreed, are of limited relevance to the current context, but were stated to be (a) oppressive, arbitrary or unconstitutional behaviour by servants of government; (b) wrongful conduct the wrongdoer has calculated will be profitable to them, despite payment of compensatory damages; and (c) punitive damages authorised by legislation.

[24] ibid 1221 (Lord Devlin), with whom all other Law Lords agreed: Lord Reid (1179), Lord Evershed (1197), Lord Hodson (1203), Lord Pearce (1238); *Broome v Cassell and Co* [1972] AC 1027, 1073 (Lord Hailsham); 1089 (Lord Reid); and 1124 (Lord Diplock).

[25] ibid 1228 (Lord Devlin), with whom all other Law Lords agreed.

[26] ibid.

[27] Law Commission (n 6).

[28] ibid 105.

[29] *AB v South West Water Services Ltd* [1993] QB 507; Law Commission (n 6) 54.

[30] *Kuddus v Chief Constable of Leicestershire* [2002] 2 AC 122.

[31] *Whitfield v De Lauret and Co Ltd* (1920) 29 CLR 71, 77 (Knox CJ).

in order to punish or deter.[32] The motivation for the defendant's actions would be relevant.[33] However, the High Court refused to follow the House of Lords decision in *Rookes v Barnard* severely limiting the categories of case in which punitive damages could be awarded.[34] In that case the High Court reasserted the broad range of cases in which punitive damages could be available, again asserting their possible applicability in cases involving the defendant's involvement in reprehensible conduct, in order to deter it.[35] Subsequently in *Gray v Motor Accident Commission* the High Court would again emphasise that punitive damages were designed to punish the wrongdoer and deter others from like behaviour.[36] Either rationale is apparently sufficient on its own, thus the fact that an award of punitive damages in a particular case would not in fact punish the wrongdoer does not necessarily mean that no such damages should be ordered. In particular, in such cases the Court has rationalised the award of punitive damages on the basis of general deterrence of undesired activity.[37] However, if *neither* punishment *nor* deterrence would be achieved by the making of a punitive damages award in a particular case, the Australian courts will not make such an order.[38]

Similarly, the Canadian case law has largely followed the English precedents. The Canadian Supreme Court has focused on the wrongdoer's behaviour, and whether they acted in a high-handed or reprehensible manner. The motivation for their actions will be relevant.[39] Their object is to punish and deter.[40] Like the Australian High Court, the Canadian Supreme Court has not accepted the limitation on punitive damages articulated by the House of Lords in *Rookes v Barnard*. It does not restrict the availability of punitive damages to particular causes of action, such as those in which the availability of such damages was previously recognised.[41]

Thus, each of the jurisdictions studied seems to describe similar types of behaviour as warranting consideration of punitive damages, leaving the three categories of case controversially articulated in *Rookes* to one side.

[32] ibid 81 (Isaacs J).

[33] *Williams v Hursey* (1959) 103 CLR 30, 83 (Fullagar J); *Fontin v Katapodis* (1962) 108 CLR 177, 187 (Owen J).

[34] *Uren v John Fairfax and Sons Pty Ltd* (1966) 117 CLR 118.

[35] ibid 138 (Taylor J), reckless and arrogant behaviour, malicious, wilful and reprehensible behaviour; (143, Menzies J), conscious wrongdoing; (154, Windeyer J), conduct actuated by malice or ill-will, reprehensible (158, Owen J).

[36] *Gray v Motor Accident Commission* (1998) 196 CLR 1, 7 (Gleeson CJ; McHugh, Gummow and Hayne JJ); 29 (Kirby J). Civil liability legislation in some parts of Australia now limits or abolishes the availability of punitive damages.

[37] *Lamb v Cotogno* (1987) 166 CLR 1.

[38] *Gray v Motor Accident Commission* (n 36).

[39] *Blackwater v Plint* [2005] 3 SCR 3, 35 (McLachlin CJ, for the Court); *Whiten v Pilot Insurance Co* [2002] 1 SCR 595; *Hill v Church of Scientology of Toronto* [1995] 2 SCR 1130; *Norberg v Wynrib* [1992] 2 SCR 226.

[40] *Norberg v Wynrib*, ibid, 263–64 (La Forest J; Gonthier and Cory JJ) and 299–300 (McLachlin and L'Heureux-Dube JJ); *Hill v Church of Scientology of Toronto*, ibid, 1208 (Cory J, for La Forest, Gonthier, McLachlin, Iacobucci and Major JJ).

[41] *Vorvis v Insurance Corp of British Columbia* [1989] 1 SCR 1085.

The next question is whether an award of punitive damages could or should ever be made against an employer who is vicariously liable in a particular case. In making this argument, I should distinguish between cases where the employer directly authorises and is aware of the behaviour which is now the subject of a punitive damages award, and cases in which the employer did not know of, or authorise, the relevant behaviour.

The first point to note is that it is a relatively novel question. Writing in 1967, Atiyah observed that:

> There appears to be no English authority in which there has been any discussion of the question whether exemplary damages can be awarded against an employer who is vicariously liable for the tort of a servant committed in circumstances in which exemplary damages can be awarded against the servant.[42]

Since Atiyah wrote this, the matter has been considered by at least two English decisions. Unfortunately, they reach different conclusions. The matter was first considered by Lord Scott in *Kuddus v Chief Constable of Leicestershire*.[43] Lord Scott said that at common law, in cases of joint tortfeasors, punitive damages could only be ordered if the conduct of all of the joint tortfeasors warranted punishment. He said it did not matter whether one joint tortfeasor was sued individually or was joined in the action with others. Either way, the common law rule applied. For this reason, the fact that the wrongdoer (employee) may have engaged in behaviour which met the description of the behaviour often warranting an award of punitive damages (malicious, reprehensible etc) would not necessarily justify an award of punitive damages against their employer through vicarious liability.[44]

Lord Scott referred to the work of Atiyah, and his observation that the deterrent effect may be sufficient to justify the imposition of punitive damages upon an employer vicariously. Lord Scott said he disagreed with the statement that a deterrent purpose was sufficient to warrant the imposition of vicarious liability.[45] Lord Scott concluded strongly that:

> The objection to exemplary damages awards in vicarious liability cases seems to me to be fundamental … the defendant should not be liable to pay exemplary damages unless he has committed punishable behaviour. This principle leaves no room for an award of exemplary damages against an individual whose alleged liability is vicarious only and who has not done anything that constitutes punishable behaviour.[46]

In this case, Lord Scott also referred to the traditional rule that where joint tortfeasors were sued, or where one joint tortfeasor was sued, it must be borne in

[42] PS Atiyah, *Vicarious Liability in the Law of Torts* (London, Butterworths, 1967) 435; to like effect, Law Commission (n 6) 159.

[43] [2002] 2 AC 122.

[44] ibid 160–61; see, to like effect, Lord Mackay (141).

[45] ibid 161.

[46] ibid 162. No other Law Lord considered the matter in detail; Lord Hutton said that Lord Scott had made a 'powerful argument' against the award of punitive damages against a vicariously liable employer (153).

mind that all wrongdoers were jointly liable for the wrong. This meant that in relation to punitive damages, only one award could be made. The conduct of each of them should be considered. If the conduct of any of them did not warrant the imposition of punitive damages, no punitive damages at all could be awarded in the case. This was because joint liability was considered one and indivisible. This point derives some support from various judgments of the House of Lords in *Broome v Cassell and Co.*[47] While this was the common law position in Australia, to some extent this has been abrogated by statute, meaning that this consideration is of lesser importance in that jurisdiction.[48] Lord Scott did not refer to United Kingdom legislation which is said to have a similar impact.[49] Similarly, in Canada the position has been taken that in cases of joint and several liability it may be possible that only one of the defendants is liable for punitive damages.[50]

In contrast, in *Rowlands v Chief Constable of Merseyside Police*[51] three members of the Court of Appeal found punitive damages against the Chief Constable on the basis of vicarious liability for the actions of his or her officers.[52] This was said to be necessary to ensure that 'adequate amounts' of awards could be made against those responsible for the officers. It will be recalled that this statement occurred in the context of the narrow categories of case in which punitive damages remains available in United Kingdom law. One of the categories in which the House of Lords said that punitive damages remained available was in cases of public officers.

While the matter has not been considered specifically by the United Kingdom courts in other vicarious liability cases, there appears wording in cases such as *Dubai Aluminium Co Ltd v Salaam*[53] which might lend support to an argument that an employer could be vicariously liable for punitive damages. For example, Lord Nicholls, with whom Lord Slynn and Lord Hutton agreed, spoke of the innocent employer 'standing in the shoes' of the wrongdoer for the purposes of liability.[54] The context there was liability under partnership legislation, but general principles of vicarious liability were applied. Lord Millett opined that the

[47] [1972] AC 1027: 'only one sum can be awarded by way of exemplary damages where the plaintiff elects to sue more than one defendant in the same action … this sum must represent the highest common factor, that is, the lowest sum for which any of the defendants can be held liable' (1063, Lord Hailsham); Lord Reid (1090).

[48] *XL Petroleum (NSW) Pty Ltd v Caltex Oil Australia Pty Ltd* (1985) 155 CLR 448; *Thompson v Australian Capital Television Pty Ltd* (1996) 186 CLR 574, 581–82 (Brennan CJ; Dawson and Toohey JJ) ('the effect of (the section) is that the cause of action against joint tortfeasors is no longer one and indivisible'); 591 (Gaudron J); and 613 (Gummow J). See, eg, s 5 Law Reform (Miscellaneous Provisions) Act 1946 (NSW).

[49] s 6 Law Reform (Married Women and Tortfeasors) Act 1935 (UK); *Bryanston Finance Ltd v deVries* [1975] QB 705 (CA).

[50] *Hill v Church of Scientology* (n 39).

[51] [2007] 1 WLR 1065.

[52] ibid, Moore-Bick LJ, with whom Richards and Ward LJ agreed.

[53] *Dubai Aluminium Co Ltd v Salaam* [2003] 2 AC 366.

[54] ibid 383.

employer's vicarious liability was 'co-extensive with that of his employee',[55] and agreed that the employer should be considered liability-wise as 'standing in his employee's shoes'.[56] Clearly these comments, though not made in the precise context of an employer's vicarious liability for punitive damages, would suggest that an employer could be liable vicariously for punitive damages.

For its part, the Law Commission was in favour of the possibility of vicarious liability for punitive damages. Though it acknowledged the force of the objections to such finding, it concluded that such an imposition could provide desired deterrence for undesirable behaviour, and an incentive for employers to control, supervise and educate their workforce.[57] It could also work to provide a remedy in cases where otherwise one might not be available.[58]

There has been little consideration of the matter in the Australian case law. On occasions it appears to have been assumed that an employer could be vicariously liable for such damages, without the point being considered in much depth.[59] In one of the cases, the employer had specifically directed the wrongdoer's reprehensible behaviour.[60] Arguably in such cases, concerns with ordering punitive damages against a vicariously liable employer are not as strong.

The other point evident in some of the cases is an attribution of the act of the wrongdoer to the defendant employer, rather than an attribution of liability for the act. So for instance in *Herald and Weekly Times Ltd v McGregor* Higgins J discusses the 'reckless conduct of the newspaper, through its contributor'.[61] In *New South Wales v Ibbett* the joint reasons distinguish the master's tort theory (which is no longer the law in Australia) of vicarious liability with the 'other theory', which 'treats the act of the servant as the indirect act of the master'.[62] In that case the joint reasons observed that previous High Court cases had assumed the availability of vicarious liability for punitive damages.[63] After referring to a lower court appellate decision in New South Wales and in Canada[64] which confirmed the availability of such a remedy, the High Court of Australia concluded that this was the approach that ought to be taken in Australia as well.[65]

[55] ibid 407.
[56] ibid.
[57] Law Commission (n 6) 161.
[58] ibid, because the plaintiff could not identify the precise wrongdoer, or where the wrongdoer lacked the resources to pay any punitive damages awarded against them.
[59] *Herald and Weekly Times v McGregor* (1928) 41 CLR 254.
[60] *XL Petroleum (NSW) Pty Ltd v Caltex Oil Australia Pty Ltd* (n 48).
[61] (1928) 41 CLR 254, 272.
[62] *New South Wales v Ibbett* (2006) 229 CLR 638, 641–42: 'counsel for the State emphasised that s8 is drawn in terms which apply the 'master's tort' theory of vicarious liability … whereby the master is liable for a breach of duty resting on the servant, not on the master, and broken by the servant. The other theory … treats the act of the servant as the indirect act of the master' (Gleeson CJ Gummow Kirby Heydon and Crennan JJ). Respectfully, the High Court's summary of the master's tort theory may not be correct.
[63] ibid 651 (Gleeson CJ Gummow Kirby Heydon and Crennan JJ).
[64] *Peeters v Canada* (1993) 108 DLR (4th) 471, 482.
[65] *New South Wales v Ibbett* (n 62) 653 (Gleeson CJ; Gummow, Kirby, Heydon and Crennan JJ).

Given the dearth of case law authority on the matter in the United Kingdom, Australia and Canada, it might be sensible to briefly consider how the matter has been dealt with in a jurisdiction with a large volume of case law—the United States—where the matter has been considered on more occasions.

The United States Supreme Court dealt with the matter early in its history in *The Amiable Nancy*.[66] There it was alleged that the owner of a ship was vicariously liable for trespass and theft committed by the ship's crew. The Supreme Court found the owner was vicariously liable for compensatory damages, but not punitive damages:

> They are innocent of the demerit of the transaction, having neither directed it, nor countenanced it, nor participated in it to the slightest degree. Under such circumstances, we are of opinion that they are bound to repair all the real injuries and personal wrongs sustained by the (plaintiffs) but they are not bound to the extent of vindictive damages.[67]

The Supreme Court again considered the matter in *Lake Shore and Michigan Southern Railway Company v Prentice*.[68] There the question concerned the possible vicarious liability of a railway company for the high-handed manner in which one of their conductors dealt with a customer. Gray J for the Court pointed out the orthodox view of punitive damages as being designed to punish and deter a wrongdoer. The wrongdoer in such cases would have acted with malice or recklessness. On this basis it was difficult to sheet it home to an employer vicariously:

> Exemplary or punitive damages, being awarded, not by way of compensation to the sufferer, but by way of punishment of the offender, and as a warning to others, can only be awarded against one who has participated in the offence. A principal therefore, though of course liable to make compensation for injuries done by his agent within the scope of his employment, cannot be held liable for exemplary or punitive damages, merely by reason of wanton, oppressive or malicious intent on the part of the agent.[69]

These cases suggest it would generally be unlikely that an employer could be held vicariously liable for punitive damages for an employee's wrongdoing. Though the way in which an employee conducted themselves might suggest that punitive damages should be payable by them, without more this liability could not be sheeted home to their employer, though the employer was liable to pay compensatory damages relating to the employee's wrongdoing.

Since that time, several approaches seem to have been taken on the question of an employer's possible vicarious liability for punitive damages. Different Court of Appeal circuits apply different rules. One approach is that reflected in the Restatement (Second) of Agency and the Restatement (Second) of Torts. Under this approach, an employer's liability for punitive damages vicariously is limited to cases where (a) the principal authorised the doing and manner of the

66 *The Amiable Nancy* 16 US 546 (1818).

67 ibid 559 (Story J, for the Court).

68 *Lake Shore and Michigan Southern Railway Company v Prentice* 147 US 101 (1893).

69 ibid 107 (Gray J, for the Court).

act; (b) the agent was unfit and the principal was reckless in employing them; (c) the agent was employed in a managerial capacity and was acting in the scope of employment; or (d) the principal or a managerial agent of the principal ratified or approved the act.[70] Often this approach would limit possible vicarious liability for punitive damages to cases where the relevant employee was at the managerial level. It is thus narrower than a general 'scope of employment' approach that would permit punitive damages with respect to the activity of any employee, provided it was within the scope of employment, not just managerial employees. A stricter approach would require that an employer only be held vicariously liable for punitive damages where they have been complicit in some way. This is apparently the approach taken by the Fifth and Sixth Circuits.[71] The First and Eleventh Circuits require some fault to be proven against the employer.[72] An attempt to resolve this split among circuits failed in *Exxon Shipping Co v Baker*, with the Supreme Court splitting 4:4 as to the correct approach.[73] Thus, it is difficult to speak of an 'American approach' to this question, and it can only be hoped that in a future case the United States Supreme Court might resolve this conflict among circuits.[74]

Reflections on Punitive Damages in the Vicarious Liability Context

The purpose of punitive damages can be difficult to square with requiring a vicariously liable employer to pay them. They are said to fulfil dual functions, to punish and to deter. This is hard to square with a doctrine that is concededly sourced in the realms of strict liability, characterised by an absence of fault.[75] So in the course of applying a no-fault principle, the court is being asked to punish the person who is, by definition, not at fault. It is difficult to accept that a court should apply a remedy that is punishment-based to someone who is, by definition, not at fault. They have done nothing wrong. It is difficult to see how punitive

[70] The Ninth Circuit applies the Restatement approach: *In Re The Exxon Valdez* 270 F 3d 1235 (2000).

[71] J Watts, 'A Confused Sea: Vicarious Liability for Punitive Damages Under Maritime Law' (2017) 91 *Tulane Law Review* 691, 694; *In re Oil Spill by the Oil Rig 'Deepwater Horizon'* 21 F Supp 3d 657, 749 (2014); *US Steel Corp v Fuhrman* 407 F 2d 1143 (1969).

[72] *CEH Inc v F/V Seafurer* 70 F 3d 694 (1st Cir, 1995); *Dudley v Wal-Mart Stores Inc* 166 F 3d 1317 (11th Cir, 1999).

[73] *Exxon Shipping Co v Baker* 554 US 471 (2008).

[74] An argument that the imposition of punitive damages on a vicarious basis was unconstitutional was dismissed in *Pacific Mutual Life Insurance Co v Haslip* 499 US 1 (1991).

[75] Sales and Cole (n 11) 1141: 'punitive damages in a strict tort liability context … would seem to be plainly illogical because neither punishment nor deterrence of conduct is at issue'; 'employers should not suffer punishment for conduct that they cannot prevent' (1160).

damages are appropriately imputed to a person who, or an organisation that, has done nothing wrong.[76] This was recognised by the New Zealand Court of Appeal in *S v Attorney-General*:

> We have earlier determined that the Crown is liable (vicariously) to compensate the plaintiff for abuse by his foster parents. But it does not follow that it would be proper also to impose liability for exemplary damages on a vicarious basis. In fact, when it is appreciated that the primary purpose of such damages is to punish a flagrant wrongdoer, not to provide additional compensation (in contrast with compensatory, including aggravated damages) it might seem to be quite unfair to inflict a punishment upon someone who has been found not to have been complicit in the wrongdoing. Exemplary or punitive damages would not then be a reflection of the culpability of the defendant. Any 'message of disapproval' would be delivered to the wrong person. It is one thing to require a principal who has without neglect created a situation leading to injury to compensate the injured person; it is quite another to punish the principal for the sins of the agent.[77]

[76] With respect, Atiyah's first impression was correct when he found that 'at first sight there seems to be much against allowing vicarious liability for exemplary damages, for if these are avowedly designed as punishment it might seem wrong in principle to punish someone other than the actual wrongdoer': Atiyah (n 42) 435 (he then went on to accept that such damages should in some cases be payable by an employer. He may have been influenced by the narrow terms in which the ability to claim punitive damages had been cast in *Rookes v Barnard* shortly before his book was published); Beever, 'The Structure of Aggravated and Exemplary Damages' (n 16) 96: 'vicarious liability for exemplary damages is an injustice of the first order as it entails punishing a defendant who has done no wrong by transferring his property to a claimant who has no right to receive it'; A Duggan, 'Exemplary Damages in Equity: A Law and Economics Perspective' (2006) 26 *Oxford Journal of Legal Studies* 303, 320: 'from the retributivist's perspective, there should be no vicarious liability for exemplary damages; B Chapman and M Trebilcock, 'Punitive Damages: Divergence in Search of a Rationale' (1989) 40 *Alabama Law Review* 741, 779: 'it is of the essence of traditional theories of retribution that individual wrongdoers are deserving of punishment but that, conversely, individuals who are innocent of wrongdoing are not. Vicarious liability by definition violates these precepts'; P Corboy, 'Vicarious Liabiity for Punitive Damages: The Effort to Constitutionalize Tort Reform' (1991) 2 *Seton Hall Constitutional Law Journal* 5, 15–16: 'there is no benefit to be gained by holding the employer liable for misconduct which is purely personal to the employee'; M Sturley, 'Vicarious Liability for Punitive Damages' (2010) 70 *Louisiana Law Review* 501, 516: 'if punitive damages punish someone who is not guilty of any misconduct they do not accomplish their stated purpose; R Parlee, 'Vicarious Liability for Punitive Damages: Suggested Changes in the Law Through Policy Analysis' (1984) 68 *Marquette Law Review* 27, 36: 'where the (evil) motive is not shared, punishment of the principal is patently irrational and unethical'. Though the Law Commission ultimately found that vicarious liability for punitive damages should exist, it acknowledged the force of arguments such as this against such imposition: Law Commission (n 6) 159: 'the second objection is that recognising vicarious liability for punitive damages imposes a burden on employers that is not warranted by the policies which serve to justify the law's recognition of claims to punitive awards … the direct, punitive, deterrent or symbolic efficacy of the punitive award is at best substantially diluted. The primary wrongdoer does not feel the punitive award in his or her pocket. We acknowledge the force of these arguments. Together they appear to entail that one should refuse to recognise vicarious liability to punitive damages' (159); Ellis (n 10) 66: 'the arguments used to justify vicarious compensatory damages are … inapplicable or lamentably weak when applied to vicarious punitive damage liability'.

[77] *S v Attorney-General* [2003] NZCA 149, [88] (Blanchard J, for McGrath, Anderson and Glazebrook JJ); to like effect Tipping J: 'far more harm and a far greater sense of injustice would be created by punishing those whose conduct did not deserve it, than by declining to do so' [122]; S Todd, 'A New Zealand Perspective on Exemplary Damages' (2004) 33 *Common Law World Review* 255.

Lord Reid dismissed them as 'palm tree justice' in *Broome v Cassell and Co*.[78]

Various concepts have been used, as discussed above, to describe the circumstances in which punitive damages are payable. They focus on the conduct of the wrongdoer. As discussed above, whether they acted in a reprehensible manner, whether they acted maliciously, how long the wrongdoing persisted, whether they acted in clear disregard of the interests of another. Evidently, none of this applies to an employer said to be vicariously liable. They did not act reprehensibly, and they did not act maliciously. The very language used to explain the circumstances in which punitive damages are payable is very difficult to apply to the context of an employer and the possibility of vicarious liability.

Even if the enterprise risk theory is appropriate to explain and rationalise the imposition of vicarious liability, a position I have challenged above, it has been pointed out that its rationale does not extend to the imposition of punitive damages on the employer:

> The entrepreneur theory … is a rationale which is built solely on the reparative function of torts … even though business practice should be found to coincide with the deductions of the entrepreneur theory, the assessment of punitive damages against masters for the wrong of their servants would not be justified. The entrepreneur theory portrays the doctrine of (vicarious liability) as a risk-shifting device … to further the reparative function of torts. The operation of the doctrine of punitive damages gives the plaintiff an undeserved windfall that has nothing to do with the reparative function, which is duly served … by the allowance of compensatory damages.[79]

The alternative purpose of punitive damages that is sometimes articulated in the case law is that such damages act as a 'deterrent'. Again, this is used in the context of deterring a would-be wrongdoer who is considering engaging in wrongful behaviour. The actual efficacy of punitive damages in achieving such a goal is itself questionable. It may be doubted whether someone considering wrongful behaviour has the law of punitive damages in the back of their mind. Others have pointed out the lack of empirical evidence that punitive damages do indeed provide a deterrent effect or an optimal deterrent effect.[80] However, that argument will not be pursued here. The point here is that the argument is stretched even further when it is said that such principles justify the imposition of punitive damages upon an employer vicariously, as opposed to the wrongdoer themselves.[81] Precisely what is the imposition of punitive damages upon an employer vicariously expected to deter? The law seeks to deter the wrongdoer's behaviour, and that goal is hardly

[78] [1972] AC 1027, 1087.

[79] C Morris, 'Punitive Damages in Tort Cases' (1931) 44 *Harvard Law Review* 1173, 1199–200.

[80] A Sebok, 'Punitive Damages: From Myth to Theory' (2007) 92 *Iowa Law Review* 957, 982.

[81] KR Redden, *Punitive Damages* (Charlottesville, VA, Michie Co, 1980) 35: 'if the purpose of punitive damages is to deter … the penalty is certainly of questionable effectiveness and justice if not imposed on the employee. The inequity is especially acute in the case of corporations where innocent stockholders ultimately bear the punitive burden'.

advanced by imposing culpability upon their employer.[82] Todd pointed out that given punitive damages are imposed for the most reprehensible kind of conduct, in the context of vicarious liability, an employee apparently intent on that kind of behaviour is most unlikely to be deterrable. This in turn presents difficulties for an employer expected to have taken steps to deter them.[83] She further points out that the inherent uncertainty around whether such damages will be awarded, and their quantum, makes it difficult to expect employers to take appropriate precautions.[84] Smillie takes a similar position, concluding that:

> If the purpose of exemplary damages is to punish and deter, surely the individual wrongdoer must be required to pay the award from (their) own personal resources. The direct punitive and deterrent effect on the wrongdoer will be lost if (they are) permitted to avoid personal responsibility for payment, and to punish an innocent person for the wrong of another violates the most fundamental principle of retributive justice.[85]

These arguments present difficulties for those who seek to justify the imposition of punitive damages on the basis of their economic efficiency, ie, they deter what would be otherwise an economically inefficient activity to the extent that efficiency is obtained.[86] Smillie responds to these arguments with the salient point that:

> The purpose of an award of exemplary damages is not merely to reduce the level of injury-producing conduct to an economically efficient (ie cost-justified) level. Exemplary damages serve to identify conduct that is presumptively devoid of social value and must be suppressed entirely, regardless of relative economic costs and benefits.[87]

I should point out that I leave to one side here cases in which the employer has specifically directed the act which results in the possible application of punitive damages, or who ratifies the wrongful acts. In such cases, I have no objection to the law imposing the punitive damages upon the employer. In a real sense it may be said that the employer in such a case is directly liable, as opposed to being vicariously liable, for acts directly authorised or ratified. A person who did so has

[82] *Couch v Attorney-General* [2010] NZSC 27, [61] (Blanchard J): 'it seems hardly principled … to punish an inadvertent wrongdoer by means of a damages award in order to provide a deterrent to someone else when a sufficient deterrent for others exists in the form of the almost inevitable criminal prosecution of the wrongdoer for negligence'; A Todd, 'Vicarious Liability for Sexual Abuse' (2002) 8 *Canterbury Law Review* 281, 307: 'in the case of a blameless employer, imposing vicarious liability is unlikely to have any significant deterrent effect, as it is unlikely to induce any significant modification of business practice'.

[83] A Todd, ibid, 311: 'employees who engage in conduct that gives rise to exemplary damages awards are likely to go well beyond the threshold standard for the type of conduct needed to justify such damages when they intentionally behave in an undesirable way. When this is so, the conduct of the employees is unlikely to be altered by any preventive measures put in place by the employer'.

[84] ibid.

[85] J Smillie, 'Exemplary Damages for Personal Injury' (1997) *New Zealand Law Review* 140, 164. He concludes that imposing vicarious liability for punitive damages will not likely have any significant deterrent effect (166).

[86] Ellis (n 10) 23–33; M Legg, 'Economic Guidelines for Awarding Exemplary Damages' (2004) 30 *Monash University Law Review* 303.

[87] Smillie (n 85) 167.

effectively committed a wrongful act, so I have no objection to punitive damages being visited upon them, if we can conceivably say that the wrongful act is theirs. However, in most of the cases, the employer did not specifically authorise or ratify the wrongful act.

As discussed in chapter four, deterrence has been utilised by the Canadian Supreme Court in vicarious liability cases as a basis for the imposition of liability upon an employer, on the basis of the enterprise risk approach. It will be recalled that in *Bazley v Curry*, one of the two rationales for the imposition of vicarious liability upon an employer is that it would assist in achieving deterrence of accidents, because employers could often reduce accidents by efficient organisation and supervision. Imposing vicarious liability upon them was said to provide an incentive for employers to take such steps.[88]

I explained in chapter six why I did not accept this justification for the imposition of strict vicarious liability upon an employer. It does not explain why strict liability is needed in that particular context, rather than a negligence standard. Negligence principles can provide appropriate incentives for the kind of behaviour that is desired. In fact the reasoning is perverse—if an employer knows it will be liable, regardless of the steps it took, this is unlikely to provide incentive for the kind of behaviour sought.[89] On the other hand, where an organisation is aware that the steps it took will be taken into account in determining whether or not it is liable, a negligence approach could be argued to provide desired incentives and deterrence. I indicated in chapter six that the United Kingdom courts have pointedly refused to accept the deterrence rationale for the imposition of vicarious liability,[90] and the Australian courts have not embraced it.

So my objections to the deterrence theory of imposing vicarious liability upon employers naturally extend to the deterrence theory of imposing vicarious liability upon employers for punitive damages. Most of the type of conduct which attracts punitive damages, reprehensible—malicious conduct actuated by ill-will and/or improper purpose—is likely to be a breach of the employee's employment contract in any event. The employer has likely already attempted to deal with unexpectedly bad employee behaviour in this contractual way. What further incentive/

[88] *Bazley v Curry* [1999] 2 SCR 534, 554–55 (McLachlin J, for the Court).

[89] This argument is also made by Paul Walker: P Walker, 'Vicarious Liability for Exemplary Damages: A Matter of Strict Liability?' (2009) 85 *Australian Law Journal* 548, 560: 'if the relevant policy for allowing a vicarious award of exemplary damages is to encourage employers to take active steps to minimise the risk of their employees acting in a high-handed or reprehensible manner, a strict liability approach is potentially counterproductive … if employers are to be subject to vicarious awards of exemplary damages on a strict or automatic basis, there may be no, or no sufficient incentive for those employers to take any steps to reduce this risk. Such employers will not only have to bear the costs of attempted minimisation of harm, but also the cost of exemplary damages, which are imposed even if these steps are taken'.

[90] *Armes v Nottinghamshire County Council* [2017] UKSC 60, [67] (Lord Reed, with whom Lady Hale, Lord Kerr and Lord Clarke agreed).

deterrent will the possibility of making them vicariously liable for this kind of behaviour provide?[91]

The Law Commission report, which favoured the availability of vicarious punitive damages, also relied on this possible deterrent rationale:

> Vicarious liability may offer a wider, if indirect, method for pursuing the aims of punitive damages. Employers who are so liable or who are potentially so liable will have an incentive to control and educate their workforce. The development by employers of some form of wrong-preventing educative process might be particularly beneficial, for example, in cases of … discrimination. Employers also possess a range of disciplinary powers which will enable them to penalise and deter individual guilty employees, or to discourage potential wrongdoers. Indeed, the loss of employment, coupled with impaired employment prospects, may be a more severe form of sanction for wrongdoing by employees than a punitive damages award could directly provide.[92]

With respect, the likely deterrent effect upon employers of the possible imposition on them of vicarious punitive damages is speculative and untested.

It might also be relevant to note that in most cases employers are able to obtain insurance against the risk of being held liable for punitive damages.[93] No doubt arguments about loss spreading and loss distribution will again be made to justify the imposition of punitive damages upon employers. I have dealt with these arguments in chapter six and will not revisit them here. Further, it is hard to see what deterrence a punitive damages liability will provide to an employer who is insured for that risk, so will not actually pay any damages awarded.[94] It was noted in chapter six that it cannot practically be argued that the employer will pay because their premiums, deductible or excess will be adjusted to accommodate a finding against them. Insurance experts have pointed out that insurance companies rarely bother getting into this level of calibrated detail in assessing a

[91] A similar position is taken by Stephen Todd: S Todd (n 77) 273: 'an incentive to take care already exists and it is difficult to see how a vicarious liability for exemplary damages could have any significant impact in this respect … closer inspection may be impossible to achieve or unlikely to be effective; the type of conduct that gives rise to an exemplary liability is unlikely to be prevented by reasonable precautionary methods; and extra monitoring may not be a cost-effective use of resources in light of the defendant's probable lack of control over the conduct in question, and therefore be unlikely to happen'; Morris (n 79) 1203: 'it may often be the case that the allowance of punitive damages against the master adds no impetus to extra-legal punishment, and results in an unnecessary burden on business'; Ellis (n 10) 68: 'there is no reason to assume … that compensatory damages alone—for which employers are vicariously liable—provide insufficient incentives for employers to undertake efficient safeguards in selecting, monitoring and disciplining employees'.

[92] Law Commission (n 6) 161.

[93] *Lancashire County Council v Municipal Mutual Insurance Ltd* [1997] QB 897; *Gray v Motor Accident Commission* (n 36).

[94] Sales and Cole (n 11) 1163: 'the allowance of insurance reduces the punishment of the wrongdoer while simultaneously imposing the effects of the punishment on all other policy holders … permitting punitive damages insurance likewise conflicts with the deterrence objective by reducing the incentive to avoid loss-creating conduct'; Beever, 'The Structure of Aggravated and Exemplary Damages' (n 16) 95: 'the alleged point (of an award of punitive damages) is to punish and deter. This cannot be achieved efficiently if the defendant has insurance'; J Kircher, 'Punitive Damages and Business Organisations: A Pathetic Fallacy' (2000) 67 *Tennessee Law Review* 971, 978–79.

particular enterprise's insurance risk and what premiums they should pay. But the likely existence of insurance further undercuts any argument that imposing punitive damages on employers can be supported on the basis that it deters them from undesired activity.[95]

Further, traditionally in punitive damages the means of the defendant are relevant in determining the amount of damages payable. But this is obviously closely linked to the punitive and deterrent purposes associated with their imposition. The idea is to make the amount significant enough to a particular defendant; their means will bear on this matter. And to deter them; again, the extent to which a particular punitive damages payout will deter them is said to depend significantly on their means. All of this serves to reinforce the highly individualised assessment of punitive damages in a particular case, and the fact that the identity and characteristics of the defendant are absolutely critical in a proper assessment of them. This makes it all the more problematic to transfer liability for punitive damages from the actual wrongdoer to their employer. The whole point of making the individualised assessment is lost if the one for whom the individualised assessment is made does not actually pay the damages; and it makes no sense to assess the employer in terms of their capacity to pay, because they have done nothing to warrant punishment or to deter, so that it is meaningless to ask what means they have, because we only ask that question because we are attempting to punish and/or to deter.[96]

The distinction between the so-called master's tort theory of vicarious liability, and the servant's tort theory of vicarious liability, is of some relevance here. I have explained above that courts in the United Kingdom,[97] Australia[98] and Canada[99] have adopted the servant's tort theory of vicarious liability, by which it is the wrongdoing of the wrongdoer, and not their act, which is attributed to the employer. Had the master's tort theory been accepted as the basis for vicarious liability, whereby the master was liable for a breach of their own duty, then the possibility of punitive damages against an employer might be acceptable. However, in such a case the focus would be on the employer's actions, and whether they were deserving of punishment and/or needed to be deterred. However, the courts' acceptance of the servant's tort theory is much more likely to make the employer automatically liable for what the wrongdoing employee would have been liable for, including punitive damages, since the employee's wrongdoing is entirely attributed to the employer.[100] Such a theory makes it more difficult to argue that an

[95] This was acknowledged by Simon Brown LJ in *Lancashire County Council v Municipal Mutual Insurance Ltd* (n 93) 909: 'to allow a defendant liable for exemplary damages to be held harmless against them by insurance must undoubtedly reduce the deterrent and punitive effect of the order upon (them)' (with whom Thorpe LJ agreed).

[96] D Travis, 'Broker Churning: Who is Punished? Vicariously Assessed Punitive Damages in the Context of Brokerage Houses and their Agents?' (1993) 30 *Houston Law Review* 1775, 1800–01.

[97] *Majrowski v Guy's and St Thomas's NHS Trust* [2007] 1 AC 224.

[98] *New South Wales v Lepore* (2003) 212 CLR 511.

[99] *Bazley v Curry* (n 88).

[100] Walker (n 89) 557–59.

employer should not be liable for punitive damages in respect of an employee's wrongdoing. I hasten to add that this does not mean I am arguing that the courts should accept the master's tort theory, just that acceptance of the servant's tort theory makes it a bit harder (though certainly not impossible) to mount an argument for imposing punitive damages upon the employer vicariously.

The Law Commission gave two other reasons for its conclusion that an employer should potentially be liable for punitive damages through vicarious liability. These were that an employee may not be able to pay a significant punitive damages payout ordered against them, and that on some occasions, plaintiffs may not easily be able to identify the precise wrongdoer.[101] I have explored these supposed rationales for vicarious liability generally in chapter seven—in essence, these reasons are essentially variations on the deep pockets rationale and the evidentiary difficulties rationale discussed there. As explained there, these arguments to support the imposition of vicarious liability upon an employer generally are not supported, and they are no more supportive in the context of a punitive damages award.

Interestingly, the Law Commission itself acknowledges major problems with the law relating to vicarious liability. It frankly canvasses that it is 'notoriously difficult to find a convincing, comprehensive justification of the doctrine', and frankly acknowledges that it may produce unfairness and unjustified outcomes.[102] With respect, this is surely correct. The Law Commission raises these issues in the context of asking whether an employer should be liable vicariously for punitive damages. Now, obviously, the primary scope of the report was the various nominated heads of damage, and not vicarious liability, so the latter was only of peripheral relevance to the Commission's report here. However, one might have thought that if the Commission were aware of the highly anomalous and contentious nature of vicarious liability, and its capacity to produce unfair and unjustified outcomes, which it clearly was, this may have made it somewhat reluctant to find that the tentacles of vicarious liability extended to punitive damages, not just compensatory ones. This was not the outcome of its deliberations. This seemed to be because the Commission felt that if an employer could be vicariously liable for compensatory damages, although entirely innocent of wrongdoing, this was somehow on an equivalent unfairness plane with ordering them also to pay punitive damages. In other words, because the law seems to accept the possible unfairness of it in relation to compensatory damages, it seemed to be satisfactory to accept the possible unfairness of it in relation to punitive damages as well.

With respect, this is not strong reasoning. I applaud the Law Commission's frankness about the anomalous nature of punitive damages, but pointing out that it is already dysfunctional is not a sound basis for arguing its reach should be extended still further.

[101] Law Commission (n 6) 161.
[102] ibid 160.

Conclusion

The courts should not impose punitive damages upon an employer vicariously, simply because their employee has committed wrong. Again, there is in that instance nothing for the law to punish or to deter. The rationales for the imposition of punitive damages are not present in relation to an employer's vicarious liability—they have done nothing that warrants punishment, and there is no behaviour of theirs that the law should be seeking to deter. As has been repeatedly pointed out throughout this book, the law risks losing its moral imperative when it punishes the innocent. Even the much discussed doctrine of enterprise risk theory does not support the imposition of punitive damages upon an employer.

Conclusion to Part III

Part III has discussed three different contexts in the law of tort in which the innocent are being punished. They are punished for the actions of their employees, they are punished (sometimes) for actions of their independent contractors, and they are liable to pay punitive damages if their employee has behaved particularly egregiously. As indicated, the law approaches, or exceeds, the limits of its moral force when it punishes those who are morally innocent.

While traditionally the law has applied a two-step test to determining vicarious liability issues, recently United Kingdom case law has suggested something of a merger between them. This part has considered there is some logical sense in merging the two. On this basis, if an enterprise risk approach were to be taken to the traditional 'second' question of the scope of liability, it might be logically defensible to apply the 'organisational' or 'entrepreneur' test to the traditional 'first' question of the kinds of relationships to which vicarious liability applies. Unfortunately, the courts have not squarely addressed the logic of this. Thus, the High Court of Australia is clearly disinclined to apply the enterprise risk approach but applies an organisational test to the first question (and answers the questions separately). The United Kingdom courts seem to have merged the questions into one but have not entirely signed up for the 'organisational' or 'entrepreneurial' approach, and still apply other tests. And the scope of contractors for whom a business might be vicariously liable is ratcheted ever upwards, as demonstrated by *Barclays Bank*, where a bank is held vicariously liable for what a medical practitioner did. This is arguably a product of a departure from the control test, unfortunately coupled with what I regard as an indefensible application of the organisational test. Respectfully, a medical practitioner is not part of a banking organisation, and the law should not treat their conduct as if they were.

The doctrine of enterprise risk liability is further weakened when the issues of non-delegable duties and of punitive damages are considered. Through the logic of enterprise risk, an employer is required to internalise its costs of doing business. Yet, through an expansive definition of 'employee' to include people like medical staff performing medicals for banks, and through the doctrine of non-delegable duties as applied to independent contractors, an employer is also being asked to bear costs that properly belong to another business. The law cannot have it both ways—one cannot at the same time laud a theory that causes the internalisation of loss within the relevant business, while in the next breath requiring them to internalise losses clearly caused by other businesses. Yet this is the current state of play, when the interplay of vicarious liability doctrine is considered with developments in the scope of non-delegable duties. The concept of non-delegable duties was created to solve a problem that no longer exists. And imposing punitive damages upon an innocent employer is completely at odds with the rationales for the imposition of such damages, and is itself at odds with notions of enterprise risk theory.

Conclusions

The notion that an employer is legally liable for the actions of their employees is one of ancient vintage and has been recognised to varying degrees by all of the common law jurisdictions being studied. However, the Achilles heel of such a doctrine has been the long-running failure of courts and academics to satisfactorily rationalise and justify the imposition of such liability. It remains anomalous, and precarious, in a world of tort dominated by fault-based negligence. At the very least, the law should hesitate before imposing liability upon the innocent, whether they are individuals or organisations, whether or not they have deep pockets, and whether or not they are insured.

The broad direction of vicarious liability since the early twentieth century has been a one-way ratchet up in terms of broadening the scope of such liability. Past limits based on the extent to which the employee was acting for the purposes of the employer and/or their benefit, or whether the employee was on a 'frolic' have either been ignored or minimalised. This has sharply increased the scope of liability upon an employer. Employers are now routinely liable for actions they never would have authorised, including deliberate, criminal wrongdoing, and even actions they specifically prohibited. Employers are liable for those who are not strictly employees. Employers can find themselves liable for actions of independent contractors. Employers can be liable for punitive damages because of what their employee did. It is doubtful that the original purveyors of vicarious liability doctrine would recognise the ever-broadening scope of vicarious liability. The extent of the ability of an organisation to bear such costs, or for them to be 'distributed' elsewhere, is little considered. The social consequences of imposing very substantial costs on an entrepreneur are little considered. Capitalism, with its faults, generally provides great benefits to society, in terms of wealth creation, creation of employment opportunities, and contribution of taxation to society to enable it to offer essential services. It is worth considering the extent to which regulatory burden, including the imposition of large-scale vicarious liability upon an employer, might adversely affect the capitalist model and the risk-taking it traditionally encourages and rewards. Further, where organisations and individuals provide for risk, for example in their employment contracts, it is submitted that these provisions should generally be respected, including by the law of vicarious liability, rather than ignored.

Three of the four jurisdictions studied have chosen to explain and rationalise the imposition of vicarious liability on the basis of an 'enterprise risk' theory, by which the cost of risks generated by a business venture should be internalised to it, the theory being that this will allow the business to operate at an efficient level.

It is part of the broader law and economics agenda, some adherents of which make the bold claim that this area of legal theory 'best explains' existing common law, including the law of vicarious liability. The search by scholars and judges for a unifying, satisfactory rationale to explain vicarious liability is lauded and encouraged.

However, the law in fastening upon enterprise risk theory has arrived at a mirage. Fatally for a theory said to explain current doctrine, it does not explain large components of the existing law. It cannot explain the long-running distinction between liability for employees and independent contractors, it cannot explain why the law of vicarious liability fastens upon a wrong, cannot explain why the common law permits a vicariously liable employer to claim back against their employee, and cannot explain the imposition of vicarious liability upon a non-profit organisation.

These deficiencies, substantial as they are, are not all. Even its adherents would have to concede the notions of 'enterprise risk' evidently do not explain how the law imposes civil liability upon an organisation generally. Exhibit A would be *Donoghue v Stevenson*, and Exhibit B would be *Bolton v Stone*. Economic analysis of the kind demanded by Posner and others is notably missing from these judgments. They were enterprises; evidently, the law found other ways to determine whether those organisations were tortiously liable for alleged wrongdoing. They are leading cases in the law of tort. Evidently, the law of tort generally, and the law relating to the liability of business organisations in particular, is not premised around notions of efficiency and the internalisation of costs to the enterprise that generated them. So it is apparently to be used only in relation to one kind of civil liability of an organisation, vicarious liability, but this is not explained or justified. It inevitably invites further uncertainty about what are the proper costs to be allocated to an organisation. Is the risk that a teacher will abuse a child a 'cost' of running a school? There is no easy answer.

Attempts to rationalise the imposition of costs upon a business on the basis that it is better placed to distribute losses are unconvincing. Because it is not practical or viable for a court in an individual case to actually consider the extent to which a given defendant can in fact distribute such losses, courts have taken the lazy way out of assuming at the macro level the ability of organisations to do so. Sweeping assumptions or generalisations are not a substitute for strong reasoning. In this context, they are dangerous. A similar pathology affects claims that imposing such costs upon employers will 'deter' them, without an explanation of how existing fault-based negligence liability does not provide the needed 'deterrence'. And the logical circuity involved in lauding a doctrine on the basis both that it will result in losses being spread around, so the immediate defendant does not pay them, and that they will be deterred, because they will pay them, is too obvious to rehash.

While it is not perfect, it is believed that notions of agency are the best way through which the liability of an employer for actions of their employees should be conceptualised. There is significant historical support for such a view, much more than the alternative of enterprise risk theory. On an agency view, which is evident in the position taken in the United States, an employer is liable for actions of an employee that are authorised either expressly or impliedly. An action of an employee will be considered authorised when it is of a kind that the employee is engaged to perform. The employee must be acting for the purposes of the employer and for their benefit, judged objectively. An employer is not liable for the consequences of an employee engaged in a frolic.

This would represent an improvement in the current situation where the employer is being held to be an effective insurer of costs associated with activities they never would have countenanced, for criminal behaviour by an employee, and for conduct they specifically prohibited. An employer should not be liable for any of this kind of behaviour. One way of intellectualising this is to say that the law should only punish wrongdoing. A defendant's actions must be morally blameworthy in order to attract legal sanction. If an employee's actions were for the benefit and purposes of the employer, being specifically directed or impliedly authorised or commanded, the employer is morally blameworthy and it is right that a legal sanction should be visited upon them. I am happy not to call this the imposition of vicarious liability. Labels do not matter. The fact that only wrongdoers should be sanctioned by the law does.

Traditionally the law has maintained a strong distinction between employees and independent contractors, and the liability of an employer for them. This sharp distinction may be defended as a decision that an employer has made about risk. In the decision of whether to engage an employee or engage an independent contractor, one relevant factor would traditionally have been the extralegal risk involved in engaging an employer, in terms of vicarious liability. At least this knowledge has permitted the employer to make an appropriate assessment of the risks and benefits of each approach, and to contract on appropriate terms. It is believed that the law should accord individuals substantial freedom in managing their risk. The law traditionally does this, including in relation to entrepreneurial and business activity.

These assessments have been disturbed by the increasing willingness of courts to impose non-delegable duties upon an employer for the actions of independent contractors. Just like with the other strict liability doctrine of vicarious liability, courts have struggled to articulate a basis for their imposition. They have sometimes engaged vague concepts such as 'dangerousness' or 'ultra-dangerousness' that defy easy description. Though the courts in some jurisdictions seem determined to maintain this category of non-delegable duty cases, they do not seem to have noticed the great inconsistency between the law in relation to vicarious liability, in particular enterprise risk, and their views on non-delegable duties. Presently, the courts in some jurisdictions are espousing in vicarious liability cases that businesses must be forced to internalise the cost of risks associated with their business. Yet in cases involving the sister strict liability tort principle of non-delegable duty, they are espousing that businesses must be forced to internalise the cost of risks associated with other people's businesses. It is respectfully hoped that one day the anomaly will be recognised and addressed.

Finally, I have considered whether my preferred approach, whereby an employer should only be liable for actions of an employee committed for the employer's purposes and for their benefit, is liable to lead to injustice. Injustice could occur because it might leave the victim without a remedy, or it might impose an undue burden upon the wrongdoing employee, given the reality that where vicarious liability exists, in most cases the victim will simply proceed against the employer, and statute may prevent the employer (or their insurer) from claiming against the wrongdoer.

Having considered this, I do not believe that injustice would generally be created. No legal rule will lead to 'perfect outcomes', and of course different people would have different views on what a perfect outcome would be in any event. However, it should be pointed out what while adoption of the rule I favour might crimp the ability of victims in some cases to claim against an employer for vicarious liability, they may well have a claim against the employer directly for negligence, for instance in relation to poor choice of staff, poor supervision or management etc. This book does not directly concern direct claims of negligence such as this, but the existence of a strong negligence tort to be applied against an employer who has breached their duty obligations in such contexts goes a long way to addressing any concerns that a victim will be left without a remedy. Of course, it will not always be possible for a victim to prove negligence, but the possibility certainly exists.

I have also considered the impact of introduction of the approach I favour upon employees. Will employees bear an unacceptable risk, if victims have a crimped ability to claim against the employer for employee wrongdoing? It is certainly likely that claims against employees directly will increase, at least to some extent, if the approach I favour is adopted. On the other hand, we are all party to contracts where we know that if we do not meet our expectations we face personal financial difficulties, or ruin. I know that, for example, my vehicle is fully insured. However, I know that if I drive contrary to the road rules, drive while under the influence of drugs or alcohol, for instance, that my insurance will be void, and I will be personally liable for the damage that I cause. The damages payable might be large. Is it so different for the law to have the effect that an employee, as long as they comply with the terms of their employment agreement, acts for the purposes and benefit of their employer, knows that effectively they will not face personal tort liability? However, an employee who acts outside their employment agreement, acts not for the interest and purposes of their employer but for themselves, and thereby causes loss to another, may be personally liable to that other. I do not wish to impose unreasonable burdens upon an employee. I do not believe that reconceptualisation of the law regarding an employer's liability for the actions of an employee in the way that I have suggested would be unreasonable.

The law faces a difficult balancing act, both to accommodate and regulate essential business and commercial activity, from which we all derive social benefit one way or the other, and to provide compensation to those who are injured as a result of such activity. However, it is believed that the law of negligence is best placed to deal with the vast bulk of the legal consequences arising from the relationship between business and society, including its members. Through a very long lens, the law has been shifting away from strict liability, and in favour of fault-based liability. This shift is supported. Strict liability is anomalous and is becoming increasingly isolated in the law of tort. The doctrines of vicarious liability and non-delegable duties should not remain in this awkward position. The liability of an employer for what their employees do is best thought of, at least going forward, as an example of agency law, in the wide sense of the concept, as opposed to an anachronistic, isolated doctrine of the law which time and circumstance have largely left behind.

INDEX

www.ingramcontent.com/pod-product-compliance
Lightning Source LLC
Chambersburg PA
CBHW071301180926
51613CB00001B/97
* 9 7 8 1 5 0 9 9 2 0 2 3 5 *